Navigating by the Southern Cross

To Leigh, Vanessa, and La Folle Journée

Navigating by the Southern Cross

A History of the European Discovery and Exploration of Australia

Kenneth Morgan

BLOOMSBURY ACADEMIC

LONDON • NEW YORK • OXFORD • NEW DELHI • SYDNEY

BLOOMSBURY ACADEMIC
Bloomsbury Publishing Plc
50 Bedford Square, London, WC1B 3DP, UK
1385 Broadway, New York, NY 10018, USA
29 Earlsfort Terrace, Dublin 2, Ireland

BLOOMSBURY, BLOOMSBURY ACADEMIC and the Diana logo
are trademarks of Bloomsbury Publishing Plc

First published in Great Britain 2021

Cover design: Terry Woodley
Cover image: The *Resolution* and the *Adventure* in Matavai Bay, Tahiti, during the second voyage of
James Cook between 1772 and 1775. Painting by William Hodges (1744–1797),
National Maritime Museum. Photo by DeAgostini/Getty Images.

A catalogue record for this book is available from the British Library.

Library of Congress Cataloging-in-Publication Data
Names: Morgan, Kenneth, 1953- author.
Title: Navigating by the Southern Cross: the European Discovery of Australia / Kenneth Morgan.
Other titles: History of the European Discovery and Exploration of Australia
Description: London; New York: Bloomsbury Academic, 2021. | Includes
bibliographical references and index. | Summary: 'In this comprehensive
new study, leading historian Kenneth Morgan provides an authoritative
account of European exploration and discovery in Australia. Introducing
new findings and drawing on the latest in historiographical research,
this book situates developments in navigation, nautical astronomy and
cartography within the broader contexts of imperial, colonial and
maritime history"– Provided by publisher.
Identifiers: LCCN 2020037971 (print) | LCCN 2020037972 (ebook) |
ISBN 9781350154773 (hb) | ISBN 9781350214545 (pbk.) |
ISBN 9781350154780 (ePDF) | ISBN 9781350154797 (eBook)
Subjects: LCSH: Australia–Discovery and exploration. |
Explorers–Australia–History. | Explorers–Europe–History. |
Navigation–Australia–History. | Nautical astronomy–History. |
Australia–History–To 1788. | Australia–History–1788–1851. |
Cartography–Australia–History.
Classification: LCC DU97 .M67 2020 (print) | LCC DU97 (ebook) | DDC 944.01–dc23
LC record available at https://lccn.loc.gov/2020037971
LC ebook record available at https://lccn.loc.gov/2020037972

ISBN: HB: 978-1-3501-5477-3
          ePDF: 978-1-3501-5478-0
          eBook: 978-1-3501-5479-7

Typeset by Integra Software Services Pvt. Ltd.

To find out more about our authors and books visit www.bloomsbury.com
and sign up for our newsletters.

Contents

Illustrations

All the illustrations are taken from the Map Division of the National Library of Australia, Canberra, with internal call numbers provided.

Acknowledgements

This book has benefited from the help of several people and from the cooperation of numerous archives and libraries. Alex Wright offered wise counsel during the commissioning process. Adrian Webb and his colleagues at the United Kingdom Hydrographic Office discussed my work with me fruitfully, and offered a model service to academic researchers. Martin Woods and his team in the Maps Department of the National Library of Australia similarly provided positive support. Quentin Slade, a member of that department, gave valuable assistance in providing the maps used in this book. Maddie Holder and Abigail Lane steered me helpfully through Bloomsbury's publication procedures. An anonymous referee for the publishers suggested useful revisions to the completed manuscript. From my home base in Twickenham, I was able to access relevant material in major institutions in libraries and archives in the Greater London area: the Humanities and Map reading rooms of the British Library, the British Museum's Anthropology Library, the Library and Archives at the Natural History Museum, the Caird Library and Archive at the National Maritime Museum, the National Archives, the Royal Botanic Gardens Library and Archives, and the main library at University College London. Information was also gathered from several English provincial repositories: the National Museum of the Royal Navy, Portsmouth; the Lincolnshire Archives; the Leicestershire and Rutland Record Office; Cambridge University Library; the Scott Polar Research Institute, University of Cambridge; the National Meteorological Archive, Exeter; the Cheshire Record Office; and the United Kingdom Hydrographic Office, Ministry of Defence Archives, Taunton. A few items were gleaned from the Archives nationales France, Paris. The remaining research was undertaken in Australian libraries and archives familiar to me from previous projects: the National Library of Australia, Canberra; the Australian National Maritime Museum, Sydney; the Archives Office of Tasmania, Hobart; the Mitchell Library at the State Library of New South Wales, Sydney; the State Library of Victoria, Melbourne; the State Library of Western Australia, Perth; and the State Library of Queensland, Brisbane. Brunel University London provided financial support for some of the research trips. I must also thank my wife and family for their support in enabling me to complete this project in the time left available after carrying out full-time university lecturing, supervising and administrative duties.

Abbreviations

ADB	*Australian Dictionary of Biography*
AJFS	*Australian Journal of French Studies*
BL	British Library
Early Days	*Early Days: Journal and Proceedings of the Royal Western Australian Historical Society*
Eisler, *The Furthest Shore*	William Eisler, *The Furthest Shore: Images of Terra Australis from the Middle Ages to Captain Cook* (Cambridge, 1995)
Flinders, *A Voyage to Terra Australis*	Matthew Flinders, *A Voyage to Terra Australis; Undertaken for the Purpose of Terra Australis Completing the Discovery of that Vast Country, and Prosecuted in the Years 1801, 1802, and 1803, in His Majesty's Ship The Investigator, and Subsequently in the Armed Vessel Porpoise and Subsequently in the Armed Vessel Porpoise and Cumberland Schooner, With an Account of the Shipwreck of the Porpoise, Arrival of the Cumberland at Mauritius, and Imprisonment of the Commander during Six Years and a Half Years in That Island*, 2 vols. (London, 1814)
HRA	*Historical Records of Australia*
HRNSW	*Historical Records of New South Wales*
IJMH	*International Journal of Maritime History*
JPRAHS	*Journal and Proceedings of the Royal Australian Historical Society*
JRAHS	*Journal of the Royal Australian Historical Society*
JRHSQ	*Journal of the Royal Historical Society of Queensland*

ML	Mitchell Library, *State Library of New South Wales*, Sydney
Mapping Our World	*Mapping Our World: Terra Incognita to Australia* (Canberra, 2013)
Mault, 'Notes on Charts'	A. Mault, 'Notes on Charts of the Coast of Tasmania, obtained from the Hydrographical Department, Paris, and copied by permission of the French Government,' *Papers and Proceedings of the Royal Society of Tasmania for 1889* (Hobart, 1890)
Mawer, *Incognita*	Granville Allen Mawer, *Incognita: The Invention and Discovery of Terra Australis* (Melbourne, 2013)
MM	*Mariner's Mirror*
Morgan, ed., *Australia Circumnavigated*	Kenneth Morgan, ed., *Australia Circumnavigated: The Voyage of Australia Circumnavigated Matthew Flinders in HMS Investigator, 1801–3*, 2 vols. (London, 2015)
NHM	Natural History Museum, South Kensington, London
NMM	National Maritime Museum, Greenwich
Pearson, *Great Southern Land*	Michael Pearson, *Great Southern Land: The Maritime Exploration of Terra Australis* (Canberra, 2005)
RO	Record Office
Tiley, *The Mermaid Tree*	Robert Tiley, *The Mermaid Tree: How a Tiny, Unknown Ship Opened Australia's North and West to Development, Dreams and Disappointment* (Sydney, 2006)
TNA	The National Archives, Kew
UKHO	United Kingdom Hydrographic Office, Ministry of Defence Archives, Taunton
Wood, *The Discovery of Australia*	G. Arnold Wood, *The Discovery of Australia*, rev. edn. (Melbourne, 1969)

Introduction

This book provides a comprehensive overview of the European maritime discovery of Australia from the sixteenth century, when geographers and voyagers searched for *Terra Australis Incognita*, until the mid-nineteenth century, by which time the continental size and shape of Australia had been identified. During these centuries, several western European powers – including Spain and Portugal but principally Britain, the Netherlands and France – supported voyages of discovery to the southern hemisphere. The book considers the following themes in detail: the characteristics of the leading explorers, developments in navigation and nautical astronomy, advances in geography and cartography, imperial and commercial policies, the emergence of scientific voyages, and the work of specialist hydrographers and surveyors.

Two books that cover some of these themes are G. Arnold Wood's *The Discovery of Australia* (1922) and Michael Pearson's *Great Southern Land: The Maritime Exploration of Terra Australis* (2005). Wood's book was lightly revised by J. C. Beaglehole for a paperback version in 1969. Though it is still lively and worth reading, the findings of modern scholarship have extended far beyond the evidence available nearly a century ago. Pearson's book is a specialist publication by the Australian government, with good illustrations but with no space to include material from primary sources. My aim in *Navigating by the Southern Cross* is to do justice to the accumulation of new material on the voyages to Australia and to how knowledge of the shape and identity of Australia evolved over time. The entire process of European engagement with the maritime discovery of Australia needs a modern overview, and I hope this book will serve that purpose.

The title of the book – *Navigating by the Southern Cross* – refers to the constellation of the bright stars in the Milky Way that were the essential guide for mariners tracing their oceanic routes in the southern hemisphere. First described by the Italian explorer Andrea Corsali in 1515, the southern cross (or crux) was not officially named until 1679 by the French astronomer Augustine Royer.[1] Books on navigation in the 1590s mentioned the latitude of the Southern Cross but at that time explorers had only a vague knowledge of the southern celestial sky and the location of the Southern Cross was unknown.[2] The southern hemisphere's absence of a single marker star, such as Polaris in the northern hemisphere, meant that the circling of the Southern Cross was a guide to the direction of the South Pole and therefore an important celestial reference point for ships proceeding in a southerly direction.[3] Thus, navigators on ships to Australia looked daily for constellations of the Southern Cross when sailing in the southern hemisphere. Those mariners were involved in elaborate calculations of coordinates, and the way in which that was handled will be discussed in the chapters below.

The extent and shape of Australia were unknown before the late eighteenth century. Throughout the Middle Ages and for most of the early modern period, geographers and cartographers referred to Australia as *Terra Australis Incognita* (the unknown Southern Land). Many theories posited that this landmass existed in the southern hemisphere, but its location and extent remained uncertain. The first chapter shows how imaginative theories about the *Terra Australis Incognita* still dominated intellectual discourse by 1600. It also considers the reasons why European explorers had failed to locate the Australian continent by that date. The circumstances of the initial landfall in Australia in 1606 of the Dutch East India Company ship the *Duyfken* are outlined at the start of the second chapter, which then covers other Dutch voyages to Australia in the early seventeenth century. Chapter 2 explains why these voyages were uncoordinated in terms of their geographical direction.

Abel Janszoon Tasman's two voyages in 1642 and 1644 represented the apex of Dutch voyaging to Australia. On the first voyage, Tasman discovered the southeastern end of Australia, which he named Van Diemen's Land. On the second voyage, Tasman sailed to a completely different part of Australia, the Gulf of Carpentaria. Chapter 3 discusses these voyages along with Tasman's encounters with Aborigines and the cartographical representation of his expeditions. One result of these voyages was that the Dutch used the name New Holland for Australia. Chapter 4 focuses on several independent expeditions that reached Australia between Tasman's voyages and James Cook's expedition in the *Endeavour*. The most significant Dutch expedition was by Willem de Vlamingh, who discovered parts of Australia's west coast in 1696/7. William Dampier was the first English navigator to reach New Holland. In 1699, he explored the northwestern Australian coast. Though he spent relatively little time on Australian soil, his published account of his voyages influenced subsequent attitudes towards Australia.

Dutch and English interest in the maritime discovery of Australia stalled in the first half of the eighteenth century, but interest in Pacific exploration increased after *c*.1750. European imperial powers became more interested in expansion into hitherto unknown parts of the globe, partly through intellectual curiosity about the wider world and partly because of a desire to expand their empires. Chapter 5 focuses on the Australian part of Cook's first Pacific voyage in the *Endeavour*. Though the voyage was mainly concerned with observing the transit of Venus at Tahiti and the exploration of Polynesia and New Zealand, Cook investigated and charted Australia's east coast. He discovered Botany Bay, found a navigable passage through the Great Barrier Reef, and claimed eastern Australia for Britain under the name of New South Wales.

Several separate voyages explored parts of Australia in the wake of Cook. Chapters 6 and 7 discuss the three most significant expeditions. Louis Aleno de Saint Alouärn explored parts of southwestern Australia in 1772 and annexed the region for the French crown as neither the British nor the Dutch had claimed Western Australia. George Vancouver's voyage around the world, beginning in 1791, explored southwestern Australia, but the expedition was mainly devoted to examination of northwest America. In 1792, the French seafarer Antoine Bruni D'Entrecasteaux's voyage in search of the lost explorer Lapérouse carried out detailed survey work along the south coast of Australia and discovered and named the Recherche archipelago. It also explored parts of Van Diemen's Land. The explorations of Matthew Flinders and George Bass in New South Wales and Van Diemen's Land are considered in Chapter 7.

Two major expeditions to explore and survey coastal Australia are examined in the next two chapters. Chapter 8, dealing with Flinders's circumnavigation of Australia in H.M.S. *Investigator*, discusses the trials and tribulations that beset this voyage, but also explains its importance in terms of cartography and firmer knowledge of Australia's maritime environment. Flinders's *A Voyage to Terra Australis* (1814) proved the capstone to the voyage's achievements, along with an atlas that provided the most accurate general chart of Australia yet undertaken. Chapter 9 discusses Nicolas Baudin's contemporaneous French voyage to survey Australia, explaining the difficulties encountered by Baudin and the reasons why the expedition's scientific and geographical results were only slowly disseminated. Baudin's expedition led to the first published chart of the Australian continent, prepared by Louis de Freycinet and printed in Paris in 1811.

Subsequent voyages of discovery in Australian waters concentrated on detailed hydrographical and surveying work. Chapter 10 concentrates on voyages undertaken by Phillip Parker King in HMS *Mermaid* and the *Bathurst* between 1817 and 1822 to survey coasts located mainly in the north and northwest Australia and to find a safe route through the Great Barrier Reef. Chapter 11 examines the work of maritime surveyors who charted Australia's coasts and offshore islands and reefs in greater detail to provide safe routes for shipping. The five hydrographers and surveyors discussed are John Clements Wickham, John Lort Stokes, Francis Blackwood, Owen Stanley and Henry Denham. They commanded voyages in the period 1837–61. These naval commanders all produced detailed charts, sheets and drawings to illustrate their navigational findings.

This book explains how Australia was gradually discovered by European navigators and incorporated onto charts, maps and atlases. The main European trading nations interested in the discovery of Australia were Britain, France and the Netherlands, with Spain and Portugal playing a limited supporting role. The contribution of these different powers in the maritime exploration of Australia will be explained. Little material is included on Aboriginal discovery of coastal Australia because Australia's main indigenous people had an oral culture in which memories were passed down from generation to generation. Very few of these memories have surfaced in relation to the European exploration of Australia, though there is one notable exception to this observation included in the chapter dealing with Cook's voyages. Lack of Aboriginal written records makes it virtually impossible to recreate the reactions of indigenous people to the intrusions made on their land by maritime explorers.

The book has three further aims. One is to show how incremental advances in geography and navigation led to advances in knowledge about the shape and size of Australia. This lengthy process covered virtually three centuries from the mid-sixteenth century until the mid-Victorian period, during which time considerable advances were made in navigation and hydrographical surveying along with greater scientific accuracy in charting and compiling maps. A second, related, aim is to explain the process of intelligence gathering that lay at the core of voyages of exploration by explaining how more accurate knowledge about Australia was embedded on maps and charts and in voyage accounts. An emphasis upon gathering objective scientific data will be emphasized.[4] Greater knowledge of navigation, astronomy and the natural world became increasingly a 'fundamental aspect of British imperial expansion.'[5] The third aim of the book is to examine and explain changing European attitudes towards the indigenous people that explorers came across in Australia. This involves consideration of European perceptions of the bodies, gestures, actions and behaviour of Aboriginal communities, all of which have to be discussed, for reasons referred to above, almost entirely through the writings of the explorers and their associates.

1

Terra Australis Incognita

The theory of the antipodes – the parts of the spherical earth diametrically opposed to the northern hemisphere – was explained frequently in geographical works written between ancient times and the Renaissance. For many centuries, the antipodes were discussed as if they existed only in the imagination rather than in the known world. By the fourteenth century, however, writers began to depict the antipodes as extensive land in the southern hemisphere. Further shifts in perception gradually occurred, for numerous geographers and writers speculated that *Terra Australis Incognita* (the unknown southern land) formed a significant portion of antipodal space. Sometimes a slightly different name was used, such as *Terra Australis Nondum Cognita* (the southern land not yet known). In the sixteenth century, *Terra Australis Incognita* (including parts of Asia and Tierra del Fuego) was always conceived of as much larger than Australia proved to be. Therefore *Terra Australis* should not be equated with modern Australia even though these designations are often used interchangeably.[1]

This chapter discusses the evidence of maps and early voyages in relation to the discovery of Australia. Most maps depicting *Terra Australis* before 1600 were based on theoretical assumptions about land unexplored by Europeans. Navigators therefore had limited accurate information to use when sailing in the Pacific Ocean. While a more precise outline of *Terra Australis* had barely emerged by 1600, some voyages across the Pacific had attempted to find land that fitted the speculative theories. Some writers have been sceptical about the results because some ventures are poorly documented and may well be fictional. This chapter will discuss whether the evidence from maps and voyages justifies these doubts.

Mapping *Terra Australis Incognita* from Ptolemy to Ortelius

The earliest significant maps to depict *Terra Australis Incognita* were based on the writings of the geographer, mathematician and astronomer Claudius Ptolemy, who lived in Alexandria, Egypt, between 90 and 168 AD at a time when educated Europeans had no definite information about lands in the southern hemisphere. Ptolemy only had knowledge of around a quarter of the globe but he accepted the existence of a spherical earth, which dated from Aristotle's time, and believed a large landmass must exist in the southern hemisphere to counterbalance parts of Asia, Europe and Africa in the northern hemisphere. This supposition was based on the notion that extensive land in the southern hemisphere maintained the earth's equilibrium on its axis and thereby prevented it from toppling over. This large land lay to the south and east of Africa but spread across the southern border of the Indian Ocean to join eastern Asia. Ptolemy did not know what proportion of the unknown world consisted of land or sea or the shape and extent of unexplored land, and he exaggerated the coordinates of the known habitable world (the *oikoumene*). Yet his theoretical insistence that a large landmass in the southern hemisphere existed to balance land in the northern hemisphere influenced geography for centuries. Drawing upon an inherited scientific hypothesis, Ptolemy posited that the Indian Ocean was landlocked. The southern coast of that ocean, in his view, was the great unknown south land and part of an Austral continent.[2]

Ptolemy's mapmaker's manual *Geographia*, originally written in Greek, survived in various versions and attracted additions by other geographers after his death. No maps to accompany this manuscript existed from Ptolemy's own time, and it is unknown whether his *Geographia* originally contained maps. This treatise presented the most detailed topography of Europe and Asia. Rediscovered in 1406/7 after centuries of neglect, a Latin translation of the *Geographia* circulated swiftly and soon became a standard work of geographical reference. Maps were produced by moveable type printing that aimed to show the world as Ptolemy understood it.[3] The first printed edition of these redrawn maps appeared in 1477, published in Bologna as part of the then only available printed world atlas. The maps soon became regarded by scholars as authoritative geographical sources.[4]

More than fifty editions of the Ptolemaic world map were published between 1477 and 1730.[5] A typical example was Sebastian Münster's *The World after Ptolemy* (1540), which showed a southern landmass enclosing the Indian Ocean with an east-west coastline at 17° longitude and an inscription of 'Terra Incognita secundum Pto' ('the unknown land according to Ptolemy'). This land, extending throughout the entire circumference of the map, joined Asia to southern Africa, following Ptolemy's stipulation that a land bridge connected those lands. The map depicted the Mediterranean Sea and North Africa reasonably accurately, but the landlocked Indian Ocean and the size and shape of the Great South

Land, based on Ptolemy's work, were erroneous. Ptolemy had erred in suggesting that the Indian Ocean was an enclosed sea, for Marco Polo's writings of *c.*1300, describing his travels through the Middle East, the coastal regions of Asia and China, had disproved this notion.[6]

Felipe Fernández-Armesto has deftly noted that Terra Australis was the 'biggest intruder from myth to the map' in the sixteenth century.[7] An oversized Terra Australis was depicted on several globes in the late 1520s.[8] The cartographers Franciscus Monachus and Oronce Finé used the phrase *terra australis* on maps in the late 1520s and early 1530s, by which time the term was beginning to be used more widely. The southern continent appeared as a monumental landmass on Finé's 1531 double cordiform map of the world.[9] This map bore the inscription 'Terra Australis recentern inventa, sed nondum plene cognita' ('Terra Australis, recently discovered but not yet fully known').[10] Finé's map became an enduring image of a vast southern continent, identified as Terra Australis rather than as the antipodes just at the time when such a distinction was first made.[11] As Alfred Hiatt has explained, by the 1530s 'the antipodes were reformulated as *Terra Australis*, a land mass that mimicked and mirrored New World discoveries by means of its position on the brink of exploration.'[12]

The Flemish mapmaker Mercator, who absorbed Ptolemy's geography and ideas, became the leading figure in the sixteenth-century dissemination of the shape and location of the southern continent, believing that it existed and was greater in extent than other parts of the earth. Mercator followed Ptolemy's belief in the theory of equipoise between the northern and southern hemispheres.[13] His small, single-sheet world map of 1538 presented both hemispheres separately in double heart-shaped frames in a double cordiform projection. The map incorporated the findings of Vasco da Gama's voyage linking Europe with Asia (1497–9) to show the true peninsular shape of India, but it also followed Ptolemy in many respects.[14] Mercator's world map (1538), globe (1541) and grand-engraved wall map of the world (1569) all included Terra Australis Incognita, though the 1538 world map included a full depiction of Terra Australis whereas only part of the southern continent was shown on his world map of 1569. Tierra del Fuego, discovered by Ferdinand Magellan in 1520, was the only fixed land among the space in the southern latitudes on these maps.[15]

On the map of 1538, Mercator's southern continent was unnamed and indicated by a hatched line. A legend stated that 'it is certain that there is a land here, but its size and the limits of its boundaries are uncertain.' Mercator had read *The Travels of Marco Polo*, which circulated widely among scholars. The

Venetian traveller's accounts of his voyage from China to the Middle East in 1292, via the straits of Malacca, his description of his six months' sojourn in Java Minor (Sumatra) and his remarks on the wealth of the Indies fascinated European readers. Polo wrote about fabulously rich countries to the south and east of today's Indonesia.[16] These included Beach/Locach, a gold-bearing province, and Maletur, which had abundant spices. Mercator incorporated these kingdoms into Terra Australis on his world map of 1538.[17]

Mercator derived several place names from Polo's travel account. On his globe of 1541, Mercator showed Polo's Beach/Locach, situated on a large promontory of the southern continent to the south of Java. This seemingly equated to the land called Jave-la-Grande, which featured on contemporaneous maps discussed below. On his world map of 1569, Mercator maintained the position of Beach/Locach on the extensive South Land, and this was copied on many subsequent world maps.[18] Thus Mercator's son, Rumold, published a world map in 1587, reissued in Mercator's atlas of 1595, depicting an extensive Terra Australis,

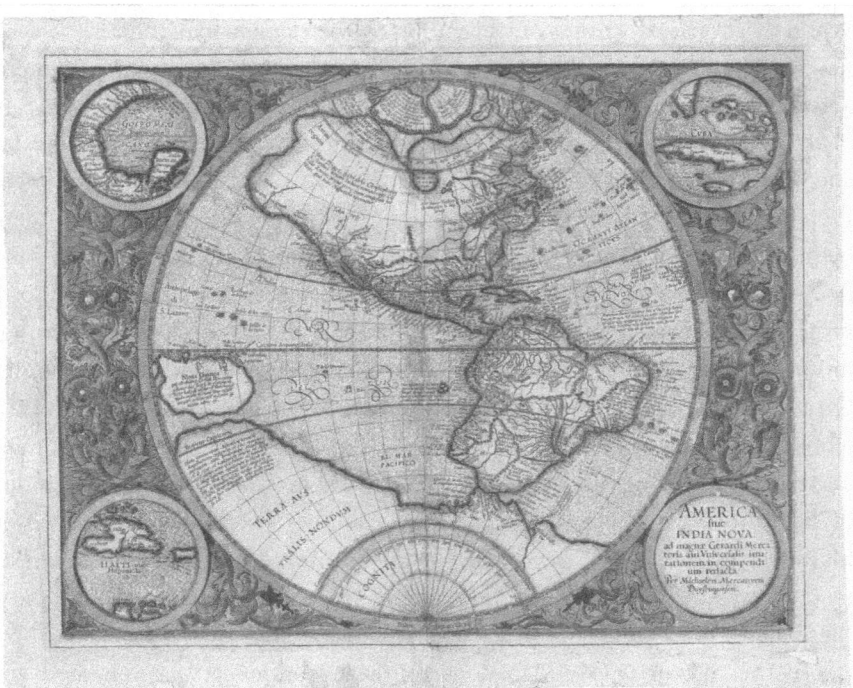

Map 1 Michael Mercator, *America siue India nova: ad magnae Gerardi Mercatoris aui Universalis imitationem in compendium redacta* (Duysburgensem: Michaelem Mercatorem, 1595) MAP NK 2078 Bib ID 2637149

encircling the entire southern hemisphere, with Beach/Locach and Maletur situated on a large promontory to the south of Java. It is now thought that Beach/Locach was situated in Thailand while Maletur was in Malaysia.[19]

Acquainting himself with other travel literature, Mercator believed that the southern continent had been sighted. He absorbed material from numerous sources to present his own cartographical understanding of the extent and location of the unknown southern land. His map of 1569 showed Terra Australis as a vast landmass lying to the south of Africa but not joined to it. It connected *Terra Australis Nondum Cognita* with the Magellan Straits and Tierra del Fuego at the southern end of South America, crossing along the bottom of the map to sweep up to New Guinea before falling away to the southwest. The Indian Ocean was now unenclosed, in contrast to the late fifteenth-century maps that followed Ptolemy.[20]

Mercator's cartographic depiction of the southern continent was followed by others, notably by his fellow Flemish mapmaker Ortelius, and it soon became commonly included on maps.[21] Ortelius, unlike Mercator, did little original work

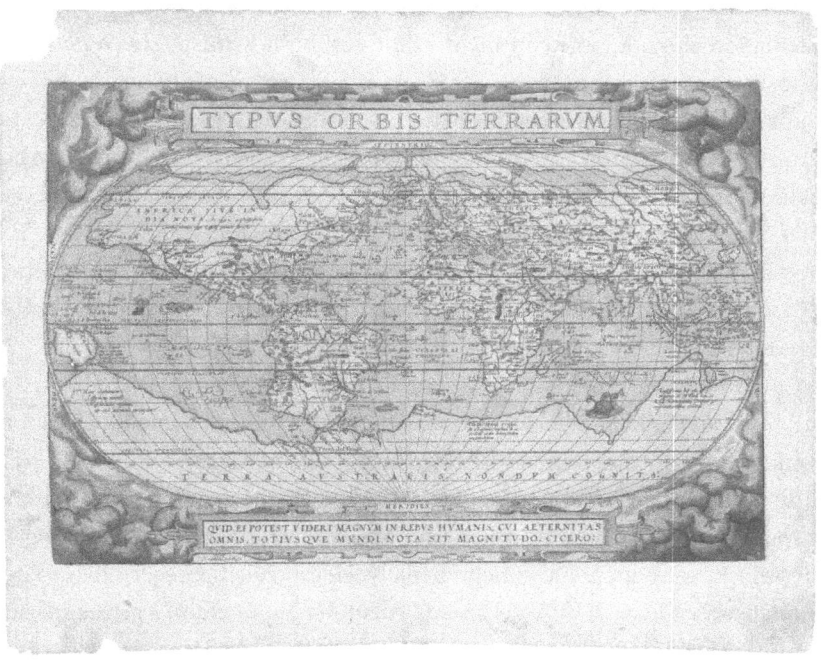

Map 2 Abraham Ortelius, *Typus orbis terrarum* (Antwerp: Coppenium Diesth, ?1570) MAP NK 10001 Bib ID 1180467

as a geographer; he focused instead on disseminating maps as a cartographic businessman. Ortelius copied or adapted seventy maps on fifty-three sheets mainly by other mapmakers for his atlas *Theatrum Orbis Terrarum* (1570). He followed Mercator in depicting Beach/Locach on his maps, continuing the supposition that a great southern landmass existed. Whether or not this large body of land was inhabited elicited various responses, with no convincing supporting evidence.[22] Ortelius's eight-leaved world map *Typus Orbis Terrarum*, included in his atlas of 1570, depicted the Ptolemaic southern continent, but exaggerated the size of the Great South Land to counterbalance the size of high polar Arctic regions. This map showed a strait between New Guinea and a large southern continent, but qualified it by a note to the effect that it was still unknown whether New Guinea was an island or part of the Great South Land.[23]

A Chinese discovery of Australia?

There is no evidence that Asian, Arabic or Indonesian seafarers discovered Australia. Arab seafarers reached Indonesian islands by the thirteenth century. They had acquired copies of Ptolemy's work, and would have been aware of speculation about a large continent in the southern hemisphere. Whether this curiosity was sufficient for their ships to explore south of Indonesia, however, is unknown. By the eighteenth century, a profitable trepang industry existed between Makassar on Sulawesi and Australia's north coast, providing sea cucumbers to Chinese markets, but there is no evidence that this traffic preceded 1700. The Chinese knew about Indonesia by the early fourteenth century, as the large map of the China Sea and Indian Ocean produced by Zhu Siben between 1311 and 1320 shows. But whether they were aware of lands to the south and east of Indonesia remains unproven.[24]

Gavin Menzies argued the case for a Chinese discovery of Australia in *1421: The Year China Discovered the World* (2002). The author claimed he had found voyages made in the years 1421–3 by four fleets of Chinese junks led by the third Ming emperor Zhu Di's captains, trained by the famous eunuch admiral Zhenge He accompanied by other admirals such as Zhou Man and Hong Bao. The voyages were apparently phenomenally widespread; they sailed to the Arctic, Antarctica, both coasts of America and Australia in pursuit of a global maritime empire. Menzies expansively asserted that the Chinese circumnavigated the globe a century before Magellan, reached America seventy years before Columbus and arrived in Australia 350 years before Captain Cook. The Chinese imperial dynasty's isolationist policy had destroyed all documents relating to the vessels. To counteract this deficiency, Menzies drew upon an eclectic and idiosyncratic mélange of supposedly Chinese artefacts, plants, animals and DNA traces relating to Australia; upon imaginative contentions concerning features on early maps; and upon unidentified shipwrecks purportedly from the fifteenth century.[25] Menzies argued that Zhou Man's fleet reached Australia, and that Hong Bao led a voyage that made a landfall near modern Bunbury, Western Australia.[26]

Menzies's *1421* has sold millions of copies, but even a cursory glance at its contents indicates that it is a work of pseudo-history. Menzies had no academic training as a historian. Nor did he read Chinese. He relied mainly on maps and charts for his evidence, yet he repeatedly misinterpreted them. In addition, three significant methodological errors undercut his findings. First, there is the basic error of supposing that the coast marked on early maps and charts had been surveyed rather than being a hypothetical or imagined construct. Second, it is claimed that Portuguese charts had been copied from earlier Chinese originals made by Hong Bao and Zhou Man, though no such charts by them have survived. Third, Menzies mistranscribed a great many place-name inscriptions on the maps he used, failed to consult the main source materials relating to Zheng He and lacked evidence confirming that the voyages of 1421–3 took place as he described them.[27] Thus, his book rested on unsustainable assumptions and interpretations.[28]

The Dieppe maps and Jave-la-Grande – a Portuguese discovery of Australia?

As part of their sphere of influence under the Treaty of Tordesillas (1494), whereby they could expand into lands east of a demarcation line near the Cape Verde islands, leaving Spain to expand west of the line, the Portuguese established a strong presence in the Indian Ocean and the East Indies in the sixteenth century. Portuguese navigators had sailed around the Cape of Good Hope by 1488 on an expedition led by Bartholomew Diaz. A decade later, Vasco da Gama successfully discovered a sea route from Europe to India. The Portuguese established a trading base at Malacca, on the Malay peninsula, by 1511 and a colony in Timor from 1516. They exploited the resources and products of the Indies, notably the trade in spices, but had little motivation to explore in Australian waters and made no territorial claims south of Indonesia.[29] Nor did Spain. In 1520, Magellan's voyage from Spain identified a sea route from the southern end of the Atlantic through a passage adjacent to Tierra del

Fuego to the Pacific Ocean. This was named after him as the Strait of Magellan. But neither Magellan nor any other sixteenth-century explorer found Terra Australis.[30]

Many historians have considered whether there was a Portuguese discovery of Australia during the sixteenth century. Sixteen maps created in the period 1540–87 by French cartographers based at Dieppe have been the main source material to support this argument.[31] The maps are scattered across various institutions; none emanate from Portugal and none are supported by written documentation. They purport to show a land named Jave-la-Grande, located south of Indonesia, that has been equated with all or part of Australia. Thus, on Pierre Desceliers' 'Royal' World Map of 1546 Jave-la-Grande is shown as extending from Indonesia to Antarctica and covering less than half of Australia, though displaced by 24°W and 5°N.[32] The inscriptions on Jave-la-Grande on the Dieppe maps are mainly written in Portuguese, Gallicised Portuguese and French.[33]

The depiction of Java on the Dieppe maps shows a fabulous, exotic realm with various birds and animals that may represent wildlife from New Guinea and Australia but may also be imaginary creatures. Ornamental scenes, with trees, huts and small human figures, are also depicted on these maps. Some animals represented on the maps, such as monkeys, elephants and camels, are more obviously related to Asia than to Australia.[34] Despite being produced by different cartographers over several decades, the landmass identified as Jave-la-Grande is portrayed consistently.[35] Australia is the only large landmass between Indonesia and Antarctica, and the outline of Jave-la-Grande has similarities (albeit very loosely) with the shape and size of Australia.[36]

The French never claimed to have discovered Jave-la-Grande; they attributed the discovery to the Portuguese. Information about a Portuguese voyage to Jave-la-Grande was obtained by the French in Sumatra during Jean Parmentier's expedition from Dieppe in 1529/30 that aimed to break the Portuguese spice trade monopoly.[37] A Portuguese expedition that might have reached Australia was a fleet of fourteen ships under the command of Cristovão de Mendonça in mid-1519, but no records have survived for this voyage. In 1521, Mendonça left Goa with three ships on another expedition to search for Pliny's legendary gold-bearing isles that the Portuguese believed lay somewhere east of Sumatra. Mendonça reached Malacca but nothing further is known about his voyage. Some historians have argued that the wreckage from the expedition has been located at a few points on Australia's coastline whence it would have drifted thousands of miles before being washed up on shore. Supporting documentation for this supposition is weak, however, and will be discussed below.[38]

Jave-la-Grande was purportedly the size of a continent. The designation of such a land followed Polo's misleading description of Java Major as the largest island in the world. Some Dieppe mapmakers depicted Jave-la-Grande as Java Major while others applied it to the unknown landmass beneath Java.[39] On the Dieppe maps, Java Major became a promontory of Terra Australis.[40] Sixteenth-century mapmakers differed in their representation of Jave-la-Grande. Jean Rotz's map in the *Boke of Idography* (1542) provided it with a northern, eastern and western border but no southern border. Desceliers' world map of 1550 joined Jave-la-Grande to *Terre Australe*, partly because no southern border between the two lands had been identified.[41] One scholar has suggested that the representation of Jave-la-Grande on this map was 'an elaboration of the southern land mass as it appeared on Mercator's 1541 globe.'[42]

In the mid-1780s, the hydrographer Alexander Dalrymple saw a manuscript of one Dieppe map showing Jave-la-Grande. Credited with having made the first reference to the Dieppe maps, he thought this proved Portuguese priority in the discovery of Australia.[43] Dalrymple claimed Jave-la-Grande was Australia.[44] He published over 200 facsimile copies of the eastern section of one of the main Dieppe maps, known as the Harleian manuscript. This whetted scholarly appetite for a putative Portuguese discovery of Australia.[45] Further maps from the same school of cartography were identified in the later nineteenth century. Matthew Flinders thought it possible that the Portuguese had seen part of the north and northwest coasts of Australia in their voyages to and from India before 1540, but he carefully noted that this was conjectural.[46]

If the Dieppe maps were derived from Portuguese evidence, they were not based on cartography because there is no indication of land that could be taken to represent Australia on Portuguese charts of the first half of the sixteenth century.[47] Toponomic evidence on the maps does not support the view that the Portuguese discovered Australia, but points to place-name corruption.[48] Rather than representing any part of Australia, it has been argued that Jave-la-Grande was a composite construction made up of parts of the coasts of Java and Vietnam.[49] Another viewpoint is that the east coast on the Dieppe maps was Sumba while the west coast represented west Java.[50] Yet another interpretation is that the Dieppe maps showed the coasts of either Java and Sumatra or Java and Sumba.[51] These views are argued with various degrees of plausibility but no certainty.

Some Dieppe mapmakers may have considered Jave-la-Grande was partly or entirely a cosmographical fiction rather than an actual part of Terra Australis. One mapmaker, Guillaume le Testu, creator of a manuscript atlas from 1555–6 and a planisphere dated 1566, depicted imaginary lands to warn navigators of the dangers of sailing in unknown seas.[52] How to interpret these maps has not reached a consensus. One historian argued that le Testu mixed up fact and fiction, including both known landmarks and conjectural places.[53] Another stated that le Testu noted that his depiction of the southern continent was based on his imagination because no-one had yet discovered such a landmass.[54] Most recently, it has been argued that le Testu accepted the reality of Jave-la-Grande but marked an imaginary coastline between Java-la-Grande and Tierra del Fuego.[55] Le Testu himself acknowledged the imaginative element in his mapmaking. His planisphere of 1566 referred to the 'part of the same land of the south called Australie which has not yet been discovered because there is no record that anyone has searched it out and because it is only drawn from imagination.'[56]

Kenneth G. McIntyre argued that Jave-la-Grande represented Australia's east coast. To support his arguments, he cited artefacts found around Australia's coastline that can be linked to early sixteenth-century Portuguese voyages.[57] But the connections made were tenuous and, in some cases, clearly wrong. Thus, McIntyre argued that two guns found in 1916 on Carronade Island, on Western Australia's Kimberley coast, were Portuguese guns cast in Seville in the fifteenth or early sixteenth centuries. However, a careful physical, chemical and x-ray examination of the guns has shown that the guns were manufactured in south-east Asia about three centuries later.[58] McIntyre further argued that wreckage found at Warrnambool, Victoria, came from the remains of a Portuguese ship commanded by Mendonça in the 1520s, and that a ruined building at Bittangabee near Twofold Bay, New South Wales, was a fortress built by the Portuguese.[59] However, ship relics at Warrnambool have not been conclusively identified, while the Bittangabee ruins are now known to be the remains of a storehouse built in 1844.[60]

Other writers have discussed the representation of Jave-la-Grande on the Dieppe maps. Lawrence Fitzgerald argued that these maps were distorted versions of Australia's coasts based on Mendonça's voyage, and that reassembling them into a different order would overcome the problem.[61] Unfortunately, Fitzgerald had no proof that the maps were based on that thinly documented voyage and his attempt to piece together the Dieppe maps at different angles from their original representation, though ingenious, lacked credibility.[62] A different and more convincing argument was that Jave-la-Grande was based on cosmographical concepts of the early sixteenth century and not derived from the discovery of Australia's coasts made by unknown voyagers.[63] While much scholarly energy has been invested into the mysteries of Jave-le-Grande, the maps had little influence on geographers or explorers outside of Dieppe and provided no stimulus to further Portuguese exploration of Australia.[64]

Spanish voyages to *Terra Australis*

Spanish conquest of the Philippines in 1565 led to the establishment of an important trade route between New Spain (now Mexico) and the western Pacific. Galleons sailed regularly from Acapulco, on Mexico's Pacific coast, to Manila with silver and returned laden with goods from the east. Spanish navigators wanted to gain material riches, such as spices from the East Indies. Spanish humanists knew about the speculation that a vast continent – Terra Australis – might lie somewhere in the Pacific. These various types of impetus led to three Spanish expeditions from Peru to the South Pacific between 1567 and 1606. Spain was the first European nation to sponsor expeditions to search for Terra Australis.[65]

The first two voyages, ordered by Peru's governor, were commanded by Spanish navigator Álvaro Mendaña y Neira.[66] In the first expedition (1567–9), he discovered and claimed for Spain the Solomon Islands, a hitherto unknown Pacific archipelago. The Spanish soldier Pedro Sarmiento da Gamboa, cosmographer on the voyage, believed, on the basis of Inca lore, that a populated southern continent existed between the east of Java and the Strait of Magellan, but the voyage failed to locate such a landmass.[67] Mendaña pressed for many years for a follow-up second voyage. Eventually, he gained financial support and royal approval for a larger expedition from Peru's viceregal government.[68] On this voyage (1595–7), Mendaña failed to reach the Solomon Islands but he discovered the Marquesas and the Melanesian island of Santa Cruz. He died there, as did many of his crew, from either disease or massacre by the natives. The remnants of his ship's company were led to the Philippines by Pedro Fernándo de Quirós, a Portuguese navigator in the service of Spain.[69]

It was not until 1606 that a Spanish expedition, led by Quirós, came within proximate distance of Australia. He believed a southern continent existed between the Strait of Magellan and New Guinea. This was partly based on his observation that light-skinned islanders he had come across on Mendaña's second expedition came from the yet-to-be-found Great South Land.[70] Quirós gained the Pope and Spanish king's support for his voyage. Setting out from Callao, the port of Lima, with two vessels and a tender, his mission was to find the austral continent or Nuevo Mondo, as he called it. Quirós as overall commander was assisted by Luis Vaez de Torres, the captain of the *Almirante*, and Don Diego de Prado, commander of the *Capitana*. The expedition reached an island north of Santa Cruz that Quirós thought was the southern continent. He named it Tierra Austrialia del Espíritu Santo.[71] In June 1606, the expedition's vessels were separated in a storm. Quirós deserted the mission, without any signal or notice to many of his crew, and sailed for Acapulco. He appears to have abandoned the expedition for several reasons: he was ill, the mid-winter weather made navigation difficult, his ship needed repair and his crew were mutinous. His second-in-command Torres, another Portuguese navigator, waited fifteen days for Quirós to return to Santa Cruz. After he failed to do so, sealed orders were opened that made Prado the leader of the expedition, with Torres as navigating captain.[72]

Torres explored the seas around Espíritu Santo, having concluded it was not a continent. He then sailed south to the 21st parallel and abandoned hope of finding the Great Southern Land. He headed north to Manila, made landfall at Tagula, in the Louisiade Archipelago, turned westwards and explored the southern coast of New Guinea as far as the Gulf of Papua. Tracing Torres's track from this point onwards is difficult to determine from surviving sources, but, en route to Manila, he came across the strait that now bears his name. He had no previous knowledge of Torres Strait and, in fact, only sailed through it because he had failed to weather the seas leading to the north side of New Guinea.[73]

Torres realized, as all later navigators confirmed, that the approach to Torres Strait was hazardous because of the submerged continental shelf he referred to as 'placel.'[74] This is one of the most treacherous sea routes in the world. Torres Strait is 93 miles wide at its narrowest extent, linking the Coral Sea in the east with the Arafura Sea in the west. It has shallow water, many reefs, shoals, sand cays and scattered small islands. Labyrinthine coral formation effectively closes southeastern approaches except for shallow, small draft vessels. Torres recorded the abundant shoals and great currents but gave no indication that he knew a strait existed there.[75] He was the first navigator to sail through the strait – something not repeated until Cook's voyage in the *Endeavour* in 1770.

Torres eventually reached Manila. Nothing is known about him after he had filed an official account of his voyage for the Spanish authorities. His contribution to the discovery of Australia is difficult to pinpoint. It has been stated that Torres sighted Australia.[76] But there is no evidence that he did so. No historian has claimed that Torres landed in Australia, but Brett Hilder argued that Torres sailed through Endeavour Strait, the most southerly route through Torres Strait, and sighted Australia's coast.[77] Exactly which track he took, and whether he saw the Australian mainland, is still debated by historians, who have no evidence of latitudes and only haphazard longitudes on the charts Torres used.[78] One interpretation is based on Torres's own evidence and that of Prado.[79]

It refers to sailing through a strait at 11°S, which suggests a passage through Endeavour Strait in the extreme south of Torres Strait. This explanation noted that Torres did not realize he was passing through a strait.[80] An alternative view is that Torres sailed through the narrow Bligh Channel, near the New Guinea coast, from which he would not have been able to see Australia.[81]

Torres's traversal through the strait was kept secret for many years by the Spanish. It was not until the eve of the American Revolution that Dalrymple, having gained documents from a British raid on Manila in 1762, translated them into English and named the strait.[82] The Spanish showed virtually no interest in the strait through which Torres sailed. This indifference extended to Torres's voyage as a whole because it offered no prospects of trade, exploration or colonization. Quirós arrived in Madrid in October 1607, and tried to persuade the Spanish authorities to support another voyage in search of the southern continent, but his pleas fell on deaf ears.[83] Nevertheless, his voyage kindled further European speculation about the existence of a southern continent. At least twenty-five books were published about this expedition in different European languages.[84] The Spanish took no further interest in voyaging towards Australia, however, and it was the Dutch instead who displayed curiosity about the southern continent immediately after the expedition of Quirós and Torres.

Conclusion

Before 1600, Australia had not been discovered or mapped, but the circulation of Ptolemy's geographic theories greatly influenced sixteenth-century mapmakers, notably Mercator and Ortelius, to depict a large southern continent they named Terra Australis. This was an imaginative construct based on theoretical geography and Marco Polo's travel accounts. The nearest equivalent to portraying part of this landmass on maps consisted of the Dieppe maps of Jave-la-Grande, derived from Portuguese origin. Interpretation of those maps has exercised the ingenuity and analytical skills of numerous modern scholars, but there is no conclusive evidence that the maps represented parts of Australia. Nor did the Dieppe maps influence Portuguese voyages of exploration, if indeed there were any, within reach of Australia's shores.

Arguments purporting to show that the Chinese, in the fifteenth century, or the Portuguese, in the sixteenth century, discovered Terra Australis or Australia founder on the grounds of unconvincing evidence. Two Spanish voyages to the

Pacific under Mendaña also failed to locate Australia. Thus, there is no reason to dispute the verdict of the geographer Oskar Spate who wrote about the discovery of Australia that 'as an exercise in historical detection it is engagingly replete with hopeful clues which lead nowhere, dark sayings which cut both ways, and suspects who have to be let off, till it all ends in a dismal verdict of not proven.'[85] In 1606, however, the Portuguese navigator Torres sailed through Torres Strait for the first time. He probably did not see the Australian mainland, let alone land on it, but this marked the first known voyage to sail within proximate distance of Australia.

Dutch exploration of seventeenth-century Australia

The Dutch dominated Australian maritime exploration during the seventeenth century. The Dutch East India Company (Verenigde Oostindische Compagnie or VOC), founded in 1602, established itself as the leading European commercial organization within a few days' sail of northwest Australia. With headquarters in Amsterdam, this large chartered trading company created a powerful base in Bantam (near today's Banten), a small port in western Java, where a governor and a full professional seafaring staff were located. Experienced navigators and maritime chart makers were among their number. In 1619 Batavia (now Jakarta), on the north coast of Java, superseded Bantam as the VOC's centre of government and trade in the East Indies (now Indonesia). It became the main Dutch base for curtailing Portuguese dominance of the Asian trading network between the Indian Ocean and the Far East.[1]

The Dutch East India Company's domain in the Indian Ocean stretched from the Cape of Good Hope to the East Indies. Commercial gains lay at its heart. VOC ships plied across the Atlantic and Indian oceans to Batavia, where they collected cargoes of spices – pepper, cinnamon and cloves – for European consumption. Their base in the East Indies enabled the VOC to engage in extensive intra-Asian trade with Ceylon, Japan and China. Dutch shipping competed with Portuguese, Spanish and English rivals in the Indian Ocean and China Sea.[2] Maritime exploration was only a relatively minor offshoot of these commercial activities.[3] That is why one historian has dubbed the VOC 'a reluctant discoverer.'[4] Nevertheless, VOC vessels made exploratory voyages in the early seventeenth century more regularly than the ships of any other European trading power. Thirty-two Dutch voyages either touched or were thought to have reached the west Australian coast in the seventeenth century.[5] They were aided by the VOC's professional charting of unknown waters.[6]

Günter Schilder has shown that the VOC were involved in two types of exploratory voyages from their base in the East Indies. First, some voyages discovered offshore islands around Australia, especially on the west coast, and sometimes touched at parts of the mainland, by accident rather than by design. These led to scattered findings about Australia's coastal geography that fitted no obvious pattern, with no indication that the places they came across were part of a large landmass. Second, on relatively few occasions VOC ships made expeditions to locate the routes to the Great South Land and to report back to the VOC's governor in Batavia about their discoveries.[7] Some voyages had instructions to explore parts of Terra Australis but others were VOC ventures that came across offshore islands and the northwest Australia by following shipping routes across the Indian Ocean to the East Indies.

The voyage of the *Duyfken*, 1606

In 1606, the VOC's *Duyfken* (*Little Dove*), a tiny ship less than twenty metres long, was the first vessel definitely known to reach mainland Australia. Its shallow draught was suitable for surveying near shorelines. In September 1605, the *Duyfken* received orders to remain in the East Indies for three years to search for new sources of trade.[8] The Director of the VOC's Bantam factory, Jan Willem Verschoor, wanted to follow up rumours that gold and trading opportunities could be tapped from land lying to the southeast of the Spice Islands.[9] Verschoor despatched the *Duyfken*, under Willem Janszoon's command, on a voyage that left Bantam on 28 November 1605 for Banda, about 1,680 miles further east, and then to New Guinea, landing several times. A skirmish with Papuans led to the death of eight crew members. Undeterred by such hostility, Janszoon continued along the same coast until he reached extensive shoals and shallow reefs that diverted the voyage to the south. The shoals were probably at the western edge of Torres Strait, though Janszoon did not realize that.[10] He may have thought the shoals marked a bay, but he did not check whether that was the case or whether a strait existed there.[11]

The *Duyfken* reached the Gulf of Carpentaria during the monsoon season in February 1606. Janszoon wrote 'Nova Guinea' on his chart, believing he had arrived at a southern arm of New Guinea. The point where the ship reached the coast was marked on its chart as 11°48′S, though the actual latitude was 12°14′, an error of forty-eight kilometres. No longitude was recorded. It is thought that this position was at the mouth of today's Pennefather River. Janszoon named it *R. met het Bosch* (River with the Bush).[12] The *Duyfken* sailed around 200 miles down the east side of the Gulf of Carpentaria as far as Cape Keerweer (Turnaround). Parts of this drab, low-lying coast were probably examined, but no log survives for the voyage to provide any specific details. We do not know for how long the ship anchored along the coast.[13]

At Cape Keerweer, Janszoon turned the vessel around to retrace her track up the west side of the Cape York peninsula. It is not known why he turned back, but possibly it resulted from a confrontation between the crew and Aborigines at the mouth of the Batavia River coupled with a lack of food and water. The men of the *Duyfken* had fired muskets on the Aborigines.[14] Captain John Saris, an Englishman resident in Bantam, recorded that men were sent on shore from the *Duyfken* to 'entreate of trade', but one was 'killed by the Heathens, which are man-eaters; so they were constrained to returne, finding no good to be done there.' After this incident and finding no trade opportunities, the *Duyfken* left the Australian coast about 30 miles to the southwest of Cape York and headed back to Banda. The crew were unaware that they were the first Europeans to set foot on Australian soil.[15]

The main contemporary information for the *Duyfken*'s expedition lies in the chart compiled on the voyage. This shows the entire course of the voyage, the southern coast of 'Nova Guinea', the landfall on the Gulf of Carpentaria and the position of Cape Keerweer. Janszoon allocated Dutch names to landmarks he came across.[16] The chart was reasonably accurate: a large bay now called Albatross Bay, for example, approximates its actual shape.[17] James Henderson has combined the information on the chart with modern exploration of the route followed to suggest the likely places where the *Duyfken* touched at the coast. This has been undertaken carefully, but of course this methodology can only indicate the possible route followed.[18]

Virtually no commercial possibilities for the VOC emerged as a result of the *Duyfken*'s voyage. Janszoon's report of unfriendly natives discouraged Dutch exploration of Australia's north coast for nearly two decades.[19] Nevertheless, the *Duyfken*'s voyage was an important staging post in the European discovery of Australia: it marked the first known landfall by navigators on that continent, and produced the first European chart depicting part of the land discovered. To commemorate the voyage, a replica *Duyfken*, constructed in Fremantle in the late 1990s, has re-enacted the original voyage and is now used regularly for public tours from Fremantle Fishing Boat Harbour up the Swan River.[20]

The next Dutch expedition to find Terra Australis occurred in 1615. Organized by the private Australische Compagnie of Hoorn in the Netherlands and led by a former VOC director, Isaac le Maire, aided by Willem Schouten, two ships, the *Eendracht* and the *Horn*, undertook a secret expedition in search of Terra Australis.[21] Le Maire reached the Tongan Islands and left a detailed description of Polynesians he encountered in the Hoorn Islands (now part of the French overseas collectivity of Wallis and Futuna). Schouten persuaded Le Maire to sail north of New Guinea because they had enough information about that route to ensure the prospect of a safe voyage. The aim of finding Terra Australis was therefore abandoned. The vessels reached Bantam, where the new Governor, Jan Pieterszoon Coen, confiscated the ships and arrested the commanders because they had breached the VOC's patent. He sent them back to the Netherlands. Le Maire died on the voyage. The Australische Compagnie did not discover any part of Australia.[22]

Dirk Hartog and the *Eendracht*, 1616

It took a decade after the *Duyfken's* voyage for another VOC vessel to reach Australia. This involved an accidental landfall on Western Australia's largest and most western island. The ship was the *Eendracht* (Unity or Harmony) under the command of Dirk Hartog. It was a large new vessel of 700 tonnes. Its skipper was already working for the VOC in Bantam by 1609, and had sailed on numerous voyages. His expedition in the *Eendracht* formed part of a small fleet of five ships. On 23 January 1616, these vessels left Texel roadstead, the anchoring place on the Zuidersee, on a voyage to the East Indies.[23]

Hartog followed the new route across the Indian Ocean established by the Dutch navigator Hendrik Brouwer in 1610. This offered a faster sailing time than earlier Portuguese voyages to the East Indies had achieved. Brouwer, who had sailed across the Indian Ocean, advocated taking advantage of strong, constant westerly winds that blew south of 36° latitude in heavy seas in the Southern Ocean. Aided by these 'roaring forties' with their very high waves, ships sailed for about a thousand miles east from the Cape of Good Hope before altering course for the north towards the Sunda Strait to reach Java. The exact location for the turn to the north was subject to the judgement of individual commanders. This route avoided sailing in the face of strong south-east trade winds that predominated in higher latitudes and it enabled Dutch ships to steer away from Portuguese territories in Africa and India.[24]

The southerly route had the advantage of being open sea, with no low-lying or dangerous islands lurking unseen in hazy or foggy weather.[25] Ships sailing along different latitudes between 35°S and 44°S, however, would end up in dissimilar longitudes. Following Brouwer's route could therefore lead to VOC vessels ending up in widely different parts of the Indian Ocean. This was inevitable in terms of current navigational knowledge. Detailed charts of that ocean were largely lacking at the time. Mariners usually relied on dead reckoning to pinpoint their location, which involved plotting the distance and direction of a ship from one point to the next, but it lacked precision in calculating longitude. Nevertheless, in 1616 the Brouwer route was made mandatory for all VOC vessels sailing beyond the Cape of Good Hope. It became a major contribution to oceanic navigation.[26]

On his voyage, Hartog followed Brouwer's instructions until he estimated it was time to head north for Java. He either missed the correct position to head north or sailed too far south with the 'roaring forties' behind him.[27] He landed at Cape Inscription on Dirk Hartog Island, in Shark Bay, in Western Australia. His arrival there was documented in several contemporary letters, though no journals are extant.[28] The location has rugged gorges, cliffs, low-lying vegetation and no surface water. Hartog only stayed there for two days.[29] Yet he realized he had reached a new land unknown to navigators. To mark the occasion, he erected a post on the cliff top at Cape Inscription and fixed to it a pewter dinner plate. The plate recorded the names of Hartog and his senior merchant (Gilles Mibais of Liège) and noted that the *Eendracht* reached Dirk Hartog Island on 25 October 1616 and left on 27 October; it made no claim to Dutch possession of the island. The plate, now deposited at Amsterdam's Rijksmuseum, is the oldest surviving artefact of a European landing in Australia.[30]

Hartog made three further brief landings on the west Australian coast at about 22°, 23° and 25°S. We do not know whether he thought this coast was continuous. The *Eendracht* then sailed towards Bantam, which was only reached after dealing with hostility at Makassar arising from an incident a year earlier when a native vice-ruler had been killed there by the Dutch. Two English ships assisted the Dutch seamen and escorted the *Eendracht* to Ambon. The rest of the *Eendracht*'s fleet sailed to Bantam. It is not known why Hartog sailed to Ambon rather than Bantam nor when and why he separated from his small fleet. In August 1617, the Dutch Governor-General in Bantam claimed Hartog had deliberately changed the sailing route of his vessel, but further explanation was not provided. Hartog himself remained in the East Indies as skipper of the *Eendracht*, but sailed back to the Netherlands in 1618.[31]

Ship logs of Hartog's voyage were returned to Amsterdam, but they cannot be located today. The *Eendracht*'s brief landings in Western Australia were located on a stretch of land represented on sixteenth-century maps, following Marco Polo's writings, as the province of Locach or Beach. It was not for several more decades that Locach/Beach was omitted from maps on the basis that it was an imaginary part of the Great South Land.[32] The *Eendracht*'s landfalls were incorporated on the first chart of Western Australia by the VOC cartographer Hessel Gerritszoon, engraved in 1618 and revised after 1627. This was based on the journals and drawings of the pilots. Gerritszoon labelled Hartog's landing site *'t Land van d'Eendracht* (the land of *Eendracht*), which stretched from North West Cape – a peninsula then thought to be an island – down to about 28°S.[33] The chart included details of other Dutch discoveries in Western Australia in the years just after Hartog's voyage.[34]

VOC voyages and Terra Australis, 1618–22

Several VOC ships accidentally reached the Western Australian coast a few years after Hartog's voyage.[35] It was increasingly clear to the Dutch that a large landmass (or possibly a series of islands) lay somewhere along Brouwer's oceanic route.[36] In May 1618, the *Zeewolf* under Haevick Claeszoon van Hillegom sighted North West Cape, easily visible from the ocean, at 21°15′S. Unaware of Hartog's voyage, the ship's officers thought they had seen an unknown land but the *Zeewolf* did not make a landfall to follow up this supposition. Two months later, however, the *Mauritius* under Lenaert Jacobszoon landed at the same cape. A future VOC governor, Anthonie van Diemen, was on board the ship. The supercargo was Willem Janszoon, the skipper of the *Duyfken* in 1606. He went ashore on what he presumed was an island. The crew located a river, which was named Willems River (now the Ashburton River). This was partially mapped. Janszoon later reported to the VOC's Amsterdam Chamber that he had found people's footprints.[37]

In 1619, Frederik de Houtman, a senior VOC officer, commanded eleven vessels sailing from Texel to the Dutch East Indies. The main ships were the *Dordrecht* and *Amsterdam*. They reached the mainland at around 32°S, located south of the Swan River, near modern Perth.[38] De Houtman sailed north-west and charted the low-lying, rocky, treeless Abrolhos Islands, situated at 28°S off the coast in the vicinity of modern Geraldton and running parallel to the west coast for 100 kilometres. Surrounded by coral reefs and shoals in shallow water, the Abrolhos were deceptive for ships in the vicinity because they were almost invisible and the coast near them had not been properly charted.[39]

De Houtman reported in a letter that they had tried to land at latitude 32°20′S, 'but could find no convenient place to make a landing by reason of the violence of the surf and the breaking of the sea.' He was convinced he had come across the same land visited by the *Eendracht* in 1616.[40] De Houtman associated this landing with Beach/Locach, partly because his supercargo Jacob d'Edel had commented that the muddy coast at 27°S (identified as Hartog's *Eendrachts* land) might be gold-bearing. They called this coast *d'Edelsland* after Jacob d'Edel, a Councillor for the Indies and the highest-ranking man on board their ships.[41] 'We are all assured,' they reported, 'that this is the land which the ship *Eendracht* discovered … and noways doubt that all the land they saw … is one uninterrupted mainland coast … This South Land … seems to be a very fair coast, but we found it impossible to land on it, nor have we seen any smoke or signs of inhabitants there, but further investigation is wanted on this point.'[42]

Individual sightings of, or landings on, the west Australian coast occurred after de Houtman's voyage. Thus, for example, in March 1622 the VOC ship *Leeuwin* (Lioness), which just avoided shipwreck, discovered the southwestern end of Australia, leading to the name of Cape Leeuwin, but the loss of the logbook from the voyage makes it difficult to know how much land, if any, the ship explored. Even the name of the commander of the voyage is unknown.[43] A Dutch map of the 1620s referred to the location as 'the Land of the Leeuwin.'[44]

The English were becoming curious about Dutch voyages towards Australia. The English East India Company vessel *Tryal* was wrecked on rocks off Australia's west coast in May 1622. It was sailing towards Java and had made a navigational error in proceeding too far east. Its master falsified his journal to show the wreck site was on the route he was supposed to have followed, many miles west of its actual location, which was later represented on maps as the Tryal Rocks near the Montebello Islands. This was the oldest shipwreck known to have occurred off Australia's coasts. Forty-four survivors sailed in a skiff and a longboat to Batavia.[45] The exact location of the *Tryal*'s wreck was elusive for several centuries, however, because there were no rocks in the position assigned by the Dutch on their charts. Underwater explorers discovered the likely wreck of the *Tryal* on the outer edge of the Montebello Islands in 1969, but the wreck site has not been conclusively proven.[46]

The voyage of the *Pera* and *Arnhem*, 1623

The *Tryal*'s wreck had an immediate impact on the next Dutch exploratory voyage into Australian waters. In Java the *Tryal*'s survivors discussed the disaster with the Dutch Governor-General. Knowing two Dutch vessels had just avoided shipwreck off Australia's west coast, he wrote instructions to send two ships to sail to 32°–33°S and follow the coast southward to 50°S, favouring the first place to be reached. The expedition would then retrace its route back to locate the northern end and east coast of the Great South Land.[47] Thus in 1622 the VOC equipped two ships, the *Hazewind* and the *Haring*, under the command of Jan Vos, to chart Australia's west coast with orders to 'discover and survey all capes, forelands, bights, lands, islands, rocks, sandbanks, depths, shallows, roads, winds and currents ... to be able to map out and duly mark everything in its true latitude, longitude, bearings and conformation.'[48] Coen hoped to extend Dutch charting and knowledge of the Great South Land and to tap commercial opportunities for the VOC. The quest for profit was the main priority. This ambitious plan, however, was not realized because the *de Haringh* and *Hasewint* were diverted instead to assist two VOC ships encountering difficulties sailing through Sunda Strait.[49]

In 1623, the Governor of Ambon, Herman van Speult, despatched an exploring expedition with Jan Carstenz in charge of the VOC ships *Pera* and *Arnhem*. He ordered Carstenz 'to sail eastwards as long as the western monsoon is blowing, and should spend as little time as possible on the investigation of various islands: on his return voyage with the east monsoon he should investigate everything carefully.'[50] Near the southern coast of New Guinea, the master of the *Arnhem*, Dirk Melisz, and nine crew were killed by Papuans. The vessels reached the shoals that marked the western end of Torres Strait where, as happened with the *Duyfken* in 1606, they turned south. Carstenz thought they had come into a shallow bight. The *Pera* under Carstenz examined the coast north from 17° to 18°S, naming landscape features and reaching a river he named van Speult after the instigator of the expedition. Carstenz returned along the same coast, found it difficult to locate fresh water and food, had some clashes with Aborigines, and then sailed back to Amboyna (Ambon), arriving there on 8 June 1623. The *Arnhem*, now led by Willem Joosten van Colsteert, was in poor condition and separated from the *Pera*. It sailed in a northwesterly direction, drifted in Indonesian waters, but was fortunately sighted and brought into Banda on 14 May 1623.[51]

Carstenz's journal in the *Pera* and his charts of the coasts visited on the voyage survive. The journal is, in fact, the earliest extant written account by a Dutch explorer. The *Arnhem*'s journal was lost. Carstenz named the east coast of Cape York peninsula 'Carpentier' after the VOC's Governor-General Pieter de Carpentier. Carstenz made seventeen landings or attempted landings on the coast.[52] His journal offered a negative account of the east side of the Gulf of

Carpentaria: 'The land between 13° and 17°S is an arid and poor tract without any fruit trees or anything useful to man; it is low and monotonous without mountain or hill, wooded in some places with bush and little oily trees; there is little fresh water and what there is can only be collected from pits specially dug.'[53] Carstensz provided the first extended description of the Cape York peninsula and its native inhabitants. The Aborigines were 'pitch-black, lean of body and totally naked, with a little knitted basket of net around their head, and further in their hairstyle and appearance like the blacks from the Coast of Coromandel.'[54] Carstenz had been instructed to bring back some native people, but an attempt to do so led to 200 Aborigines preventing his crew from carrying out the seizure.[55]

Carstenz charted and described parts of the Gulf of Carpentaria, which he thought was part of New Guinea, but did little to advance knowledge about the Great South Land. The *Arnhem* had come across the east coast of Arnhem Land. Neither ship found anything potentially profitable for the VOC: no gold or silver was discovered, the land appeared unsuitable for growing spices and the native people were savage and uncivilized.[56] The discoveries of the *Pera* appeared on Dutch maps in the late 1620s, but those of the *Arnhem* did not appear on any map until Tasman drew attention to them in his voyage of 1644.[57]

Dutch voyages in Australian waters, 1623–8

Several VOC voyages came across small parts of the west Australian coast between 1623 and 1627. They briefly glimpsed fragments of land but did not explore further. On 21 June 1623 the *Leiden*, with Klaas Hermanszoon as master, saw 'the Land of the Eendracht' at 27°S and sighted nearby coasts. Another ship to reach the west coast, in 1624, was the *Tortelduiff*, which gave its name to the Turtledove shoal south of the Houtman Abrolhos. Two further Dutch voyages came within sight of Western Australia in 1627. In one, Jan Pieterszoon Coen on the *Gallias*, sailing towards Batavia, nearly collided with two companion vessels, the *Utrecht* and *Texel*, near the Abrolhos archipelago. On 17 September 1627 the '*t Wapen van Hoorn*, under David Pieterszoon de Vries, sighted Dirk Hartog Island and corrected Hartog's chart of Shark Bay.[58]

Another voyage in Australian waters was undertaken in 1628 by Gerrit Frederikszoon de Witt in the *Vianen*. The vessel ran aground near Barrow Island off Australia's northwest coast, becoming perhaps the only VOC ship to have been driven on to the Australian coast en route from Batavia to the Netherlands. After throwing excess cargo overboard, the *Vianen* resumed her voyage and charted the northwest coast of Australia as far as Port Hedland in the Pilbara region. This stretch of coast later appeared on maps as 'de Witt's Land', named after the captain of the *Vianen*.[59] He referred to de Witt's Land as 'a foul and barren shore, green fields, and very wild, black, barbarous inhabitants.' The *Vianen* eventually sailed back to Zeeland.[60]

Altogether, the Dutch voyages near the north and west Australian coasts between 1623 and 1628 were piecemeal, disjointed affairs. Many of them came across coastlines by accident, underscoring the need for more accurate, comprehensive charting of Australia's shores. None of these voyages had significant commercial outcomes. How the individual sightings of islands and coastlines of disparate parts of Australia fitted together, if indeed they did, remained unknown: no-one had yet shown whether the section of the Gulf of Carpentaria charted by the Dutch had any relation to Eendracht Land or de Witt's Land, or what were the size and shape of the Great South Land.[61]

Our knowledge of many early Dutch voyages to Australia is advanced by the map of 1627 by Hessel Gerritsz, the expert professional artist, engraver and chartmaker for the VOC's Amsterdam Chamber. His map depicted the Land of Eendracht, located between the 21st and 26th parallels south, based on VOC vessel logs and journals. The details on the map are important because of missing written records for some of the voyages on which it was based – for instance, the voyage of the *Leeuwin* in 1622.[62] Nevertheless, there are some puzzles on Gerritsz's map, notably the absence of North West Cape which had been identified by several Dutch voyages mentioned above.[63]

The voyage of the *Gulden Zeepaard*, 1627

The voyage of the VOC's *Gulden Zeepaard* (Golden Seahorse) under François Thijssen came across a new coast in Australia by chance. Sailing towards the East Indies, the ship was propelled by strong winds far to the south and east of all previous Dutch voyages. Thijssen made landfall at Point Nuyts (116°40′E), situated on the Southern Ocean, and continued eastwards until he reached the islands of St Peter and St Francis near modern Ceduna, South Australia. Stormy seas were hazardous but Thijssen was able to turn around the ship to sail with easterly winds behind him. The *Gulden Zeepaard* proceeded safely to its destination in Batavia, which it reached on 10 April 1627.[64]

The *Gulden Zeepaard*'s voyage was noteworthy because Thijssen, sailing sufficiently near the coast, charted almost 950 miles of Australia's south coast from Albany in Western Australia as far as 133°5′E. Named the 'Land of Pieter Nuyts' after the VOC council member present on the voyage, it was represented on Gerritz's map showing Dutch discoveries in Terra Australis up to 1628.[65] Nuyts was on his way to take up the position of Governor of Formosa (Taiwan) and Ambassador to Japan. The failure of Thijssen to proceed further eastwards meant that the south coast of Australia beyond the islands of St Peter and St Francis remained unknown. This situation did not change until the voyages of Matthew Flinders and Nicolas Baudin just after 1800.[66]

The wreck of the *Batavia*, 1629

The wreck of the *Batavia* near Beacon Island among the perilous Houtman Abrolhos was the main disaster for the Dutch off the west Australian coast in the seventeenth century. This ship, commanded by Francisco Pelsaert, had left Texel in October 1628 with 316 people and a cargo worth 260,000 guilders.[67] The *Batavia*'s instructions warned her to look out for the Houtman Abrolhos but, despite this admonition, on 4 June 1629 the ship hit those rocks. Pelsaert abandoned ship, passengers and goods were ferried to nearby small islands, but forty people drowned. Pelsaert and some officers and crew left the wreck site, made their way to Batavia to seek help, returned in a rescue vessel, and spent over three weeks trying to find the wreck. When they did so, they discovered a mutiny had recently occurred in which 125 people had been killed. Pelsaert partially salvaged the *Batavia* and sailed with the survivors to the Dutch East Indies. A board of enquiry accused him of neglecting to exercise his authority appropriately, his financial assets were seized, and he died within a year.[68]

The *Batavia*'s voyage advanced knowledge of Terra Australis in two ways. First, it illustrated dramatically the dangers in sailing near to reefs and islands in the Houtman Abrolhos, which were far from easy to see until one came perilously near them, and which could lead to wrecks especially after nightfall. Second, the *Batavia*'s voyage established the continuity of the mainland coast from the area near the Houtman Abrolhos as far north as North West Cape.[69] The drama of the *Batavia*'s disaster and the grisly details of murder and sacrifice have been recorded in modern fiction, poems, opera and screenplays.

The rescue of items from the wreck has also given the *Batavia* a high profile among shipwreck disasters off the west Australian coast. In the 1950s, there were efforts to locate the sunken vessel. Its wreck site was rediscovered in 1963. Recovery dives and archaeological investigations took place over the next thirteen years. Some of the cannon, an anchor and other artefacts were salvaged; they are conserved at the Western Australian Shipwrecks Museum, Fremantle.[70]

After the disaster of the *Batavia*, the next Dutch voyage known to have sailed near the west Australian coast was of virtually no significance for maritime exploration. This involved the VOC yacht *Grootenbroeck*, engaged in 1631 in a voyage from Texel to Batavia. The vessel reached the southwestern end of Australia and coasted for 600 miles from Cape Leeuwin north. It sailed past the latitude of the Abrolhos rocks but did not see them. The vessel reached its destination safely. This voyage, which was not intended to explore Australia's shores, was soon forgotten.[71]

Conclusion

Dutch VOC voyages began to explore and chart parts of Australia in the first three decades of the seventeenth century. Without knowledge of the existence of either Terra Australis or Australia, these voyages made a series of probes to locate disparate parts of the Australian mainland. The main achievements were to chart part of the Gulf of Carpentaria and the Cape York peninsula in the *Duyfken* (1606) and the *Pera* (1623), to discover Dirk Hartog Island and selective mainland parts of Australia's northwest coast in the *Eendracht* (1616), and to explore and chart the south coast from Point Nuyts to the islands of St Peter and St Francis in the *Gulden Zeepaard* (1627). Many other VOC voyages sighted parts of Australia but did not make landfall. Navigational hazards abounded, such as the low-lying Houtman Abrolhos off west Australia's coast and numerous rocks and reefs in the Indian Ocean, which wrecked the *Tryal* (1622) and the *Batavia* (1629).

Dissemination of the Dutch discoveries in Australia in the period 1606–40 largely came through incorporating details from charts onto maps by the VOC's expert cartographers. Gerritz's map of 1627, representing the known discoveries of the Dutch in Australia, was a particularly important cartographic landmark in this regard. Journals kept by the skippers of the various VOC voyages were either lost, as in the case of Hartog's voyage, or less widely available. The survival of Carstenz's journal for his voyage in the *Pera*, however, pointed to the significance of written descriptions for future navigators. Only scraps of evidence survive from these early VOC voyages to Australia about the Aboriginal population. And at this stage of Australian maritime exploration, no emphasis was laid upon scientific investigation. The most important navigational discovery made by the VOC was the adoption of the Brouwer route for sailing along the latitudes in the Indian Ocean for ships approaching Australia from the west.

3

Tasman's voyages

Dutch voyaging to Australia resumed in the first half of the 1640s with expeditions led by Abel Janszoon Tasman. Commissioned by the VOC to command two voyages of discovery, he became the first European navigator to see any part of Van Diemen's Land (named after the sponsor of his voyages, Governor Anthonie Van Diemen, and nowadays renamed Tasmania after Tasman himself) and to chart part of the coastline of the Gulf of Carpentaria. The fact that these two voyages, in 1642 and 1644, reached completely disparate shores, separated by several thousand miles, reflected the fact that the shape of Australia as a continent, and indeed whether it was one single landmass or divided in two, was unknown in Tasman's lifetime. Tasman's expeditions were the two most significant deliberate voyages of discovery (rather than accidental sightings) dealing with Terra Australis in the seventeenth century.[1] This chapter discusses the reasons for Tasman's selection as commander, the motivation behind his voyages and their outcomes.

Abel Janszoon Tasman

Tasman, born to humble origins in 1603 in the Groningen province of the Netherlands, was employed by the VOC for about a decade before his first voyage to Australia. Mainly based at Batavia, he spent time cruising in the Moluccas.[2] Tasman rose up the seafaring ranks from common sailor to high office in the VOC. He was an experienced navigator, often in poorly charted or uncharted waters. Between 1634 and 1636, he patrolled the waters of Ambon and nearby islands at the eastern end of the Indonesian archipelago.[3] He returned briefly to Amsterdam in 1637, but in the following year went back to Batavia. Sailing as second-in-command on an expedition in 1639–40 via the Philippines to locate rich islands supposed to lie to the east of Japan and to explore the coasts of north China and Korea, he gained valuable experience as a navigator in waters unknown to the VOC. Further expeditions in 1640 involved sailing near Formosa (Taiwan), Japan, Cambodia and Laos. In 1641, he returned to Cambodia, took on board a cargo for Japan, but the voyage was curtailed by a violent storm. In 1642, Tasman undertook another voyage, from Batavia to Sumatra.[4] These missions made him familiar with the main shipping routes from Europe to India, and with navigation of the seas of China and Japan.[5]

Anthonie Van Diemen

Anthonie Van Diemen, since 1636 the VOC's Governor-General at Batavia, was instrumental in the choice of Tasman to lead his two voyages to Australia.[6] Van Diemen was an experienced administrator who wanted to pursue commercial interests for the VOC in the fabled Great South Land to determine whether gold, silver, spices or other riches could be found. He also wanted to plunder Spain's rich colonies in Chile. At the time only isolated islands had been found by navigators in the vast expanse of the southern Pacific where geographical theorists had long thought the great southern continent could be found.[7] How the parts of Australia fitted together, or whether they all formed part of a larger landmass, possibly the great Terra Australis Incognita, was unknown.[8] But there was also a political and strategic motive: the Dutch wanted to increase their hold on the East Indies and, to do so, they needed a safe oceanic route to Chile away from threats posed by the Spanish.[9]

Van Diemen wanted to increase the VOC's wealth and power through systematically planned voyages of discovery.[10] He realized that much land and a great expanse of ocean needed exploration to the south of the East Indies. A passage through the Pacific to Chile for the commercial benefit of the VOC could lead to acquiring bullion from Spanish settlements on America's west coast, and help to stage privateering raids against the Spanish in the Pacific.[11] The search for bullion was an important motive for commissioning the voyages because the Dutch were short of gold and silver in the East Indies despite their commercial success in the region. These precious metals were important for paying for Asian goods. There is no evidence that Van Diemen thought a Dutch colony of settlement in the South Land could be established as a result of an expedition.[12]

Soon after he became Governor-General, Van Diemen despatched Gerrit Thomaszoon Pool to command an expedition of 1636 to Arnhem Land and Speult Land, in northern Australia, which he assumed formed one whole with the

South Land.[13] The two ships involved in the mission were the *Klein Amsterdam* and *Wessel*. Pool was instructed to look for passages into the Pacific. He did not get that far because he was attacked by natives on the coast of New Guinea and killed along with some of his crew. His second-in-command, Pieter Pieterszoon, took over the leadership of the voyage, headed south and reached a coast at 11° that he identified as Arnhem Land and Speult Land. The outline of the Cobourg Peninsula and Melville Island was added to maps as a result of this voyage. Worried about sailing further to the east, Pieterszoon headed westward and back to Banda. The northern coast he discovered was named after Van Diemen.[14]

Instructions for Tasman's voyage of 1642

Van Diemen wanted to send out further voyages from Batavia to confirm that a Great South Land existed. He also hoped to find an oceanic route from Java to Chile. Another expedition became possible after the Dutch conquest of Malacca from the Portuguese in 1641, a military assault that removed Portuguese control over the Malay Archipelago. Van Diemen could now proceed with a voyage without major impediment. This led to plans to send Tasman and the experienced Dutch geographer and pilot Frans Visscher on such an expedition.[15] Based at Batavia by the early 1640s, Visscher possessed, according to a contemporary assessment, 'greater skill in surveying of coasts and the mapping out of lands than any of the steersmen present in these parts.'[16] He had produced improved maps of the coasts of China and Indochina and parts of Japan, and was one of the most talented cartographers employed by the VOC.[17] Visscher had nearly twenty years' experience in navigation in the Indian and Pacific oceans, in the China Sea, and along the coasts of Japan and Cambodia.[18]

In January 1642, Visscher composed a detailed scheme for a successful discovery of the unknown South Land.[19] This was the most ambitious exploratory voyage yet undertaken by the Dutch, who wanted to find out what lay beyond the meridian where ships turned north on the Brouwer route across the Indian Ocean. In 1814, Matthew Flinders wrote that Tasman's 1642 voyage resulted from 'the anxiety of the Dutch government at Batavia, to know how far the SOUTH LANDS might extend towards the Antarctic circle.'[20] Van Diemen's words to Tasman about the purpose of the voyage were that he should 'sail to the partly known as well as the undiscovered South and East lands, to discover them and find some important lands, or at the very least some practicable passages to well-known rich places, to be used eventually to enhance and enlarge the general welfare of the company.'[21] Van Diemen appears to have been the first person to use the name New Holland ('Nieuw Holland') for the South Land. The unsolved geographical problems needing resolution were whether the South Land was part of a larger continent, where and how New Guinea was joined to it, and whether a sea passage ran through the continent from the point reached by Cartensz in 1623 in the Gulf of Carpentaria to Nuyts Land on the south coast.[22]

Detailed instructions for Tasman's 1642 voyage drawn up by Julius Schouten, a VOC councillor, included a summary of the VOC's entire knowledge of the South Land to that date.[23] Tasman was given two vessels, the yacht *Heemskerck* and the fluyt *Zeehaen*, with crews of sixty and fifty, respectively.[24] Gerrit Jansz commanded the *Zeehaen* and Visscher was first mate (or pilot-major). The highly competent surveyor and cartographer Isaack Gilsemans, the ship's merchant, was charged with providing a visual record of discoveries made on the voyage. The expedition was 'assigned to the discovering of the unknown and found Southland, the South East coast of Nova Guinea, together with the islands located thereabout.'[25] The *Heemskerck* was to carry two important navigational aids: a 'Great Chart of the South Sea,' which was probably a revised version of Hessel Gerritsz's Pacific chart of 1622, and a terrestrial globe made by Joan Blaeu in the first decade of the seventeenth century.[26]

Aware of the prior European discovery of the Americas and extensive parts of Asia, the instructions deplored any serious attempt 'to discover the remaining unknown part of the globe,' where it was supposed that many 'fruits of gain' could be found. Tasman and his ships were to sail westward from Batavia across the Indian Ocean to Mauritius, deliver goods there, and supply the *Heemskerck* and *Zeehaen* with water, firewood and supplies. Mauritius was then a Dutch possession and a frequent stopping point for the refreshment of Dutch ships on long oceanic voyages. The voyage eastwards across the Indian Ocean was to continue until Tasman encountered 'the unknown Southland' as far as the latitudes of 52° to 54°. If no land was discovered in those latitudes, the vessels were to sail eastwards to the east end of New Guinea or perhaps as far as the Solomon Islands.[27]

The instructions continued with possible directions based on limited knowledge of parts of Australia and on speculation about what passages or channels might be found. The instructions make plain that it was not yet known whether New Guinea was attached to the Australian mainland. Tasman was to sail along the north coast of New Guinea and then along its south coast to find out whether there was a passage between New Guinea and Cape York. If he arrived at Cape Keerweer, identified on the *Duyfken*'s voyage of 1606, he was to sail westwards to Willem's River, located in the land of Eendracht, to identify passages or channels to the south. When the instructions were written, it was unknown whether the west side of the Cape York peninsula, explored by the Dutch in 1606 and 1623, was joined to the land of Eendracht (the northern part of Australia's west coast), discovered by Hartog in 1616. Tasman was directed to keep a navigational record, to record details of the products and people encountered, to find out whether gold and silver could be acquired, and to take possession of any lands for the States General of the Netherlands by planting its flag in the soil, for 'such lands rightly belong to the finder and taker.'[28] Tasman was warned to be cautious when landing, for 'it is well known that the southern regions are peopled with fierce savages.'[29]

Tasman's voyage of 1642

Tasman's surviving journal from the voyage includes estimated geographical coordinates on an almost daily basis that enable us to follow his course. For longitudes, the expedition followed the then-current practice of basing readings on a meridian in Tenerife rather than Greenwich.[30] The *Heemskerck* and *Zeehaen* left Batavia on 14 August 1642 and arrived at Mauritius on 5 September. This long detour for the ships was necessary because the VOC at Batavia had been careless about the condition of the vessels: the *Zeehaen* had half-rotten upper work while both ships were poorly equipped. It took a month at Mauritius to repair and restock the ships.[31] The *Heemskerck* and *Zeehaen*, victualled for a maximum of eighteen months, left Mauritius on 8 October, and headed southeast across the Indian Ocean aided by the roaring forties.[32]

The plan was to sail as far south as 52° or 54° latitude into sub-Antarctic waters. No previous European navigator had sailed further south than 27°S. Encountering dense fog, stormy weather, hailstorms and snow on reaching 49° latitude, however, Tasman departed from his instructions. On Visscher's advice, he decided to sail to 44°S and continued east. The plan was to sail to 150° longitude, northward to 40°S and eastward to 220° longitude towards the Solomon Islands.[33] The ships proceeded to the south of Australia, but were so far from land that they did not realize they were sailing beneath an extended landmass. On 17 November, they calculated they had reached the furthest point of Pieter Nuyts's exploration of Australia's south coast in 1627. They thought the west side of New Guinea must be to their north.[34] This indicates the rudimentary state of their geographical knowledge. In late November, land was sighted at

42°30'. The land seen was near Macquarie harbour, on Tasmania's west coast. This was the first European sighting of Van Diemen's Land.[35]

Tasman's journal indicated that the longitude to be assigned to Van Diemen's Land's west coast was 3°E of its true position at Point Hibbs – an error of 155 miles. Given that the sextant and the chronometer had not yet been invented, and that correction tables for nautical astronomy were not very accurate, this was not too erroneous for a location in unknown waters. We do not know the method of calculation followed by Tasman and Visscher, but the longitude was probably determined by taking lunar distances in relation to Jupiter's moons.[36]

Tasman named the land Anthonie Van Diemen's Land, in honour of the VOC's leading official in Batavia, but he had no idea Van Diemen's Land was an island.[37] The voyage continued around the southeastern Van Diemen's Land. Strong winds frequently drove the ships away from the coast. Tasman mistook some peaks for islands. He named Wits, Sweers and Maetsuijker islands after members of the VOC's Council of the Indies. On 29 November, he tried to anchor in a bay, but was obliged to head out for sea in the face of a gale. It took almost two days for the *Helmskeerck* and *Zeehaen* to reach land again, owing to a severe storm. Tasman later named the location 'Storm Bay.' He failed to detect either the Derwent estuary or whether Van Diemen's Land was connected to the South Land.[38]

Tasman anchored in North Bay, in southeast Van Diemen's Land, on 1 December 1642. On the next day, he sent Visscher with a sloop and four musketeers and six rowers to a nearby small inlet to search for freshwater and food. They came ashore at what they named Frederick Henry Bay (now Blackman Bay). This was relatively sheltered, and lay just east of present-day Hobart. Visscher and his men gathered green vegetables, found running water, and 'heard some sound of People, also playing almost like a horn or small gong, which was not far from them.' They did not see anyone but thought they were being watched. Numerous trees were hollowed out by fire. One curiosity they came across consisted of trees containing flint notches in the shape of steps about five feet from one another. When this was reported to Tasman, he thought that a race of giants had cut these steps in the trees. The notches had actually been made by Aborigines to catch possums.[39]

On 3 December, a storm prevented Tasman from landing at Frederick Henry Bay, but he ordered a carpenter to swim ashore with a stake, with the VOC's mark cut on it, along with a flag to claim the newly found land for the Netherlands. This was a signal to all who came after that the Dutch had been there and had claimed possession of Van Diemen's Land. It was the only occasion when the Dutch formally claimed part of Australia.[40] After carrying out this task, the carpenter returned to the *Helmskeerck* 'leaving posterity and the Inhabitants of this land (who did not show themselves, although we surmise some were not far from there and were with watching eyes on our proceedings) the above mentioned as a memorial.'[41] Tasman never set foot on the island that now bears his name. His journal offers no indications why further exploration on land was not undertaken.[42]

On 4 December 1642, Tasman sailed north past islands that he named Maria (after Van Diemen's wife) and Schouten (after the prominent VOC councillor who had drafted his voyage instructions). Failing to find gold, spices or any trade items, on the following day Tasman sailed eastward from near St Patrick Head, Van Diemen's Land, towards New Zealand, which was sighted on 13 December. Tasman gave New Zealand the name of Staten landt after the leading politicians of the States-General of the Netherlands.[43] His initial exploration of New Zealand was not followed up, possibly because of the hostility encountered from the Maoris.[44] The Dutch never again sent out a voyage of discovery to New Zealand.[45]

The *Helmskeerck* and *Zeehaen* proceeded up the west coast of the South Island, and encountered Maoris who attacked one of their boats and killed four of Tasman's crew. Tasman failed to explore Cook Strait, which divides New Zealand's two islands, but sailed up the west coast of North Island. He did not land. By failing to circumnavigate New Zealand, he was unable to prove whether it was insular or part of the South Land.[46] The voyage continued to Tonga and Fiji. Gilsemans drew interesting drawings of the people encountered in New Zealand and Polynesia.[47] The ships reached Batavia on 15 June 1643. At the end of May, Tasman had decided it was too late in the season to follow the instructions to explore the land between Cape Keerweer and Willem's River. Thus, he did not attempt to determine whether New Guinea was joined to the land that the Dutch had identified in the Gulf of Carpentaria several decades previously.[48]

The entire voyage was a considerable feat of navigation and endurance. Tasman and his officers displayed superior abilities in oceanic voyaging and dealt with stormy conditions at sea while ensuring they did not run out of freshwater and victuals. Good communications were maintained between the two vessels. VOC officials praised Tasman for the extent of his voyage, the discovery of Van Diemen's Land and New Zealand, and the safe return of his vessels to Batavia. Tasman had contributed towards a more complete geography of the world. He and his pilot Visscher had made extensive charts. After the voyage ended, Tasman and his officers were rewarded with two months' additional pay; the common seamen received one month's extra pay.[49]

Tasman had added more to the nautical knowledge of the southwest Pacific than any other navigator before the age of Cook.[50] He had proved that a sea route to Chile was possible from the western Pacific.[51] He had removed the probability that New Holland might be part of the fabled southern continent, and had shown that the landmass of that continent could not begin until at least the western coast of New Zealand.[52] Flinders later noted that Tasman's voyage of 1642 deprived the 'Great South Land' 'of its pretensions to be a continent, but not of its name.'[53]

The VOC's reaction, however, was not entirely favourable. Their officials criticized Tasman's lack of curiosity in exploring further the lands he came across and his failure to examine the region between New Guinea and the Gulf Carpentaria as laid down in his instructions. Tasman had established the existence of Van Diemen's Land without determining its configuration. He had failed to ascertain how far Van Diemen's Land extended to the northwest and northeast, and had made no attempt to communicate with the natives.[54] The Dutch historian J. E. Heeres, writing at the end of the nineteenth century, echoed this assessment by noting that Tasman 'had left everything to be more closely inquired into by more inquisitive successors.'[55] Helen Wallis was similarly critical: after the voyage 'it was still not known whether Van Diemen's Land was connected westward with St Pieter and Francois, and northward with the South Land, and whether there was a passage to the South sea, questions which Tasman had been asked to answer.'[56]

Instructions for Tasman's Voyage of 1644

Despite their criticism of the outcome of Tasman's 1642 voyage, Governor Van Diemen and his associates almost immediately appointed Tasman as commander of a second expedition. This was intended to clear up some missing parts of the jigsaw of the disconnected lands known to the Dutch in the Southern Seas. Visscher was again the pilot on the voyage, which involved three ships sailing together – the *Limmen*, *Zeemeeuw* and *Bracq*.[57] The inclusion of the small flyboat *Bracq* indicated that Van Diemen envisaged a close reconnaissance of lands discovered.[58] The itinerary of the proposed voyage was less ambitious than for the 1642 expedition but still wide-ranging. Tasman and Visscher would set out from Batavia to New Guinea and continue westward from the west side of the Cape York peninsula, identified from Dutch voyages earlier in the seventeenth century, 'to find out whether the known South land is continuous with it, or in fact separated, which on the further remaining investigation will give much light.'[59] In making the case for this voyage, the VOC councillors argued that the failure of Tasman's first Australian voyage resulted from encountering hostile native people.[60]

The voyage instructions were drafted once again by Schouten and signed by six members of the Governor and Council of the VOC, including Van Diemen, on 29 January 1644. They ordered Tasman to sail close to the south coast of New Guinea towards a roadstead at 'the High Island' (now Prince of Wales Island), on the west side of Torres Strait. It was hoped that he could surmise from the set of the current whether a passage led into the South Seas. If so, Tasman was to sail down it to the newly discovered Van Diemen's Land and determine whether it was an island or connected to New Guinea or to Nuyts' Land. The *Limmen* and *Zeemeuw* were to remain anchored at Prince of Wales Island for two or three days while the shallow-draught *Bracq* searched for a passage to the South Sea. Any islands or channels were to be identified, but if New Guinea was joined to the Great South Land, as the authors of the instructions believed, Tasman was to sail along and fully discover that coast. This referred to the western Cape York peninsula, discovered by Jan Carstenszoon in 1623, which the Dutch did not then know was separated from New Guinea.[61]

Various alternatives were set down for the return voyage, including sailing south along Australia's west coast to the Houtman Abrolhos, and searching for the large haul of silver dollars from the wreck of the *Batavia* in 1629, or sailing from the Gulf of Carpentaria to Java's south and then via Sunda Strait to Batavia. The geographical breadth of the instructions indicates that the VOC at Batavia had little idea of the vast distances that separated known parts of Australia. The voyage was expected to last five months, and Tasman was instructed to keep a detailed journal. A draughtsman was included on the expedition to draw the lands seen on the voyage.[62]

Tasman's voyage of 1644

Tasman's journal from the 1644 voyage has not survived, but several maps and references in other documents enable us to piece together his route. He set out in February 1644 and found no open channel on the western side of Torres Strait. Instead, he came across a large spacious bay or gulf (the Gulf of Carpentaria). Lacking a ship's log or journal, we do not know how long Tasman looked for a passage. He may have undertaken probes into the western side of Torres Strait and then abandoned them; or, given his lack of curiosity on his previous voyage, possibly he failed to explore the location thoroughly. He concluded that Torres Strait was a bay, as the water was shallow or consisted of shoals. Earlier Dutch voyages in the *Duyfken* (1605) and the *Pera* and *Arnhem* (1623) had also concluded it was a bay.[63]

Tasman's vessels sailed down the west side of the Cape York peninsula past Cape Keerweer and Carstenzoon's 17° cut-off point for his earlier voyage, looking for a passage to Van Diemen's Land and the Pacific. Cape Keerweer was the furthest point reached by previous Dutch explorers. Unfortunately, Tasman did not have copies of Carstenzoon's journal and chart of his voyage to help him. The voyage continued along the southern and western sides of the Gulf of Carpentaria. The approximate route can only be conjectured. A map produced after the voyage shows that Tasman landed briefly on at least ten occasions. Lack of documentary evidence means that we do not know how much exploration on land occurred.[64]

Tasman passed between Groote Eylandt and the Australian mainland, rediscovered Arnhem Land, and traced the coast as far as Willem's River just south of North West Cape. He found out that the 'islands' of Arnhem and Van Speult, discovered in 1623, belonged to the mainland.[65] But he made errors in detail, identifying the Wellesley and Sir Edward Pellew as capes rather than islands and thinking that present-day Melville, Goulburn and Bathurst islands were on the mainland. One wonders how often he deployed the *Bracq* for minute coastal exploration. On reaching the Tropic of Capricorn, Tasman returned to Batavia in August 1644.[66]

The absence of primary written documentation for this voyage makes it difficult to evaluate Tasman's achievements in exploring the Gulf of Carpentaria. We do not know his exact route. The capes, islands and other landmarks on his charts were not investigated systematically until Flinders spent several months in this locality during his Australian circumnavigation of 1802–3. Flinders respected Tasman as a navigator, but was sceptical about the accuracy of Dutch charting of the Gulf of Carpentaria owing to the lack of written records.[67] Flinders noted, circumspectly, that 'although conjecture had assigned' the 'early examination' of the Gulf 'to Tasman, yet geographers knew not what credit ought to be attached to the form it had assumed in the charts.'[68] After he had surveyed the Gulf thoroughly, however, Flinders believed that 'the whole of the Gulf of Carpentaria has really undergone an examination of some former period, and I believe that the old Dutch charts contain a faithful delineation of what was seen.'[69]

The VOC reaction to Tasman's voyage of 1644

The VOC in Batavia reacted unfavourably to Tasman's 1644 voyage. Tasman, it was concluded, had failed to follow his instructions properly. In a report dated 23 December 1644, the VOC summarized the route followed by Tasman's vessels, noting that it had not found a 'through channel between the half known Nova Guinea and the known land of the Eendracht or Willem's river in the southern latitude of 22⅔ and longitude of 119 degrees, but in fact a large spacious bight or Gulf'. The report then became critical: they 'have found nothing profitable, but only poor naked beach-runners, without rice, or any noteworthy fruits, very poor, and in many places evil natured people'. The VOC did not censure Tasman for failing to discover Torres Strait because they were unaware of its existence. But they expressed disappointment that Tasman and his associates had not explored inland at the Gulf of Carpentaria, especially as his two voyages had circumnavigated the 'as yet unknown Southland', which appeared to contain 2,000 miles of land. It concluded that further investigations should take place in future 'by more vigilant and more courageous persons'.[70]

Tasman's voyage had explored parts of the northern coast of Australia, adding to geographical knowledge a largely unknown part of the world to Europeans. Specifically, he had competently demonstrated the continuity of land from Torres Strait to the Tropic of Capricorn, and had mapped much of the southern and western shores of the Gulf of Carpentaria.[71] The VOC were not inclined, however, to send out a third voyage of discovery from Batavia to fill in missing gaps on the world's map. Governor Van Diemen was disappointed with the results of the 1644 expedition. Far from being a source of gold and silver, Australia appeared to be of no utility to Dutch commerce.[72] Tasman's voyages led to no commercial finds for the Dutch, no exploration of the land and no contact with Aborigines. It is therefore unsurprising to find that Tasman was not sent out on a third voyage.[73]

Van Diemen died in Batavia on 19 April 1645. Later governors lacked interest in voyages of discovery. The managers of the VOC's Council of the Indies eschewed further exploration: enough gold and silver mines had already been found to enable them to trade with India, Japan and Formosa/Taiwan.[74] Tasman remained in Batavia where, in 1644/5, he held the position of supervisor of navigation.[75] In 1648, Cornelis van der Lijn, Van Diemen's successor, placed Tasman in charge of a Dutch fleet to attack the Spanish and blockade Manila in the Philippines, but he failed to capture the Spanish silver ship sailing from America. Tasman was accused of hanging two young sailors from the expedition who had committed a crime but had not received a trial. The Court of Justice in Batavia was not convinced by Tasman's explanation of what really happened. Tasman was accordingly suspended from his office and functions, but reinstated to his rank in 1651. He became a large landowner in Batavia and died in October 1659.[76]

Tasman's legacy

Tasman's record of geographical discovery in Australia was mixed. Within two years, he had made progress in the European knowledge of the southern continent, but many parts of the puzzle still needed to be pieced together. Tasman had discovered part of Van Diemen's Land, but had not circumnavigated it and therefore did not realize it was an island separated from the mainland by Bass Strait. He had explored the Gulf of Carpentaria, but did not enter Torres Strait (which he believed was a bay). He had shown no inclination to linger when he confronted adverse winds, being concerned to preserve his food and water. He had no knowledge of Australia's east coast and failed to explore places, such as Van Diemen's Land, where he could have gathered additional information with greater perseverance.[77] Though Tasman was the first navigator to circumnavigate Australia, he had no knowledge of the size or shape of Australia and was unaware that he had sailed around a continent well out to sea. The verdict that Tasman 'carried out instructions rather taking the initiative' seems fair.[78]

Beyond Australia, Tasman had discovered and mapped most of the west coasts of both of New Zealand's islands. He had shown that the landmass he had sailed around was much smaller than Eurasia, and that the vast continent that theorists supposed existed must lie between New Zealand and South America, if it lay anywhere at all. His two voyages of 1642 and 1644, however, had not found any precious minerals or commercial possibilities that would induce the VOC in Batavia to support further voyages to Australia. The Dutch interest in the maritime discovery of Australia thus came to an abrupt halt after Tasman's voyage of 1644 ended.[79] The VOC did not promote further maritime exploration in the Pacific in the decades after Tasman's voyages; their priorities lay rather in conducting trade with India, Formosa/Taiwan and Japan.[80] However, the Dutch kept details of Tasman's two major voyages secret because the information he had collected was considered to be of possible commercial benefit for the Netherlands.[81]

Dissemination of Tasman's findings from his voyages was made possible by first-hand written documentation and spread through maps, charts and globes. His original journal from the 1642 voyage has not survived. But two journals probably written by Tasman and Visscher and based on Tasman's notes are extant. One is held by the National Archives of the Netherlands at The Hague, which is signed by Tasman. The other is deposited in the Mitchell Library, Sydney, which is neither signed by Tasman nor in his hand. The latter is known as the Huydecoper Journal, named after a Dutch family with strong VOC connections. It includes six coastal drawings of land sighted on 4–5 December 1642 in Van Diemen's Land.[82] The masters' logs of the *Zeehaen* and the *Heemskeerck* have not survived.[83]

The printed dissemination of Tasman's voyages in England was rather slow. The first published account of Tasman's voyages in English was in a translation of 1671 by John Ogilby of an account of the voyage prepared by Hendrik Haalbos, ship's barber and surgeon.[84] Extracts from the Dutch version of Tasman's journal were printed in Amsterdam in 1674, translated into English, published by Robert Hooke in the proceedings of the Royal Society for 1682 and reprinted at least five times in the next sixty years.[85] Flinders noted the absence of a log for the voyage was a 'great obstacle to tracing correctly the progress of early discovery in Terra Australis.'[86]

Cartographic material for the two voyages can be found. Gilsemans drew a chart of Van Diemen's Land in November and December 1642.[87] This was known by 1657 to some Dutch cartographers, who incorporated it on their maps.[88] A similar chart of the south coast of Van Diemen's Land for 1642/3 exists among the VOC's miscellaneous marine records.[89] A chart showing the routes of the 1642/3 and 1644 voyages was drawn up under Tasman's eyes soon after the conclusion of the second voyage.[90] A rough sketch map of Van Diemen's Land was sent home in January 1644, emphasizing the Dutch discovery of that location. On the voyage of 1642–3, Gilseman's drawings of natives in New Zealand, Tonga, New Ireland and Jamna, an island north of New Guinea, represented the physiognomy and material culture of people all but unknown to Europeans.[91]

An important piece of evidence for the 1644 voyage is the Bonaparte Tasman Map, held by the Mitchell Library, Sydney, where it is also reproduced as a floor mosaic in the entrance vestibule. The map is so-called because it was once owned by Prince Roland Bonaparte, the great-nephew of Napoleon.[92] Probably compiled half a century after Tasman's expedition, it was based on an original map made during the voyage. In the absence of written information from the ship's log, this map is crucial evidence in showing Tasman's route along the Gulf of Carpentaria.[93] The Bonaparte map shows the Dutch discoveries in

Australia prior to and including 1644, it includes a more detailed depiction of the eastern shore of the Gulf of Carpentaria than earlier maps, and several new rivers and one bay are named on the chart for the first time. These features of the map suggest that Tasman had resurveyed the Gulf's coast.[94]

In the late 1640s, Tasman's discoveries of Van Diemen's Land and the Gulf of Carpentaria were given wider circulation by their inclusion in Joan Blaeu's revision of his father's large world map of 1619. As cartographer to Amsterdam's VOC Chamber, Blaeu had access to charts generated by Dutch oceanic voyages. Blaeu's map incorporating Tasman's voyages was entitled *Nova et Accurata Totius Terrarum Orbis Tabula*. It appeared in 1645/6, and was copied by many other mapmakers.[95] This was the earliest printed cartographical record of Tasman's voyage. Information about Tasman's voyages was also included on Blaeu's two large globes of *c*.1647 and on his world map of 1648 made on the occasion of the Peace of Westphalia that concluded the Thirty Years' War.[96] Blaeu's map was the first to show Tasman's discoveries and the first to include the name 'Nova Hollandia' to represent Australia. Blaeu must have based his map on charts from Tasman's 1644 voyage or from copies of that material. Only one original copy of the map survives – at the Maritime Museum Rotterdam.[97]

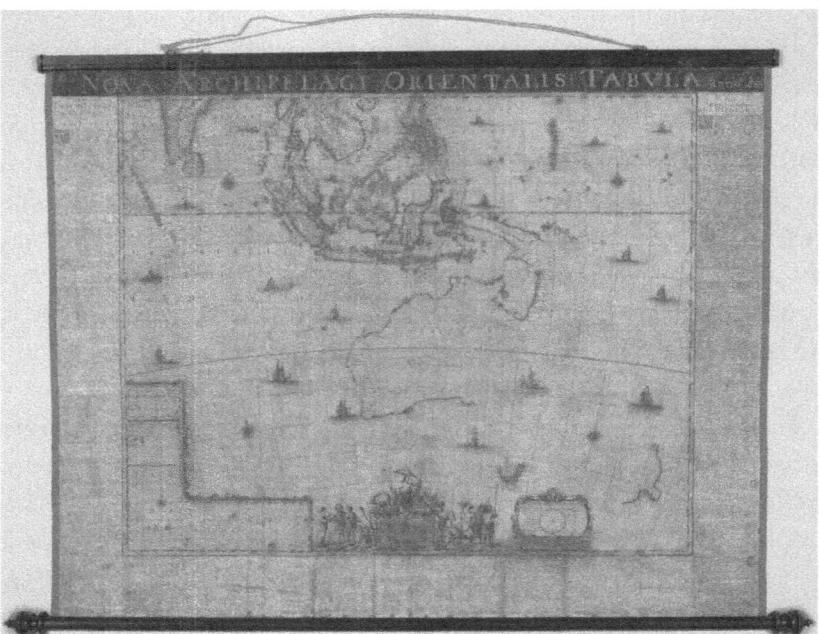

Map 3 Joan Blaeu, *Archipelagus Orientalis, sive Asiaticus* (Amsterdam: Joannem Blaeu, 1663) PIC Rowan stack on Row 1 Bib ID 6264405

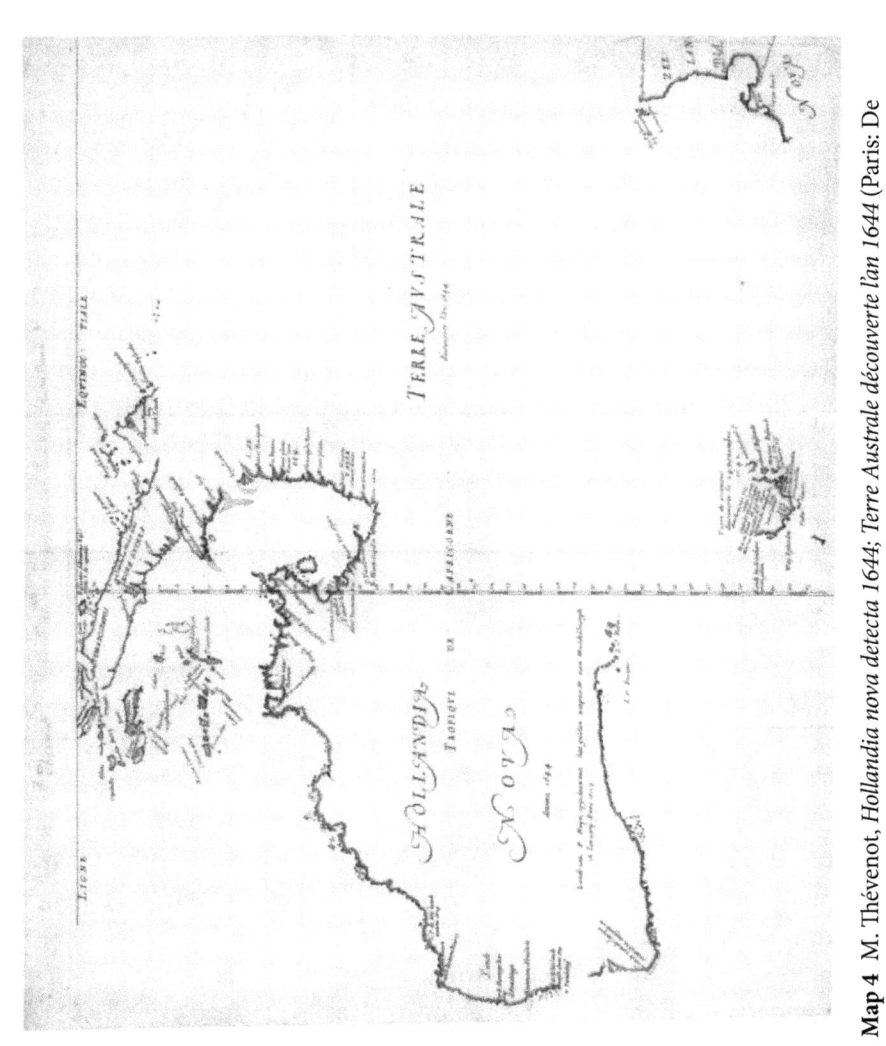

Map 4 M. Thévenot, *Hollandia nova detecta 1644; Terre Australe découverte l'an 1644* (Paris: De l'imprimerie de Jacques Langlois, 1663) MAP 689A Bib ID 1537852

Blaeu's map was widely copied. It was included in the Klencke Atlas, one of the world's largest atlases presented by a Dutch scholar and merchant to Charles II in 1660. Another rare map by Blaeu included for the first time the landfall of the *Zeehaen* at Van Diemen's Land on 24 November 1642. This is Blaeu's *Archipelagus Orientalis sine Asiaticus* (Eastern and Asian archipelago), purchased for the Rare Maps Collection of the National Library of Australia, Canberra, in 2013. This map includes early references to the Dutch language names for New Holland ('Nieuw Hollant') and New Zealand ('Nieuw Zelandt').[98] The earliest known world map to illustrate the results of Tasman's two voyages involving Australia was undertaken by Cornelis Danckert in the Netherlands in 1648. In the mid-seventeenth century, the best-known map of Tasman's discoveries was that of the French geographer Melchisédec Thévenot in his *Relations de divers voyages curieux qui non point esté publiées*, published in Paris in 1663. Thévenot copied material from the charts and globes published by Blaeu between 1645 and 1648. It was the first European work on Australia and the Pacific to gain a wide international readership.[99] In 1684, Thomas Bowrey, a merchant attached to the English East India Company, created a map of Tasman's discoveries based on maps shown to him by the VOC.[100]

Conclusion

Tasman's voyages of 1642–3 and 1644 were the most important VOC expeditions sent out in search of the southern continent in the seventeenth century. The personnel despatched on these voyages were highly skilled, experienced seafarers. Before setting out on these expeditions, Tasman and Visscher had strong credentials as a navigator and a pilot and chartmaker, respectively. The VOC issued very detailed voyage instructions, with a number of options to follow, though these were over-optimistic in their geographical breadth. Tasman's achievements were to discover Van Diemen's Land and New Zealand and to continue Dutch charting of the Gulf of Carpentaria. Despite these important advances in geographical knowledge, Tasman proved a better navigator than an explorer. He did not prove that Van Diemen's Land was an island, and made no attempt to land there. On both voyages, he misidentified capes, peaks, islands and parts of Australia's mainland. He failed to explore Torres Strait. He circumnavigated the Australian continent so far out to sea that he did not realize he had achieved a circumnavigation. The VOC were disappointed with the lack of commercial opportunities arising from his voyages, and they sent out no third exploratory voyage to Australian waters after 1644.

Tasman's voyages nevertheless left an important legacy in Australian maritime exploration. Extensive charts were produced from both voyages to show the discoveries in Van Diemen's Land and northern Australia. These included Dutch names bestowed on places and landscape features identified from shipboard observation or landfall. The surviving journals of the 1644 expedition added further details, but the loss of the journals for the 1642–3 voyage and of the ship's log for the 1644 voyage meant that charts were more influential for future navigators following up Tasman's ventures than the written record. Between the late 1640s and the 1680s numerous charts, maps and globes depicted the two voyages. Initially, these were mainly the work of Dutch specialists but they were copied in other parts of Europe, notably in France and England. These were the means through which Tasman's discoveries were perpetuated, and they were extensively utilized by later navigators.

From Tasman to Cook

Tasman's voyages to Terra Australis had shown that the 'known Southland,' including the south and east coasts of Van Diemen's Land, was separate from any world-balancing southern continent.[1] His suspicion that rough people inhabited Van Diemen's Land and that no profitable trade or resources could be found in Australia meant that, in Campbell Macknight's pithy summation, 'the lure of a golden province had lost its immediate appeal. Australia looked like a useless discovery.'[2] Small wonder that Dutch interest in pursuing further exploratory voyages to Australia virtually disappeared for several decades. Nevertheless, Dutch voyages to Australian waters were made in the second half of the seventeenth century and in the early eighteenth century. This was also the period when England despatched its first significant exploratory voyage to Australian shores. The Dutch and English voyages to Australia made between the era of Abel Tasman and James Cook are the focus of this chapter.

Dutch voyages to Australia, 1656–94

The loss of the VOC ship *Vergulde Draeck* (Gilt Dragon) in 1656 stimulated further Dutch exploration of Australia's west coast. This vessel, commanded by Pieter Albertszoon, was sailing across the Indian Ocean towards Batavia on the Brouwer route when she struck a reef near Cape Leschenault, about 80 miles north of Perth. Seventy-five of around 193 passengers reached the shore. The ship was carrying a valuable cargo of bullion worth 185,000 silver guilders. A small boat was sent to Batavia for help; two ships were sent to search for the wreck, but they found neither it nor the survivors.[3] Jan van Riebeeck, the Governor of the Dutch colony at the Cape of Good Hope, was ordered to send a ship to search for survivors. He despatched the *Vincq* from Table Bay on 28 April 1657. This voyage failed to find the wreck, the bullion or the survivors of the

Vergulde Draeck. In 1658, another search for the vessel in coastal waters between the Swan River and the Houtman Abrolhos found wreckage, thought to be from the *Vergulde Draeck*, near Rottnest Island. No survivors were found. In 1658, van Riebeeck sent another ship, the *Immenhorn*, to carry out a similar search. It reached Western Australia, failed to find anyone, and made no landings. The wreck of the *Vergulde Draeck* was not found until 1963.[4]

Subsequent occasional Dutch voyages touched at the Western Australian coast. In February 1678, the *Vliegende Zwaan*, commanded by Jan van der Wall, left Ternate, an eastern Indonesian island, on a voyage via Timor to Batavia. No written records survive for the voyage, but a copied chart indicates that the ship visited northwest Australia near Exmouth Gulf. On 5 February 1694, the *Ridderschap van Holland* (the Nobility of Holland) left the Cape of Good Hope bound to Batavia but disappeared. Rumours circulated that it had been captured by pirates near Madagascar, but it was possible that it had been wrecked off the coast of the South Land. The VOC in Amsterdam decided to send out an expedition under Willem de Vlamingh to search for the vessel or its wreck and any survivors.[5]

Willem de Vlamingh's voyage, 1696–7

De Vlamingh's voyage was a substantial expedition and the only major one in the seventeenth century to sail from the Netherlands rather than Batavia. Intended, as noted above, to search for two VOC vessels wrecked off the west Australian coast, it was also charged with charting and scientific investigations, the first time a Dutch exploratory voyage had included a scientific agenda. De Vlamingh had made two VOC voyages to Batavia, in 1688 and 1694. After the second voyage, he was asked by Nicolaes Witsen, the administrator of the VOC and mayor of Amsterdam, to lead an expedition to search for the *Ridderschap van Holland*. Vlamingh was placed in command of three vessels – the *Geelvinck*, the *Nijptangh* and *Weseltje*.[6]

De Vlamingh was instructed to sail to the latitude of 37°S and explore Tristan da Cunha and then continue to Cape de Bonne Esperance and the islands of St Paul and Amsterdam, situated in the south Indian Ocean more than 3,000 kilometres from any continent. The location of the *Ridderschap van Holland*'s wreck was unknown, but it was hoped that survivors would be found. The voyage was then to proceed across the Indian Ocean to 'call at the South Land or Nova Hollandia' at 32° or 33°S 'in order not to fall south of same about the Land of Pieter Nuyts and there to founder through west winds and currents.' He was warned that 'the coast is inhabited by very savage, barbaric and cruel people.' To facilitate his expedition, de Vlamingh was furnished by the VOC with written reports and charts relating to previous Dutch voyages to Western Australia.[7]

The expedition left Texel on 3 May 1696, and first sighted land off the west Australian coast on 29 December. De Vlamingh named the landfall Rottenest (now Rottnest) Island because of many bush rats seen there. Members of the ship's company explored the island for three days. De Vlamingh was impressed with the island, referring to it in his personal journal as 'a paradise on earth' and 'pleasurable above all islands I have ever seen.'[8] Between 4 and 12 January 1697, an exploration party, led by Gerrit Colsaert, the skipper of the *Weseltje*, investigated the Swan River, named after the black swans seen there. The party came across huts, footprints and other signs of the Aboriginal presence. Cockatoos, parrots, cormorants, geese and possibly emus were sighted, but no kangaroos, which are common in that vicinity, were seen. On 23 January, the crew of the *Geelvinck*'s longboat sighted ten Aborigines, described by de Vlamingh as 'quite naked and black, without any weapons.'[9]

After leaving the Swan River, the expedition sailed north and anchored next to Dirk Hartog Island on 30 January. Charting and coastal drawings were undertaken. Though not all of the locations can be identified, the expedition probably touched at Island Point, south of Jurien Bay, and Gantheaume Bay. De Vlamingh found Hartog's pewter plate from 1616 at Cape Inscription. He removed this and took it with him as an object of historical importance, and erected another pewter plate in exactly the same spot. He added Hartog's complete text to the details he supplied on the new plate. This conformed with the Dutch seafaring tradition of erecting signs with text at places where discoveries were made, a practice that did not have the purpose of claiming land. De Vlamingh took Hartog's plate to Batavia, whence it was transferred to Amsterdam. It is now among the collections of the Rijksmuseum there. The expedition's ships left Dirk Hartog Island and reached their final destination, Batavia on 17 March 1697.[10] De Vlamingh left Batavia in poor health on 3 February 1698, reached the Cape on 17 April, and set sail for the Netherlands on 8 May. He appears to have died on the voyage, for nothing more is known about him.[11]

The expedition found no remains of the *Ridderschap van Holland* nor any survivors. Thus, one of the main objectives of the voyage had been unsuccessful. In addition, nothing of commercial value was found; no live specimens were taken back to the Netherlands; and a box containing shells, fruits and plants proved of little value. De Vlamingh found Dirk Hartog Island barren and desolate, with only an abundance of turtles and turtle eggs to detract from a sterile coast. These negative results of the voyage occurred even though de Vlamingh was a dutiful explorer who followed his instructions carefully, taking every opportunity to record nautical detail, sending landing parties to explore coasts where landfall was made, and collecting as much information on geography and natural history as he could find.[12]

Nicolaes Witsen, the VOC's administrator, was unimpressed by de Vlamingh's reports of New Holland, observing that nothing had been discovered that could be serviceable to the company.[13] A letter to the VOC's managers emphasized the expedition's disappointing results: 'nothing has been discovered but a barren, arid and wild land, both near the shore and so far as they have been inland. Without meeting any human beings, only now and then some fires ... nor have they found there any remarkable animals or birds, except especially in the Swan river, a sort of black swans.'[14]

In other respects, however, the expedition yielded positive results. De Vlamingh had charted minutely and accurately about 1,500 kilometres of coast, a larger portion of west Australia – indeed, of any part of the entire Australian continent – than any previous explorer. His detailed charts appear to be no longer extant, but four outline charts of the voyage exist – two held at the Dutch National Archives and two at the National Library of Australia, Canberra. The two charts now in Australia were prepared by the mapmaker Gerard van Keulen in Amsterdam. Accurate to a tenth degree of latitude, they include the places located in west Australia during the voyage and include text on the search for water, mountains and sightings of Aborigines near Geraldton. Flinders incorporated many details from these charts on his 'General Chart of Terra Australis or Australia,' published in 1814.[15] Seven watercolour profiles of the west Australian coast, by Victor Victorszoon, have survived from the voyage; these are the oldest set of coastal views of Australia. It is not known whether the botanical specimens collected are now extant.[16]

De Vlamingh led the last significant Dutch expedition to Terra Australis. The VOC considered it now had sufficient evidence that no profit could accrue from Dutch interests in the South Land. Seventeenth-century Dutch voyages had charted about 55 per cent of Australia's coastline, from Cape York in a clockwise direction to the Nuyts Archipelago, but they had conferred relatively few place names because they had no intention of forming settlements in Terra Australis or pursuing scientific expeditions there.[17] Details of de Vlamingh's voyage were not published in full until 1753. The watercolours from his voyage did not reach the public domain until 1970.[18]

After de Vlamingh's expedition, Dutch interest in Australia rapidly faded while British and French curiosity about the South Land increased. In 1705, the Dutch sent an expedition from Timor under Maarten van Delft in the ships *de Vossenbosch*, *Waaier* and *Nova Hollandia* to north Australia that remained for three months off Melville Island and the Cobourg Peninsula.[19] A summary report and a good chart were produced. Dutch Eastindiamen, however, continued to be shipwrecked off the west Australian coast. In 1712, the *Zuytdorp*, carrying a large cargo of specie, was wrecked near today's Zuytdorp Cliffs.[20] In 1727, another VOC vessel, the *Zeewijk*, ran aground in the Houtman Abrolhos, while en route from the Netherlands to the East Indies. The crew constructed a sloop out of timbers from the wrecked ship and managed to sail to safety in Batavia.[21] Neither of these voyages was significant in the history of exploration. The Swiss entrepreneur and geographical theorist Jean Pierre Purry, working for the VOC in Batavia, proposed a scheme in 1717 whereby the Dutch would settle Nuyts Land in south and southwest Australia, but this fell upon deaf ears.[22] 'New Holland had had nothing that could be fitted into the commercial policy of the VOC,' Günter Schilder has concluded, adding: 'The VOC lost interest in the barren coasts of the fifth continent and deliberately abandoned the idea of exploring them further.'[23]

Dampier's voyages

England, unlike the Netherlands, had shown virtually no interest in exploring Terra Australis for most of the seventeenth century. The English East India Company had no base in the East Indies to rival the VOC's establishment in Batavia. It is therefore unsurprising that the first English navigator to undertake exploration in Australia was not an employee of the English East India Company but a jack-of-all-trades with extensive sailing experience on the oceans. This was William Dampier, a Somerset man who had briefly served on an East Indiaman followed by a spell in the Royal Navy, employment as a logwood cutter in the Bay of Campeche, and experience as a buccaneer in Jamaica and Panama and on privateers in the Pacific. Dampier participated in two voyages that explored parts of Australia's west coast and left a detailed written and pictorial record of his expeditions. He had previously undertaken amateur natural history and scientific observations on voyages to other parts of the world.[24] He was interested in exploring New Holland largely because it could serve as a base for England to gain access to Spain's South American markets.[25]

Dampier's first voyage to touch at Australia was in the *Cygnet*, a privateering vessel that set out on 31 March 1686 from New Spain (Mexico) to raid the East Indies. The ship called at Guam, Mindanao, the Philippines, China, the Spice Islands and Timor before reaching Australia's northwest coast on 5 January 1688. 'We fell in with the land of New Holland,' Dampier recorded in his journal, adding 'we sent our boat ashore to speak with the natives but they would not abide our coming.'[26] The decision to make an Australian landfall appears to have been spontaneous. Dampier did not have charts from Tasman's Australian voyages to guide him, but he did have a nautical chart of the eastern part of the East Indies from John Seller's *Atlas Maritimus* (1675) depicting part of Hollandia Nova.[27] With winds encouraging a southern track from Timor, Dampier wrote that 'we stood off South, intending to touch at New-Holland, a part of *Terra Australis Incognita*, to see what the Country would afford us.'[28]

The exact position where the *Cygnet* anchored and was careened is unknown, but Dampier stated it was at latitude 16°50′S at a place open to the northwest.[29] Dampier was careless in describing landfalls accurately. The location may have been Karrakatta Bay, behind Swan Point at the eastern entrance of King Sound, situated to the northeast of Broome. However, the landfall might also have been on an island east of King Sound where there are suitable bays for careening a vessel.[30] Extant primary sources cite different time periods for the *Cygnet*'s stay in northwest Australia: one states five weeks, while the other gives nine weeks.[31] Dampier was uncertain about the features of his geographical location. 'It is not yet determined,' he wrote, 'whether it is an island or a main continent, but I am certain that it joins neither Africa, Asia nor America.'[32] After leaving Australia on 12 March 1688, the vessel sailed to the Nicobar Islands in the Indian Ocean where Dampier left her, continuing his voyaging in Malacca, Vietnam, Cambodia and Madras before returning to England in 1691.[33]

Dampier published impressions of northwest Australia in a picaresque narrative entitled a *New Voyage Round the World* (1697), which provided a vivid account of his peregrinations across the globe in the *Cygnet* and other vessels, including a section describing his impressions of Australia's environment and native people. A *New Voyage Round the World* became popular, being printed in a fourth edition in 1699 with an additional volume that included material omitted from the original edition. Dampier shrewdly dedicated the book to the Earl of Orford, the first Lord of the Admiralty. This proved instrumental in enabling him to undertake a second voyage that visited Australia. Dampier was introduced to Orford in 1698, and asked to prepare a plan for a future voyage of discovery. He came up with a plan to sail to 'ye remoter parts of the *East India Islands* and the Neighbouring Coast of *Terra Australis*' to search for valuable commodities. During 1698, the Admiralty accepted the plan. This was to be the Navy's first expedition devoted to science and exploration.[34] Dampier's intention to explore the region of New Guinea and northwest Australia was his own rather than a government initiative.[35]

Having requested two ships for the expedition, Dampier was provided with one, a vessel of 290 tons with twenty-six guns named the *Roebuck*. No contemporary plans of its appearance have been found. Dampier was appointed commander of the expedition even though he had had no previous experience of being a ship's master.[36] The vessel was not in the best state of repair, and most of the crew were inexperienced in sailing across the oceans.[37]

The *Roebuck* set out on its voyage on 14 January 1699. Dampier faced trouble from many of his crew, whom he thought might mutiny, and he had several altercations with his lieutenant. The route followed was by way of the Canary Islands, Cape Verde Islands, Brazil, the Cape of Good Hope and the Indian Ocean. It appears that Dampier estimated his longitude by dead reckoning and measured the depth of ocean water with a hand lead line and a deep-sea lead line.[38] Dampier had been provided with a Dutch map showing Tasman's two voyages. He intended to reach Terra Australis but he seems to have been somewhat muddled about where he might find a landfall.[39]

Even though Dampier did not publish a chart of his route, the course followed by the *Roebuck* can be verified more easily than the *Cygnet*'s route. The *Roebuck* approached the west Australian coast near the Houtman Abrolhos, turned north and reached the north side of Dirk Hartog Island on 16 August 1699.[40] Dampier did not find de Vlamingh's pewter plate. On 31 August, the voyage reached islands later named the Dampier Archipelago where Dampier landed on Rosemary Island and at East Lewis Island. He took an armed party ashore and fended off some aggressive Aborigines, but then had no more contact with them. Sailing north-eastwards on 2 September, the *Roebuck* anchored at Lagrange Bay on 9 September and left the west Australian coast six days later for Timor.[41]

Dampier discussed his nautical position in relation to his copied chart of Tasman's voyages to Terra Australis. Coming across tides, Dampier used the navigational knowledge he had distilled into his published discussion of hydrographical matters.[42] He suspected he might be near an archipelago of islands with 'a passage possibly to the S. of N. Holland and N. Guinea into the great S. Sea eastward.'[43] In making this comment, Dampier implicitly challenged the reliability of Dutch charts of New Holland. He thought they were wrong to depict New Guinea as joined to Australia: that is why he referred to a channel running between them in the above quotation.[44] He nevertheless failed to locate such a passage.[45]

Dampier's voyage gave more definition to parts of northwest Australia, but added nothing essential to geographical knowledge. It did not determine, for instance, the relationship between New Holland and Terra Australis: it remained uncertain whether they were fully joined or part of a larger landmass. Dampier's limited geographical contribution to knowledge of New Holland 'was to make its western shoreline a real, if unattractive, place rather than a wavering line on the map.'[46] Dampier left west Australia's coast, continued eastwards, and came within about 100 nautical miles of Australia's east coast – then unknown to navigators – before severe leaking and unfavourable winds forced the ship to turn back. Thus, Dampier was unable to sail for Torres Strait.[47] The *Roebuck*'s voyage had not lived up to its expectations. It had 'promised to open up the South Pacific to the active development of British policy' but 'ended with the mysteries of that region still largely unsolved.'[48]

In February 1700, on the voyage home, the *Roebuck* was wrecked near the isolated Ascension Island in the South Atlantic; the crew were taken to the shore by raft. Dampier lost most of his books and papers but saved his dried plant

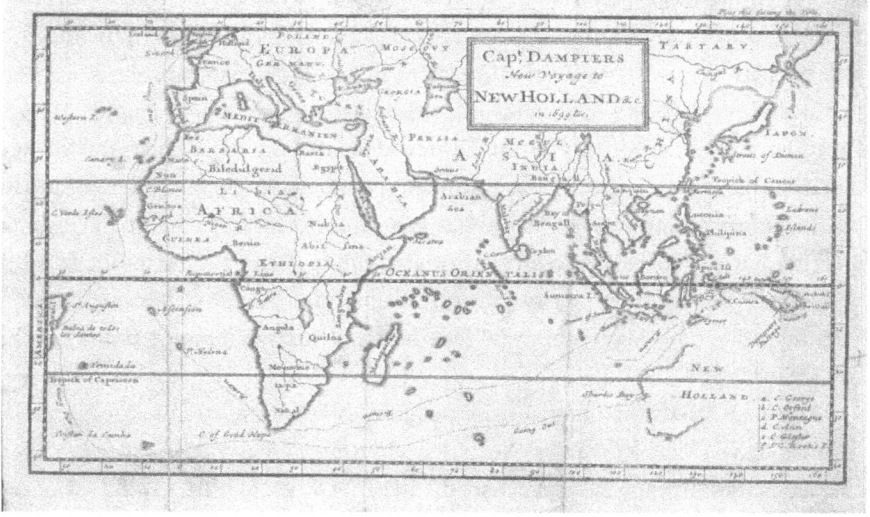

Map 5 William Dampier, *Capt. Dampier's New Voyage to New Holland etc. in 1699* (London: for James and John Knapton, ?1729) MAP NK 11185 Bib ID 2825581

specimens from New Holland.[49] The wreck site was located by a salvage team from the Western Australian Maritime Museum in March 2001, though the wreck itself remains to be recovered, examined and conserved.[50] After Dampier returned to England in 1701, he faced a court martial for his cruel treatment of a lieutenant, George Fisher, with whom he had clashed during the outward-bound part of the voyage. Dampier was found guilty; his pay was docked and he was dismissed from the Royal Navy.[51]

Dampier published two accounts of his voyage – *A Voyage to New-Holland* (1703) and *A Continuation of a Voyage to New Holland* (1709). The first book included drawings of coastal profiles, plants and animals by an unnamed artist on the *Roebuck*'s voyage.[52] Maps drawn by the London cartographer, engraver and publisher Herman Moll made the outline of New Holland familiar in England for the first time.[53] The books were embellished by anonymous editorial additions, possibly by his publisher James Knapton, though this is not certain. Additions and changes to Dampier's manuscript account of Aborigines, for example, were more than stylistic polishing.[54] Plant descriptions at the end of the first volume of *A Voyage to New-Holland* may well have been written by the botanist John Ray. The books sold well when first published, running rapidly into various editions. Appearing in French, German and Dutch editions, they provided impetus for a flourishing literary genre of writing sea narratives, and influenced later perceptions of Australia by explorers such as James Cook and Charles Darwin.[55]

Dampier's two books included more extensive narrative material on the Australian environment, its flora, fauna, wildlife and native people, than any previous publications based upon first-hand experience. His impressions of New Holland influenced many literate Europeans.[56] His commentary on Australia's environment was unflattering. On his first voyage in the *Cygnet*, he described a monotonous landscape on the Dampier Peninsula, west Australia, noting the gum trees and dry, sandy banks and soil. In *A Voyage to New Holland*, his descriptions of the landscape were similar; they offered little prospect of fertile soil suitable for settlement or readily available food resources.[57] Australia's northwest coast disappointed Dampier: 'if it were not for that sort of pleasure which results from the discovery even of the barrenest spot upon the globe,' he wrote, 'this coast of New Holland would not have charmed me much.'[58] As Adrian Mitchell has put it, 'the whole of Dampier's encounter with New Holland is characterised by negatives – by remoteness, by vacancy, by insufficiency, by indefinition.'[59]

Dampier's natural history collections in Western Australia were gathered on the *Roebuck*'s voyage. He was an observant recorder and collector of fauna, flora, animals, shells and fish, but not a trained scientist. Thus, he did not undertake botanical research, name and describe new species of plants or publish scientific articles.[60] Nevertheless, *A Voyage to New Holland* includes interesting descriptions of trees and shrubs seen in Western Australia, of curlews, waterfowl, cormorants, gulls, sharks, humpback whales, bottle-nosed dolphins, and green turtle, many of them illustrated with pictures to whet the reader's curiosity. Dampier included a long section describing a stumptail lizard he came across.[61] He identified three separate species of birds at Shark Bay in 1699, one of which, the water bird, had eight different varieties.[62]

Dampier had sufficient botanical knowledge to ascribe genera to plants. On returning from the *Roebuck*'s voyage, he handed over his specimens to the botanist John Woodward who passed them to John Ray and Leonard Plukenet, botanist to Queen Anne.[63] Among Dampier's surviving specimens are twenty-three species of Australian flowering plants and a seaweed. The most vivid flower he discovered is known as the Sturt Desert Pea – a creeping vine with a recognizable deep red blossom.[64] Dampier's collections are preserved in the Sherardium Herbarium in the department of Plant Sciences at Oxford University. They comprise the earliest documented collection of Australian flora. The plant specimens are still in a very good state, having been pressed soon after collection. The Scottish botanist Robert Brown examined the collection in the early nineteenth century and commemorated Dampier by naming a genus after him – *Dampiera* in the family *Goodeniaceae*.[65]

Among the most influential sections in *A New Voyage Round the World* and *A Voyage to New Holland* are those dealing with Aborigines. In his published version, though not so much in his manuscript account, Dampier's view of these natives (probably members of the Bardi people) was highly negative: 'the inhabitants of this country are the miserablest people in the world,' he observed, adding that 'setting aside their human shape, they differ but little from brutes. They are tall, straight-bodied, and thin, with small long limbs. They have great heads, round foreheads, and great brows.' Dampier considered that Aborigines had unsightly facial features. He observed that all Aborigines had two fore teeth missing, but did not know whether that was deliberate or coincidence.[66] Their skin colour was 'coal-black like that of the Negroes of Guinea.' They wore no clothes, had no houses, did not understand a word of English, and seemed not to worship anything. Dampier found the Aborigines were shy and tended to run away from his ship's company.[67] On his second visit to Western Australia in 1699,

Dampier referred to the Aborigines as having 'the most unpleasant Looks and the worst Features of any people that I ever saw.'[68] Despite this negative verdict, Dampier stopped short of referring to Aborigines as brutes or cannibals.[69]

Dampier's ethnographic comments on Aborigines were partly influenced by medieval lore and partly based on empirical observation. Notions of fabulous monstrously large people from the Middle Ages are reflected in his published descriptions of Aborigines as having 'great heads,' 'great brows' and 'bottle noses.' Dampier also compared the grin of Aborigines with that of monkeys.[70] Dampier's observations had a lasting impact on European explorers: James Cook and Sir Joseph Banks referred back to his comments some seventy years later when they reached Australia's east coast in the *Endeavour*.[71] Dampier's perception of the Aborigines appears to have been influenced by the notion of a 'great chain of being' in which God was placed at the apex, white men immediately below, non-white people beneath them, and animals at the bottom of the scale. Aborigines were looked down upon as an uncivilized human group, a lower element of humanity. Dampier's views were also partly influenced by his assumption that civilized people would have plenty of worldly possessions.[72]

After Dampier

No further British voyages of exploration to Australia occurred between Dampier's *Roebuck* expedition of 1699 and Cook's traversal of the east coast in 1770. Nevertheless, Dampier's voyages had a lasting effect on imaginative literature. Daniel Defoe's novel *A New Voyage Round the World by a Course Never Sailed Before* (1724) echoed the title of Dampier's book. Jonathan Swift's best-selling *Gulliver's Travels* (1726), a satire on the travellers' tales literary sub-genre, situated the Land of the Houyhnhnms near the Nuyts archipelago off Australia's southern coast.[73]

Although these books catered for curiosity about Terra Australis, that was not their main purpose. Such interest was stimulated more by John Campbell's *Navigantium Atque Itinerantium Bibliotheca*, an extensive and enlarged version of John Harris's *Collection of Voyages and Travels* (1702–5). These large tomes presented a positive fantasy of the rich spices, diamonds and silver that could be found in Terra Australis to add to Britain's commercial wealth. They offered a speculative, optimistic account of how Australia could increase the power and status of the British Empire.[74] In the first volume, it was claimed

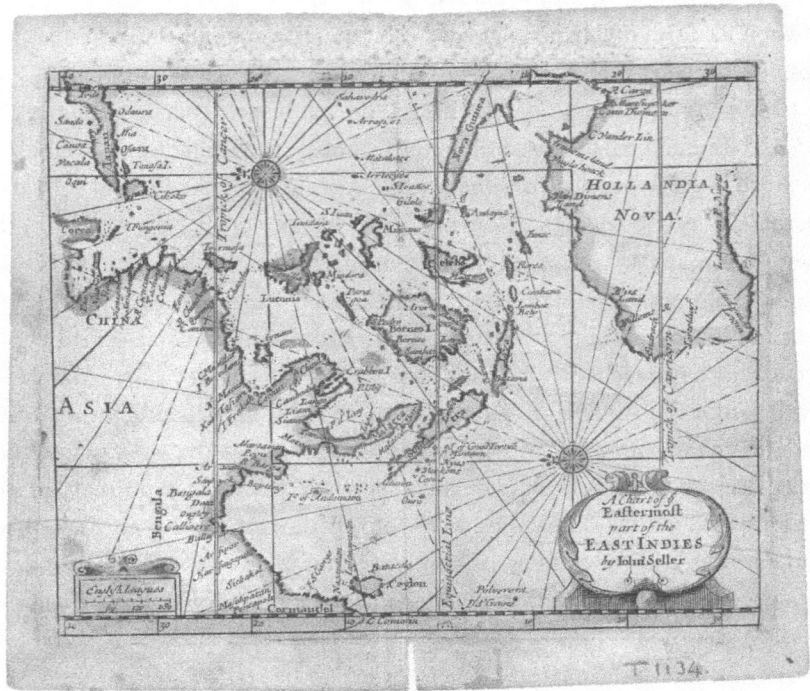

Map 6 John Seller, *A Chart of the Easternmost Part of the East Indies* (Wapping: The Hermitage, ?1690) MAP T 1134 Bib ID 1481604

'there is a great Continent, and many Islands' to the south of Asia, 'and those islands are very probably rich and well peopled, to which if a Trade could be opened, it might, nay, must, be very commodious, and produce as great or greater Advantages, than those which have resulted from the Discoveries of America.'[75]

Geographical knowledge of Australia advanced little between the time of Dampier and Cook. Most maps of Australia were based on Tasman's discoveries in the 1640s. Joan Blaeu's map of the world (1645–6) and Thévenot's copy of a map depicting Tasman's two voyages in his *Relation de divers voyages curieux* (1663) have been referred to in Chapter 3.[76] The Thévenot map was recopied to form the best-known British map of Terra Australis produced before 1750: this was Emanuel Bowen's *Hollandia Nova-Terra Australis* (1744), which only showed discovered territory. This first English map devoted to Australia depended heavily on information provided on seventeenth-century Dutch charts; its two legends drew attention to the supposed land fertility and mineral

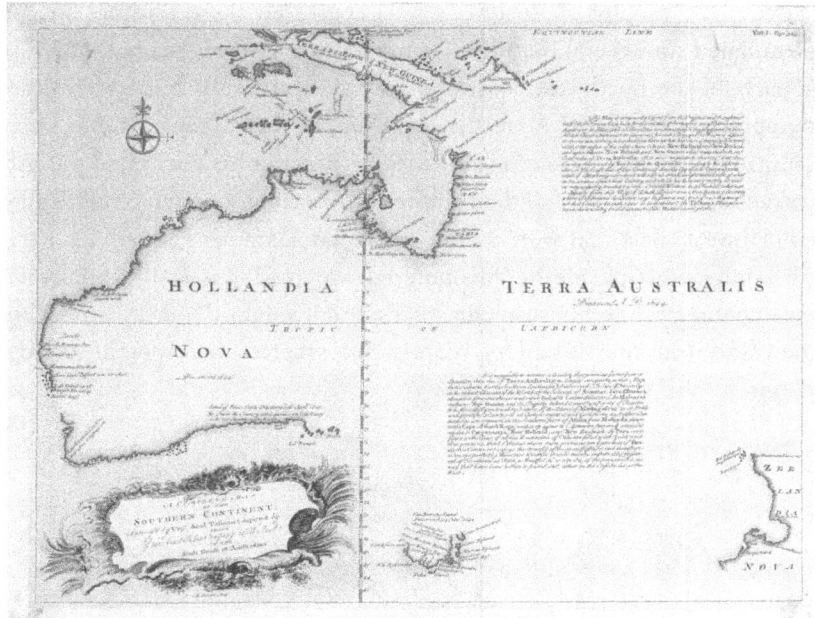

Map 7 Emanuel Bowen, *A Complete map of the Southern Continent: survey'd by Capt. Abel Tasman & depicted by order of the East India Company in Holland in the Stadt House in Amsterdam* (Amsterdam: East India Company, 1744) MAP NK 10147 Bib ID 2650522

wealth to be found in the southern continent. One legend also noted that it was 'impossible to conceive a Country that promises fairer from its Situation, than this of Terra Australis; no longer incognita, as this Map demonstrates, but the Southern Continent Discovered'.[77]

Conclusion

On the last major Dutch voyage and the first significant English voyage to Australia, ships concentrated on exploring the northwest and west coasts. De Vlamingh's expedition explored Rottnest Island, Dirk Hartog Island, and the Swan River and its vicinity. The natural history collections from this voyage were relatively insignificant; little contact occurred with Aborigines; and after the voyage was over, the Dutch concluded that no substantial commercial gains were to be had from Australia. They therefore lost interest in sending further vessels there. De Vlamingh's voyage was notable for its extensive and accurate charting of Australia's west coast, but these findings were not disseminated for several decades. Dampier's two voyages made landfall in a few parts of the northwest coast and its offshore islands but added little to geographical knowledge. Nevertheless, Dampier left a considerable imprint on future maritime exploration of Australia because his illustrated published travel accounts included full descriptions of Aborigines and natural history of the northwest coast that were widely consulted. Dampier's negative portrayal of the indigenous people he encountered was read closely by explorers for over a century, while his suspicion that a strait might divide Australia from somewhere near the Rosemary islands also whetted the appetite of future explorers.

Cook, the *Endeavour* and the East Coast

During the eighteenth century, Enlightenment thinking emphasized human progress via greater discovery of the globe. Scientific curiosity was strongly connected with maritime exploration. After many years when fresh knowledge about Terra Australis had dried up, navigators, geographers and scientists renewed their interest in Pacific exploration. Britain and France were at the forefront of voyages of discovery to the Pacific after 1750 through the work of various institutions and individuals. The distinguished learned society the Institut de France, with headquarters in Paris, and several French monarchs were keenly interested in maritime exploration. In Britain the Royal Society, with headquarters in London, the patronage of Sir Joseph Banks for collectors of new knowledge, and the Admiralty and Board of Longitude were also closely involved in promoting oceanic exploration.[1] Thus, for example, the Royal Society, the most prestigious British scientific institution, produced detailed instructions to seafarers and travellers about how to gather accurate data on coastlines, ports and weather patterns.[2] By the late eighteenth century, potential strategic and economic advantages for European trading nations combined with the quest for new knowledge about the human world to stimulate Pacific exploration.[3]

Britain and France competed for power and new resources in remote areas of the South Seas. French writers discussed the potential benefits of increased voyaging to the Pacific. The Comte du Buffon's first volume of his *Histoire naturelle* (1749) discussed the existence of potentially large lands in the southern hemisphere, while Charles de Brosses's *Histoire des Navigations aux Terres Australes* (1756) collated a large amount of information about voyages to the Pacific.[4] John Callender's English edition of de Brosses's book pointed out that much confusion had arisen in Pacific exploration from misidentifying islands, bays, straits, and from rudimentary nautical charts and inaccurate geographical descriptions.[5] Yet the impulse to explore further, in the hope of finding riches, remained strong. Writers such as John Campbell, Alexander Dalrymple and James Mario Matra speculated about the prospects of trade, exchange and products that Terra Australis could provide in an optimistic, favourable way. This added to contemporary interest in the Great South Land.[6] In 1767, Dalrymple, following Mercator's notion of equipoise, reiterated the view that a large southern continent must exist as a counterweight to land in the northern hemisphere: 'Having shewn that there is a seeming necessity for a Southern Continent to maintain a conformity in the two hemispheres, it rests to shew, from the nature of the winds in the South Pacifick Ocean, that there must be a Continent on the South.'[7]

The main object of British voyages after the conclusion of the Seven Years' War was related to British dominance as a seapower. That is why the Admiralty organized nearly all the voyages and why the commanders were Royal Navy officers. Scientific exploration was another major impetus in Pacific exploration as European powers pursued a quest for new knowledge about geography, botany, zoology, ethnography, hydrography and astronomy in diverse parts of the globe. These branches of scientific knowledge experienced considerable development and progress in the era of the Enlightenment. All of them, in different ways, could be advanced by the findings of oceanic explorers.[8]

Pacific exploration, however, was only partially related to an attempt to find out more about *Terra Australis*. Commodore John Byron, who had sailed on Anson's voyage around the world (1740–4), led his own circumnavigation of the globe in 1764–5 in HMS *Dolphin* and HMS *Tamar*. He was charged with finding an island for a permanent British naval settlement in the south Atlantic. In January 1765, he surveyed the Falkland Islands, claiming them for Britain, unaware that the French had already created a small settlement there. Byron sailed around Cape Horn but made no discoveries of note in the Pacific. From the absence of great swells, he thought there might be a large landmass to his south, possibly Terra Australis, but he came across no land that fitted that description. His expedition arrived back in England by May 1766, having achieved the swiftest circumnavigation yet known.[9]

As soon as Byron arrived home, the Admiralty fitted out another voyage of discovery to the Pacific. Led by Philip Carteret in the *Swallow* and Samuel Wallis in the *Dolphin*, this expedition of 1766–9 included instructions to search for the landmass that Byron thought he had missed: 'There is reason to believe [*sic*] that Lands, or Islands of great extent, hitherto unvisited by any European Power may be found in the Southern Hemisphere between Cape Horn and New Zealand, in Latitudes convenient for Navigation, and in Climates adapted to the product of Commodities usefull in commerce.'[10] These were the first official instructions ever issued in Britain to search in the Pacific for the Southern Continent. The Admiralty hoped British ships would find such lands before any of their continental European rivals.[11]

The *Swallow* and the *Dolphin* lost touch with one another in the Strait of Magellan and continued separately for the rest of their voyages. Neither commander came across any land that could be Terra Australis, but their voyages had some positive results. Carteret discovered Pitcairn Island, the Carteret Islands and the Duke of York Islands (off the eastern end of New Guinea). Wallis sighted Tahiti and thought he saw mountain tops 60 miles to the south of his position.[12] George Robertson, the master of the *Dolphin*, believed this was a tantalizing glimpse of Terra Australis. At sunset on 19 June 1767, in thick and foggy weather, he noted that 'we now suposd we saw the long wishd for Southern Continent, which has been often talkd of but neaver before seen by any Europeans.'[13] The *Dolphin* never sailed near enough to the supposed mountains, however, to confirm this sighting. Less than a year later, in March 1768 Louis Antoine de Bougainville's expedition around the world reached Tahiti and eventually publicized the beauties of this tropical paradise in the Pacific.[14] The cartographic results of these voyages were modest. No maps published from Wallis's expedition and only small-scale maps appeared in Bougainville's volume published after his voyage.[15]

Cook and the *Endeavour*, 1768–71

In 1767, the Admiralty, with the support of the Royal Society and King George III, planned a major scientific expedition to the Pacific, the largest such enterprise yet undertaken. The voyage's ostensible purpose was to observe an astronomical phenomenon, the transit of Venus across the Sun, which was next expected to occur in June 1769. This was a relatively rare occurrence, scheduled to happen twice within eight years after gaps of 121½ and 105½ years.[16] Samuel Wallis, on the basis of the *Dolphin*'s voyage, recommended Tahiti as a suitable observation transit site because it had plenty of fresh water and friendly natives, and was a secure place for undertaking scientific observations.[17] By calculating the distance of Venus from the Sun, it was thought the distances of other planets could be estimated from their orbits. If the transit could be timed accurately within a couple of seconds, calculations could be made about the Sun's diameter, the distance of the Sun from the Earth, and the size of the solar system. Calculation of the distance of the Earth from the Sun was required for determining longitude at sea via any lunar theory.[18]

The voyage had another objective, namely to search further for *Terra Australis*, which Byron and Wallis thought they might have been near on their voyages a few years earlier. This part of the voyage was based on secret instructions to remain unopened until the expedition had left Tahiti – something which suggests that the voyage's findings were intended primarily for use by the British state.[19] By the time these instructions were written, scientists and geographers distinguished between Terra Australis (i.e. Australia) and *Terra Australis Incognita*, the unknown continent which was expected to be more fertile than Australia and to have new vegetables and spices, new tropical fruits along with diamonds, silver and gold.[20] Cook's secret instructions were intended to ensure that Britain discovered Terra Australis before rivals such as France so that in the future this might be the base for a flourishing Pacific trade.[21]

The Royal Society wanted the Scots navigator and hydrographer Dalrymple to lead the expedition because of his strong interest in the quest for a Great Southern Continent. However, the Admiralty refused to accept him because he was not a naval officer. The Yorkshireman James Cook, an experienced navigator with a good working knowledge of astronomy, was the somewhat surprise choice as commander. Cook had extensive nautical experience, having served on coastal voyages in the coal trade between Newcastle and London, on journeys across the North Sea to Baltic lands, and on naval vessels in Canada.[22] The middle-aged Cook was only promoted to lieutenant just before the voyage began. The vessel selected for the expedition was HMS *Endeavour*, a three-masted, flat-bottomed ship of 368 tons burden. This ship was converted to hold almost one hundred crew, marines and civilians. Originally built for the coal trade in north-east England, the *Endeavour* was large enough to carry plenty of provisions, but also designed for her capability in navigating shallow waters. Both would be essential for her exploratory voyage.[23]

The *Endeavour* expedition was an important landmark in oceanic voyaging, covering an impressively large swathe of the Pacific and coming across many people, plants and artefacts unknown to Europeans. No exploratory voyage of this scope had preceded it. Cook undertook a more thorough search for the missing continent, thought to lie somewhere between New Zealand and South America, than any previous voyage.[24] While it is important to include commentary that reflects the breadth of the voyage, this chapter concentrates on the relationship of the voyage to the exploration of Australia, which was only one part of the remit pursued on the *Endeavour*'s voyage.

The *Endeavour* was fully fitted out for a major scientific expedition. Charles Green, who had worked with the Astronomer Royal Nevil Maskelyne, was the astronomer. Sydney Parkinson, a Scottish botanical illustrator, was the artist. Dr Daniel Solander, a Swedish naturalist, friend and pupil of Linnaeus, shared botanical collecting with Joseph Banks, a rich English amateur who had been influential in getting George III to establish the Botanic Gardens at Kew. Banks brought a party of associates with him at his own expense, including two servants and two greyhounds. Additional accommodation was built in the *Endeavour* for this entourage. The voyage was supplied with the latest scientific instruments, including reflecting telescopes, an astronomical quadrant and clock, Hadley's sextant and a dipping needle designed by renowned instrument-makers. The scientific experts were expected to collect fauna and flora, to take astronomical observations, to record details of the peoples they came across, and to paint people and landscape views. The results of the expedition were intended for public dissemination after the completion of the expedition.[25]

Cook and Banks had an extensive library on board ship. The *Endeavour* carried de Brosses's *Histoire des Navigations aux Terres Australes* (1756), which included material on all Pacific exploration yet carried out; George Anson's *A Voyage Round the World* (1756); Charles Clerke's *A Voyage Round the World, in His Majesty's Ship the Dolphin* (1767); copies of Tasman and Dampier's writings relating to New Holland; and Dalrymple's *An Historical Collection of the Several Voyages and Discoveries in the South Pacific Ocean* (1770). These summarized the discoveries of European navigators, but they indicated that most of the charting of the Pacific and surveying of its lands remained to be done.[26]

The *Endeavour* left Plymouth on 25 August 1768 and sailed via Cape Horn into the Pacific. During this first phase of the voyage, Green taught Cook the lunar distance method of calculating longitude.[27] The voyage reached Matavai Bay, Tahiti, on 13 April 1769, allowing Cook plenty of time to prepare for the transit of Venus. This was duly observed on 3 June, but Cook was dissatisfied with the astronomical observations taken. Staying at Tahiti until late July allowed Cook to record impressions of the local Polynesians and Parkinson to draw portraits of these people. Cook took aboard ship Tupaia, a priest and navigator from the western Society Islands, to help as an interpreter with Polynesians. During August and September, the *Endeavour* explored many Pacific islands and then headed due south in search of the Great Southern Continent. No signs of land were seen after many days' sailing. Cook therefore decided to change to a westward course to find New Zealand, which had not been visited by any navigator since Tasman but which was marked on the French mapmaker Robert De Vaugondy's 1756 chart, of which Cook had a copy.[28]

On 8 October 1769, Cook made landfall at Poverty Bay on the north island of New Zealand. Over the next five months, the *Endeavour* circumnavigated both islands of New Zealand for the first time, naming many landmarks and compiling a highly accurate chart. This proved that New Zealand was not part of a Great Southern Continent, an important advance in geographical knowledge. After initial skirmishes, involving some deaths, friendly relations were established with the Maori. Tupaia helped to communicate with the Maori, who respected him as an important religious leader. On 9 November, Cook and Green observed on shore the Transit of Mercury across the Sun at Mercury Bay by observing and recording the times when the disk of Mercury was in contact with the Sun's limb. Cook discovered the passage between the two main islands of New Zealand, which Tasman had missed. Banks named it Cook Strait. Cook took possession of some districts he explored but not of New Zealand: his instructions had not requested that he do so, presumably because Tasman had been the first discoverer. The *Endeavour* left New Zealand on 31 March 1770 to return to Britain.[29]

Cook and his associates had a choice of three possible sailing routes. One was to return to Cape Horn in high latitudes to determine whether a Great Southern Continent existed. This option was discarded because it was likely that the ship's sails and rigging could not withstand the hard gales that would be encountered. A second possibility was to steer the ship south of Van Diemen's Land and head for the Cape of Good Hope. But the *Endeavour* had plenty of provisions and this scheme was not followed because, as Banks put it, 'the over plus was not to be thrown away in a Sea where so few navigators had been before us.'[30] The third option was selected, which was to sail westwards, fall in with the coast of New Holland, and follow that as far north as possible in the hope of locating the lands seen by Quirós in 1606 – namely 'Austrialia del Espiritu Santo' or the New Hebrides. Following this scheme meant that the voyage had to abandon its 'first grand object, the Southern Continent.'[31] However, Cook had arrived at the conclusion that there was only a relatively small space northwards of 40° where such a land might exist, while Banks continued to believe in the possibility of a southern continent though not on the scale imagined by 'the theoretical continent-makers.'[32]

Cook's knowledge of the extent and shape of Australia was largely informed by maps mainly founded on Tasman's voyages. These showed an almost continuous coastline on the north and west coasts of Australia, a southern coastline from the southwestern end of Australia to the islands of St Peter and St Francis, an unknown south coast for the eastern half of Australia's shores bordering the

Southern Ocean, and a large gap on the east coast between Espiritu Santo and Van Diemen's Land. How the missing parts of the jigsaw fitted together had whetted the curiosity of navigators and geographers since the early seventeenth century. The blank spaces could join up to comprise a continental landmass, or they might turn out to be chains of islands. No consensus existed. John Campbell, writing in 1744, thought 'that New Guinea, Carpentaria, New Holland, Van Diemen's Land, and the countries discovered by Quirós make all one continent.' But de Brosses's volumes represented New Holland and New Guinea as separate lands divided by a strait while joining Van Diemen's Land to New Holland. Cook had with him a copy of Dalrymple's *Chart of the South Pacifick Ocean Pointing Out the Discoveries Made Previous to 1764*, published in 1767, which showed a clear passage between New Guinea and New Holland.[33]

Margaret Cameron Ash has recently argued that Cook deliberately avoided sailing across the Tasman Sea to Van Diemen's Land from New Zealand, which he left on 31 March 1770, because he wished to conceal the existence of Bass Strait for the purposes of British state secrecy.[34] Proving this point is virtually impossible, however, because the written sources are silent on this matter. What is known is that on 19 April 1770 Cook, following a course in latitude 38°, saw Point Hicks, on the Australian mainland. That particular coordinate is well out to sea, so Cook either made an error or deliberately recorded a wrong location.[35] Cook commented that the current longitude meant that Van Diemen's Land ought to be due south of their position, though they did not see it, as it lay well beyond the horizon. Cook doubted whether Van Diemen's Land was joined to the land they saw, but he had no proof of this.[36] His supposition would mean that a strait divided Australia and Van Diemen's Land. But he made no attempt to follow this up because he had been at sea for one year and eight months, his supplies were depleted, and it seemed more sensible to run up Australia's east coast to explore rather than proceed in a southwest direction towards the supposed location of Van Diemen's Land.[37]

As Cook sailed up Australia's east coast, he looked out for harbours, places of shelter and supplies of fresh water. He named various coastal features.[38] Cook saw Bateman's Bay but thought it had too little protection from the elements to anchor there. He passed Jervis Bay, which appeared to offer shelter but the shore did not seem sufficiently interesting for the *Endeavour* to stop there. Cook attempted to land a few miles north of Red Point (Port Kembla) but the surf made this impossible.[39] The *Endeavour* reached what Cook eventually called Botany Bay (on account of the numerous plants collected there) on 30 May 1770. During the stay there, Cook arranged for 'the English colours to be display'd ashore every day.'[40] Cook came across Aborigines at Botany Bay, but no formal possession ceremony was undertaken.[41]

After remaining for a week at Botany Bay, the ship proceeded a few miles north where Cook named an inlet Port Jackson (modern Sydney) but did not stop there. Cook's journal merely noted that the location appeared to offer a safe anchorage for ships – rather an understatement.[42] The *Endeavour* continued northwards up the east coast, keeping as near the mainland as possible. Cook named geographical features, allowed his scientists to botanize, took daily coordinates, and conducted a running survey that was recorded on charts. During this part of the voyage, Cook sailed past and named Broken Bay, Moreton Bay and Bustard Bay. He largely remained on board ship, only pausing occasionally to land on the mainland and offshore islands.[43] Altogether, Cook spent 100 days on or off Queensland's coast, landing at nine places.[44]

Cook navigated through extensive shoals and coral reefs between the Whitsunday Isles and the Cape York peninsula. He did not realize that a huge expanse of coral polyps – the Great Barrier Reef – covered 1,200 miles from below the Tropic of Capricorn to the coast of New Guinea.[45] On 10 June 1770, while sailing away from the shore gently on a clear moonlit night, the *Endeavour* unexpectedly struck sunken coral reefs at high tide.[46] Cook had more confidence in the situation than was warranted as he had recently visited two places in New Zealand where he had sailed into trouble on moonlit nights.[47]

When the *Endeavour* struck the reefs, Cook immediately came on deck and he and the ship's company threw many heavy items overboard. Banks heard a violent noise as the ship crashed into rocks, and feared he would die by drowning. Twelve hours later, despite the lightening of the ship, the *Endeavour* would not move.[48] The reefs were 'the most dreadfull of all others on account of their sharp points and grinding quality which cut through a ships bottom almost immediately.'[49] As Cook explained, 'the coral rock had cut through the plank, and deep into one of the timbers, smoothing the gashes before it, so that the whole might easily be imagined to have been cut with an axe.'[50]

The location was near Endeavour River on the coast of modern Queensland. The ship was repaired at this location (near today's Cooktown) for several weeks. During this sojourn, Cook and his ship's company came across Aborigines and discovered and described kangaroos, which became the subject of drawings by Parkinson.[51] Banks recorded that he had seen 'an animal as large as a greyhound, of a mouse colour and very swift,' but it was several weeks before speculation about the animal could be identified. Banks expressed his curiosity at the sight of a kangaroo: 'To compare it to any European animal would be impossible as it has not the least resemblance of any one I have seen. Its fore legs are extremely short and of no use to it in walking, its hind again as disproportionately long; with these it hops 7 or 8 feet at each hop.'[52] Cook also came across a dingo and flying foxes.[53]

In reaching this location, Cook did not realize he was sailing within the Great Barrier Reef. The dangers of coral rocks were scarcely known in Europe.[54] Sandbanks and shoals lay all around this part of the Australian coast. A passage out to sea would have to be found between the reefs after the ship had been repaired.[55] On 14 August, Cook noted that he had been entangled among shoals and reefs almost since 26 May, having sailed a distance of 360 leagues.[56] He had struggled to cope with such unknown navigational difficulties. 'I have ingaged more among the Islands and shoals upon this coast,' he wrote, 'than may be thought with prudence I ought to have done with a single ship.'[57] After attempting over several days to sail from Endeavour River, Cook found a clear passage to the open sea. But, with only three months' provisions left, which were sufficient to reach the East Indies but only without further damage and delay, he agreed with his officers that the *Endeavour* should sail away from the coast until the danger of reefs had passed.[58]

Cook considered an explorer should not shy away from 'leaving a coast unexplored he has once discover'd,' dealing pragmatically with 'all the dangers and obstacles he meets.'[59] His traversal of the coral reefs certainly met those criteria. Within the Great Barrier Reef, he named 'Magnetical Island' (now Magnetic Island, 8 miles off Townsville) in the belief that magnetic ore caused variations in his compasses at this location.[60] Cook acknowledged Dutch discoveries of New Holland, but proudly noted in his journal that no European navigator before him had seen Australia's east coast. On what he called Possession Island, situated near Torres Strait, he hoisted the Union flag in the name of George III and 'took possession of the whole Eastern Coast…by the name of New South Wales.'[61] He claimed that part of Australia's coast not previously visited by Dutch navigators, from Point Hicks (38°S) to Cape York; he did not want to antagonize the Dutch.[62] Cook's arrival at Possession Island prompted Banks to write, with relief, that the *Endeavour* had accomplished the 'safe completion of the most hazardous piece of navigation of the voyage.'[63] An open sea to the westward convinced Cook that New Holland and New Guinea were two separate lands or islands 'which until this day hath been a doubtfull point with Geographers.'[64]

Cook intended to prove or disprove whether Torres Strait existed. The rulers of Spain had kept Torres's discovery of the strait secret: Cook therefore approached it without having a detailed chart to follow.[65] He sailed through Endeavour Strait, its southernmost and most extensive western entrance, situated between Possession Island and Prince of Wales Island, the largest of the Torres Strait islands. Sailing conditions were difficult: numerous small banks of coral with a couple of fathoms between them were invisible until they were almost reached and, even then, they appeared as though they were reflections of dark clouds on the water.[66]

By 26 August 1770, the *Endeavour* had passed between New Holland and New Guinea and there was open sea to the westward. This was the only occasion that Cook sailed through Torres Strait. He later reported to the Admiralty that on 22 August, in the latitude of 10°30′, he had found a passage into the Indian Ocean between the northern extremity of New Holland and New Guinea. He had proved that New Guinea and New Holland were 'not one continued land.'[67] Dalrymple later claimed that Torres' track, which he laid down in his chart supplied to Banks, had enabled Cook to pass between New Holland and New Guinea.[68] Cook hoped that one day a better route through the strait would be discovered among islands he could see to the north. As G. Arnold Wood put it, Cook had been the first known navigator to sail through Torres Strait but 'apart from this one passage, the huge chaos of the strait remained unexplored.'[69]

Leaving Possession Island on 22 August 1770, the *Endeavour* proceeded to Batavia, where repairs were undertaken. Tupaia died there from either dysentery or malaria.[70] While the *Endeavour* remained in Batavia, Cook forwarded copies of his journal and charts via a Dutch ship to the Admiralty in London. He also wrote a modest letter to the secretary of the Admiralty about his achievements on the voyage:

> Altho' the discoveries made in this Voyage are not great, yet I flatter myself that they are such as may merit the attention of their Lordships, and altho' I have failed in discovering the so much talk'd of southern Continent (which perhaps do not exist) and which I myself had much at heart, yet I am confident that no part of the failure of such discovery Can be laid to my Charge...had we been so fortunate not to have run a shore much more would have been done in the latter part of the Voyage than what was, but...I presume this Voyage will be found as Compleat as any before made to the South Seas.[71]

The *Endeavour* left Batavia on 26 December 1770, lost twenty-four men while crossing the Indian Ocean, and arrived near Durban, South Africa, on 5 March 1771. The voyage continued to the Cape of Good Hope and St Helena, and arrived back in England on 13 July 1771 after an expedition of over three years.[72] Cook, again modestly, wrote to the Admiralty, noting 'that the discoveries we have made, though not great, will apologize for the length of the voyage.'[73] Cook was promoted from lieutenant to commander at the end of the voyage, and was presented to the king. Banks's role in the expedition was acclaimed in well-connected London society circles.[74]

Cook and the *Resolution*, 1772–80

Cook's two further Pacific voyages between 1772 and 1780 only had a limited bearing on Australia: their focus was much broader in geographical scope. In neither voyage did he land on mainland Australia, though he discovered Norfolk Island on 10 October 1774.[75] In his second Pacific voyage (1772–5), Cook led the *Resolution* and the *Adventure* in search of the Great Southern Continent. This involved three separate searches for that elusive goal. The *Resolution* visited numerous Pacific Islands such as the Marquesas, Tahiti, the Cook Islands and the New Hebrides, many of which Cook charted. This was the first European voyage to cross the Antarctic Circle, though it did not discover Antarctica. Cook also returned to New Zealand. The voyage finally disproved the long-held speculation that a Great Southern Continent existed. The expedition returned to England in July 1775.[76]

On his third Pacific voyage, which began in 1776, Cook was charged with sailing into the north Pacific to find out whether the Northwest Passage, an ice-free opening around the top of Canada, existed for ships to sail from the Pacific to the Atlantic or vice-versa. This voyage proceeded well away from Australia, and it was not part of its remit to explore it. Navigators had been searching for the Northwest Passage since the sixteenth century without any success. A good many of their voyages had been misguided in their navigation, and ended in failure.[77] Cook, again in command of the *Resolution*, failed to find such a passage, despite several attempts to do so. He spent the summer of 1778 charting the northwestern American coastline from Nootka Sound to Bering Strait. He himself was unexpectedly killed on a Hawaiian beach by hostile natives in February 1779. The *Resolution* made its way back to England under the direction of Cook's second-in-command. Cook's death was widely reported and commemorated, and he became elevated to posthumous fame as a renowned navigator and explorer.[78]

Cook's second Pacific voyage had one footnote that related to Australia. Tobias Furneaux, the commander of HMS *Adventure*, which accompanied Cook's *Resolution*, rounded Van Diemen's Land from the south in 1773 and had an island group named after him by Cook. Different versions of charts of Van Diemen's Land were drawn up by Furneaux and his associates.[79] Furneaux, after separating from Cook, was not convinced that a strait existed between Van Diemen's Land and southeastern Australia. Others on the ship, including the midshipmen Richard Hergest and Samuel Kemp and the astronomer William Bayly, were more inclined to think that it might be found.[80] If their supposition had been followed up, Furneaux could have discovered Bass Strait (which, in that case, would have had a different name) before George Bass and Matthew Flinders located it in 1798.[81] Furneaux had anchored briefly in Frederick Henry Bay, Van Diemen's Land, where he saw deserted huts but no people. According to Daniel Solander, he was 'desirous of seeing that part of New Holland which lays between Van Diemens Land whe[re] Tasman left it, and Point Hicks where we fell in with it.' However, a strong southwest gale made it necessary for him to leave the coast when he was within 15 or 20 miles of Point Hicks.[82]

Cook and the Aborigines

Cook and his ship's company had more contact with Aborigines than any previous European voyagers. Even so, the interaction was sporadic and occupied only a few days. Some contact with indigenous Australians took place when the *Endeavour* stopped for a week at Botany Bay, but more sustained interaction occurred during the repair of the damaged ship at Endeavour River. At Botany Bay, Cook came across the Eora people. At Endeavour River, he encountered the Guguyimithiar natives. In each location, the meetings of Cook and his ship's company with Aborigines were fragmentary, hesitant and marked by mutual incomprehension. No-one on board the *Endeavour* understood any Aboriginal vocabulary; nor, of course, could any indigenous people speak English. Both sides of the racial and cultural divide therefore relied on perceptions of the meanings of each other's gestures and behaviour.[83]

Cook's secret instructions for the voyage had enjoined him to 'cultivate a Friendship and Alliance' with local inhabitants and to 'observe their Genius, Temper, Disposition and Number.'[84] Cook's fascination with non-European people had already been manifest in his interaction with Terra del Fuegans,

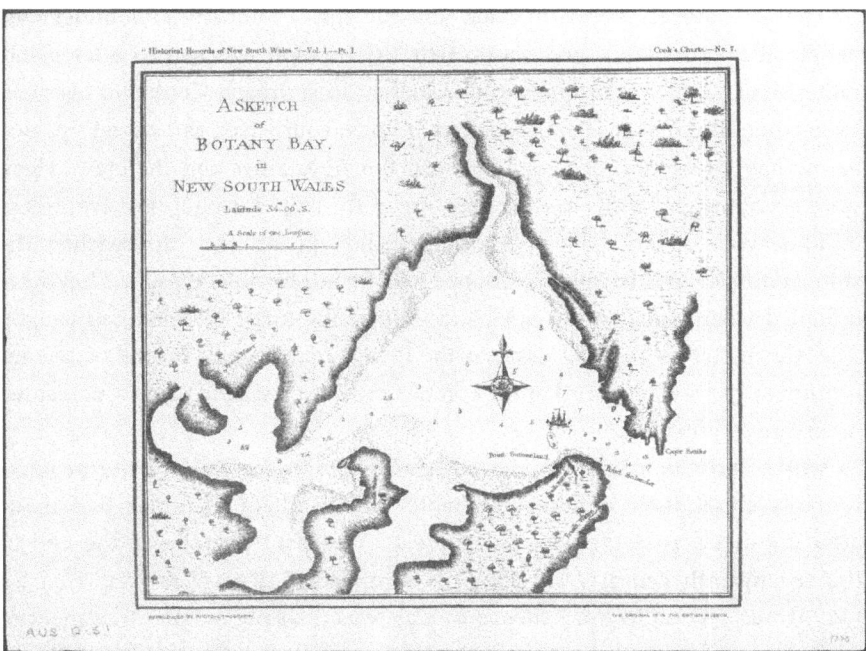

Map 8 James Cook, *A Sketch of Botany Bay in New South Wales* (Sydney: Charles Potter, Government Printer, 1893) MAP RM 2456D Bib ID 3916542

Tahitians and Maori; it continued with his encounter with Aborigines.[85] The initial meeting between Cook and the Aborigines at Botany Bay, however, was not encouraging. On his first attempt to go ashore, Cook fired his musket in what seems to have been an attempt to demonstrate that he and his mariners would use force if necessary and that resistance would be futile.[86] There was no immediate reaction to this martial overture. Banks provided a little more detail. After seeing two Aborigines from the deck of the ship, he explained that 'they called to us very loud in a harsh sounding Language of which neither us [n]or Tupaia understood a word, shaking their lances and embracing, in all appearance resolvd to dispute our landing to the utmost tho they were but two and we 30 or 40 at least.'[87]

At Botany Bay, Cook and Banks found the Aborigines were reluctant to accept the gifts and garments offered to them, displaying no interest in European goods.[88] Moreover, no sooner did natives appear than they retreated to the bush and remained out of sight. Though the British explorers did not know it, it was a common Aboriginal practice to ignore strangers.[89] Cook saw Aborigines but wrote in his journal that we 'could by neither words nor actions prevail upon them to come near us.'[90] The Aborigines remained elusive throughout the eight days and eight nights that the *Endeavour* remained at this location.[91]

The separateness between Cook and his ship's company and indigenous people at Botany Bay is one reason why the location was named after plants rather than people. Aborigines were reluctant to approach Cook and his men. Even when the ship was being repaired at Endeavour River, three weeks passed before any interaction occurred between the Aborigines and the crew. There were no Aboriginal visits to the repair site of the ship during its last two weeks at Endeavour River.[92] When Aborigines did appear, they approached the ship cautiously and frequently disappeared for no obvious reason. They were offended when Cook would not hand them some turtle his men had caught. The Aborigines set fire to grass near the British mariners on several occasions, presumably to warn them that they would protect their land against unwanted incursion by outsiders.[93]

Banks and Cook initially viewed Aborigines in the light of the negative remarks about their culture and habits that William Dampier had made after coming across indigenous people in Western Australia at the end of the seventeenth century.[94] A copy of Dampier's *A Voyage to New Holland* (1699) was carried in the *Endeavour*. This was the only lengthy treatment of Aborigines in print then available.[95] It influenced the perceptions of Banks and Cook about indigenous people. At Botany Bay, Banks saw five natives, whom he referred to as 'Indians,' and 'so far did the prejudices which we had built on Dampier's account influence us that we fancied we could see their Colour when we could scarce distinguish whether or not they were men.'[96] However, on closer encounter Banks and Cook gradually discarded a negative view of Aborigines and took a more positive approach. They commented in their journals, with fascination, on the appearance, language, throwing sticks and lack of clothing and possessions of Aborigines, and they both provided a summary of their views about these people as they were about to leave New Holland.[97] Banks collected aboriginal spears at Botany Bay; these were brought back to England. He put together a lexicon of thirty-eight Aboriginal words. Parkinson also compiled a vocabulary of words used by Aborigines on Australia's east coast.[98]

Banks concluded his observations on the Aborigines with cautious praise: 'thus live these I had almost said happy people, content with little nay almost nothing.'[99] Cook, in an oft-quoted phrase, was enthusiastically optimistic:

> From what I have said of the Natives of New-Holland they may appear to some to be the most wretched people upon Earth, but in reality they are far more happier [*sic*] than we Europeans; being wholly unacquainted not only with the superfluous but the necessary Conveniences so much sought after in Europe,

they are happy in not knowing the use of them. They live in a Tranquillity which is not disturb'd by the Inequality of Condition: The Earth and sea of their own accord furnishes them with all the things necessary for life, they covet not Magnificent houses, Household-stuff &c, they live in a warm and fine Climate.[100]

In several publications, Cook's chief biographer John C. Beaglehole considered this to be an atypical panegyric that made idealistic claims about Aboriginal life.[101] Glyndwr Williams has reappraised Cook's views on Aborigines, however, to argue that his glowing account of their culture and lives reflected eighteenth-century notions of the virtues of primitivism in the 'noble savage' tradition.[102] Cook appears to have approved of people who had few possessions and had no interest in luxury.[103]

Cook's importance in the indigenous experience of white settlement is remembered throughout Australia in Aboriginal oral tradition. In 1982, an ethnographer recorded collective memories of Cook's presence in Australia by Hobbles Daniyeri, a ceremonial man of the Yarralin peoples. In his discourse, Daniyeri took Cook as a representative of all European intruders coming to Australia. Unwanted by the indigenous people, the 'whitefellows' acquired the land, often by violence, without asking for Aboriginal consent. This is an imagined collective memory of the impact of white explorers and settlers on Australia, emphasizing the destruction caused by colonization. In Daniyeri's storytelling, the white colonists are depicted as bringing their own law with them that conflicted with the morality of Aboriginal law. In this indigenous narrative, Cook is a symbol of white power and a destroyer of 'blackfellow' communities.[104]

Cook's charts of Australia's east coast

Cook's Pacific voyages left a legacy of new knowledge in terms of astronomy, oceanography, natural history and linguistics along with observation and evidence on various peoples that in the nineteenth century would be a central feature of the new disciplines of ethnology and anthropology. The publication of edited versions of his journals in the 1770s and 1780s also brought Cook fame and publicity.[105] Charts were compiled that delineated Australia's east coast accurately for the first time, naming bays, capes, rivers, offshore islands and other landscape features, and inserting the ship's route on charts for the benefit of future navigators. Cook used quadrants and sextants, calculated lunar distances, and used Maskelyne's *Nautical Almanac* to compile the geographical coordinates for his charts. His running survey of the coastline meant that calculations had to be made expeditiously when the ship was either at anchor or in a stationary position.[106] Cook spent fifty-four days in Botany Bay and Endeavour River and seventy-two days on his survey, which progressed at about 30 miles a day.[107] The astronomer Green played an essential role in calculating latitude and longitude on Cook's running surveys by following the method of lunar distances.[108]

Cook's latitudes and longitudes between his landfall near Point Hicks and Endeavour River were highly accurate, but between Cape Flattery and Booby Island, in Torres Strait, there was a considerable loss of accuracy. This appears to have been the result of the illness of his astronomer, Green. Cook's calculations of the height of tides were also commendably accurate, given the complexity of the tidal regime on Australia's east coast.[109] With the probable help of a draughtsman, Cook prepared a set of fair charts and coastal views on the return voyage of the *Endeavour* to England.[110] Cook's nomenclature on his charts identified ninety-four features named in his journals and a further thirty names from his manuscript charts and coastal views. In 1773, the book editor John Hawkesworth published an important chart showing these discoveries in his account of Cook's voyage.[111]

When he anchored in Adventure Bay, Van Diemen's Land, in late January 1777, on Cook's second Pacific voyage, Furneaux surveyed its east coast and named about a dozen features. Bligh carried out a further survey at Adventure Bay on Cook's third Pacific voyage. Their findings were published in the official accounts of Cook's last two voyages. Furneaux, however, made errors in locating places. When his ship passed the channel separating Bruny Island from the mainland, he thought he was in Storm Bay. When he anchored off Bruny Island, he thought he was in Tasman's Frederick Henry Bay, though he later wrote that this bay was further north. Furneaux also mistook Tasman's peninsula for Maria Island.[112] First lieutenant James Burney made similar errors about the geography of Van Diemen's Land. He noted that South East Cape was the southwest point of Storm Bay whereas it was the southwest end of the D'Entrecasteaux Channel. He wrongly concluded, as did Furneaux, that the bay in which the *Adventure* anchored was on the east side of the Tasman peninsula whereas it was on the eastern side of Bruny Island that corresponded to Tasman's Storm Bay. Furneaux and Burney both tended to identify land masses as islands. Their charts of the east coast of Van Diemen's Land were less accurate than Tasman's.[113] It was not until later French voyages of exploration that these geographical errors were rectified.

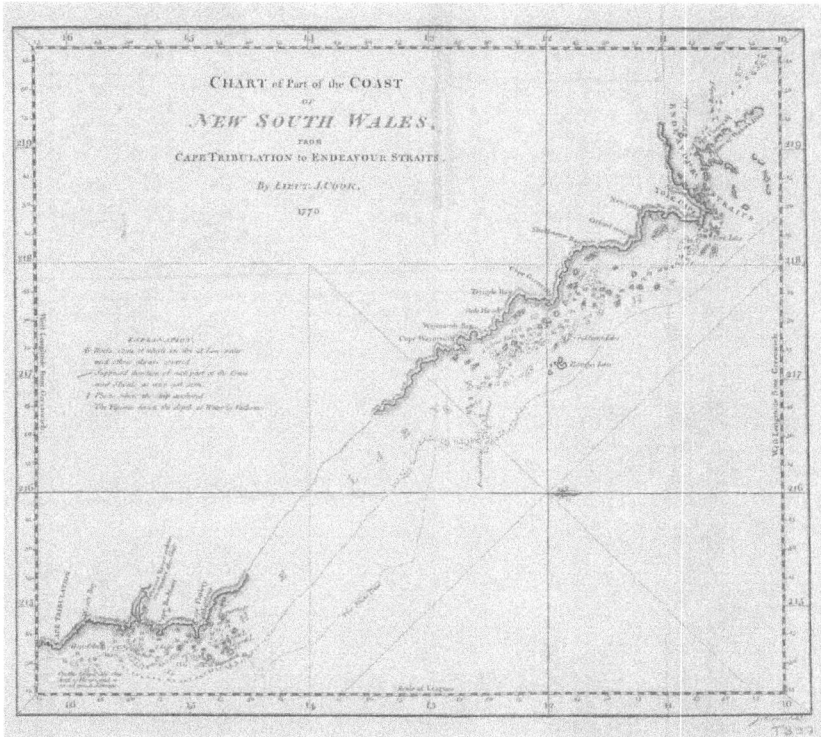

Map 9 *Chart of part of the coast of New South Wales, from Cape Tribulation to Endeavour Strait by Lieut. James Cook* (London: W. Strahan & T. Cadell, 1773) MAP T 327 Bib ID 1185163

Natural history results

Banks and Solander collected a large number of plant specimens in Australia, including 132 species at Botany Bay and more than 200 species at Endeavour River. Among the plants were varieties of wattle and eucalypt, deciduous trees, perennial climbers, annual herbs and many different flowers. Specimens were dried and preserved – a laborious task – and brought on board the *Endeavour* as quickly as possible so that Parkinson could make pencil sketches of them. He made colour notes on his sketches son that he could later paint the leaves, buds, flowers and fruit of plants accurately. Parkinson wrote a manuscript name on the reverse of his sketches and noted the locality where the specimen was collected.[114] Working single-handedly, Parkinson found it difficult to keep up the pace required to deal with the specimens.[115]

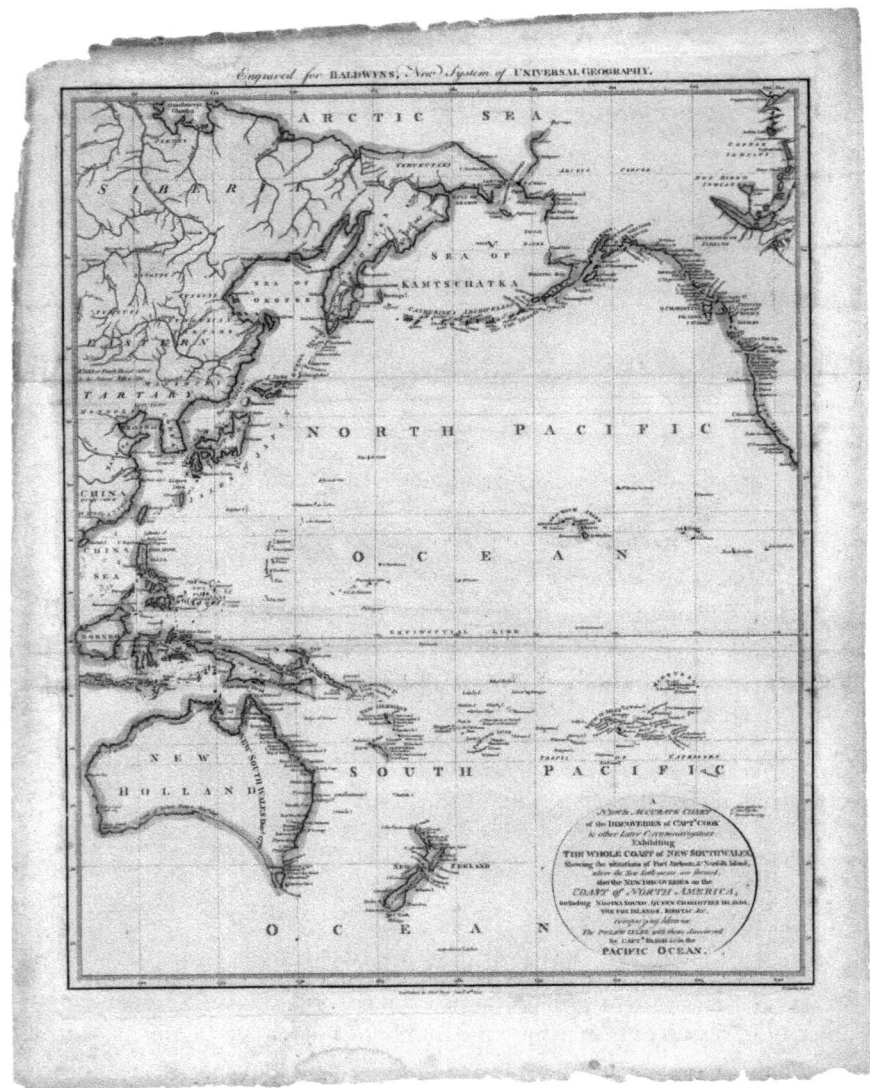

Map 10 Thomas Conder, *A new & accurate chart of the discoveries of Captn Cook & other later circumnavigators: exhibiting the whole coast of New South Wales, shewing the situations of Port Jackson, & Norfolk Island, where the new settlements are formed; also the new discoveries on the coast of North America, including Nootka Sound, Queen Charlottes Islands, the Fox Islands, Kishtac &c. comprising likewise the Pelew Isles with discoveries by Captn. Bligh &c. in the Pacific Ocean* (London: Sold by ?A. Hogg, 1794) MAP RM 514 Bib ID 3513459

After the voyage ended, Banks kept the botanical material in own herbarium at his home in London's Soho Square. Before his death in 1782, Solander wrote meticulous descriptions of about 400 Australian plants collected. He had mastered the Linnaean system of classification and nomenclature, and had expertise in assigning genera and species.[116] The failure to publish his work in the years after his death diminished its immediate value, but his descriptions were used in a piecemeal fashion in later scientific publications. Banks welcomed visitors to his house who wished to consult the notes, specimens and descriptions, and bequeathed the collection to the botanist Robert Brown, who donated them to the British Museum.[117] Parkinson died from dysentery on the return voyage of the *Endeavour*. This loss of the artist who had seen and described the plants was a blow to the dissemination of the flora and fauna sketches. Banks employed artists to produce finished drawings from Parkinson's sketches; these were later engraved but not published until well into the twentieth century.[118]

The zoological material collected on the *Endeavour*'s voyage was not kept together but was widely dispersed. Today it can be found scattered in at least eleven institutions.[119] Parkinson's published voyage account described the birds, reptiles, quadrupeds and fish seen on Australia's east coast.[120] Parkinson also produced drawings of mammals, fishes, birds and insects. Most of the bird drawings, some sketched in pencil and others in partial colours, concentrated on sea birds such as petrels, shearwaters and frigate birds. After the voyage ended, Banks employed the artist George Stubbs to undertake an oil painting of a kangaroo, using the skin and skull and Parkinson's sketches. This painting was engraved and included in the third volume of the 1773 edition of Hawkesworth's voyage account.[121]

Conclusion

Cook's voyage in the *Endeavour* was the most important single expedition to Australia yet mounted – to say nothing of the broader discoveries it made in the Pacific in terms of geography, ethnography and natural history. Substantially prepared and equipped with a highly skilled commander, a team of scientists and artists, and a knowledgeable amateur botanist in the person of Joseph Banks, the *Endeavour* expedition marked the European discovery of Australia's east coast and the possession of the eastern half of Australia by Britain. Cook named numerous places he discovered and produced extensive, highly accurate charts of the east coast that soon became essential for navigators. The scientific haul from the expedition included substantial collections of botany and zoology that were transmitted to London. Nautical astronomy advanced during the voyage. The descriptions of Aborigines were more extensive, despite rather limited contact, than any previous voyage had mustered. Drawings of plants by Solander and of animals by Parkinson were among the artistic achievements of the voyage. Cook and Banks kept detailed journals of their explorations, supplemented by the logs and journals of several other officers on board the *Endeavour*. The interest and curiosity aroused in metropolitan circles by Hawkesworth's books on the expedition, available in print by 1773, tapped into a burgeoning public appetite for published narratives of voyages of discovery.[122] Cook's second Pacific voyage, in the *Resolution* and *Discovery*, only made an Australian landfall in Van Diemen's Land, but it added some geographical details to what was known about that area to add to Tasman's findings.

French Voyages to Terra Australis

Before 1700, the French had limited interest in the Pacific. During the reign of Louis XIV, the French search for new lands was subordinated to a preoccupation with the cost of warfare. Thereafter the French took more interest in Pacific exploration, but their efforts were scattered and disjointed because they focused too much on the notion that a French navigator, Captain Binot Paulmier de Gonneville, had discovered part of Terra Australis *c*.1504. This speculative belief led to an almost-obsessive French quest to find that locality. In the mid-seventeenth century, the writings of the Abbé Jean Paulmier de Courtonne, Canon of Lisieux Cathedral in Normandy, influenced voyages connected to this objective. A descendant of de Gonneville, he had studied various geographers and cartographers and was convinced that *Terres australes* existed. The first two chapters of Paulmier's *Mémoires*, published in the 1660s, discussed the Gonneville story in relation to his proposal for France establishing a Christian mission in Australia, depicted as a fertile and attractive country. Paulmier failed to gain support for the project, but his *Mémoires* influenced French interest in the South Seas for more than a century.[1]

The evidence that Gonneville had discovered part of Terra Australis was decidedly slight. He had sailed from Honfleur on an expedition to the East Indies, but after reaching the Cape of Good Hope he was diverted to an unknown land in a storm. Gonneville claimed to have found the great Austral Land, but took no accurate coordinates or bearings of his position.[2] The only evidence to support his claim consisted of an affidavit he signed before the French authorities, which was accepted at face value.[3] The absence of any mention of Gonneville's voyage in sources before Paulmier's account or on the sixteenth-century Dieppe maps suggests that the authenticity of the voyage can be challenged.[4] Nevertheless, the French despatched several voyages of exploration over several decades to search for Gonneville Land.

In 1738, the French East India Company supported Lieutenant Jean-Baptiste Bouvet de Lozier's expedition in search of Gonneville Land in the

Southern Ocean. Bouvet de Lozier had been influenced by reading Paulmier's *Mémoires*.[5] The company thought such a location could serve as a convenient place for their vessels to stop for repairs and refreshment en route to India. On 19 July 1738, Bouvet's ships *Aigle* and *Marie* steered a course from Lorient into the Atlantic and eventually sighted what they took to be a cape at 54°S 11°E, about 1,500 miles to the south-east of the Cape of Good Hope, but the fog was too thick to follow up this discovery. Bouvet de Lozier named the location Cape Circumcision after the feast day on which he discovered it. Unrealistic as it might seem, he thought the cape was the edge of a continent that could be the elusive Terra Australis: it was, in fact, a small, remote island, which was later named after him. The expedition was a failure. Bouvet de Lozier mislabelled the island's coordinates and abandoned the expedition because most of his crew fell ill. One ship sailed for Ile de France while the other returned via the Cape of Good Hope to France.[6] The main finding was that no habitable land existed in the waters where the South Atlantic flowed into the Indian Ocean.[7]

After Bouvet's botched venture, French geographers maintained their interest in the southern continent. The publication of the *Encyclopédie* between 1751 and 1772 provided stimulus to explore the world beyond Europe.[8] Charles de Brosses's *Histoire des navigations aux terres Australes* (1756) set down a very detailed plan for the scientific exploration and settlement of Australia. This major contribution to European knowledge of the South Seas was the first publication to translate, summarize and synthesize over 250 years of European voyaging in the Pacific.[9] De Brosses believed Gonneville had found a southern land, and argued that further French exploration in the South Seas was vital for French wealth, prestige and commerce in the continuing rivalry with British seapower.[10] In 1756, Robert de Vaugondy produced a chart of Australasia to accompany a lecture by de Brosses. The chart included place names for locations in northern and Western Australia, but it lacked a delineation of the east coast, omitted two large gulfs from the south Australian coast, and depicted some named places in Van Diemen's Land as part of the mainland.[11]

Bougainville's voyage around the world, 1766–9

French voyages of discovery to the Pacific in the 1760s were heavily influenced by de Brosses's ideas that further exploration of *Terres australes* would be beneficial. These expeditions were led by the navigator and explorer Louis Antoine de

Bougainville, a military officer with no naval training. In 1764–5, he was in charge of two voyages to deliver people expelled by the British from French Canada to settle on the Falkland Islands. On the second voyage, he sighted the ships of a British expedition led by John Byron.[12] Returning to France, Bougainville convincingly argued that France should challenge the British in exploratory voyaging in the Pacific.[13] Action soon followed. In 1766, Bougainville was commissioned by the French government to sail around the world, with most of the voyage intended to explore the Pacific. He followed de Brosses's idea that a great southern continent could be found whose northern and western shores were known as New Holland.[14]

Bougainville left Nantes with the ships *La Boudeuse* and *Etoile* in November 1766 and sailed towards the South Atlantic. He reached the Falkland Islands and formally handed them over to France's ally Spain, who had exercised her sovereignty rights. Continuing his voyage into the Pacific, he discovered several islands, some of which are now part of French Polynesia. Bougainville's brief visit to Tahiti, which he praised as a paradise, was the capstone to his voyage. The European discovery of Tahiti, with its exoticism and tropical allure, was much discussed in subsequent years. Bougainville searched for Terra Australis, hoping to follow up the findings of Quirós, but he did not locate a continent and wondered on what basis geographers had claimed there was one in these largely uncharted waters.[15]

Bougainville sailed from Tahiti towards southern Samoa and the New Hebrides and then towards New Guinea, discovering the Louisiade Archipelago. He only had enough water on board his ships to last a month and three months' food supplies. Bougainville was familiar with de Vaugondy's map in de Brosses's book that showed a strait between New Holland and New Guinea, but he did not search for Torres Strait because rumours were the only information then available on Torres's voyage. Bougainville eventually returned to France. He kept an open mind about whether a Great Southern Continent existed, though he concluded that previous explorers would have found it if that were the case.[16]

Bougainville received favourable publicity after returning to France. His discoveries in the Pacific and his navigational information attracted attention from ministers, cartographers and promoters of French seapower and influence. He quickly prepared an account of his voyage. This was published in 1771 as *Voyage autour du monde*, which appeared in an English translation the next year. This had clear defects as a factual report on Bougainville's travels: it contained few navigational details, some inaccurate charts, and rather limited descriptions of the Pacific islands visited and of the indigenous peoples and flora and fauna of various locations. Bougainville's failure to find a southern continent was a disappointment to de Brosses. Nevertheless, Bougainville's voyage and the positive reception of his travel account sustained French interest in the Pacific even though Bougainville himself showed no interest in another expedition.[17]

St Aloüarn and Australia's west coast, 1771–2

Between 1770 and 1800, several French navigators explored parts of Australia's coast on expeditions with a much broader remit motivated by the quest for new knowledge of unknown parts of the globe and by Anglo-French diplomatic and strategic manoeuvres.[18] Though de Bouvet had failed to confirm the existence of Terra Australis in latitude 55°S in 1738–9, French writers continued to think that a southern land existed, and that geographical and scientific discoveries could promote opportunities for trade and settlement by France in the southern hemisphere.[19] In 1771, Yves de Kerguélen de Trémarec, an ambitious French explorer and naval officer, asked his colleague Louis François Marie Aleno de St Aloüarn to join him in a search for Gonneville Land and the southern continent. Hoping to emulate Cook's first Pacific voyage, Louis XV and the French government supported this expedition. They provided secret instructions that Kerguélen should search for Gonneville Land and hence, it was thought, *Terres Australes*. Kerguélen was ordered not to allow anyone on his ship know the true purpose of the voyage.[20]

Kerguélen and St Aloüarn began the expedition at the Ile de France on 30 April 1771. Kerguélen was on board the *Fortune* while St Aloüarn sailed in the storeship *Gros Ventre*. Kerguélen saw a mountainous island in the southern Indian Ocean that he wrongly supposed was part of Terra Australis; it was later named after him. Separated from the *Gros Ventre* in bad weather for several days, Kerguélen decided to return to the Ile de France as there seemed only a minimal chance of coming across St Aloüarn's ship. Kerguélen was well received by the Intendant of the colony, and later, without knowing the fate of St Aloüarn and his ship, he returned to France where he was presented to, and personally decorated by, Louis XV on 18 July 1772. Despite these accolades, the Intendant at the Ile de France was privately critical of Kerguélen abandoning St Aloüarn and failing to land in person on the island he supposed to be part of Terra Australis.[21]

On 14 February 1772, St Aloüarn, while separated from Kerguélen, landed briefly on Kerguelen Island. He proved that no significant land lay in the southern Indian Ocean north of the 50th parallel, and that Gonneville Land, if it existed, could only be further south in icy waters. St Aloüarn advanced across the Indian Ocean to an intended rendezvous with Kerguélen at Cape Leeuwin.

But not finding his colleague's ship there, he sailed north to Dirk Hartog Island where charts indicated known anchorages.[22] At Turtle Bay on that island on 30 March one of St Alouarn's officers, Jean Mengaud de la Hage, took possession of the land for France by hoisting a white ensign in the name of the French king and burying a proclamation and two French coins in a bottle. This was placed within sight of de Vlamingh's commemorative plate left there in 1697. This was the first time France had claimed any part of Australia. The proclamation document has never been found, however, and there was no French attempt to settle in that area.[23]

Impeded by scurvy spreading among his crew and the loss of two anchors at Shark Bay, St Alouarn guided the *Gros Ventre* along the northwest coast of Australia before heading north in stormy weather for Timor and Java in search of fresh water, provisions and a place for the sick crew to recuperate. The return voyage to the Ile de France was marked by further illness for St Alouarn and his crew. St Alouarn was treated for putrid fever in hospital at the Ile de France, where he dictated a letter to Kerguélen advising him that he had annexed Western Australia for France. This was not recognized in international law, however, because France never followed up the claim with a colony or settlement. St Alouarn died shortly afterwards, on 27 October 1772. Mengaud de la Hage, sick from a fever contracted in Batavia, died a day later.[24]

Louis XV, unaware of these occurrences, sent Kerguélen to search for St Alouarn. Three vessels were under his command – the *Roland*, the *Oiseau* and the storeship *Dauphine*. Kerguélen arrived in Port Louis, Ile de France in October 1773, less than a year after St Alouarn's death, and was received there sceptically by administrators. Ignoring orders to sail towards the Pacific, he proceeded towards Kerguelen Island but failed to land there or to secure it as a French colony. Kerguélen sailed for Madagascar in search of provisions but eventually returned to France. An investigation into the handling of the voyage found Kerguélen guilty of negligence and misconduct: he was imprisoned as a result.[25]

Kerguélen and St Alouarn's voyages had few positive results. Kerguélen never sailed anywhere near Australia. The island named after him was of no use commercially or strategically to France. The details of his voyages indicate his failings as a navigator. St Alouarn's annexation of Western Australia was virtually unknown for well over a century, and his voyage added nothing to knowledge of Terra Australis. In 1998, archaeologists from the Western Australian Maritime Museum excavated his landing site on Dirk Hartog Island. They found a French coin dated 1766, a French wine bottle and other material assumed to be relics from St Alouarn's expedition.[26]

Marion Dufresne and Van Diemen's Land, 1771–2

In 1771, the Breton explorer and former naval officer Marc-Joseph Marion Dufresne was assigned the task of returning home the Tahitian native Aotourou who had accompanied Bougainville to France in 1768. The authorities at the Ile de France chartered two government vessels for this voyage. Marion Dufresne raised private money to support this endeavour. The voyage had other motives, which appear to have been the hope of finding new spice islands and locating the southern continent supposedly sighted by Gonneville in the sixteenth century.[27] The French authorities thought Terra Australis might offer an alternative base to the Cape of Good Hope for voyages to India. They also wanted to find out whether Tasman's route to New Zealand was viable for merchant ships. No significant scientists or scientific equipment were attached to this expedition.[28]

Marion Dufresne commanded the store ship *Le Mascarin*, with Julien-Marie Crozet as his second-in-command. The naval officer Ambroise du Clesmeur commanded the accompanying ship, the *Marquis de Castries*. Aotourou died of smallpox when the voyage reached Madagascar. Though this removed a major motive for the voyage, it was too late to abandon the expedition.[29] The vessels continued towards Australia, sailing along latitudes well beneath the mainland of that continent. Van Diemen's Land was sighted on 29 February 1772. Jean Roux, one of the officers, noted in his journal that they doubted their position because 'Tasman, who drafted a map of the coast, has erred by not marking the points exactly.' On 6 March the ships entered Frederick Henry Bay, where Tasman had anchored 130 years earlier. 'We presume that our vessels must have seemed extraordinary,' wrote Roux, 'because we have no knowledge of any navigators, since Tasman, to have frequented these waters.'[30]

Marion Dufresne and his officers briefly explored Frederick Henry Bay, becoming the first Europeans land on Van Diemen's Land. Marion Dufresne was wounded when some Aborigines pelted him with stones.[31] Unable to find fresh water, he decided to leave after a six days' sojourn and headed to New Zealand. Marion Dufresne and his crew explored the north island for nearly two months, but the expedition ended in disaster. Marion Dufresne and twenty-six of his crew were attacked and cannibalized by Maori after they had cut down a sacred tree without realizing its significance for native people. Crozet took command of the expedition, which he led back to the Ile de France.[32]

Marion Dufresne's stopover in Van Diemen's Land produced useful results in charting and recording the characteristics of native peoples. Some surveying was undertaken on the south and east coasts, and maps were drawn to depict the findings. Marion Dufresne's personal account of the expedition has disappeared, but several journals by his officers survive that describe their stay in Van Diemen's Land and their encounters with Aborigines. Crozet mapped the east coast of Bruny Island and the entrances to d'Entrecasteaux Channel. The mapping of Marion Bay was notably accurate. Crozet drew a chart of southern Van Diemen's Land that was published in his book *Nouveau voyage à la mer du sud* (1783). Clesmeur charted the south coast of Van Diemen's Land from South West Cape to Tasman's Head, and from Storm Bay eastward and northward to the anchorage in Frederick Henry Bay.[33]

On 7 March 1772, the day of their landing in Van Diemen's Land, Marion Dufresne's crew came across about forty Aborigines, who were naked and carried long spears. An initial friendly meeting between the crew and the Aborigines descended into conflict.[34] The Frenchmen tried to cultivate good relations with these people, but Crozet recorded that 'they rejected with disdain all that we offered, even iron, mirrors, handkerchiefs, and pieces of cloth.' An Aborigine presented Marion Dufresne with a firebrand to light a pile of wood whereupon he did so and the 'Savages withdrew hastily onto a hillock, from which they threw a shower of stones, by which M. Marion, as well as an officer who was with him, was wounded.' The French fired muskets in return. At least one Aborigine was killed. The French then withdrew to their boats. A later excursion on shore led Crozet to note, with surprise, that there was no indication that the Aborigines lived in houses, and that the usual food of these people was shellfish, a conclusion reached from the numerous piles of shells seen.[35]

The French officers recorded negative views of the Aborigines they encountered in Van Diemen's Land. Lieutenant Le Dez compared them 'with the inhabitants of New Holland of whom Dampier speaks.' The French observers viewed them as savages who differed little from animals. Du Clesmeur summed up the reaction of the Frenchmen to the Aborigines:

> They are the most miserable people in the world, and the human beings who approach closest to brute beasts; they are in general small, not well-built, skinny, have a large head, sunken and bilious eyes, and thick eyebrows…It appears that they live in troupes of 50 or 60 men and women all together, having no fixed abode in any place, as long as they have enough to live on.[36]

These unflattering remarks were made without awareness of the more favourable reaction of Cook and Banks to Aborigines on Australia's east coast, made two years previously.[37]

Overall, Marion Dufresne's voyage was poorly planned, with just the two aims of repatriating Aotourou and searching for rich islands. The new information gathered on Van Diemen's Land was helpful for future explorers, but the voyage did not stop elsewhere in New Holland. A legacy of failure was the main result of French exploratory voyages of the 1770s. The French monarch and his government officials were fully aware that the expeditions by Kerguélen, St Aloüarn and Marion Dufresne were minor, unsuccessful attempts at exploration compared with the substantial achievements of Cook's first Pacific voyage.[38]

Lapérouse's Pacific voyage, 1785–8

In 1785, Jean-François Galaup, the Comte de Lapérouse, an experienced naval officer, was appointed by Louis XVI and the Marquis de Castries, the Secretary of State for the French Navy, to lead a large-scale voyage to complete the Pacific discoveries made by Cook, to continue mapping the Pacific Ocean, and to search for future trade opportunities there. Over a million livres tournois were spent preparing the voyage.[39] This project followed a failed proposal by William Bolts, a Dutch-born merchant, to interest Louis's brother Joseph II, the Holy Roman Emperor, in such an expedition.[40] Extensive planning for the voyage was undertaken by the Director of Ports and Arsenals, Charles Pierre Claret de Fleurieu. The French king had a strong interest in the voyage: he was a great reader of Cook's published voyage accounts, and arranged for a French edition of his writings. Fleurieu liaised with the king about the voyage, drew the charts to be used, and drafted detailed geographical notes for Lapérouse to follow. There was a strong desire to promote a successful voyage that would eradicate memories of failed French expeditions to the Pacific in the 1770s.[41]

The voyage had political, commercial, scientific and imperial motives; it was much more ambitious than previous French Pacific expeditions. Anglo-French commercial rivalry influenced the French to imitate British penetration of the Pacific, with the hope that this voyage would surpass Cook's achievements. This appears to have been a more important motive for the expedition than serious French interest in Australia. Lapérouse was instructed to investigate the China trade and the North Pacific fur trade. It was also hoped that France might find a base in the Philippines where she could link up with Spanish allies.[42] Lapérouse was expected to undertake careful coastal surveys through detailed hydrographical work. He had ten scientists on board the voyage. The intention was that they should calculate longitude through combining lunar observations with the use of precision watches, and that their mapping should be as accurate as Cook had achieved on his voyages.[43]

Lapérouse's voyage left Brest on 1 August 1785 with two large ships, the *Boussole* and the *Astrolabe*. Lapérouse visited Chile, Easter Island, the Sandwich Islands, Alaska, other coasts of northwest America and the Kamchatka peninsula. While anchored there, on 26 September 1787 he received instructions from France's Minister of the Marine that changed the expedition's geographical focus. Lapérouse had originally been instructed to explore the north and west coasts of New Holland, but the new instructions took account of the infant British colony at Botany Bay and therefore redirected the expedition to head there because France now knew about the new British penal colony in New South Wales. Lapérouse was instructed to send his observations on this settlement to his promoters in France. Louis XVI's government was keenly interested in the strategic implications of Britain's new colony at Botany Bay.[44]

Following his new instructions, Lapérouse set sail towards Australia's east coast. At Samoa, in December 1787, a group of Samoans attacked his men, killing twelve and wounding twenty. The expedition left for Tonga for help and new supplies, and then set out for Australia, arriving at Botany Bay on 24 January 1788. Remarkably, the First Fleet of convicts, led by Arthur Phillip, had arrived there from Britain just a few hours earlier to form Britain's first permanent settlement in Australia. The British colonists were surprised to see the two large French ships, but provided them with supplies and other assistance over the next six weeks. Though Lapérouse and Phillip did not meet, eleven recorded visits occurred between the British colonists and the French crew.[45] According to David Collins, judge-advocate of New South Wales, the French had an unfavourable view of the Botany Bay area and its native inhabitants, 'the officers having been heard to declare, that in their whole voyage they nowhere found so poor a country, nor such wretched miserable people.'[46]

Lapérouse thought Cook, whom he regarded as a great navigator, had already explored the east coast thoroughly, leaving little for others to follow up. Moreover, his secret instructions focused on gathering information on Botany Bay but with no remit to explore the east coast. Lapérouse was keen to leave expeditiously to proceed with his voyage.[47] He left Botany Bay on 10 March 1788, intending to head for New Caledonia, Santa Cruz, the Solomon Islands, the Louisiades and the western and southern coasts of Australia. He and his ships were never seen again: his opinions of the Botany Bay settlement perished with him. It was nearly another forty years before evidence was found that his ships had been wrecked, with presumably the loss of life of Lapérouse and most of his crew at Vanikoro in the Santa Cruz Islands.[48]

D'Entrecasteaux's expedition, 1791–3

Disappointments arising from the above French voyages to Australia were mitigated by the greater success of voyages in the 1790s. A major expedition of the early 1790s was led by the nobleman and naval officer Antoine Raymond Joseph de Chevalier D'Entrecasteaux. In January 1791, the Société d'Histoire Naturelle petitioned the National Assembly to organize a voyage to search for Lapérouse and his vessels.[49] There had been much speculation but no evidence about his fate after he left Port Jackson in 1788. Fleurieu discussed Lapérouse's voyage with Louis XVI in April 1790, when it was clear something was seriously awry. Fleurieu, the Minister of Marine, instigated a rescue mission to search for survivors. This was intended to be 'a humanitarian and patriotic enterprise.'[50] There was considerable pressure from scientific groups in France to find Lapérouse, his vessels and his crew.[51]

D'Entrecasteaux's expedition was the largest French scientific voyage ever assembled. Apart from searching for Lapérouse, it was also intended to find out more about the geography and the scientific potential of Terra Australis. Interest in these matters had stalled after Cook's discovery of Australia's east coast in 1770, but the establishment of the Botany Bay colony in 1788 gave impetus to further expeditions to Australia. Much remained to be discovered. In many Australian locations, there was plenty of scientific investigation to be undertaken in terms of nautical astronomy, the gathering and classification of plants and seeds, and observations of native peoples.[52]

D'Entrecasteaux was an experienced hydrographer and explorer who had been Assistant Director of Ports and Arsenals in France, Commander of the Indian Ocean Squadron, leader of a survey expedition to the northeastern Indian Ocean and western Pacific (1785–7), and Governor of the Ile de France (Mauritius) and Bourbon (Réunion) (1787–9).[53] D'Entrecasteaux was probably the most experienced French captain available with knowledge of oceanic navigation. He was provided with full information about Lapérouse's planned itinerary to guide him where to concentrate his search for the lost explorer, but the vastness of the Pacific Ocean meant the task was likely to be unachievable.[54] D'Entrecasteaux's expedition set sail during a turbulent period in the French Revolution. The personnel on board ship were divided between loyalists and republicans. This caused, as might be expected, political tensions during the expedition, but the divisions only became serious towards the end of the mission.[55]

D'Entrecasteaux had a talented group of sixteen scientific officers for his expedition. The main surveyor and mapmaker was Charles François

Beautemps-Beaupré, who had drawn charts of the Baltic region. Felix Lahaie of the French Royal Botanical Gardens led a team charged with bringing back living plants and seeds to Paris for research. Jacques Julien Houtou de Labillardière, who had worked on Australian flora and fauna with Banks, was the leading botanist. He sought advice from Banks on botany before the expedition began, and was encouraged to collect samples from unexplored environments. The astronomer, who joined the voyage at the Cape of Good Hope, was the skilful navigator and mathematician Elisabeth Paul Edouard, Chevalier de Rossel.[56]

D'Entrecasteaux's two vessels, the *Recherche* and the *Espérance*, shared resources, which meant it was not realistic for them to carry out separate investigations. Fleurieu anticipated that the expedition would follow Lapérouse's proposed route from Botany Bay to Tonga, New Caledonia, New Guinea and the Ile de France.[57] This search inevitably led to lengthy traversals of thousands of miles of ocean. Long searches for Lapérouse included six months from May to December 1792 and from February to October 1793 in the Western Pacific and East Indies. Only two locations in Australia were visited by the expedition: Esperance, Western Australia (9–17 December 1792) and Van Diemen's Land (21 April–28 May 1792 and 21 January–27 February 1793).[58]

In December 1792, d'Entrecasteaux missed the opportunity of taking shelter in King George Sound because his ships were too far down wind to tack their way back into the sound. This was unfortunate because this was a roadstead where ships could anchor and replenish their supplies of wood and water, as Vancouver discovered in 1791.[59] D'Entrecasteaux encountered violent winds from the west and south-west at Esperance Bay, which had blown unceasingly for a month, so he was unable to reconnoitre the southwest west coast of Australia. He discovered the bay, which he named after one of his ships, and entered it as a refuge to avoid being wrecked on coral reefs. He concluded that the southern coast could only be surveyed when winds were favourable in January or February.[60]

D'Entrecasteaux was disappointed not to find the mouths of large rivers on the south coast, which Fleurieu's instructions had identified as needing detailed exploration.[61] Reflecting on the voyage of Pieter Nuyts in 1627, he found it unsurprising that the Dutch voyage had 'not provided any details of this sterile land, the aspect of which is so uniform that even the most fertile imagination would have nothing to say about it.' However, he believed the 'lack of fresh water, and contrary winds, forced Nuyts, just like us, to end his discoveries at the islands of Saint Francis and Saint Peter.'[62] D'Entrecasteaux therefore decided to head straight for southern Van Diemen's Land.

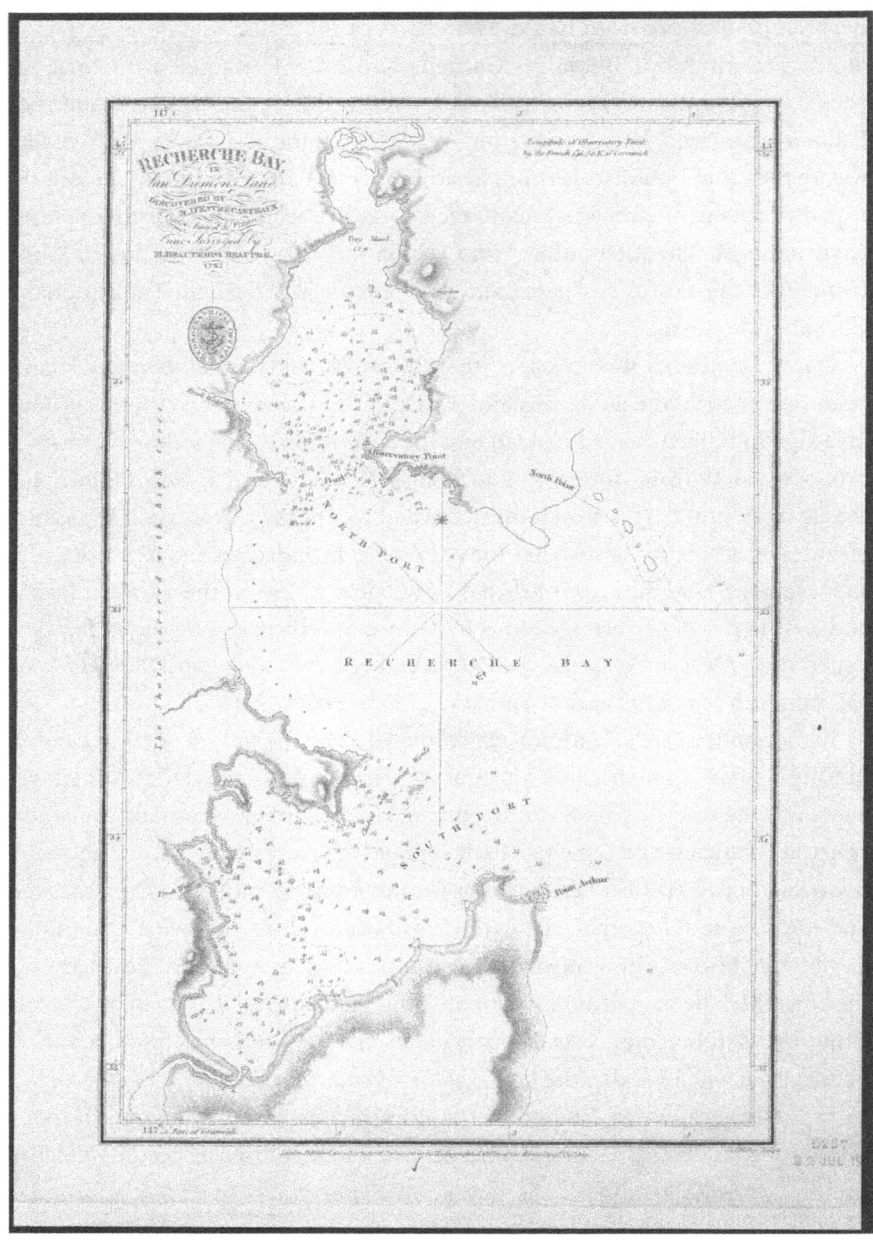

Map 11 C. F. Beautemps-Beaupré, *Recherche Bay in Van Diemen's Land discovered by M. d'Entrecasteaux, Contr'e Amiral de France, 1792* (London: Hydrographical Office of the Admiralty, 1829) MAP RM 674 Bib ID 3534002

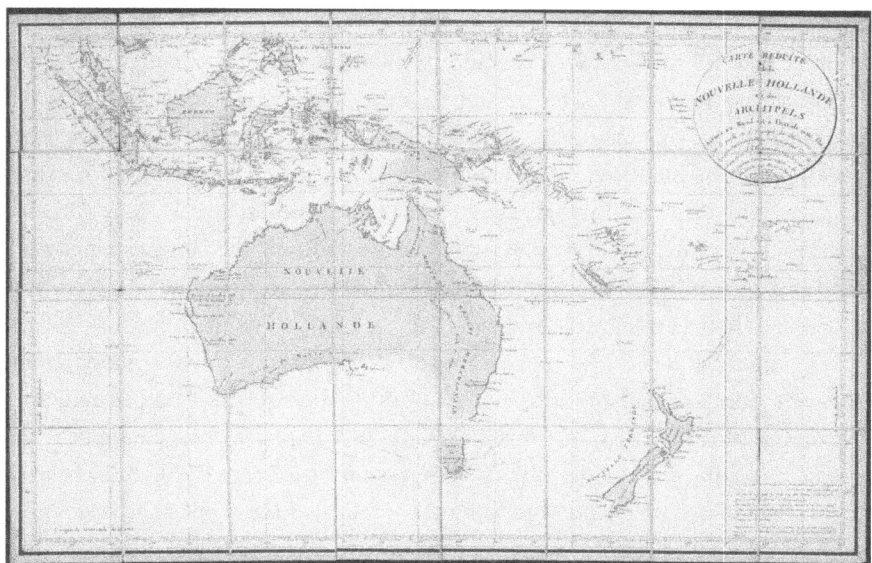

Map 12 C. F. Beautemps-Beaupré, *Carte réduite de la Nouvelle Hollande et des archipels: situés au nord et à l'est de cette île sur la quelle on a marqué les découvertes et reconnaissances faittes en 1792 et 1793 par le Contre Amiral d'Entrecasteaux, Commandant des fregattes Françaises envoyée a la récherche de M. de la Pérouse* (Paris, 1796) MAP RM 3852 Bib ID 3300329

When he returned to the south coast in January 1793, d'Entrecasteaux was short of water and facing continuous winds, so he abandoned his plan to reach St Peter and St Francis and again sailed towards Van Diemen's Land.[63] Nevertheless, he explored part of the Recherche archipelago, where Beautemps-Beaupré undertook important mapping. The archipelago comprised 130 granite islands and rock islets covering a distance of 143 miles. Given its numerous islands, d'Entrecasteaux admitted he could not guarantee that all the archipelago's reefs were marked on their maps. In his opinion, the unimpressive coast and the low land beyond the Recherche archipelago would not lead someone to 'suspect them of being part of a vast continent which can be considered to be a fifth part of the world. One would be inclined to believe that they belonged to small islands.'[64]

D'Entrecasteaux's expedition made significant advances in geography, charting, botany and ethnographical observation. Maps and charts by previous explorers were used but checked for accuracy. Newly found places were added. The expedition discovered the Derwent River, the site of Hobart, the future capital of Tasmania. D'Entrecasteaux spent much time in and around Recherche

Bay and the D'Entrecasteaux Channel.[65] The Channel had been seen by James Burney in 1773 in the *Adventure* and by Bligh in the *Providence* in 1792, but d'Entrecasteaux was the first person to enter it. Detailed hydrographic work established that this channel, situated between the east coast of Van Diemen's Land and Bruny Island, had safe anchorages. Time was spent revising Cook's chart of Adventure Bay.[66] D'Entrecasteaux found that Cape Frederick Henry, named by Cook, was much nearer to Penguin Island than on the English navigator's map and a few minutes south of the latitude given by Cook. Numerous bays were discovered between Maria Island and latitude 42°42′ to the east of Cape Pillar.[67]

The highly skilled Beautemps-Beaupré was the chartmaker. Renowned for his superior draughtsmanship and analytical skills, Beautemps-Beaupré relied on astronomical rather than terrestrial bearings as a base for observing places. He used a reflecting circle rather than a compass for measuring the angular bearing of landmarks from his base observation. He repeated these bearings from other points to provide a set of triangles for the area to be investigated. The reflecting circle enabled him to take multiple horizontal angles to prominent points much more easily than by using either a sextant, which had a restricted arc, or a theodolite, which needed a stable land base for optimum use. With the aid of these instruments, Beautemps-Beaupré mapped D'Entrecasteaux Channel, Huon River, Bruny Island, the Derwent estuary and the general outline of Storm Bay. This enabled the map of the shores of Van Diemen's Land, comprising Cape South-West to Cape Pillar, to be completely redrafted. Beautemps-Beaupré's charts were published after the voyage as the *Atlas du voyage de Bruny Dentrecasteaux*.[68]

During five weeks in Van Diemen's Land, d'Entrecasteaux's scientists collected 5,000 natural history specimens, consisting of 30 genera and about 100 new species. Labillardière led the botanizing in the southeastern corner of the island. He found many specimens but lacked an assistant to help him with the fieldwork. With cooperation from other colleagues, Labillardière made several exhausting excursions into the mountains and rainforest to gather lichens, pines, geraniums and other plants. His finds included the native cherry (*Exocarpuos cupressiformis*) and the flag iris (*Diplarrena moraea*), which were new genuses.[69] He was impressed by the broad leaves and indented edges of the celery top pine (*Phyllocladus aspleniifolius*). The proportion of live as opposed to dried plants, or how many samples were simply seeds, is unknown.[70]

Members of d'Entrecasteaux's expedition left impressions of their encounters with Aborigines. This accorded with the voyage instructions, which called for an investigation of the customs and habits of the Aborigines (referred to as *sauvages*), their weapons and warfare, and what they had in common with other indigenous peoples and civilized nations.[71] Some ethnographical accounts from the expedition recorded observations of indigenous people. Labillardière, for instance, described the way in which Aborigines threw their spears. He compiled a vocabulary of eighty-four Aboriginal words, and noted that Aboriginal women sometimes had initiation marks on their breasts and shoulders. He also remarked, without providing an explanation, that the Tasmanians did not remove any upper front teeth in contrast to other Aboriginal groups seen by earlier European visitors.[72]

Other members of the French exploring party had cordial exchanges with the Aborigines in locations such as Bruny Island, readily acknowledging the friendly interaction.[73] The French voyagers made perceptive comments about Aboriginal families.[74] There were some critical voices: Louis-Auguste Deschamps, for example, characterized the Aborigines as brutish and uncivilized. But such a negative remark was the exception rather than the rule. The expedition's artist, Jean Piron, sketched Aborigines in groups and individually. Engravings of his sketches appeared later in Labillardière's published voyage account. They included examples of Aborigines being industrious and bonding with their families and of the French approaching the natives while they ate.[75]

D'Entrecasteaux offered different, somewhat contradictory, views of the Aborigines he encountered. He thought the hostility of his initial meeting with them was irreconcilable with the 'the apparent simplicity and meekness of the inhabitants of Van Diemen's Land observed at Adventure Bay by Captain Cook, and at Oyster Bay by Captain Cox.' However, he later reported a friendly meeting with Aborigines who treated the French voyagers with 'candour and kindness,' a contrast to 'the vices of civilization.' The Aborigines' lack of property and devotion to their tribes singled them out, in terms reflecting Rousseau's ideas, as 'the most perfect image of positive society' living in natural harmony and thereby uncorrupted by civilization's excesses. D'Entrecasteaux described the family groups and eating habits of the Aborigines. Like Labillardière, he also recorded some Aboriginal words, noting that the natives' language in the Port du Sud area was different to that recorded by Captain Cook at Adventure Bay.[76]

Leaving Van Diemen's Land at the end of February 1793, d'Entrecasteaux continued to search for Lapérouse in largely uncharted Pacific waters, but he died of scurvy near New Guinea on 20 July 1793. As his second-in-command had already died, the expedition's leadership passed to Jean-Louis d'Hesmity d'Auribeau, a Royalist sympathizer, who reached the Dutch East Indies where he handed the ships over to the Dutch after learning that France was now a republic. Auribeau did not want the new French government to profit from the expedition. He died a month later and Rossel took over as commander.[77]

The political changes of the French revolutionary wars had a direct impact on other aspects of the expedition. Labillardière and his republican scientific colleagues were interned at Java in 1794 by the Dutch authorities at the request of the loyalist officers of the expedition. Labillardière was released in 1795, and returned to France the following year. His scientific collections were placed for safe keeping in a Dutch vessel returning from Batavia to Europe, with the intention of sending them to Louis XVIII, the titular French monarch. The ship was captured by the Royal Navy off the Shetland Islands and the collections and charts were seized. Sir Joseph Banks inspected the collections in March 1796, and the contents were copied. In the spirit of scientific international cooperation, he then arranged for their return to France. This occurred after the Peace of Amiens in 1802.[78]

Long after the voyage ended, Labillardière produced the first flora of Australia in *Novae Hollandiae Plantorum*, published in fascicles between 1804 and 1807. This described 265 species from Western Australia and Van Diemen's Land, far fewer than Robert Brown's collection of Australia's flora and fauna in the *Investigator* expedition of 1801–3.[79] Labillardière followed the Linnean system of plant classification. His account includes examples of all major plant groups, including mosses, lichens, liverwort, fungi and seaweeds. Among the species identified from the sojourn in Van Diemen's Land, seven were different eucalypts, but there is no reference to the myrtle beech or alpine plants found in the island.[80] Labillardière provided generic names for Australian plants such as Chorizema, Exocorpus, Lepisdosperma and Atherosperma.[81] He was the first botanist to describe many common Tasmanian plants, including musk (*Olearia argophylla*), native laurel (*Anopterus glandulosus*) and waratah (*Telopea truncate*).[82]

Labillardière's plant collections ended up being widely dispersed; most are now in Florence while others are deposited in Geneva, Leiden, Paris, Vienna, Uppsala and elsewhere. They are still consulted by botanists.[83] Rossel had returned to France in 1802 with d'Entrecasteaux's journal and the remaining material from the expedition. He embarked on a state-sponsored publication about the voyage. This appeared under the title *Voyage de d'Entrecasteaux* in 1808. This volume had poor sales, largely because Labillardière's published account of the voyage was already available in print. Rossel complained, however, that Labillardière had concentrated on natural history at the expense of the expedition's geographical studies.[84]

Conclusion

For two centuries after 1500, French perceptions of Terra Australis were dominated by the notion that the French navigator Gonneville had landed somewhere in Australia *c*.1504, but there was no verification that his voyage achieved this goal. Nevertheless, Gonneville Land, as the French termed it, had a strong imaginative hold over geographers. In the late 1730s, Bouvet de Lozier conducted a search for Gonneville Land that was abandoned after he reached no farther than waters south of the Cape of Good Hope. De Brosses's large tome of 1756 accepted that Gonneville Land could be found, and this provided stimulus for further French voyages in search of Terra Australis. Successive voyages, however, yielded paltry results. De Bougainville's expedition of 1767 discovered Tahiti, the Louisiade archipelago and several Pacific islands but did not locate Australia. In 1771, Kerguélen and St Aloüarn set out to discover Gonneville Land and Terra Australis, but after a series of miscalculations only St Aloüarn made an Australian landfall, and a fairly brief one at that, in a few locations in Western Australia. Marion Dufresne's voyage in 1772 continued the vain search for Gonneville Land. This expedition included a short stay in Van Diemen's Land notable for gathering information on local Aborigines and for some useful surveying and charting.

Aware that voyages in search of *Frances Australes* were largely unsuccessful ventures, the French monarch and his administrators in the 1780s planned and assembled larger, better-equipped expeditions to the south hemisphere. Lapérouse's voyage received instructions in 1788 to visit the nascent British colony in New South Wales. This was undertaken, but information gathered about that settlement never reached France because Lapérouse's ships were lost in the Pacific Ocean, with no known survivors. Fortunately, for the French their last attempt to sail in Australian waters during the eighteenth century was much more successful. D'Entrecasteaux's fully equipped scientific expedition of the early 1790s redeemed the failures of earlier French voyages to Australia. Focusing mainly on southwestern Australia and Van Diemen's Land, Beautemps-Beaupré prepared highly professional charts of newly discovered bays, river and other coastal features; Labillardière gathered thousands of natural history specimens to return to France for further study; and members of the expedition undertook ethnographic observations of Aborigines that greatly extended what was previously known by Europeans about Australia's indigenous inhabitants.

English Voyages in the Age of Bligh and Vancouver

Cook's discovery and charting of Australia's east coast were not followed up systematically by any British expedition to Terra Australis for thirty years. Nevertheless, between 1789 and 1800 several discrete voyages set out from Britain that ended up exploring and charting parts of Australia's coastline while also being concerned with other activities on the world's oceans. All the voyages discussed in this chapter made a significant contribution to piecing together the jigsaw of the shores and islands surrounding Australia's shores before any navigator had ascertained the size and scope of the whole. The voyages of the 1790s were therefore significant for the incremental advances made to the knowledge of Australia's coastal geography.

John Henry Cox and Van Diemen's Land

This English captain led a nominally Swedish expedition in 1789 in an armed brig *Mercury* that was intended to raid Russian fur trade posts in the north Pacific. In voyaging out via the Cape of Good Hope, John Henry Cox, who had a commission in the Swedish Royal Navy, sailed under the south coast of Australia and stopped to refresh his supplies and water in Van Diemen's Land. He ended up near the mountainous Maria Island, situated off the east coast of Van Diemen's Land, mooring in Oyster Bay. There he came across Aboriginal huts, and made some observations of these people.[1] Cox remained in Van Diemen's Land for three days (8–10 July 1789); he drew a sketch map of Oyster Bay.[2] After his brief stay in Van Diemen's Island, Cox sailed across the Pacific, stopping at Tahiti and Hawaii, and eventually reaching Canada.[3] Cox's voyage was a small footnote in Australian maritime exploration, but his sketch map was quickly disseminated. Thus, Cox's plan of Oyster Bay was published by Dalrymple in 1791.[4]

Navigation through Torres Strait

Two British voyages after Cox's expedition improved knowledge of the passage through Torres Strait, a potentially important channel for shipping sailing from Australia's east coast to Indonesia and the Indian Ocean. Locating a safe passage through Torres Strait was beset by navigational and geographical problems. Torres Strait links the Coral Sea in the west with the Arafura Sea in the east. It has shallow water, many reefs, shoals, sand cays and scattered small islands. Altogether, there are 274 small islands in Torres Strait. Many of its islands and reefs have never been named or charted accurately. East-west movement through the strait, with a choice of around nine channels, is restricted to draughts of 12.2 metres; north-south movement can only cope with much shallower draughts. The strait is situated at the intersection of two oceanic tidal systems that can cause dangerous, rapid tidal streams. During the wet season from December to April, strong southeasterly winds can cause storms.[5]

No British navigator after Cook passed through Torres Strait until William Bligh traversed the passage in unexpected, desperate circumstances in 1789.[6] Master of the *Resolution* on Cook's second Pacific voyage, Bligh had gained further naval experience before being appointed commanding officer in HMS *Bounty*. This vessel left Spithead on 23 December 1788 with instructions to sail via Cape Horn to Tahiti to collect breadfruit as a nutritious, staple foodstuff for West Indian slaves. The first part of the voyage passed uneventfully. But on 28 April 1789, nearly three weeks after leaving Tahiti with his cargo, some of Bligh's crew rose up in revolt against their commander's draconian discipline on board ship. This was the most famous naval mutiny in British history. Bligh and eighteen loyal crew members were cast adrift in the *Bounty*'s launch, a 7 metres' longboat. In this small craft, Bligh made a remarkable voyage of 3,168 nautical miles from Tofoa (now Tofua), where the mutiny occurred, to Timor, the nearest known place for refreshment and shelter. During forty-one days at sea, Bligh and his crew sailed through Torres Strait.[7]

Bligh, who had learned about hydrography and surveying under Cook in the *Resolution*, compiled a running survey of his track. He had taken with him all the necessary navigational instruments save for a timekeeper and a nautical almanac. Bligh and his crew sailed through Torres Strait in dreadful weather, suffering from thirst and starvation. Distress and fatigue among the crew on the launch did not prevent Bligh from concentrating on improving geographical and nautical knowledge of Torres Strait.[8] He discovered a new route through Torres Strait that later became known as Bligh Channel, the northernmost of all known channels through the strait.[9] Commenting on the charts drawn by Cook and himself, Bligh hoped future navigators of these seas would derive 'more advantage ... from the possession of both our charts, than from either of them singly.'[10]

Bligh was proud of charting Torres Strait, as he carried out complex nautical calculations in a situation of great danger.[11] In a modern study, Andrew David has demonstrated that Bligh's longitude on his open boat passage varied only by 11' compared with a modern chart and his latitude was only 4' in error; the equivalent differences for Cook were a 41½' error in longitude and a 9½' error in latitude. Thus, Bligh's chart was 'considerably more accurate for scale and orientation than Cook's.'[12]

Another voyage connected with Bligh's expedition in the *Bounty* was expected to sail through Torres Strait. This involved the frigate *Pandora* commanded by Edward Edwards. This expedition, which began on 7 November 1790, was intended to search for the *Bounty* mutineers. The *Pandora* sailed to Tahiti, where many mutineers were rounded up. The voyage continued through the Pacific in a fruitless search for the rest of the *Bounty*'s men. Edwards abandoned the search on 2 August 1791 and headed towards Torres Strait, as he had been instructed, en route to the Indian Ocean and a voyage home. On 27 August, the *Pandora* struck on a coral outcrop and was wrecked. Thirty-one crew and four prisoners died. Eighty-nine crew and ten prisoners survived the ship's sinking. Edwards and his crew sailed from the wreck in four open boats as a flotilla towards Torres Strait and Timor.[13] Edwards and his open boats reached latitude 11°23′S and sailed to the north of Horn Island and Prince of Wales Island.[14] Despite encountering hostile Torres Strait islanders, Edwards eventually made his way back to England with some of the mutineers.[15]

The small cutter *Matavy*, which was the *Pandora*'s tender, escaped shipwreck and sailed through Torres Strait. This was an open boat voyage that was almost as miraculous in avoiding danger through a difficult shipping route as Bligh's open boat voyage.[16] A midshipman's account of this part of the voyage referred to the dangers encountered: 'so dangerous & intricate is the navigation of these straits, that we were buffeting about a whole week, before we had completely cleared them. Our passage was impeded by numerous shoals, sandy keys, and small islands, under shelter of which we generally brought up during the night.'[17]

Bligh had another opportunity to sail through Torres Strait on his second breadfruit voyage in the *Providence*, accompanied by the brig *Assistant*, under Nathaniel Portlock, in 1792. Supported by the Admiralty, Bligh's voyage successfully transplanted breadfruit from Tahiti to the Caribbean. The passage through Torres Strait was accomplished expeditiously. The passage followed involved encounters with hostile, armed natives.[18] A landing took place at

Cook's Possession Island. On 19 September, the *Providence* and *Assistant* had sailed out of Torres Strait. Flinders drew a chart of the strait that was intended to accompany his log. Bligh also drew a manuscript survey of the passage through Torres Strait, showing the tracks of the *Endeavour*, the *Bounty's* launch and the *Providence* (but not the *Pandora's* track).[19]

The first known merchant ship to sail through Torres Strait was the East Indiaman *Shaw Hormuzear*, commanded by William Wright Bampton, accompanied by the whaler *Chesterfield*, under Captain Matthew Bowles Alt.[20] Bampton commanded a Bombay country ship that had made a speculative voyage to Sydney with stores and livestock. On the return voyage, he was accompanied by Alt; they intended to pass through Torres Strait via a route not previously attempted.[21] It was later claimed that the voyage of the *Shaw Hormuzear* and *Chesterfield* showed that the passage through Torres Strait should never be undertaken near the New Guinea coast.[22]

Vancouver and southwest Australia

In 1789, the British government planned a scientific expedition to the Pacific and northwest America under the leadership of Henry Roberts, who had served under Cook in his last two Pacific voyages. George Vancouver, another participant on those voyages, was appointed as second-in-command. The expedition was postponed, however, when Spain committed depredations on British shipping and trade at Nootka Sound, near modern Vancouver, in April 1790. After the Spanish gave up rights to American waters north of the Gulf of California, as part of the Nootka Convention of 1790, the British government's expedition was reassembled under Vancouver's leadership. It was hoped to extend Cook's achievements in Pacific exploration; to examine the possibilities of greater fur trade between North America and China; to ensure that territories seized by the Spanish at Nootka Sound were returned to Britain; to chart and map the bays, harbours and coasts of northwest America; to collect botanical specimens; and to use the newest scientific instruments to aid with navigation and nautical astronomy.[23]

The expedition began on 1 April 1791. Vancouver commanded the *Discovery*, a 340-ton sloop with 100 men, named to honour the vessel that had sailed on Cook's final expedition. The naval captain William Robert Broughton was in charge of the armed tender *Chatham*, with a ship's company of forty-five. The two ships were to sail together, but in the event when they accidentally parted Broughton was furnished with a copy of Vancouver's instructions, a copy of the intended shipping route, and a list of rendezvous points. On the recommendation of Sir Joseph Banks, the surgeon Archibald Menzies was appointed as the botanist for the expedition. Banks wrote botanical instructions for Menzies to follow.[24]

The west coast of New Holland was not mentioned in Vancouver's instructions, but he wanted to explore this little-known coast. Vancouver also hoped to examine 'the unknown coast' from the eastern limit of seventeenth-century Dutch explorers to Van Diemen's Land, and to determine whether the latter was part of the mainland or an island.[25] Vancouver thought the lack of knowledge about much of Australia was 'a real blot in geography, particularly when we reflect on the many vessels that in this improved age of navigation have passed the meridians.'[26] Vancouver followed an Indian Ocean route for New Holland between the tracks of Dampier and Marion Dufresne. He was steering towards an 'ill defined' part of the coast of New Holland and therefore proceeded carefully, 'not choosing to make too free with a coast entirely unexplored.'[27] In late September 1791, he made landfall in Western Australia near Chatham Island.[28]

Vancouver explored over 300 miles of the southwest Australian coast. Faced with southerly gales, outlying reefs, contrary winds and lack of time, he abandoned further exploration of the coast when he reached the Great Australian Bight.[29] Vancouver discovered a spacious bay that he named King George the Third's Sound (later abbreviated to its modern name of King George Sound). He took possession of the country for Britain from the land northwest of Cape Chatham as far as they might explore to the east. Small parties were sent out from the ship in boats to explore and survey the Sound. To commemorate the visit, a sealed bottle was placed in a pile of stones. It contained a parchment on which were written the names of the ships, their commanders, the name given to the Sound, and the date of arrival and departure. Another bottle, containing a similar document, was left on Seal Island, situated close to King George Sound.[30]

Two weeks spent in King George Sound included some fruitful research, notably the exploration and charting of harbours and waterways. Midshipman Henry Humphreys signed a manuscript chart of the Sound; three other, unsigned, charts from the expedition exist. The main anchorage was depicted in the same place on each chart, but the coastal outlines varied considerably. The charts provide information on the geographical coordinates of the Sound and descriptions of the landscape. Vancouver found plenty of fresh water and wood in King George Sound, which had deep water suitable for large ships to anchor.[31] Vancouver discovered and named Cape Chatham, Cape Howe, Mount Gardner, Green Island and Eclipse Island. Vancouver curtailed his investigation of the coast at the appropriately named Termination Island.[32]

Vancouver was detained by unexpected easterly winds while examining the coast from Cape Chatham to Termination Island and by the labyrinth of rocks and islets in the Recherche archipelago; together with 'the advanced season,' these factors militated against his exploring the coast in detail. 'I was therefore compelled to relinquish, with great reluctance,' he wrote, 'the favourite project of further examining the coast of this unknown though interesting country.' Vancouver sailed south of Van Diemen's Land and continued the voyage to New Zealand, America's northwest coast and the Sandwich Islands before returning to Britain via Cape Horn.[33] This five-year voyage was the longest expedition ever undertaken by a British maritime explorer.[34]

Vancouver and his ships' companies came across relatively few Aborigines during their survey of southwestern Australia.[35] 'The natives appeared to be a wandering people, who sometimes made their excursions individually, at other times in considerable parties,' Vancouver concluded, adding that 'this was apparent by their habitations being found single and alone, as well as composing tolerably large villages.'[36] Vancouver attributed the use of fire to burning the bush to alarm kangaroos out into the open, where they could be captured for food. He had probably witnessed the remains of Aboriginal fire-stick farming.[37] Menzies considered that evidence of fire around the trunks of the largest Eucalyptus trees, along with notches cut in the bark, suggested that the Aborigines extracted a nutrient sap from the trees.[38]

Menzies made five botanical excursions in King George Sound between 29 September and 11 October 1791. He collected 145 taxa on these surveys, including 132 flowering plants, four ferns, three mosses and four marine algae.[39] He recorded many new discoveries in flowering plants that were not listed in his edition of Linnaeus. They included *Eucalyptus marginata*, the Holly-leafed Banksia and various mimosas. Five species of Banksia, a genus unique to Australia, were discovered.[40] Luxuriant vegetation in many places indicated that fertile soil could support growing European grains and fruit, though that later proved to be an incorrect assumption.[41] Menzies also left descriptions of many bird species, including ducks, shags, eagles, penguins, gulls, curlews and black swans.[42]

John Hayes and Van Diemen's Land, 1793–4

A minor contribution to greater geographical knowledge of Australia occurred in 1793 when Lieutenant John Hayes of the Bombay Marine visited Van Diemen's Land with the ships *Duke of Clarence* and *Duchess*. Hayes's voyage was financed by Calcutta merchants, and intended to determine the economic potential of New Guinea. But adverse winds had led him to sail around Australia to reach that destination via a long detour.[43] A chart of southeastern Van Diemen's Land from South-West Cape to South-East Cape was drawn by an East India Company hydrographer from information conveyed in a letter from Hayes supplemented by information from Hayes's letters to fellow officers in the East India Company and the Indian Navy.[44] The chart included the Derwent River, which Hayes discovered and named, as well as Storm Bay, Risdon Cove and Cornelian Bay. The chart was, unfortunately, defective. There were major omissions, names were included carelessly, several bays were poorly identified, and the latitudes contained errors. However, the name 'Admiral D'Entrecasteaux's Bay' on his chart indicates that Hayes had heard of the French navigator's voyage to Van Diemen's Land made shortly before his own. After leaving Van Diemen's Land, Hayes sailed to New Caledonia and the Louisiades.[45]

Peter Heywood and northwest Australia

Peter Heywood, who had sailed as a midshipman in HMS *Bounty* under Bligh and who was found guilty of taking part in the mutiny but then pardoned from a capital sentence, was a skilled hydrographer who charted the Timor Sea in 1801. After pursuing a naval career successfully in the wake of his pardon, in August 1800 he was stationed at Amboyna (Ambon), the main capital and island of the Moluccas, as commander of HM vessel *Vulcan*. Heywood discovered two shoals, a small island (now Red Islet), Vulcan Point (now Vulcan Islets) and a reef, but he did not touch the Australian coast. His survey of the Timor Sea took place between January and March 1801; Heywood returned to England in 1805. His manuscript survey of the Timor Sea was engraved by Dalrymple in that year, and was considered sufficiently accurate for Flinders to incorporate the findings (with some changes in longitude) in plates 1 and XVI of *A Voyage to Terra Australis*.[46]

The cruise of the *Kingston* and *Elligood* in 1800

Two British whaling vessels made an exploratory cruise off the coast of northwest Australia between September and December 1800. Sailing in company from London on 19 January 1800, these ships were charged with testing whether untried waters were suitable for whaling. The ships were supplied with Dampier's descriptions of northwest Australia, indicating that he had seen 'an abundance of whales' near the coast at latitude 22°22'. They also carried Vancouver's survey of southwest Australia from his voyage of 1791. The *Kingston* and the *Elligood* reached King George Sound on 11 August and then headed north past Perth, Geraldton and Shark Bay, on Dirk Hartog Island. The captains of the ships found that available charts of northwest Australia were very inaccurate. This impeded their attempts to locate the Tryal Rocks and Dampier's Rosemary Islands. They did at least see some whales before heading home for London, which they reached in December 1801.[47]

Bass and Flinders in New South Wales and Van Diemen's Land

Several British voyages explored coastal New South Wales and Van Diemen's Land in the 1790s. Early governors of New South Wales wanted to promote exploration of those waters to facilitate the future commerce and prosperity of their colony. Two young explorers, George Bass and Matthew Flinders, took advantage of the opportunities for maritime surveying in New South Wales between 1795 and 1800. They carried out the first voyages ever devoted to coastal exploration from a base in Australia.[48] In 1794, Flinders was given the opportunity by his friend Henry Waterhouse, second captain of the *Reliance*, to join a voyage to Sydney.[49] He was joined by Bass, a young naval surgeon, and John Hunter, sailing to his post as governor of New South Wales. Bass was three years older than Flinders; he was widely read and shared Flinders's penchant for geographical discovery.[50] Hunter, a former naval officer, was an experienced maritime surveyor, who had compiled charts of Sydney harbour.[51] Flinders noted that parts of coastal New South Wales to the north and south of Port Jackson 'were little further known than from captain Cook's general chart; and none of the more distant openings, marked but not explored by that celebrated navigator, had been seen.'[52]

Hunter had so many preoccupations as governor that he lacked the time to pursue his own interest in surveying.[53] Flinders and Bass, however, were in a position to carry out maritime surveys, and, with Hunter's support, they undertook several voyages that increased maritime knowledge of New South Wales. The first two excursions were made in very small boats both called *Tom Thumb*.[54] On the first *Tom Thumb* voyage, Flinders and Bass, accompanied only by a boy assistant, made a short excursion of nine days to determine whether a large river flowed into Botany Bay. They sketched George's River and presented it to Hunter, along with a favourable report of the land. Hunter followed up their report by visiting the vicinity twice, in November 1795 and June 1796.[55] On the second *Tom Thumb* voyage in 1796, Flinders and Bass sailed as far south as modern Port Kembla, discovered a fresh water creek they named Canoe Rivulet, and came across some islets.[56] Flinders's charts of the area were sent back to England by Hunter and published by the London commercial map seller Aaron Arrowsmith, along with a topographical plan of New South Wales prepared by Charles Grimes, the Deputy Surveyor General for the colony. This was Flinders's first published chart.[57]

Hunter had plans for further exploration of coastal New South Wales. He was keen to determine whether a strait existed off the southeastern end of Australia. If proven, this would have important consequences because vessels sailing through such a strait could shorten the sea route to Port Jackson, then usually undertaken around the southern coast of Van Diemen's Land, by 685 miles. Bass Strait had not yet been discovered and maps showed Van Diemen's Land joined to the mainland. With six volunteers, Bass took a whaleboat from Port Jackson in December 1797 to reconnoitre previously unexplored parts of New South Wales. Flinders's naval duties in Port Jackson ruled him out from joining the voyage.[58] Bass and his party discovered Western Port, in modern Victoria. Bass sketched the harbour, including the island that sheltered its entrance, later named Phillip Island. As the voyage had now taken seven weeks and provisions were running low, Bass reluctantly turned homewards. The whaleboat arrived back at Port Jackson on 25 February 1798.[59] The excursion surveyed the mainland coast from Point Hicks to Western Port, and discovered Jervis Bay as a fine harbour.[60] In *A Voyage to Terra Australis* (1814), Flinders paid tribute to the voyage, noting that Bass had sailed along 600 miles of coast in a small boat 'exposed to the buffeting of an open sea' and had returned 'in no doubt about the existence of a wide strait separating Van Diemen's Land from New South Wales.'[61]

Three weeks before the arrival of the whaleboat in Port Jackson, Flinders had sailed in the colonial schooner *Francis* to the wreck of the *Sydney Cove*, a stranded merchant vessel in the Furneaux Islands at the eastern end of Bass Strait. Flinders discovered the Kent Group of islands and undertook a detailed hydrographical survey of the Furneaux Group. He did not have an azimuth compass or a chronometer, but produced a chart of the area and wrote a careful description of his findings. From observation, he speculated he was situated in a strait 'dividing New South Wales from Van Diemen's Land.'[62]

On returning to Port Jackson, Flinders sought out Bass. The two friends agreed, from their respective recent voyages, that a strait probably existed between the southeastern mainland of Australia and Van Diemen's Land.[63] Flinders drafted the first sketch to delineate Victoria's shoreline from the eastern entrance of Bass Strait to Western Port. He incorporated Bass's whaleboat material into his sketch plan, at Hunter's request, but gave due credit to Bass.[64] Hunter informed Banks about the wreck of the *Sydney Cove*, and forwarded to the Admiralty the chart that combined the findings of Bass (in the whaleboat) and Flinders (in the *Francis*) in the Furneaux Islands and along the coast to Western Port. Hunter considered verification of a strait to be an important matter, as he had long believed it existed.[65]

Circumnavigating Van Diemen's Land

Action soon followed to determine the matter. Hunter fitted out the *Norfolk* sloop, of about twenty-five tons, and placed it under Flinders's command, with Bass and eight volunteers on board, to sail southwards from Port Jackson to determine the extent of Van Diemen's Land and whether a strait existed. Flinders was supplied with a theodolite, azimuth compass and brass sextant, but not a chronometer.[66] The *Norfolk*'s voyage lasted from 7 October 1798 until 11 January 1799.[67] Flinders and Bass circumnavigated Van Diemen's Land, proving for the first time that it was an island and correcting casual and sometimes inaccurate geographical references. Flinders took great satisfaction in having his friend Bass accompany him on this voyage.[68] But the two men soon parted ways. In early 1799, Bass decided to leave New South Wales to join a merchant expedition that planned to sell goods in China. Flinders and Bass never met again.[69]

Several months after Bass's departure from Port Jackson, Flinders asked Hunter whether he could explore the northern coast of New South Wales. Hunter readily agreed because he wanted to find out whether rivers led into the interior of New South Wales.[70] Flinders was again assigned the *Norfolk*, and the voyage occurred between 8 July and 21 August 1799. Flinders wanted to find a major river into the continent's centre to improve geographical knowledge and to prove his own credentials as a maritime explorer who could amplify Cook's findings.[71] Flinders identified some differences between his own observations and Cook's recording of coastal features on his chart. Flinders described headlands and Shoal Bay, and clarified Cook's account of this coastline.[72] He was disappointed by the results of the expedition, finding there was no river of importance intersecting the east coast between 24° and 39° of latitude south between Breaksea Spit and Wilson's Promontory.[73]

Hunter and Flinders independently informed Banks and the Admiralty of the discovery of Bass Strait, the circumnavigation of Van Diemen's Land and the *Norfolk*'s voyage to northern New South Wales. In June 1799, Hunter noted that Flinders's and Bass's survey of coastal Van Diemen's Land would provide impetus for further exploration of Australia.[74] Hunter despatched to London Flinders's chart of Bass Strait.[75] Some months later, he wrote to Banks to praise Flinders's work as a maritime surveyor, and hoped that the British government could support further examination of Australia's coastline in a suitable vessel.[76] Flinders later contacted Banks to seek permission from the Admiralty to publish and engrave the charts.[77] The Admiralty selected Arrowsmith, who knew Banks well, to undertake the task. On 16 June 1800, Arrowsmith published *A Chart of Bass's Strait between New South Wales and Van Diemen's Land, Explored by Matthw. Flinders 2nd Lieut. of His Majesty's Ship Reliance, by Order of His*

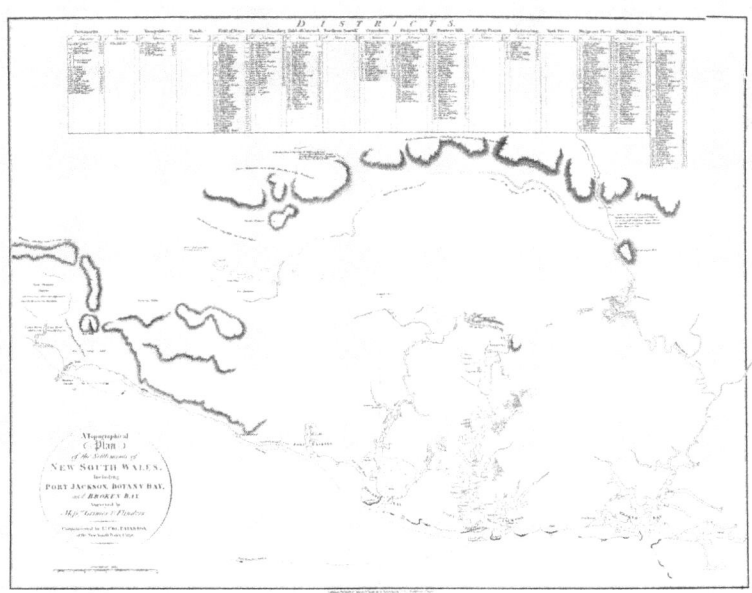

Map 13 Charles Grimes, *A Topographical Plan of the Settlements of New South Wales, including Port Jackson, Botany Bay and Broken Bay; surveyed by Messrs. Grimes & Flinders; communicated by Lt. Col. Paterson of the New South Wales Corps* (London: A. Arrowsmith, 12 March 1799) MAP RM 711 Bib ID 1012168

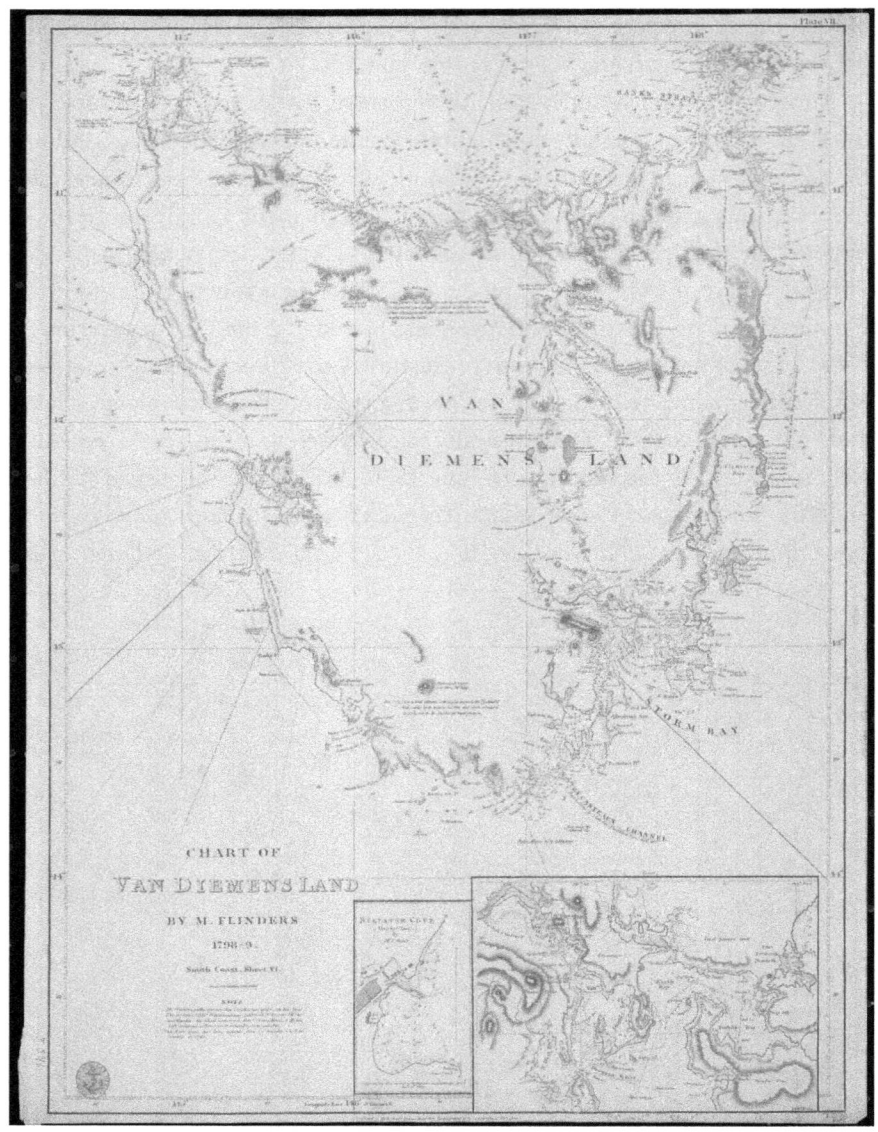

Map 14 Matthew Flinders, *Chart of Van Diemen's Land. Sheet VI, South coast, 1798–9* (London: Hydrographical Office of the Admiralty, ?1843) MAP T 596 Bib ID 620320

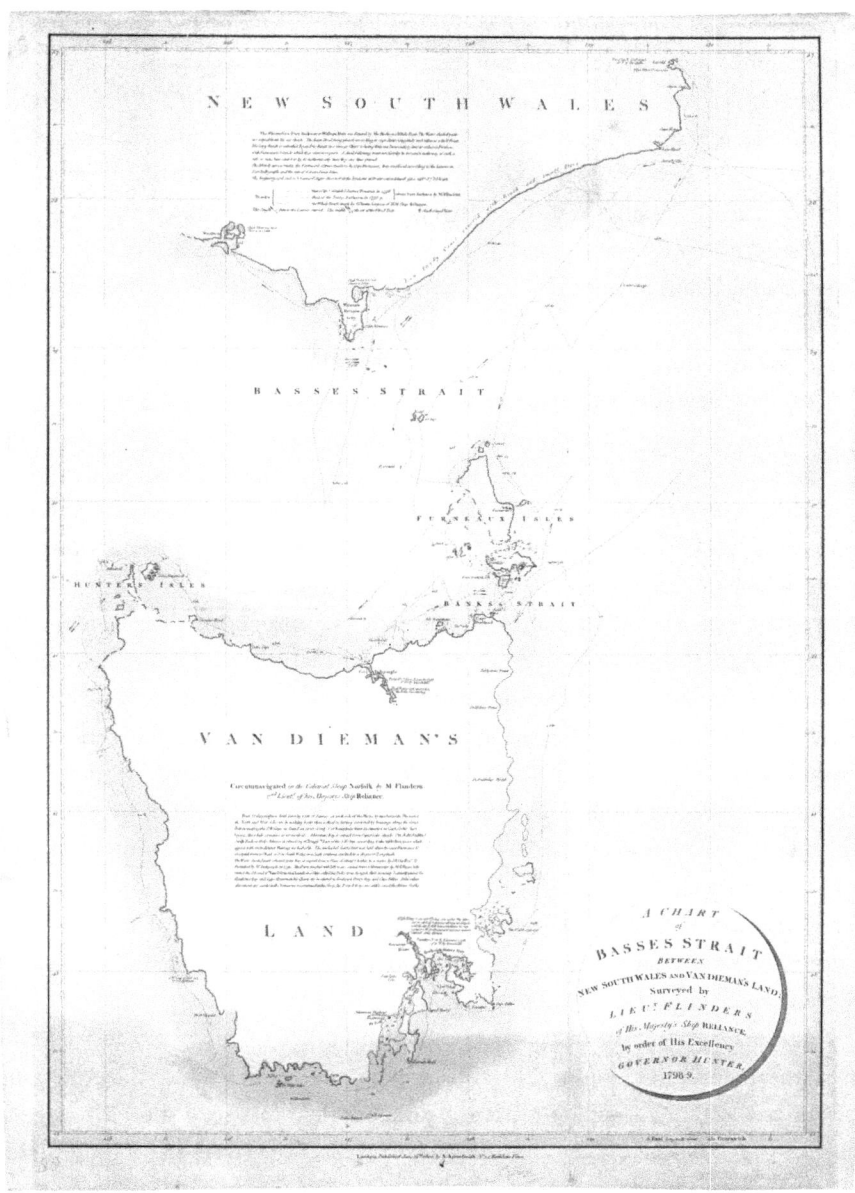

Map 15 Aaron Arrowsmith, *A Chart of Basses Strait between New South Wales and Van-Diemen's Land: survey'd by Lieut. Flinders of His Majesty's ship Reliance, by order of His Excellency, Governor Hunter, 1798–9* (London: A. Arrowsmith, 16 June 1800) MAP RM 684 Bib ID 151507

Excellency Governor Hunter 1798–9. The chart carefully followed Flinders's topography, nomenclature and notations.[78] Arrowsmith also published a *Chart of Part of the Coast of New South Wales, from Ram Head to Northumberland Isles, by M. Flinders, 2nd lieut. of H.M.S. Reliance, 1800* – the most extensive and accurate chart of coastal Australia ever published.[79] Arrowsmith published two further charts by Flinders on 20 February 1801, depicting on one Port Dalrymple, in northern Van Diemen's Land, the southernmost of the Furneaux Islands and Western Port, and on another the area from Ram's Head to the Northumberland Isles.[80]

By the beginning of 1800, Flinders was nearing the end of his stint in New South Wales. He knew the British government was considering further examination of the Australian coast, and he hoped his achievements in Australian maritime exploration might be rewarded by his being given command of an expedition.[81] This had already been proposed, in fact, by very influential people who knew about his work in New South Wales. Banks had briefly met Flinders twice in 1793 when matters connected with the second breadfruit voyage needed to be settled.[82] In May 1798, Banks had already recommended that Flinders – 'A Countryman of mine, a Man of activity & information, who is already there' – should be entrusted with the command of a vessel to continue exploring New South Wales.[83] Philip Gidley King, a former naval captain about to take over from Hunter as Governor of New South Wales, echoed this view.[84] Flinders knew about these recommendations. 'We are now given to understand,' he wrote to a friend on 17 January 1800, 'that it is the contemplation of Government to send out one or two vessels to carry on the examination of this still immense ("still immense" even when Van Diemen's Land was found to be separated) Island, the command of which, report has given to me, although the material discoveries already made must be unknown to them.'[85]

Flinders was correct in thinking a British voyage of discovery to Australia was imminent, but he did not know that the *Lady Nelson*, under the command of James Grant, a young Scots naval lieutenant, had just set out on a voyage to survey the coastline of New South Wales and discover rivers that might divide the mainland or allow access to the interior. Banks wrote the expedition's instructions, which envisaged that Grant would hand over command of the *Lady Nelson* to Flinders at Port Jackson.[86] This expedition arose after Banks and Hunter had corresponded about the need for further exploration of New South Wales so that the small British bridgehead at Port Jackson might expand into a broader territory to benefit the mother country.[87] While the *Lady Nelson* was sailing out to Port Jackson, Flinders had come to the end of his service in

New South Wales. He left there on 3 March 1800 and arrived at Plymouth on 27 August, having been away from home for five-and-a-half years.[88]

Flinders must have gleaned information about the *Lady Nelson*'s voyage soon after he returned home. Only eleven days after returning to England, he wrote a bold letter on 6 September 1800 to Banks requesting support for a major voyage of maritime discovery to Australia. Flinders knew Banks was virtually the 'managing director' of all British proposals concerning Australia.[89] Banks had extensive connections with leading figures in departments of government, and his personal library and herbarium were stocked with the literature and natural specimens associated with British voyages of discovery.[90] Without Banks's support, Flinders's proposal for a voyage of discovery stood little chance of acceptance.[91] Flinders's letter of 6 September 1800 – probably the most important one he ever wrote – referred to his charts of Van Diemen's Land and Bass Strait and discussed his work in surveying the coast of New South Wales. It emphasized the importance of a further, more ambitious voyage to promote British imperial interests, to extend knowledge of Australian geography and natural history, and to complete the exploration of New South Wales and New Holland. Flinders tapped Banks's interest in botany by noting that the voyage to Australia 'should examine into the natural productions of this wonderful country.'[92] The letter also referred to a conjecture that 'a still larger than Bass' Strait dismembers New Holland.'[93] This was a much-discussed idea at the time, stemming from distrust about the accuracy of maps depicting Australia.[94] Banks willingly supported Flinders's proposal for a voyage of discovery and became the main patron of the ensuing expedition.[95] Towards the end of 1800, Banks coordinated most of the arrangements necessary to find a ship and prepare for the Australian circumnavigation.[96]

Conclusion

English voyages to Australia in the age of Bligh and Vancouver were disparate and uncoordinated, but they managed to advance geographical knowledge in discrete areas. John Henry Cox and John Hayes led voyages that increased the charting of portions of southern Van Diemen's Land, naming several new locations they discovered. Bligh, in difficult circumstances, navigated through the treacherous Torres Strait and produced a chart of his route. Heywood undertook a survey of the Timor Sea. In the most ambitious of these voyages, Vancouver, engaged on an expedition that encompassed the Pacific, undertook maritime exploration in King George Sound, which he discovered, and among the islands of the Recherche Archipelago, naming coastal features as he sailed eastwards along Australia's south coast. Bass and Flinders combined their curiosity about exploration to undertake several voyages from their base in Port Jackson, with the support of the New South Wales governor, to improve geographical knowledge of southeastern Australia. Flinders's exploration of coastal New South Wales and Bass's whaleboat voyage through Bass Strait added more place names, bays, coves and rivers to the mapping of Australia. The two most significant findings by Bass and Flinders were to prove the existence of Bass Strait and to demonstrate that Van Diemen's Land was an island through undertaking a complete circumnavigation of its coasts. Maps and charts of these discoveries were produced promptly in London by professional map sellers, pointing to a market displaying the fruits of maritime discovery. Flinders's contribution to these voyages convinced him that a more ambitious, comprehensive expedition to Australia was needed, and the next chapter shows that this wish was soon taken up by the British Admiralty.

Flinders and the Investigator

Flinders's detailed proposal for a major voyage of exploration to chart the entire coast of Australia was highly ambitious. In a letter of 16 November 1800, Banks agreed to discuss Flinders's plans for the voyage.[1] Action followed quickly because Banks influenced government departments needed to support the voyage. In an era when colonial issues lacked firm government direction in Britain, Banks's connections with various government departments were essential for promoting scientific voyages in the British Empire.[2] One of Banks's suggestions, HMS *Investigator*, was selected by the Admiralty.[3] The Navy Board ordered provisions for six months.[4] Flinders later wrote that his plan to carry out a full exploration of Australia's coast was approved by Banks, 'that distinguished patron of science and useful enterprise.'[5] While the *Investigator* expedition was being planned, Banks and the Admiralty were aware that a rival French expedition, led by Nicolas Baudin, was being assembled; this is discussed in Chapter 9.

The *Investigator* was a converted collier. Deploying a bulk cargo ship for a voyage of discovery had famous precedents in the vessels used by Cook for his voyages of Pacific exploration. Copper sheathing took place, as was then becoming common in the navy to protect the wooden hull from being destroyed by the *teredo navalis* – saltwater clams or shipworms that were a destructive pest of submerged timber.[6] After repairs were made, the *Investigator* was described in Admiralty records as 'fitting out for a voyage to remote parts.'[7] The *Investigator* carried a launch, two cutters, a gig and a whaleboat for exploration of inlets, rivers and creeks along the shores of Terra Australis. She was a 334-ton three-masted square-sterned ship, with only one deck.[8]

Voyage preparations

In December 1800, Banks recommended Flinders as commander of the vessel to Earl Spencer, the first Lord of the Admiralty. Banks emphasized the need to anticipate Baudin's voyage and to examine the Gulf of Carpentaria between

130° and 140° longitude 'where the coast of new Holland is not lain down as Continuous.'[9] Banks provided a detailed itinerary for the expedition. He hoped Flinders would investigate any creeks, rivers or other openings on the mainland shore to find out whether any of them led to an inland sea or strait. Banks also wanted those parts of the Australian coast surveyed that were most likely to be reached by East India Company vessels in the expectation that an Australian base could be located for shipping.[10] Banks hoped that 'new articles of importance to the trade & manufactures of the united kingdom may be discovered' in Terra Australis.[11] This was a voyage in which botany and charting were also major objectives and in which Flinders and his crew were enjoined to look out for commercial possibilities for the future.[12]

Banks identified a naturalist and natural history painter for the voyage; these were Robert Brown, connected with the Linnaean Society in London, and William Westall. Banks also recommended Peter Good, who had previously collected plants for Kew Gardens, as gardener.[13] Brown worked regularly in Banks's London herbarium before the voyage began, studying Australian plants brought back to England by earlier collectors. Over 1,000 duplicates of these plants were mounted on tough brown cartridge paper for reference during the voyage.[14] Westall, aged nineteen, was the youngest scientific member of the expedition. His name was forwarded to Banks through the auspices of Benjamin West, the President of the Royal Academy.[15]

Banks contacted the Astronomer Royal Dr Nevil Maskelyne, who sought a suitable astronomer and identified the scientific instruments needed for the voyage. The Admiralty selected John Crosley as astronomer, following Maskelyne's advice. Crosley was employed by the Board of Longitude, and had sailed on a surveying voyage of the North Pacific in the *Providence* between 1795 and 1797. Maskelyne quickly arranged to acquire chronometers by leading makers such as Jesse Ramsden, Thomas Earnshaw and John Arnold.[16] Banks appointed a gifted Austrian, Ferdinand Lukas Bauer, whose elder brother had worked for Banks, as the expedition's artist.[17] Banks engaged a practical miner, John Allen, to investigate rocks and minerals.[18] Hugh Bell, who had interests in science and natural history, was recruited as surgeon on the recommendation of Sir Gilbert Blane, the Royal Navy's most notable physician.[19] Flinders helped to enrol his younger brother, Samuel Ward Flinders, as second lieutenant.[20]

Preparations for the voyage took place in the spring of 1801. Flinders clarified his ambitions for the *Investigator*'s expedition: 'My greatest ambition is to make such a minute investigation of this extensive and very interesting country that no person shall have occasion to come after me to make further discoveries.'[21]

This was an over-ambitious statement, for it was virtually impossible to complete the circumnavigation in a single voyage.[22] Flinders realized the importance of Banks's patronage in attempting his Australian circumnavigation, referring to the President of the Royal Society as 'my greatest and best friend.'[23] Banks expected his protégé would in his future conduct do credit to himself 'as an able navigator, and to me as having recommended you.'[24]

Australia's unknown south coast

The *Investigator* began her voyage at Spithead on 18 July 1801 and reached the Cape of Good Hope, then under British wartime control, on 17 October. The astronomer Crosley was ill and decided to leave the expedition. As there was no other trained astronomer on board the ship and no substitute could be found, Flinders and his brother Samuel took over these duties.[25] Flinders used his spare time to extend his knowledge of nautical astronomy. In early November, the *Investigator* sailed from the Cape of Good Hope and sailed across the Indian Ocean to reach the southwestern end of Australia near Cape Leeuwin on 7 December 1801. Late on the next night, she anchored in King George Sound. Approaching the western part of the Sound, Flinders stopped at Seal Island in order to search for a sealed bottle and parchment left by Vancouver to commemorate his visit there on 11 October 1791, but nothing was found.[26]

Flinders remained at King George Sound for a month, carrying out a detailed survey of the Sound and its two adjacent harbours and making preparations for the start of the Australian circumnavigation. He had Vancouver's account of his voyage to aid him in his survey.[27] Flinders left King George Sound on 3 January 1802. Five days later, he reached the Recherche archipelago. Using a fairly accurate chart of these islands compiled by Beautemps-Beaupré on D'Entrecasteaux's voyage of 1792, Flinders carried out additional charting.[28] Brown botanized on these islands, while Flinders took a party to Goose Island, in the archipelago, where they saw western grey kangaroos, geese, penguins and ducks.[29] The first encounter with Aborigines on the voyage occurred at King George Sound. Brown and his associates carried out botanizing in that location, collecting more than 500 plant species from the Albany area and another 100 from the Lucky Bay area and the islands of the Recherche Archipelago.[30]

Leaving this location, the *Investigator* sailed towards the Great Australian Bight and the islands of St Peter and St Francis – the farthest points reached by a previous navigator of this coast, François Thijssen in the VOC ship *'t gulden*

Zeepaard in 1627.[31] Flinders knew that sailing eastwards from those islands was 'totally unknown.'[32] His exploration of this coast made two important geographical discoveries in locating two deep gulfs: Spencer Gulf and Gulf St Vincent. Charting and surveying these gulfs were undertaken for the first time. Flinders identified the Sir Joseph Banks Group of islands, giving them names associated with his home county, Lincolnshire. Flinders and his ship's company visited Kangaroo Island where they were impressed by the local wildlife. At Flinders Island, the first group of Aborigines since King George Sound were seen. This stage of the voyage was marred, however, by the loss of several mariners, including John Thistle, the master, on a small boat sent to locate an anchorage. Flinders named the site Memory Cove as a tribute to the men who disappeared.[33]

In a remarkable coincidence, on 8 April 1802, Flinders and his ship's company unexpectedly saw an unknown ship ahead and showed her colours. Flinders later called the location Encounter Bay.[34] As Flinders drew near to the other vessel, he recognized the vessel as *Le Géographe*, commanded by Nicolas Baudin, also engaged on a voyage of exploration to Australia, backed by Napoleon Bonaparte.[35] Flinders was sailing eastwards while Baudin was proceeding

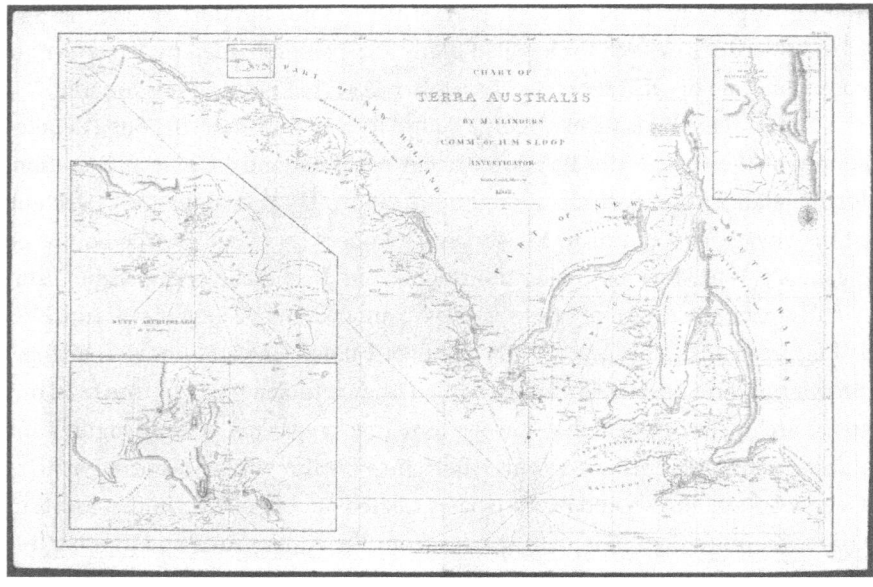

Map 16 Matthew Flinders, *Chart of Terra Australis, Sheet III, South coast, by M. Flinders, Commr. of H. M. Sloop Investigator, 1802; with additions from Commanders Wickham and Stokes, 1841* (London: Admiralty Hydrographic Office, 1814, 1841) MAP British Admiralty Special Map Col./17 Bib ID 3791265

westwards, having surveyed parts of Van Diemen's Land and a relatively small section of the Victorian and southern Australian coasts.[36]

Flinders went on board the French vessel twice, on 8 and 9 April 1802. The two commanders exchanged the passports they had been issued with as a diplomatic caution in the event of an encounter with the enemy during the Napoleonic wars. Baudin was, at the first meeting, more forthcoming about his discoveries so far on his voyage, whereas Flinders was more tight-lipped. These different approaches were underscored by the fact that Baudin had no reason to suppose that Flinders was engaged in an exploratory expedition that overlapped the French mission whereas Flinders knew from Banks that a French expedition to Australian waters was imminent. Flinders was more forthcoming about his voyage at his second meeting with Baudin. The exchange of information suggests that neither party had strategic imperatives: these were mainly scientific and geographical expeditions. The ships parted after two days and continued on their respective voyages. Flinders came across King Island at the opening of Bass Strait, a large island unseen by the French, and then entered Port Phillip Bay on the mainland (later the site of Melbourne). He and his party spent four days exploring the bay and its shores. They then sailed on to Port Jackson, arriving there on 9 May.[37]

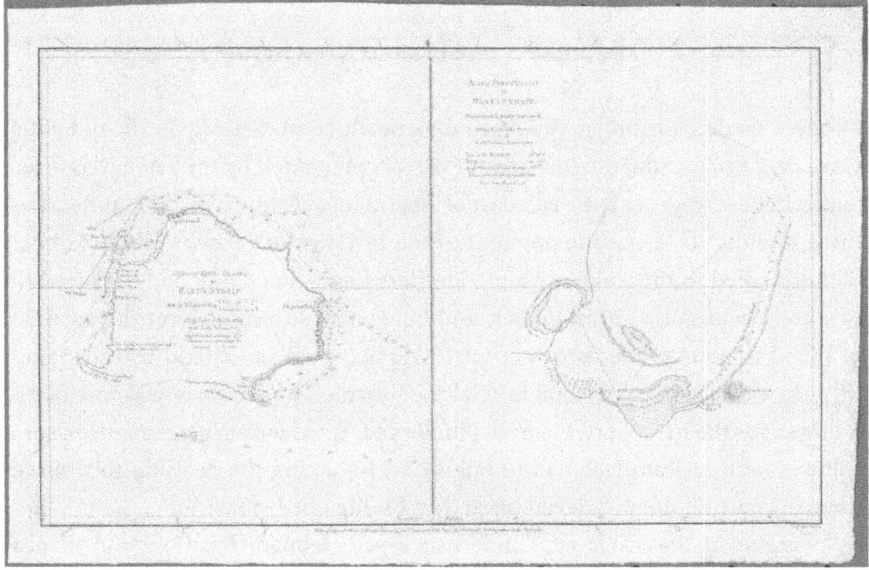

Map 17 *Chart of King's Island in Bass's Strait in Elephant Bay … by acting Lieut. John Murray, in the Lady Nelson, January 1801* MAP RM 1863 Bib ID 1766191

The *Investigator* spent nearly all of May and June 1802 in Sydney harbour. Flinders consulted with Governor Philip Gidley King about the plans for his Australian circumnavigation. Flinders was informed that the *Lady Nelson*, first under the command of James Grant and then under John Murray, had made voyages under King's direction between 1800 and 1802 to explore Bass Strait and parts of the south Australian coast. Grant came across and named Cape Bridgewater and Cape Schanck while Murray discovered a spacious harbour on the mainland coast at Port Phillip and explored and produced a sketch map of King Island in Bass Strait. Flinders acknowledged this prior discovery of Port Phillip, though he noted that Murray had only made a cursory examination of the bay.[38]

While at Port Jackson, Flinders completed charts of the south coast for transmission back to the Admiralty. Baudin's expedition was also present at Port Jackson at this time. Flinders and his ship's company fraternized and ate with their French counterparts. One of Baudin's associates referred to Flinders as 'a most distinguished officer' who freely talked to the French about his voyage along the south coast. Flinders and Baudin agreed on their respective claims to parts of the south Australian coast they had recently explored. Flinders claimed that his own area of discovery stretched from the south coast of Nuyts to Encounter Bay. Baudin had vested in himself and the French nation about 150 miles of coast from Encounter Bay (35°43′) to Cape Northumberland (38°3′).[39]

The east coast and Torres Strait

Flinders made plans to survey Australia's north coast. Setting out from Sydney Cove on 21 July 1802, the *Investigator* was accompanied by the *Lady Nelson* as a tender. The voyage up the east coast of Australia, a distance of 2,000 miles, took three months. This was the one part of the *Investigator's* voyage where Flinders literally sailed in the wake of Cook. Flinders knew that Cook had surveyed the east coast without a chronometer, and he wanted to improve on the accuracy of his illustrious predecessor's charts.[40] He accepted most land features along this coast discovered by Cook and later confirmed by Bass. He was justified in doing so for the most part. Even so, Flinders accepted wrong placements of some features such as Ram Head and Long Nose. By taking the decision to resurvey the east coast, Flinders delayed his arrival on the north coast.[41]

Voyaging up the east coast, Flinders surveyed mainland locations and offshore islands such as Hervey Bay, the entrance to Port Curtis, Keppel Bay, Port Bowen (now Port Clinton), the Northumberland Isles and Broad Sound. The scientific party botanized in several places. Flinders came across reefs that were 'a barrier to the coast.'[42] He sailed for about 500 miles inside the reefs, but could find no large opening. An exit was eventually found through a course now known as Flinders Passage into the open sea.[43] Flinders had followed the outer route of the Great Barrier Reef with more persistence than any previous navigator. He was uncertain whether his route followed 'the labyrinth of captain Cook,' but suspected the reefs reached as far north as Torres Strait.[44] The voyage up the east coast was hampered by the repeated failure of the *Lady Nelson* to keep near to the *Investigator*. After reaching the Great Barrier Reef, Flinders decided to send the *Lady Nelson* back to Port Jackson, expecting no further impediments from reefs.[45]

Flinders followed a course close to the Cape York peninsula. On 31 October, he anchored at Wednesday Island and took bearings. The *Investigator* was now at the entrance to Torres Strait. Flinders proceeded with caution owing to the formidable nautical dangers there. Despite hazards to navigation, he concluded, after finding clear water for most of his passage, that the challenges of sailing through Torres Strait were much less formidable than steering a passage through the Great Barrier Reef. Flinders sailed through Torres Strait in six days, but he believed it could have been accomplished in three.[46] He opted for a central route through the Strait, and established that this was the safest way of taking ships from the Pacific to the Gulf of Carpentaria.[47] Flinders later reported to Banks that finding a safe route through Torres Strait was one of the main navigational achievements of his expedition.[48]

The Gulf of Carpentaria and the North Coast

Flinders now headed for the Gulf of Carpentaria, a remote area for European navigators: no maritime explorer had entered it for nearly half a century. Flinders intended to examine it minutely. His running survey of the Gulf of Carpentaria occurred between 3 November 1802 and 6 March 1803. Flinders had a copy of an old Dutch chart of the Gulf, supplied to him by Dalrymple, but he did not have access to narratives of the Dutch voyagers who explored this coastline between 1623 and 1644.[49] The Dutch map proved problematic in identifying landmarks, however, because it had inaccuracies and relatively few names and details.[50] Flinders later stated that this map 'was considered little better than a representation of fairy land.'[51]

Flinders arrived in the Gulf of Carpentaria towards the end of the dry season when rivers experienced their minimum flow. He only identified one river in the Gulf – the Coen River, now known as the Pennefather River. He only made one landing on the eastern side of the Gulf where the water was deep enough to anchor his ship within reach of the shore.[52] On 16 November, Sweers Island was discovered. Flinders named it after Cornelius Sweers, a member of the Dutch Council in Batavia in 1644 and a signatory to Tasman's orders. A nearby well-sheltered passage was named Investigator's Road, which Flinders thought was the best place for a ship to anchor in the Gulf if an expedition was ever planned into the interior of Terra Australis.[53]

The *Investigator* remained at Investigator's Road for a week because its rotten timbers needed caulking. To identify the extent of the problem, the master and chief carpenter examined the physical state of the ship. Their report concluded that the ship could run for six months with little risk provided that she remained sailing in fine weather and had no accidents. Flinders was mortified to receive the report, as it placed his ambitious voyage in jeopardy. He reassessed the options available to him, should the ship's condition deteriorate. There was no possibility of turning back eastwards and heading back through Torres Strait owing to the prevalence of storms there at that time of the year and summer cyclones on the east coast.[54]

Flinders sailed on a westerly course, landing on several islands and surviving three small incidents of grounding. He took the whaleboat to explore passages between the islands. Near North Island two broken bark canoes and a piece of black rope were seen. Further signs of human activity were apparent on Wheatley Islet where Flinders and his companions found a small shade made of palm trees, with part of a bamboo cane lying nearby. On North Island, Brown reported seeing fire places with pieces of bamboo, coconut shells, small fragments of blue striped calico, a few baskets and small pieces of wood cut by an edged tool.[55] These were clearly signs of visitors. Flinders suspected that they were from China, but he had no idea why they were drawn to the Gulf of Carpentaria.[56]

After sailing around Groote Eylandt between 5 and 14 January 1803, Flinders and his scientific gentlemen landed on a small island with deep cavities between the cliffs. Flinders named this Chasm Island. An important find on this island comprised some Aboriginal art in caverns, consisting of drawings of porpoises, turtle, kangaroos and a human hand. Westall identified the representation of a kangaroo with a file of thirty-two people following after it, apparently done in charcoal. Flinders thought this painting had a symbolic meaning because the leader of the chase after the kangaroo was nearly twice as tall as the others.[57] Westall copied the paintings and made a watercolour copy of the scene with the kangaroo hunt. This is the first known European discovery of Aboriginal rock and cave paintings.[58]

Flinders now sailed in a north-east direction to Caledon Bay and Arnhem South Bay.[59] The *Investigator* had one of its most notable encounters when on 17 February 1803, it came across some Malay trepangers in the English Company Islands, situated to the north of the peninsula between Melville Bay and Arnhem Bay. The vessels were Malay praus from Makassar, on Sulawesi, formerly the territory of the Rajahs of Bone. Praus were the ships used in the Makasar trepang fleet. The trepang were taken to Timor and sold to Chinese ships for sale as a delicacy.[60] The meeting between Flinders, his ship's company and the trepangers was the first known occasion when Europeans and Asians met in Australian waters.[61]

Flinders met Pobassoo, the leader of the fleet of praus, who indicated he had been among the first of the Malays to trade for trepang on the coast of New Holland twenty years beforehand. Pobassoo had never seen a European ship on this shore before and did not know about the British settlement at Port Jackson.[62] Flinders named Malay Road (a roadstead) and Pobassoo Island to commemorate the meeting with the trepangers.[63] He recorded his meeting with the Makasars in detail partly because he thought the East India Company might want to enter into the trepang trade with Chinese markets.[64]

Leaving Malay Road on 27 February, the *Investigator* continued to Arnhem Bay. On 5 March, near the Wessel Islands, Flinders terminated his coastal survey of Australia owing to concerns about an exhausted crew and the seaworthiness of his vessel.[65] Flinders had probably carried on the survey too long. There had been indications for some time that the length of the voyage, wet weather and humid conditions had caused health problems for the sailors. Yet Flinders felt a duty to complete the survey and his personal ambition compelled him to carry out exploratory work for as long as possible. His prime duty now was to get the *Investigator* and her crew safely back to Port Jackson. The charts and descriptions of Australia's coastal landform and its flora, fauna and minerals could then be stored safely. It would also enable Flinders, or so he hoped, to have his ship repaired and to resume his survey.[66]

The return to Port Jackson

Fresh provisions were brought on board the *Investigator* in Timor and repairs made to the ship. Leaving Timor on 8 April, Flinders searched unsuccessfully for the Tryal Rocks where the English ship *Trial* had been wrecked in 1622. Owing to the state of the ship and the crew's health, Flinders was unable to conduct a running survey of Australia's north-west and west coasts. After rounding Cape Leeuwin, he continued along Australia's south coast and abandoned his intention to explore Kangaroo Island further. Disagreements arose between Flinders and the ship's surgeon, Hugh Bell, over the delays to the voyage on the north coast and their implication for the health of the crew. These recriminations led Flinders to write formal letters of admonishment to Bell.[67]

Several crew members died as the *Investigator* sailed from the south Australian coast towards Port Jackson. On arrival Flinders arranged for twelve sick crew members to be placed in the colonial hospital. Four were too exhausted to be removed and died within a few days. They included Good, the gardener, who died of dysentery.[68] The astronomer James Inman joined the *Investigator* at Port Jackson. He had been sent out by the Board of Longitude to replace Crosley, who had left the expedition at the Cape of Good Hope. Inman had been waiting nearly a year for the *Investigator* to arrive at Port Jackson. Now he began his work immediately by checking survey data gathered on the voyage in an observatory at Garden island in Sydney harbour.[69]

Flinders wrote letters to London about the progress of the voyage, and also persuaded Governor Philip Gidley King to approve of a detailed examination of the *Investigator*.[70] The ship was thoroughly investigated by two commanders of other vessels and by Thomas Moore, the master boatbuilder in New South Wales. Their signed report to Governor King came to an unequivocal conclusion: the ship was so defective 'that she is not worth repairing in any country, and that it is impossible in this country to put her in a state fit for going to sea.'[71] After negotiating with the governor for a replacement vessel, Flinders accepted the offer of the *Porpoise* for a return voyage to England where it was hoped that the Admiralty would supply another ship for him to return to Australia to complete his coastal surveys. On 22 July 1803, the *Investigator* was decommissioned. This marked the end of her voyage. Flinders agreed to the suggestion that Brown, Bauer and Allen would be best employed by remaining in Australia and awaiting Flinders's return. This would give them further opportunities to examine flora, fauna and minerals and to sketch and paint plants and wildlife.[72]

The aftermath

Flinders's return to England was unexpectedly eventful. The *Porpoise* left Sydney on 10 August 1803, with Flinders as a passenger. About five weeks later, it struck coral rock in the Great Barrier Reef and was wrecked. Most of the crew were stranded on what became known as Wreck Reef while Flinders took a cutter with a few associates to return to Port Jackson to seek help from Governor King. Three ships were provided to pick up the stranded crew – the *Cumberland*, the *Rolla* and the *Francis*. It took the ships six weeks to reach Wreck Reef. Some of the ships' companies stranded there decided to join the *Rolla*, which sailed to Canton and then returned in a fleet to England. But most of the *Investigator*'s crew stayed with Flinders in the *Cumberland*, which proceeded through Torres Strait and via Timor on a voyage across the Indian Ocean back towards England.[73]

When the *Cumberland* approached the Ile de France, Flinders decided to call there for fresh water, provisions and repairs. But the French governor of the island thought Flinders was a British spy and detained him there for six-and-a-half years before releasing him. The Napoleonic wars had resumed as Flinders was sailing across the Indian Ocean, and on arrival at the Ile de France he was shocked to be treated and imprisoned as an enemy. Flinders suffered physically and emotionally during this long confinement. However, after the initial upset of being detained, he spent his time at the Ile de France productively by compiling charts of his Australian circumnavigation and writing up a fair copy of his voyage log. Only after returning to London in the autumn of 1810 was Flinders able to arrange via Banks for the official publication of a voyage account accompanied by an atlas. Flinders spent the last four years of his life preparing these materials meticulously. His voyage account entitled *A Voyage to Terra Australis ...*, along with an atlas, was published just before he died in July 1814.[74]

The scientific gentlemen who remained at Port Jackson in August 1803 fared rather better. Brown and Bauer botanized and sketched in the Port Jackson area between August and November 1803. From then until August 1804, Brown visited Port Phillip and Van Diemen's Land and some islands in Bass Strait. He gathered 733 plants in Van Diemen's Land, including 230 specimens from the Port Dalrymple area and 248 from the River Derwent and Mount Wellington. Brown and Bauer sailed from Port Jackson back to England in October 1805, arriving with thirty-eight cases of natural history specimens and drawings. Banks arranged for employment for both Brown and Bauer so that they could consolidate their Australian work. Brown's appointment as librarian of the Linnaean Society, London, in January 1806 gave him time to classify, describe and catalogue thousands of Australia plants he had brought home. Bauer coloured his pencil sketches of life-size representation of plants, comparing his drawings with Brown's and Banks's herbaria in London and with living plants grown at Kew Gardens.[75]

Encounters with Aborigines

The extent of the encounters with Aborigines on the *Investigator* expedition was greater than on Cook's voyage in the *Endeavour*. Flinders and his colleagues came across Aborigines at King George Sound, Port Phillip, Sandy Cape and the Gulf of Carpentaria. But whereas Cook offered philosophical reflections about the state of happiness of the Aborigines in New South Wales, Flinders and his associates did not follow suit.[76] They nevertheless offered perceptive comments on the indigenous people they came across. Flinders usually described the Aborigines generically as Indians or natives; he rarely used collective nouns such as race, nation or tribe.[77]

Flinders and his associates perceived similarities and differences in the appearance and behaviour of Aborigines in different locations. Flinders reported that neither the males nor the females among the Aborigines he encountered at Caledon Bay wore clothing, that all the men had been circumcised, and that the upper left tooth of the men had been knocked out as a rite of puberty. At King George Sound, Flinders drew attention to the different words used for the same objects by natives at Port Jackson and Van Diemen's Land. He found their language was very different from the Aboriginal words he had previously heard at Botany Bay and Broken Bay – an accurate reflection of the considerable variation in Aboriginal language and dialects in different parts of Australia.[78]

Communication between the British explorers and the Aborigines was difficult because, in several places, the natives deliberately kept their distance from Flinders and his associates. Flinders used his trusted Aboriginal crew member, Bongaree, to communicate with indigenous people, but invariably he could not make himself understood by them, and vice versa. At Sandy Cape, when Bongaree, stripped naked as the natives were, tried to communicate with the Aborigines, he could not understand a word of their language. Further mystification followed when Bongaree used his woomera to throw a spear and the natives watched with incomprehension.[79]

Most encounters between Flinders and his party and different groups of Aborigines were friendly and peaceful. At King George Sound, Aborigines approached the tents of the European visitors, undertook some parleying, and exchanged implements for manufactured ironware. At Sandy Cape, about thirty Aborigines followed Flinders and his party back to their ship. Flinders gave them presents of red caps and tomahawks while the Aborigines handed over some buckets and nets.[80] But meetings between the personnel from the *Investigator* and the Aborigines were not always sweetness and light; occasionally clashes occurred. On such occasions, Flinders tried to defuse the friction. At Port Curtis, on the Queensland coast, a skirmish took place with Aborigines after they attacked Flinders's crew with a war whoop and a discharge of stones. This was the first unfriendly encounter with the Aborigines on the voyage.[81] At Caledon Bay, relations between the ship's company and local people deteriorated after Flinders detained an Aborigine called Woga in retaliation for an axe being stolen. But though there was a tense encounter between both groups, Flinders calmed down the situation by ordering Woga to be released.[82]

Encounters between Flinders and his associates and the Aborigines were compromised by misunderstandings. The best example of this in the entire voyage occurred at King George Sound when on 30 December 1801, after the marines landed on the shore, they staged a military parade. The Aborigines watched their red coats with white belts and their exercises, with fife and drum, with delight. The volleys of firing did not scare them. Curiosity and astonishment were conjured up in the 'vociferation and wild gestures' of the Aborigines.[83] This military exercise appears to have been staged to assess the Aborigines' response. The Aborigines appear to have interpreted the military drill as an appropriate contact ritual. In 1908, the anthropologist Daisy Bates met an elderly man near Albany called Nebinyan. He told her that the Nyungar Aborigines of King George Sound believed Flinders and his party were ghosts of their own dead ancestors who had returned from Kooranup, the home of the dead across the sea. They thought the full dress parade of the marines was a Kooranup ceremony. The ritual was considered sacred, to be handed down the generations.[84]

Scientific achievements

The *Investigator* expedition made a major contribution to the scientific knowledge of Australia and to the pictorial depiction of the flora and fauna seen there. Altogether Robert Brown collected 3,600 specimens of plants, one case of insects, three boxes of minerals and about 150 dried skins of birds in Australia. His rough estimate of his plant collection suggested that he had gathered 700 species from the south coast of Australia, 500 from the east coast, another 500 from the north-east coast, 1,000 from Port Jackson and its neighbourhood, 700 from Van Diemen's Land and 200 from Timor.[85] Brown's animal specimens from Terra Australis included twenty-three mammals, including five different kangaroo species, an echidna and three bats. He also brought back to England 217 samples of birds (150 species), 39 fish, 33 reptiles and amphibians, a platypus and 29 invertebrates other than insects.[86] Bauer undertook 2,073 sketches of plants, fungi and animals in Australia.[87]

With financial support from the Linnaean society and the Navy Board, Brown spent four years dealing with the botanical matters raised by the *Investigator* expedition. He lived a stone's throw from Banks's London residence in Soho Square, and liaised with his patron over the classification of his Australian natural history findings.[88] Brown found interesting novelties for the botanist, which were 'chiefly contained in the natural orders of *Protacae, Rubiacea, Companulcae & Orchidea*, each of which has afforded several new genera.'[89] Brown began to prepare a prodromus with full details of the genera. He hoped the French botanists from Baudin's expedition would not anticipate this by publishing their findings about New Holland.[90] Around this time, Bauer submitted to Banks a catalogue of his finished Australian drawings. He had coloured the sketches by following a code that was linked to the many sets of numbers on his sketches. The secret of his code has never been found.[91]

By April 1811, Brown had completed his arrangement and classification of Australia's fauna and flora; he had finished one volume and was working on a second. Bauer had completed 150 of the 2,000 drawings that Banks thought were most interesting for knowledge of botany and zoology. Among the Australian creatures sketched by Bauer were koala bears, the duck-billed platypus, the wombat, the butterfly cod fish, the southern bell frog and the black-footed rock wallaby. Brown was particularly interested in the Protea family of plants, which are common throughout Australia but are especially found in the region of the Great Barrier Reef. Brown examined the pollen grains from these plants with a microscope in order to assign the taxonomy of these genera. Brown's pollen studies were new branches of Botany while his microscopy laid foundations for the modern approach to plant anatomy.[92]

Brown identified and described over a third of the 12,000 plant species known in Australia today.[93] He liaised closely with Bauer in order to achieve his classifications by concentrated perusal of the botanical artist's detailed watercolours of floral and seed structure.[94] Brown examined plants at different stages of their development, and classified them according to families and genera. This led him towards the use of the Jussieu's natural system of classification, based on plant anatomy and physiology, rather than the Linnean method based on the reproductive organs of the stamen and pistils.[95]

In 1810 Brown, now Banks's librarian, produced a preliminary volume on his field investigations entitled *Prodromus Florae Novae Hollandiae et Insulae Van-Dieman, exhibens characters planterum quas innis 1802–1805...collegit descripsit R. Brown.* Unfortunately, the *Prodromus* had extremely poor sales. Brown, dismayed at the lack of interest in his work, withdrew it from sale. He decided not to publish the remainder of his findings. Nevertheless, Brown's botanical collections in Australia proved of lasting significance. His *Prodromus* described 464 genera and about 1,000 species.[96] Brown's work on Australian flora and fauna pioneered botanical arithmetic, which examined mathematical ratios between different families of plants in different latitudes. Botanists were strongly influenced by his work on plant anatomy and distribution studies.[97] Part of Brown's Australian collection is now housed at the Natural History Museum, London. In addition, Sydney's Royal Botanic Gardens has a Robert Brown building where researchers are still working on many matters related to plant classification and ecology which Brown pioneered.[98]

Bauer's finished plant drawings were notable for their botanical accuracy of the smallest and intricate parts of plant structure. They depicted not just the general form of the plant but the flowers, leaves, seeds, stamens, pollen grains and root structures. His drawings have a three-dimensional quality. They are very fine examples of artistic achievement as well as scientific accuracy. Bauer's watercolours are highly refined and precise depiction of plants. He was one of the first artists to depict the complete reproductive system of each plant. Several of his botanical illustrations were named after Banks, Brown and Bauer himself.[99]

Ten of Bauer's engraved plates were included in the atlas accompanying *A Voyage to Terra Australis*. Bauer also published, at his own expense, some botanical illustrations and engravings in *Illustrationes Florae Novae Hollandiae: sive icons generum quae* in *Prodromo Florae Novae Hollandiae et Insulae Van-Diemen descripsit Robertus Brown/Ferdinandi Bauer* (1813–16).[100] They were hand-coloured to an excellent standard and Bauer himself prepared the engraved plates. But, as with Brown's *Prodromus*, they sold only a few copies. Bauer completed his botanical drawings for publication between 1806 and 1819 in accordance with Admiralty instructions. His finished watercolour paintings are now in the Natural History Museum, London. Most of his sketches of Australian flora and fauna are deposited in Vienna's Natural History Museum.[101]

Artistic achievements

The young painter William Westall, aged only nineteen, complained that the *Investigator* expedition had not met his expectations. He noted that the Australian coast lacked sufficient variety to employ his 'pencil with any advantage to myself or my employers.'[102] To some extent, this sour judgement stemmed from the misfortune of seeing much of his topographic and descriptive artwork either lost or severely water damaged in the *Porpoise*'s wreck in 1803.[103] Nevertheless,

Westall had kept around 160 sketches, drawings and watercolours; these were returned to England in 1804. In 1809, Banks obtained a commission for Westall to prepare oil paintings to illustrate Flinders's published voyage account. Westall produced nine paintings that were engraved in copperplate for *A Voyage to Terra Australis*. Three of the oil paintings were exhibited at the Royal Academy in 1812. They attracted attention because of their novel depiction of a continent which few Europeans had visited.[104] The engraved illustrations featured in *A Voyage to Terra Australis* were issued separately by Rudolf Ackermann in February 1814, about five months before Flinders's voyage account was published, in de-luxe and cheaper editions. Westall's Australian art also appeared in his pencil field drawings on paper and some oil paintings on canvas.[105]

Westall sketched Australia's coastal landscape and its flora and fauna. He exercised a certain amount of artistic licence in these drawings. Thus, for example, his view of King George Sound in *A Voyage to Terra Australis* included drawings of trees seen by the artist at Port Jackson and in Spencer Gulf. Westall often provided more realism in his sketches than in his more stylized paintings.[106] He drew Aborigines, including two sketches of a native in Spencer Gulf and the body of an Aborigine shot on Morgan Island. He was the first European artist to make images of the indigenous cave paintings seen at Chasm Island in the Gulf of Carpentaria. He also drew a portrait of Pobassoo, the leader of the Makasar trepangers.[107]

As Bernard Smith has shown, Westall's Australian sketches reflected the concerns of the scientific gentlemen aboard ship and the main focal points of Flinders as commander of the voyage. Brown and Bauer's influence can be detected in Westall's detailed rendering of vegetation in his Australian landscapes, while Flinders's interest in geology and coastal surveys appears to have influenced Westall's sketching of the terrain. Though Westall never revisited Australia, he never forgot his sketches from the *Investigator* expedition. Just before his death in 1850 he was working on a painting of *Wreck Reef a Few Days after the Wreck of the Porpoise and the Cato*, now on loan to the National Museum, Greenwich, from the Ministry of Defence.[108]

Nautical achievements

Flinders and his brother Samuel undertook the astronomical calculations during the circumnavigation of Australia. This demanding task combined taking lunar observations with the times recorded on the chronometers. Timekeepers made by leading instrument makers John Crosley and Thomas Earnshaw were taken on the voyage. Arithmetical skills were needed to calculate longitude by lunar observations to allow for atmospheric refraction and lunar parallax. Chronometers needed to be regularly checked and wound up so that they gave correct readings. The occultation of stars, of Jupiter's satellites and of the aurora australis could not be recorded with the same exactitude and timeliness that a qualified astronomer could bring to the task. During daylight, astronomical calculations were made with sextants from the altitude of the Sun; at night-time, the altitudes of a fixed star were used to calculate longitude.[109]

Flinders's hydrographical expertise was vital for plotting the track of the *Investigator* and for indicating soundings for future navigators. Data gathered during the running surveys also provided essential information for maps, charts and survey sheets. To conduct running surveys, Flinders sailed as closely as possible to the coastline. When he had the opportunity to set up fixed stations on shore, he took more precise astronomical observations with the scientific instruments supplied by the Board of Longitude. Flinders was aware of the problem of magnetism affecting the compass readings on board ship. He therefore adjusted the record of his bearings before plotting his survey sheets.[110]

Flinders drew charts from his survey sheets in captivity at the Ile de France. The sheets included several innovations on previous practice by most hydrographers. Flinders showed the fixed points of his survey on land and the places from which bearings were taken. He distinguished between night-time and daytime tracks, something Dalrymple had suggested to him. He marked the difference between coasts he had examined and those parts copied from other sources. He distinguished his own soundings from those recorded by other hydrographers, and differentiated his own place names from those conferred by other explorers. He used arrows to indicate the strength of the tides, currents and winds.[111] Flinders wrote a detailed 'Memoir' in which he explained the marks used in his charts of Australia along with comprehensive material on obtaining and applying latitude and longitude and commentary on other nautical subjects connected with the expedition. The 'Memoir' serves as an explanatory text for the construction of his charts and atlas.[112]

After Flinders returned to England in 1810, it became clear that the astronomical data from the *Investigator*'s expedition would need to be completely recalculated before his charts and voyage account could be published. This was necessary owing to errors in the published *Nautical Almanac* that had been taken on the *Investigator*'s voyage. The astronomical recalculations were eventually undertaken by Crosley, but it took two years to carry out this task properly. Some 1,365 entries for each month had to be verified. Flinders insisted that the data checking should be undertaken accurately and comprehensively to preserve his reputation as a navigator, hydrographer and mapmaker.[113]

A voyage to Terra Australis

Flinders did not have the opportunity, or the authorization from the Admiralty, to compose and publish a voyage account or his charts until he returned to England in 1810. It was quickly agreed in January 1811, however, that he should proceed expeditiously in both tasks. The Admiralty liaised with Banks to oversee the draughtsmen and engravers employed to help with the task, and it was envisaged that Banks and Flinders should cooperate closely over preparation of the published voyage account. In keeping with the publication of Pacific voyages undertaken by Byron, Wallis, Carteret and Cook, it was expected that Flinders's volumes would be detailed tomes addressed to a professional readership. The main title of his voyage account was *A Voyage to Terra Australis*.[114] Flinders regularly visited Banks's London home to discuss progress. Through Banks's influence, the Arrowsmith firm was contacted to

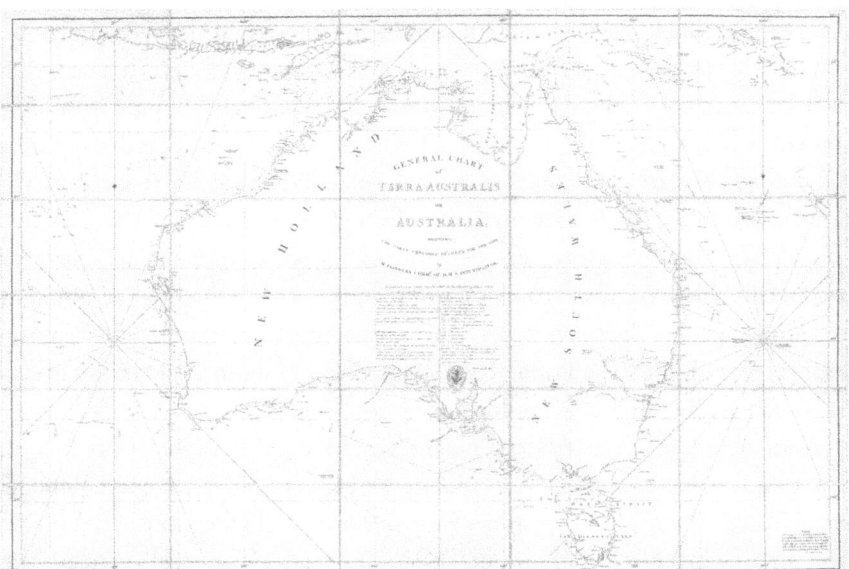

Map 18 *General Chart of Terra Australis or Australia: showing the parts explored between 1798 and 1803 by Matthew Flinders, Commander of H.M.S. Investigator* (London: Hydrographical Office of the Admiralty, 1822) MAP RM 1777 Bib ID 1729377

publish the charts and atlas. Flinders had maintained a cordial relationship with the Arrowsmiths since they published his charts of Bass Strait and Van Diemen's Land in 1800–1. The arrangement made with Arrowsmith over the publication was for eleven large charts and four smaller ones to be produced for the atlas. Flinders determined the scales of the charts and the number of copper plates needed.[115]

To write his voyage account and to produce his atlas, Flinders continued his long-established method of gathering all relevant cartographical information done by others and then synthesizing such findings with his own records of the voyage, which comprised his rough and fair journals, Bearing Book, survey sheets and astronomical calculations of the *Investigator* expedition. Flinders named 347 places he had discovered in Australia. These were all included in *A Voyage to Terra Australis*.[116] Flinders wrote an introduction to his book that, at over 200 pages, far exceeded the introductions to previously published voyage accounts.[117]

There were disagreements over the name to be attached to the Australian continent. Banks, Arrowsmith and Brown did not approve of the designation Terra Australis and used the name New Holland in their publications. Flinders, however, preferred the name Terra Australis on his charts, and he considered it would now be difficult to make alterations. By 1813, Flinders had convinced Banks that Terra Australis was an appropriate name to represent the existing New Holland and New South Wales by a collective name, though his own preference would have been to convert it to Australia.[118] Banks continued to use the appellation New Holland until 1820, but Governor Lachlan Macquarie used the name Australia in all of his correspondence. Official recognition of the name Australia was granted in 1830 with the publication in England of *The Australian Directory*.[119]

Two men who sailed with Flinders in the *Investigator* paid him handsome posthumous tributes. John Franklin, later a colonial governor and Arctic explorer, noted that Flinders's observations in *A Voyage to Terra Australis* were written 'with the greatest nicety and precision', while his charts were 'very superior' and 'will gain for him what he most desired, the character of a good navigator a man of perseverance and science'.[120] The botanist Brown considered that the thoroughness and accuracy of *A Voyage to Terra Australis* placed Flinders 'next to Cook among modern navigators'.[121] Flinders's atlas was widely used by maritime voyagers for well over a century and was not superseded until the era of aerial surveys.[122]

Conclusion

The *Investigator* expedition was a major landmark in the history of Australian maritime exploration. Never before had such a comprehensive voyage of discovery been assembled in relation to the discovery of Australia's coasts and offshore islands. Flinders, as commander of the voyage, displayed great expertise in handling the nautical and scientific aspects of the mission. Though misfortune beset him at various stages of the expedition, notably his detention as a suspected spy at the Ile de France on the homeward voyage, the investigations made by the *Investigator* were a substantial advance in the geographical knowledge of the Australian continent. Flinders added the names of hundreds of new places he explored to charts and maps and disproved the widely held contemporary belief that Australia was intersected by a great dividing strait. Among the new areas surveyed for the first time were the two great gulfs on Australia's south coast, many parts of the northern coast and islands in Bass Strait. Flinders navigated passages though Torres Strait and the Great Barrier Reef that located safe routes for navigators.

The *Investigator* expedition also had important scientific, artistic and literary outcomes. The botanical collections brought back new genera to Britain for research and classification. The assemblage of zoological specimens included animals unknown to Europeans. Brown began to produce a detailed prodromus of the botanical findings. Flinders acquired expertise in nautical astronomy and demonstrated that a combination of chronometers and lunar readings could pinpoint longitude accurately. He recorded his readings for coordinates systematically, and, after the expedition had ended, ensured that the data were professionally checked before they were disseminated. Westall produced paintings of coastal scenes in Australia that were exhibited and reproduced in Britain. Bauer's exquisite sketches and paintings of Australian flora and fauna were a further outcome of the voyage. Flinders toiled, while gravely ill, to complete his large tome dealing with the voyage – *A Voyage to Terra Australis* – and this was published, along with a detailed atlas, shortly before he died. And it was Flinders who urged that the name 'Australia' should be applied to the continent. In all these respects, the *Investigator* expedition gathered a greater amount of new factual information about Australia than any previous exploratory voyage.

9

Baudin's expedition

The most extensive French voyage of exploration to Terra Australis arose through the enthusiasm of its commander, Nicolas Baudin. Born a commoner, he was an officer in the French navy by 1778 but resigned two years later after being replaced by an officer from the nobility. In the decade after 1787, he sailed as an amateur botanist under the French and Austrian flags to the Caribbean and Mauritius, gaining valuable experience in transporting living specimens on long oceanic voyages. Serving as a post-captain in the French navy in 1798, he lobbied the French authorities for a scientific voyage of global discovery. He gained the support of the eminent naturalists Antoine Laurent de Jussieu and Bernard Germain de Lacépède, but did not receive the budget needed. Baudin was not deterred. He presented a more ambitious project, more deeply rooted in the Natural Sciences, to members of the Institut de France; to the First Consul, Napoléon Bonaparte; and to the Minister of Marine, Pierre-Alexandre-Laurent Forfait. Baudin made a strong case for the furtherance of French scientific endeavours and the need to compete with British voyages of exploration. Napoleon accepted Baudin's revived proposal in 1800, and plans were swiftly made to mount the expedition.[1]

Baudin's mission was the climax of French voyages to the South Seas in the Enlightenment, but also the most complex, volatile French expedition ever mounted to Australia. Unharmonious relations existed during the voyage between Baudin and his associates, particularly the scientific experts. Baudin had a much larger group of scientists than he wanted. Moreover, many of his officers and midshipmen were young, inexperienced and not well disposed towards an older commander.[2] But tensions also stemmed from quarrels between those associates and from dissemination of the expedition's findings by two of the scientists, François Péron and Louis de Freycinet, who were hostile to Baudin. Their voyage account, published after Baudin's death, denigrated their commander's reputation as a navigator and leader. Only in recent decades has the Baudin's mission been reevaluated, bringing out the merits and demerits of the voyage's leadership and its legacy.[3]

Forfait drew up instructions for the geographical scope of the expedition. He provided details and a schedule for Baudin to explore the southeastern, western and northern coasts of New Holland in what would effectively be a circumnavigation of Australia. The east coast was omitted because Cook had already undertaken that task thoroughly. Baudin was enjoined 'to determine precisely the geographical position of the principal points along the coasts that he will visit and to chart them exactly, as to study the inhabitants, animals and natural products of the countries in which he will land.'[4] The instructions offered the hope that Australia might be not just one continent but two, with a strait running from the Gulf of Carpentaria to the islands of St Francis and St Peter off the south coast. If this were proven, Australia might be shown to consist of two very large islands. A similar suggestion also lay behind Flinders's contemporaneous voyage.[5]

Forfait's instructions singled out particular parts of Australia's coasts that needed exploration: a general survey of Bass Strait; an examination of the east coast of Van Diemen's Land and its offshore islands, as far north as Banks Strait near the Furneaux Group; the south coast from the 145th to the 129th meridian, especially the St Peter and St Francis Islands; the west coast between the 21st and 22nd parallels; and, if possible, an examination of the Gulf of Carpentaria.[6] A strict time schedule was laid down. The expedition was to leave Le Havre in October 1800, arrive at Van Diemen's Land by late March 1801, and to have charted the mainly unknown coast of New Holland by the end of June 1801.[7]

Experts at the Institut de France planned the expedition's scientific objectives. The scientific staff selected for the voyage included the zoologist and doctor François Péron; the zoologist René Maugé; two geographers who also undertook hydrography, Charles-Pierre Boullanger and Pierre Faure; the natural history painter Charles Alexandre Lesueur; the genre painter Nicolas-Martin Petit; the gardener Anselme Riedlé; and the astronomer Pierre Bernier. Baudin took sixty scientists on the expedition and 251 men altogether. His ships had the 'largest and best-qualified team ever to leave Europe on a voyage of discovery.'[8] Baudin's expedition carried four chronometers by Ferdinand Berthaud, the official supplier for the French navy.[9]

Sir Joseph Banks played a significant role in obtaining passports for Baudin's expedition. Though concerned that France was stealing a march over Britain in terms of exploration, his scientific interests and belief in the Enlightenment Republic of Letters led him to offer his influential cooperation.[10] As the previous chapter has shown, Baudin's expedition was contemporaneous with the expedition led by Flinders to circumnavigate Australia. But though the two sets of voyages had connections, which will be referred to below, it is simplistic and erroneous to view them as participating in a race to chart Australia.[11]

Despite Anglo-French imperial rivalry, Baudin's mission was a scientific expedition rather than a voyage motivated by political ends.[12] It is unknown whether Napoleon considered any political implications for Baudin's expedition. The only section in Fleurieu's instructions that could be viewed in a political light was the order to verify whether Britain had established a settlement in the D'Entrecasteaux Channel in Van Diemen's Land.[13] Yet there is no evidence that Baudin had secret instructions to establish a place of settlement there.[14] Though Baudin's mission was not motivated by political objectives, the political allegiance of its participants was a latent factor in the connections between the officers and scientists.

On 18 October 1800, the expedition got under way from Le Havre. Baudin was the commander of the *Géographe*. His second-in-command, Emanuel Hamelin, was in charge of the accompanying vessel, the *Naturaliste*. They were extensively rebuilt before the expedition began, with the numbers of guns reduced and an extra deck provided in each case.[15] Before starting the mission, Baudin had emphasized to Hamelin that their two vessels should stay within sight of one another, avoid the risk of separation, and assist one another when needed. Baudin prepared a system of signals for the two ships to communicate with one another, and also named the rendezvous points, should a separation occur.[16] In the first weeks of the voyage, the *Naturaliste* proceeded slowly and Baudin criticized Hamelin's failure to send frequent signals.[17]

The vessels arrived at the Ile de France on 15 March 1801, having lost about six weeks' sailing time through not observing the optimal route. Discontent had arisen among many men on board the vessels. Baudin clumsily tried to instil discipline on his officers, midshipmen and scientists. As a result of poor navigational choices and an inability to quell dissent among the ships' company, rumours circulated that Baudin was an incompetent commander. Ten scientists left the voyage and twenty-one crew deserted. To lose so many of the ship's company at an early stage of the voyage is testimony to the bickering and dissatisfaction that were rife.[18] The French authorities on the island were largely uncooperative. Storehouses at the Ile de France were depleted because war with Britain had interrupted connections with the Cape of Good Hope, then under British control, from which fresh provisions were normally sought. Baudin was forced to borrow supplies from an old acquaintance serving as Danish Consul at the Ile de France.[19]

On 25 April, the expedition resumed, crossing the Indian Ocean expeditiously and arrived at Cape Leeuwin on 27 May 1801, two months behind schedule. Baudin headed for Western Australia. On 30 May the *Géographe* and *Naturaliste* anchored north of Cape Leeuwin in a bay that Baudin named after his ship. Geographe Bay was the first major geographical discovery of the expedition in New Holland. Baudin came across Aborigines there. Though they were fairly passive and did not threaten the French intruders, Baudin found they were indifferent to presents – something previous explorers had found – and of little use as a source of trade supplies. The *Géographe* and the *Naturaliste* were separated in a gale on 9 June. Baudin did not see Hamelin's vessel for another three months.[20]

Exploring Western Australia

On reaching an Australian landfall, Baudin departed from his instructions and began an exploration of the west coast in order to avoid stormy winter weather sailing under Australia's south coast. Perhaps he realized, in addition, that bad weather would increase the chances of becoming separated from the *Naturaliste*. Péron and the expedition's naval officers were disappointed at this decision, believing the winter season was not so advanced as to preclude a passage to Van Diemen's Land.[21] Their criticisms were unheeded. On 14 June, Baudin left Geographe Bay, having agreed with Hamelin that if their vessels became separated they should rendezvous at Rottnest Island. The *Géographe* approached Rottnest Island twice in bad weather but missed the *Naturaliste*, which was anchored between the island and the mouth of the Swan River on the mainland.[22] While waiting for Baudin at Rottnest Island, Hamelin surveyed the island and sent a boat to the mainland to investigate the Swan River. The river was found unsuitable for supplying the water needed for a ship: the entry into its mouth was difficult and its course was obstructed by many sandbanks and shallows.[23]

Baudin sailed north to the west of the Houtman Abrolhos. He did not stop at Dirk Hartog Island because it 'looked arid, disagreeable and dreary'.[24] The *Naturaliste*, by contrast, stopped there and found a corroded plaque of lead or tin commemorating the visits of Hartog and Vlamingh. Hamelin arranged for the plaque to be restored to its former position on a new post. The *Géographe* reached Shark Bay on 27 June, a second place of rendezvous agreed with Hamelin.[25] Baudin spent two weeks there, noting that 'the Dutch were very careful in taking the bearings of this whole coastline.'[26] Dampier's work in this vicinity was treated more critically. Baudin was surprised that Dampier had given the name Shark Bay to gulfs, harbours and bays that stretched beyond what would normally be given those designations. In and around Shark Bay, the gardener Riedlé found seventy plant specimens and the zoologist Maugé collected ten species of birds which he thought were new. However, Baudin made no attempt to leave a message at a signal flag on Shark Bay for Hamelin to find, should he arrive there.[27]

Failing to come across the *Naturaliste* at Shark Bay, Baudin set out on 14 July for North West Cape. The *Naturaliste* arrived at Shark Bay three days after Baudin had sailed, and stayed there for forty-nine days. Baudin hoped to determine the exact location of North West Cape and to survey the northwest Australian coast. He derived readings for the position of the cape, an important visible landmark for mariners approaching Western Australia from the Indian Ocean. Unfortunately, his readings were incorrect because his chronometer had increased significantly since his observations at Shark Bay.[28] Baudin, in fact, placed North West Cape 10' of latitude north of its actual location, a significant error.[29]

The *Géographe* was hampered by contrary winds and strong currents on Australia's northwest coast and, consequently, the hydrographical achievements were limited. The lack of a longboat, which had been lost in Geographe Bay, ruled out investigations of shores. Poor navigational conditions made it impossible to attempt an accurate survey of the coast. Coastal waters were full of coral reefs, banks and shoals that impeded surveying. Despite these difficulties, Baudin identified various islands and islets, especially in the Bonaparte archipelago, in dangerous, largely uncharted waters.[30] He found the sterile and monotonous landscape of much of the west Australian coast desolate: it was dominated by sand dunes, bald cliffs and low-lying scrub.[31]

Baudin checked his copy of Dampier's *A Voyage to New Holland* against his own observations. He was not convinced by Dampier's accuracy. The chain of islands referred to by Dampier off northwest Australia 'does not run, as he says, from East to South of the Rosemary Islands.' Moreover, the English navigator had written that the tides were not very strong in Semau Strait, near Timor, but Baudin found a fairly swift current there.[32] Péron's account of the voyage, continued by Louis de Freycinet, was scathing about the 'absolute ignorance' displayed in Dampier's details of Shark Bay.[33]

On 19 August 1801, Baudin headed for Timor because his supplies of wood and water were running dangerously low. The *Naturaliste* arrived there a month later. Baudin and Hamelin's reunion appears to have been friendly, with no bad feelings expressed about the separation of their vessels. Baudin became seriously ill with a fever and several crew members died at Timor from dysentery, including Riedlé. Both ships left Timor for a voyage to the south on 13 November. Illness and death continued to occur, with eleven men dying on the voyage. Baudin headed for Van Diemen's Land, reaching the narrow D'Entrecasteaux Channel, on the south of the island, on 13 January 1802.[34] Approaching an anchorage in Recherche Bay, Baudin encountered bad weather but 'the map given in the account of D'Entrecasteaux's voyage seemed to us to have been extremely carefully done, so we put all our trust in it and were guided by it.'[35]

Van Diemen's Land

D'Entrecasteaux's expedition left a positive account of the fertility of Van Diemen's Land. Baudin stayed there for nearly two months. On 14 January 1802, small boats were sent to explore the Huon River, Port Esperance and the Swan River. Baudin had strained relations with many of his crew and associates during this period: he openly criticized the inefficiency and indiscipline of many among his ship's company.[36] The friction partly arose because Baudin, though an amateur naturalist, believed he was as qualified scientifically as the experts who sailed with him.[37] Despite the lack of harmony between the commander and his crew, the stopover in Van Diemen's Land led to significant hydrographical work, the naming of new landscape features, the collection of botanical specimens, and encounters with Aborigines.

Baudin's instructions for exploring the D'Entrecasteaux Channel were to follow Beautemps-Beaupré's charts drafted during the d'Entrecasteaux expedition's stay in Van Diemen's Land and to explore the rivers and poorly charted coast to the north-east of the channel. Baudin and Hamelin discussed the surveys needed to complete d'Entrecasteaux's observations in 1793. They agreed to send two parties to achieve this. One was despatched to follow the course of the Derwent River to its source. The other was tasked with examining Tasman's Frederick Henry Bay, which Beautemps-Beaupré's charts showed as a possible strait leading to the open sea.[38]

Fleurieu's instructions had pointed out that the east coast of Van Diemen's Land, from Cape Pillar to Banks Strait, needed investigation. The expedition accordingly surveyed Frederick Henry Bay, the Tasman peninsula, Norfolk Bay, North Bay, Oyster Bay, the Freycinet peninsula and the coast as far as

42° latitude south. It was discovered that the Tasman peninsula was not an island, as d'Entrecasteaux thought; that Frederick Henry Bay did not exist where Beautemp-Beaupré's chart had placed it; and that Marion Bay was only a roadstead in front of Frederick Henry Bay. Despite these corrections, members of Baudin's expedition had great respect for the overall accuracy of Beautemps-Beaupré's geographic work.[39]

The southern part of the east coast was mainly explored in boat parties.[40] Baudin knew that Furneaux was the first to discover that coast in 1773 but was unable to examine it carefully because of bad weather. Furneaux had omitted the observations that provided the basis for constructing his chart. Flinders had sailed fairly close along the east coast in 1799, but he altered nothing in Furneaux's work and provided no nautical or topographical details of his own. Numerous low-lying, narrow isthmuses meant that 'one must explore these coasts from very close quarters in order not to be mistaken as to their real formation.'[41] Baudin noted that north of Maria Island 'it seems that Tasman and Furneaux sailed too far out from the land to study it well, and that sighting some isolated bluffs and being unable to see the low-lying lands connecting them, they made islands of them.'[42] Péron and some associates inspected Maria Island and found many errors in John Henry Cox's survey of the vicinity in 1789. These investigations enabled Baudin and his associates to produce accurate charts that advanced the capable work undertaken on the east coast of Van Diemen's Land by d'Entrecasteaux's expedition a decade earlier.[43]

Several crew members encountered Aborigines. They proved 'to be gentle and affable' but 'long conversations ensued of which no-one understood anything.' Baudin's crew offered gifts to the natives and spent a day in their company. The Aborigines were interested in the Frenchmen's meals but refused to accept any food. Second-in-command in the *Naturaliste* Pierre Bernard de Milius and his companions noted the nakedness of the 'hideously unclean' women.[44] After a few days at Recherche Bay, the two ships moved to an anchorage on the southern end of Bruny Island and then to Oyster Bay on Maria Island.[45]

Further encounters with the Aborigines in Van Diemen's Land were largely harmonious except for two incidents where, respectively, a spear and stones were thrown at the French intruders. The indigenous people accepted presents willingly and displayed an interest in the newcomers. The French navigators 'mingled together without any distrust or fear of each other.'[46] The Aborigines were worried at the sight of guns carried by the French men, but fascinated by the metal buttons they wore.[47] The French explorers recorded the Aborigines' way of life. Baudin noted that the natives were familiar with firearms; out of curiosity, he recorded their eating habits.[48] Péron thought the Aborigines on Maria Island were 'very intelligent and they easily grasped the meaning of all my gestures and seemed to understand both their object and their purpose.'[49]

Baudin's expedition made a poor haul of botanical and zoological specimens in Van Diemen's Land. Inland excursions from the D'Entrecasteaux Channel only located forty shrubs. There were, it is true, some significant finds. At Maria Island, for example, Péron gathered specimens of the Tasmanian marsupial mouse and probably the Australian water-rat.[50] However, the scientific results of the stay in Van Diemen's Land were hampered for various reasons. The senior zoologist Maugé and his assistant became seriously ill and died.[51]

On 2 March 1802, the *Géographe* lost sight of the *Naturaliste* in the mist.[52] The two ships headed off in different directions. Baudin sailed for the south coast of New Holland, while Hamelin sailed south from the north coast of Van Diemen's Land in search of Baudin.[53] The separation of the two ships lasted for four months. Hamelin looked for Baudin in several locations. The *Naturaliste* and the *Géographe* were both looking out for each other in Banks Strait in mid-March 1802, but without luck. After concluding he would not come across the *Géographe*, Hamelin headed in the *Naturaliste* for Port Jackson.[54]

The south coast

Baudin sailed with the *Géographe* to explore the southern coast of New Holland to the vicinity where Nuyts had curtailed his voyage sailing from the west in the 1620s. Baudin was unaware that James Grant had made two voyages to Bass Strait in 1800–1, but he was able to survey the south coast of New South Wales and Victoria more carefully than Grant. Manuscript charts of this coast were produced, with place names supplied by Baudin.[55] When Baudin reached 140°44'E on 2 April 1802 and sighted the inland peak of Mount Schanck, he had come to a coast previously uncharted by any European. Baudin was ill for much of this stage of the voyage, suffering from tuberculosis, the effects of malaria and colic pains in his lower abdomen.[56] Whether these complaints impinged on his appetite for discovery is difficult to say, but he showed no interest in examining Port Phillip Bay. There may have been other reasons why he made that decision, however, including the need to adhere to the timings expected for his itinerary and perhaps the desire not to impinge too much on British colonial interests.[57]

A surprise encounter, recounted in detail in the previous chapter, occurred on 8/9 April 1802 when the *Géographe* sighted a ship in Encounter Bay. Initially,

Baudin and his ship's company thought they had found the *Naturaliste*, but the ship sighted was the *Investigator*, under Matthew Flinders, engaged on a circumnavigatory voyage of Australia. Baudin must have been disappointed to find that Flinders had pre-empted him in surveying much of the unknown coast because the French mission, if it had kept to its original schedule, would have completed its survey of the south coast before Flinders.[58] One of the French officers, Henri de Freycinet, later blamed Baudin for the delays when he remarked to Flinders: 'Captain, if we had not been kept so long picking up shells and catching butterflies at Van Diemen's Land, you would not have discovered the south coast before us.'[59] This was a disloyal, though factually correct, comment to Baudin by one of his officers.[60]

John West-Sooby and Jean Fornasiero have recently argued that the meeting in Encounter Bay had several significant implications for Baudin's expedition. First, because the *Investigator* had made discoveries on the south coast before the French arrival there, it reinforced the view held by the French officers that their commander was incompetent. Second, numerous comments by the French scientists and officers indicate their consternation at finding out that their expedition had a serious rival who was ahead of them in exploring Australian waters. Third, Péron's unpublished remarks on Flinders show that he was impressed by him as a navigator and explorer and that he wrongly believed Flinders was following a British plan to colonize the entire Pacific region. Fourth, Baudin reacted to his meetings with Flinders at Encounter Bay and later at Port Jackson by attempting to complete the exploration of parts of Australia not yet seen by Flinders – the charting of the Hunter Islands in Bass Strait and the north coast of Van Diemen's Land and the circumnavigation of Kangaroo Island.[61]

After the meeting with Flinders at Encounter Bay, Baudin sailed westerly to explore the south coast.[62] Shallow water prevented him from penetrating the upper reaches of Gulf St Vincent and Spencer Gulf, which Flinders had already surveyed. The sickness of many crew members impeded the voyage's progress. Yet Baudin continued westerly to explore the mainland behind the islands of St Peter and St Francis. He was determined to see these 'almost legendary islands' that marked the end of the unknown coast.[63] It was later noted that one object of the voyage was to resolve 'the question of New Holland's being one land mass and that of the presence or absence of any big river on this vast continent.'[64] Circumstances, however, made this difficult to pursue. On 8 May, Baudin altered his plans and headed first for D'Entrecasteaux Channel and then Port Jackson.[65]

On 20 May, the *Géographe* anchored at Adventure Bay on the east side of Bruny Island. This was considered the best-watered part of Van Diemen's Land

and possibly the only one where, in all seasons, one could easily obtain fresh water.[66] The weather was so bad that an attempt to survey the uncharted part of the east coast of Van Diemen's Land was abandoned. Nevertheless, it was later claimed that the exploratory work undertaken by Freycinet and Boullanger in Van Diemen's Land meant that 'the coastal geography of this, great southern island was entirely completed by our efforts.'[67]

Port Jackson

Baudin left his anchorage on 4 June and headed north to Port Jackson, which he reached on 20 June. This was the first official French visit to New South Wales.[68] Coincidentally, the *Naturaliste* also arrived there a week later.[69] Banks had contacted Philip Gidley King, the New South Wales governor, with a hunch that the Baudin expedition would visit the British convict colony at Port Jackson. The first French ship to arrive there was the *Naturaliste*, which remained in the harbour between 26 April and 18 May 1802. Hamelin hoped to find the *Géographe* at Sydney Cove, but on arrival there was no sight of Baudin and his ship. Governor King, a Francophile who had met Lapérouse at Port Jackson in 1788, greeted the French visitors with a dinner reception at Government House.[70] This was a relief to Hamelin, who had been apprehensive that he might not receive a friendly welcome.[71]

The French spent their time productively at Port Jackson. They set up tents for an observatory at Green Point in Sydney harbour. Their scientists collected shells and plants. New provisions were taken on board the *Naturaliste*. On 11 May, news that the Treaty of Amiens had led to a cessation of hostilities between Britain and France reached Port Jackson, where it was greeted favourably by both the British colonists and the French visitors. Flinders arrived in port during Hamelin's stay at Port Jackson, bringing news that Baudin intended to come there. But Hamelin did not wait for his commander, leaving Port Jackson possibly because he felt uncomfortable in a British colony even though civilities were courteously observed between himself and Governor King.[72] As mentioned above, however, the *Naturaliste* returned to Sydney in late June.

After the *Géographe* and the *Naturaliste* were reunited at Port Jackson, where they remained for more than five months. Governor King received them cordially.[73] Baudin stopped writing his journal during this pause in the voyage. But at Timor in 1803, he submitted a detailed report to the authorities in France with observations on the growth and prosperity of the English colony based around Port Jackson. He was impressed by the growth of the British settlement there, then just fourteen years old, and recognized that this was part of Australia that could be colonized successfully.[74] Baudin and his crew realized that the coasts they had seen were part of one continent, and it was apparent that the main commercial centre was Port Jackson.[75]

Péron and Freycinet spent time at Port Jackson compiling information on the British settlement there. They observed details of the population and trade at Port Jackson, the organization of daily life and the implications of the success of this settlement for France. Freycinet later produced a private, unsigned report outlining how the French might invade Port Jackson. After the end of the expedition, Péron wrote a report that highlighted the strategic position that Britain had achieved through its presence at Port Jackson. Péron and Freycinet, it must be assumed, were spying on the British outpost for political purposes. This was later the view of Governor Lachlan Macquarie of New South Wales. There is no evidence that Baudin was party to the spying.[76]

At Port Jackson, Baudin prepared for the next stage of his voyage to the south, west and north coasts of New Holland. He arranged for his sick crew to be treated in the local hospital; ordered food and drink supplies for his ship; arranged for repairs for the *Géographe*; and oversaw his scientists' collection of animal, plant and mineral specimens.[77] Lesueur and Petit painted portraits, ethnographic landscapes and settlement scenes depicting the Aborigines of Port Jackson.[78] Peron considered that Port Jackson's Aborigines differed in their origins from indigenous people he had observed in Van Diemen's Land.[79]

The sojourn at Port Jackson also witnessed a fuller emergence of animosity between Baudin and some of his officers, who resented their commander's lower social status. Baudin ordered several troublemakers to leave the voyage to return home, but this only exacerbated existing tensions between him and his men.[80] The Frenchmen intermingled with Flinders and his ship's company while in Port Jackson. 'Captain Flinders…often had us to dinner on board his ship,' Milius noted. 'He seemed to be a most distinguished officer and to be very well educated. He had already made several voyages along this coast and we were grateful to him for some very useful information for the next stage of our trip.'[81]

At Port Jackson, Baudin rethought the next part of his expedition, relying on fewer men, greater efficiency, and the intention of revisiting parts of Australia already seen to produce charts of high quality. He bought a schooner of thirty tons, the *Casuarina*, for exploring coves and inlets in shallow waters. A few weeks later, he informed Hamelin that the *Casuarina* would replace the *Naturaliste*, which he was sending back to France with a substantial number of specimens collected by the scientists. The *Géographe*, the *Casuarina* and the *Naturaliste* sailed from Port Jackson on 18 November 1802. They anchored at King Island, in Bass Strait, where preparations were made for the return of the *Naturaliste* to France. The island had never been properly surveyed so Baudin sent the geographer Faure in a longboat to carry out that task.[82]

Governor King, believing the French might plan a settlement in Bass Strait, sent the *Cumberland* to follow the French vessels to King Island. Baudin was surprised at the arrival of this English colonial vessel at King Island. He dined with its officers but noted that their motive for the voyage was not mentioned even though he himself realized that the purpose of their arrival was to watch the French explorers.[83] Baudin sent a letter to King to discount suspicions that the French intended to form a settlement at King Island.[84] Charles Robbins, in command of the *Cumberland*, placed an English flag on King Island near the French tents in order to claim British possession. Baudin did not request an explanation from Robbins, but noted that 'the incident confirmed that he had been dispatched to observe us, rather than to hand me the unimportant letter that Governor King sent me on that occasion.'[85]

Péron enquired from sealers about the emus he came across on King Island. The *Casuarina*, under Louis de Freycinet's command, charted the Hunter Group of islands, including detailed inshore surveying.[86] Flinders had been unable to determine the exact number of these islands, their relationship or their particular configuration, so this exploratory work was able to provide new geographical information. By the end of 1802, Baudin had completed his work in Bass Strait. He had lost his longboat there. His naturalists had not gathered an impressive haul of specimens on King Island.[87]

From Bass Strait to Timor

After wishing the *Naturaliste* a safe passage to the Ile de France, the *Géographe* and the *Casuarina* sailed in a westerly direction from Bass Strait. The two ships sailed together to Kangaroo Island and surveyed its south side, which neither Baudin nor Flinders had seen. The west and south coasts of the island were surveyed and charted for the first time.[88] New species in groups ranging from seals and lizards to birds and fish were identified at Kangaroo Island. The western grey kangaroo and the dwarf emu were two animals collected there. Exploration on Kangaroo Island provided Péron with 336 specimens of mollusc, crustacean, arachnid, insect, worm and zoophyte.[89]

Freycinet in the *Casuarina* surveyed Spencer Gulf and Gulf St Vincent while Baudin in the *Géographe* examined the southern coast of Australia between the islands of St Peter and St Francis and Denial Bay.[90] However, a disappointment came with the failure to locate a vast strait separating New Holland from New South Wales on the mainland behind the Nuyts archipelago. It was found that Nuyts's chart of 1627 relating to the islands of St Peter and St Francis was inaccurate.[91] In his journal, Baudin noted that at the St Francis Isles 'we finished our bearings of the South and South-Western coasts of New Holland, and I have no doubt that the chart we shall provide of them, combined with the published one of General d'Entrecasteaux's voyage, will supply exact knowledge of the whole of this area, so long unknown to Europeans.'[92]

Baudin and Freycinet were separated between Spencer Gulf and the St Peter and St Francis islands. The *Géographe* and the *Casuarina* continued to sail westwards separately. They did not meet again until they reached King George Sound in mid-February 1803. Freycinet and Péron held Baudin responsible for the ships' divergence. When Baudin and Freycinet were reunited at King George Sound, they were on poor terms with one another. Baudin decided to remain there to survey the area because D'Entrecasteaux had sailed past it in 1792. Baudin sent out a boat to explore the coast minutely between Vancouver's Mount Gardner and D'Entrecasteaux's Bald Island to locate a haven for future navigators.[93]

Before leaving King George Sound on 1 March 1803, Baudin handed sealed orders to Freycinet that were only to be opened at sea. It is unsurprising that he wanted the contents undisclosed before sailing as the orders stated that, in the event of another separation between the *Géographe* and the *Casuarina*, Freycinet would be responsible for the expenses incurred.[94] Heading north from Cape Leeuwin, Baudin seemed undecided whether to survey the west coast thoroughly or to proceed to the Gulf of Carpentaria. The *Géographe* did not undertake a running survey of the mainland coast; instead, it made several coastal contacts and left the *Casuarina* to undertake a small amount of inshore work.[95]

Baudin thought his second reconnaissance of the land between Cape Leeuwin and Rottnest Island was more satisfactory than that made a year earlier. He did not follow the coast from Rottnest Island to Shark Bay, however, because it had already been well charted by the Dutch. At Shark Bay, he found an anchorage that was 'the most secure and commodious of all that we had been in on the coast of New Holland.'[96] A hostile confrontation occurred here between Baudin's ship's company and more than a hundred Aborigines who prevented a fishing party from the *Géographe* from landing. Baudin had anticipated such trouble might arise somewhere during the voyage. To his credit, he had briefed his men carefully about avoiding bloodshed and calming down the natives.[97]

Baudin's plans underscored the need for a thorough investigation of Australia's northwest coast from North West Cape to the Bonaparte Archipelago. He had surveyed this coast earlier in the voyage. He now redid that work to provide more accurate charting but encountered the same impediments as on the previous occasion: a plethora of offshore islands were difficult to distinguish from one another because of extensive reefs and sandbanks. Baudin covered 1,000 miles of the northwest coast but admitted that a thorough survey of all the inlets, islets, capes and coves would take ten years. On 29 April 1803, with weak winds, a sick crew and feeling seriously unwell himself, Baudin interrupted his survey of northwest Australia to head for a second time to Timor.[98]

Baudin reached Timor on 7 May 1803. Baudin wanted to resume the survey of Australia's northwest coast, but he became seriously unwell. On 7 July, Baudin curtailed his survey and headed for the Ile de France. Biscuit rations ran low, serious sickness continued among the crew, and Baudin was so unwell that he remained mainly confined to his cabin. The *Géographe* reached the Ile de France on 7 August. Most of the ship's crew were taken immediately to hospital on arrival, including Baudin. Several deaths occurred. Baudin himself died, probably of tuberculosis, on 16 September.[99] Despite the ill health and crew deaths, Baudin's expedition fared better than some others in maintaining the crew's lives: the overall death toll on the expedition was 13.5 per cent. This compares well with the 25 per cent loss of men on Flinders's circumnavigation of Australia and the voyages of Cook and d'Entrecasteaux, where the figures were nearer to 40 per cent.[100]

The *Casuarina* arrived at the Ile de France on 28 September where she was decommissioned and the crew transferred to the *Géographe*, now under the command of Milius. The *Géographe* returned to France, with a large haul of natural specimens, arriving at Lorient, Brittany on 25 March 1804. The *Naturaliste*, commanded by Hamelin, had returned to Le Havre almost nine months earlier, in June 1803. Some thirty-three large cases of botanical specimens and preserved animals were disembarked. Most of these cases were transported to the Muséum d'Histoire naturelle, Paris. Ethnographic collections and live animals, however, were taken to Malmaison, the Empress Josephine's Paris retreat and park.[101]

Attitudes towards Aborigines

The time spent in Van Diemen's Land enabled the voyagers to study several groups of Aborigines closely, namely the Nuenonne band of Bruny Island, the Lylquonny of Recherche Bay, the Tyredeme of Maria Island and the Pydairrerme of Tasman peninsula.[102] Baudin approached the Aborigines cautiously, insisting that his ship's company should be careful with their guns when they saw natives because the Aborigines were frightened by a gun 'even if one just touches it.' Such restraint was mixed with a somewhat negative view of Aborigines that Baudin appears to have derived, at least in part, from Dampier's reflections in *A Voyage to New Holland*, which Baudin had in his library on the *Géographe*. But Baudin also knew that previous French voyages had received hostile reactions from native peoples in the Pacific, notably the killing of some of Lapérouse's men in Samoa and the murder of Marion Dufresne in New Zealand. Baudin was therefore uneasy about how Aborigines might react to French intruders.[103] During the entire voyage, however, open hostility by the Aborigines to the French occurred only twice. On one occasion, a spear was thrown; on another, stones.[104]

Péron initially regarded Aborigines as a benign people living in harmony with their surroundings. He was clearly influenced by the noble savage tradition in European thought. Péron changed his views, however, as the expedition proceeded. Encountering indigenous people on Maria Island, he thought they were very intelligent and understood his gestures. Yet the indifference of Aborigines on Bruny Island to reciprocate friendship led to a more negative view of their behaviour and a sense that mutual trust would be difficult to establish.[105] Péron's unease in the presence of Aborigines eventually made him reluctant to approach them when he was alone. He commented on the physiognomy of the Aborigines, and made judgements on their character based on their appearance.[106] His observation of Aboriginal women on Bruny Island was critical of their body shape, skin, hair, clothing and facial attitude; they failed to meet his view that such women should have a more pleasant, desirable appearance as 'natural women.'[107] In addition to comments on the appearance of the Aborigines, Péron also discussed their graves and tombs.[108]

Baudin and Péron understood the anthropological questions to explore about native peoples.[109] Baudin was familiar with the work of the Société des Observateurs de l'Homme, of which he was a founding member, while Péron had been trained at the Muséum d'Histoire Naturelle and the École de Santé, the prominent Parisian medical school. However, the results achieved through these anthropological investigations were mixed. Péron used an instrument called a dynamometer to measure the muscular strength of the Aborigines' arms and legs. Unfortunately, his results were compromised because he was unaware that the instrument only measured a particular set of muscles in a specific way.[110] In addition, he could not persuade the Aborigines to test their lower back strength with the dynamometer.[111]

Péron used his findings, however, to argue that Van Diemonian Aborigines, and by implication other primitive peoples, were weaker than those who lived in civilized society. Péron's collection of Aboriginal vocabulary was disappointing: he only gathered seventy-five words. His observation of Aboriginal customs, however, brought interesting practices to light, especially his discovery of tombs on Maria Island and his observations on the burial practices of the native people there.[112] Modern anthropologists have shown that these tombs had bark linings covered in symbols that were inextricably linked to group identity.[113] Boullanger also made detailed observations about the Aborigines in his journal, focusing on their marriage, funeral and sexual rites.[114]

Scientific achievements

Baudin had established a reputation as an informed collector of natural history specimens during a voyage of 1796–8 in *La Belle Angélique* to the Caribbean, in which he worked harmoniously with other collectors on board ship.[115] However, on his expedition to Australia Baudin clashed with the young scientists, notably but not exclusively Péron, who thought they were better qualified to oversee the collection of specimens.[116] Relations between the captain and his scientists deteriorated as it became apparent that Baudin's scientific preferences and procedures differed from theirs. Baudin criticized the hazardous conjectures of the young scientists while they increasingly treated him contemptuously. Baudin annoyed the scientists on board the *Géographe* by insisting, as he was entitled to do, that they should submit their findings to him and that he would be solely responsible for the official account of the voyage's scientific results.[117]

Baudin and Péron were separated by their 'unspoken rivalry for scientific authority over the voyage.' Baudin, who had owed his appointment partly to the notable French botanist Jussieu and to his previous scientific work, came into conflict with his scientists on the *Géographe* because he considered himself as well qualified a natural historian as them.[118] Péron and others falsely accused Baudin after his death of attempting to steal specimens belonging to the expedition.[119] The divisions between Baudin and the scientists were a major distraction during the voyage.

The *Géographe* arrived back in France with an extensive haul of natural history items. The total number of specimens collected in all scientific disciplines exceeded 100,000, including 2,542 new zoological species.[120] There were cases of dried plants and shells, fishes and reptiles preserved in alcohol, stuffed or dissected birds and quadrupeds, seventy large boxes filled with natural plants, and six hundred types of seeds. The *Géographe* also carried seventy-two rare or new animals, including two kangaroos. Jussieu praised this fascinating and extensive shipment of natural history collections.[121] Live animals and plant specimens taken to Malmaison included two emus from King Island and Kangaroo Island.[122] There were also mineralogical finds from the expedition.[123]

Within a year after the end of the voyage, Péron published five zoological papers in prestigious scientific journals.[124] However, he spent more time writing up his voyage account (see below) rather than analysing his scientific findings. Many of his notes and drawings remained unpublished.[125] No complete botanical or phycological report on Baudin's expedition was prepared.[126] The turbulence in government that occurred in France soon after the scientific specimens were brought to Paris, during which Napoleon became Emperor and established the French empire, partly explains their slow examination. It was not until decades later that details of the new species were described and disseminated by a natural historians.[127] Péron's zoological work strongly influenced the comparative anatomical work undertaken by Jean-Baptiste Lamarck.[128]

Cartographical achievements

Hydrography and nautical astronomy on Baudin's expedition followed the successful practices of Beautemps-Beaupré on d'Entrecasteaux's voyage. Astronomical and terrestrial observations were undertaken with a reflecting circle refined by Jean-Charles le Borda rather than compasses. Daily readings from chronometers and lunar distances were combined and reference made to the tables included in the volumes of the *Connaissance des Temps*, the official yearly publication in France dealing with astronomical matters. The Baudin expedition carried one astronomical clock, four chronometers, one counter, four compasses, two sextants and two graphometers.[129] Challenging weather conditions often impeded astronomical observations and calculation of coordinates. At Hunter Islands, for example, Freycinet and Boullanger had to cope with choppy seas, extensive rain and violent winds while they were charting. In such circumstances, it was difficult to hold their instruments steady. Whatever the difficulties of carrying out these observations, the expedition's latitude and longitude readings have been checked against updated maps and found to be highly accurate.[130]

Baudin, unlike Flinders, did not draw his own charts, but he commented in detail on the quality of the surveying undertaken on his expedition. Hamelin in the *Naturaliste* carried out thorough surveys of the Swan River region and offshore islands and of Shark Bay. Freycinet in the *Casuarina* undertook close

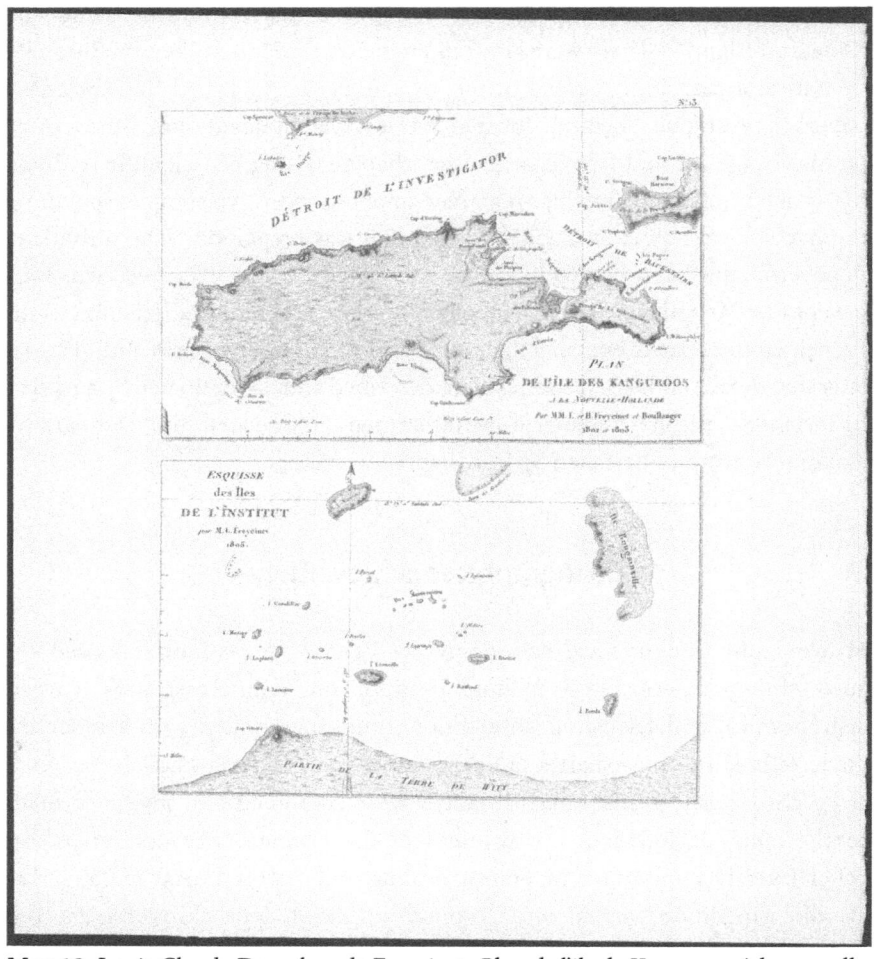

Map 19 Louis Claude Desaulces de Freycinet, *Plan de l'ile de Kanguroos à la nouvelle-hollande; Esquisses des iles de l'Institut par M.M.L. et H. Freycinet et Boullanger*, 1802 et 1803; par M. L. Freycinet, 1803 MAP RM 2077 Bib ID 628875

inshore surveys and charting of the coast from Bass Strait westward to Melville Island. Baudin's expedition added important details to knowledge of the coasts of Van Diemen's Land. The circumnavigation of King Island and of Kangaroo Island indicated the potential of those locations for the sealing trade. Surveys in Bass Strait and along parts of the southern and western coasts of Australia, notably in Denial Bay, the Nuyts archipelago and Shark Bay, identified unknown parts of Australia's coastline. The expedition tried to fix the location of North West Cape, but this was not done correctly.[131] Despite this concentrated activity, the only part of the Australian mainland that Baudin's expedition discovered was a small part of South Australia's coast between Mount Schanck and Encounter Bay.[132]

Louis de Freycinet found it difficult to raise funds to engrave the charts of the voyage.[133] But in 1812, in collaboration with Boullanger, he produced an atlas of thirty-two maps. Baudin's name is nowhere mentioned in the atlas, and the reasons for this will be discussed below.[134] Freycinet's full map of Australia, with many coastal and regional names supplied, was published separately in 1811 before appearing in the atlas. It includes almost the entire coastline of Australia for the first time in a published map, with only a few small gaps in marking the

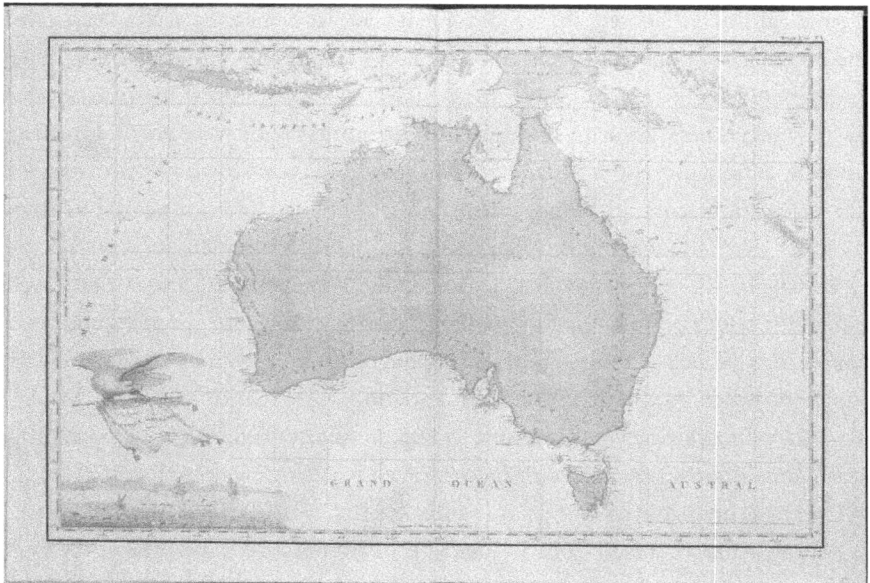

Map 20 Louis Claude Desaulces de Freycinet, *Carte generale de la Nouvelle Hollande: dressee par M. l. Freycinet, Comandant la Goelette, le Casuarina, an 1808* (Paris: Publie par Decrès Imperial sous la Ministère de son excellence le vice-amiral comte Decrès, 1812) MAP RaA2 Plate 1 Bib ID 779904

coast where detailed surveys had not been possible. Freycinet's map took no account of Flinders's discoveries on the south coast; it appeared in print three years before Flinders's map of 'Terra Australis or Australia' was published.[135]

Freycinet and Péron applied the name Terre Napoléon to the stretch of the south coast they had explored. French names were supplied to individual places on the Terre Napoléon; these were different to the names chosen by Baudin.[136] Péron believed the discoverer should have first right to name a new landscape feature identified. But he was pressurized by the Napoleonic regime (whose cooperation was needed to secure the finance and publication for his work) to use 'Terre Napoléon' and similar Napoleonic nomenclature for parts of Australia's south coast.[137] The second edition of the official atlas to the Baudin expedition, prepared by Lesueur and Petit, was revised and expanded to include sixty-eight plates. In that edition, published in 1824, there was no reference to Terre Napoléon, the only French names retained for the south coast were for places first identified on Baudin's expedition, and Flinders's names for most of the south coast were included.[138]

Artistic work

Three official artists left the voyage on its outward journey from France but two talented young artists, Lesueur and Petit, stayed with the expedition. They contributed significantly to the voyage's artistic work with drawings of Australia's flora, fauna, landscapes and indigenous inhabitants. They were adept at realistic representation, incorporating anatomical features in their drawings with a concern for scientific accuracy.[139] They drew animals in their environmental settings. Lesueur drew the tents and buildings of the British settlement at Port Jackson. Petit sketched Aborigines at Port Jackson and in Van Diemen's Land.[140] Some were portraits; others were ethnographic depictions of huts, canoes, dances and ritual gatherings, as well as drawings of Aboriginal couples in coitus. Lesueur drew the shape of heads, body hair, facial features and bodily markings. Petit started to complete his drawings on his return to France, but he died only six months after returning home. Over a third of the engraved plates in the second edition of the atlas, based on original watercolours and sketches, were devoted to Aborigines.[141]

Péron worked closely with Lesueur on his illustrations. Together they went on expeditions, and took particular delight in marine life. Lesueur sketched meticulous drawings of molluscs, jellyfish, fish and gastropods, emus, the platypus, echidnas, numerous birds, as well as producing watercolours of possums. He worked swiftly and productively, amassing nearly 1,000 animal illustrations. Wombats, emus and kangaroos were drawn in family groups. Zoological drawings incorporated anatomical details, including dorsal and ventral views of fish and stingrays and the jaw structure and teeth of shark. After returning to France at the end of the expedition, Lesueur worked on his drawings in close liaison with Péron until the latter's death in 1810. Lesueur lived on until 1846, just long enough to see his drawings and illustrations lodged at the Muséum d'histoire naturelle in Le Havre.[142]

The voyage account

Baudin of course did not live to write an account of his expedition. Authorization from Napoléon for the writing of official volumes on the voyage only occurred in 1806, two years after the *Géographe* had returned to France. The publication was entrusted mainly to Péron and Louis de Freycinet, who were close friends. The Muséum d'histoire naturelle persuaded navy ministers that they had the ability to write the volumes. This was a bold step because it handed the official publication of the voyage's discoveries to scientists rather than naval officers.[143] The Napoleonic government funded and published three volumes dealing with historical, physical, anthropological and metereological matters; a volume on natural history was published by subscription. Péron, who loathed Baudin, deliberately omitted his commander's name from the voyage account; instead, he referred only to 'the commandant' or 'our leader.'[144] Péron had clashed with Baudin over the scientific collections on the expedition, but, like other members of the crew, he had criticized Baudin for his carelessness and what appeared to be a perversity in decision-making.[145]

Mutual animosity had hardened as the voyage proceeded, and Péron did not forgive Baudin after his death. Baudin had been exasperated by Péron's habit of wandering off on shore in search of botanical specimens and holding up the expedition: he summed him up as 'the most thoughtless and most wanting in foresight of everyone aboard.'[146] Péron's shipboard manuscripts contain no criticisms of Baudin, but his attitude changed to repeated sarcasm after he read the deceased commander's derogatory comments about him in his unpublished logbook. Baudin seemed to take pleasure in recording stories about his squabbling scientists. Péron's published writing about the voyage was very much parti pris: he wanted to boost his own scientific contributions to the voyage and to criticize Baudin's leadership.[147] Other scientists and officers returning from the expedition had critical views about Baudin's handling of the voyage, and would have approved of Péron's strictures. Hamelin, by contrast, was held up in *Voyages de découvertes aux terres australes* as the ideal naval officer.[148]

A complete account of the expedition, however, was never published. Baudin, who had kept a personal voyage account, had hoped to publish volumes in which reportage of the scientific findings was interwoven with the narrative of the mission.[149] But this never occurred, partly because of his death and partly because it proved to be impossible given the sheer task of pulling together disparate strands of the expedition's documentary evidence.[150] Péron's first volume was published in 1807 as *Voyages de découvertes aux Terres Australes*. This covered the first part of the voyage up to the stay in Port Jackson between June and November 1802. A printed English version appeared in 1809.[151] The published voyage account was highly subjective: the voyage's disputes were reported to exonerate Péron from blame, to criticize Baudin's deficiencies, and to present Péron as the leading scientific intellectual on the expedition. Péron was a civilian scientist who sought to claim greater expertise for his findings than naval officers could produce.[152]

Péron was unable to complete the remaining volumes because he died from tuberculosis, aged thirty-five, on 14 December 1810. The second volume was completed by Louis de Freycinet, but not published until 1816.[153] A zoological atlas was never completed, and Péron and Freycinet's two published volumes lack the taxonomic descriptions and scientific detail that would have enhanced the expedition's scientific legacy. In addition to the official published volumes of the voyage, a vast amount of additional paperwork was generated and preserved from Baudin's expedition.[154]

French voyages to Australia after Baudin

After the end of the Napoleonic wars in 1815, the French resumed Pacific voyaging for another three decades. They concentrated on scientific work rather than the discovery of new lands and coasts. Naval personnel rather than trained scientists were given responsibility for most of the scientific work on these voyages.[155] Visits to parts of Australia occurred on several voyages, but they played an unimportant part in such missions. In 1816, Louis XVIII approved the plans for Louis de Freycinet's expedition in the *Uranie*, a corvette of 350 tons. A crew of 125 was recruited, but with no scientists in lieu of whom the measurement of the globe's southern hemisphere and experiments relating to magnetism, metereology, air pressure and the ocean's temperature – all stated objectives of the voyage – were entrusted to naval officers.[156]

During a three-year expedition (September 1817–November 1820), Freycinet only stopped twice in Australia. In September 1818, the *Uranie* reached Shark Bay on Dirk Hartog Island. There was no time to survey the bay, but Freycinet removed de Vlamingh's pewter plate, discovered and restored by Baudin in 1801, and took it to France at the end of the voyage. Freycinet ignored instructions to sail southwards to King George Sound. He reported back to France that Western Australia lacked the resources to refit ships and their crew. In November and December 1819, the *Uranie* anchored in Sydney harbour. Botanical samples were collected from Sydney's hinterland. After the *Uranie* was wrecked near the Eastern Falkland Islands on her homeward voyage, Freycinet and his crew returned to France in a rescue vessel with a haul of animals, insects, shells and botanical specimens from different places in the Atlantic and Pacific, but the expedition had made no new discoveries in Australia.[157]

French enthusiasm for voyages to Australia and the Pacific was not dampened by Freycinet's expedition. In August 1822, the *Coquille*, commanded by Louis-Isadore Duperrey with the assistance of Jules Sébastien-César Dumont d'Urville, began a voyage of scientific research partly intended to locate an Australian site for a French convict settlement. No such location was found even though the expedition did not end until March 1825. The *Coquille* barely touched at Australia. Duperrey failed to observe his instructions to investigate the area between King George Sound and the Swan River as a possible site for a French settlement, blaming poor weather for his failure to do so. The voyage was nevertheless a success in other respects as it brought back to France many zoological specimens from the Pacific islands and measurements of temperature, sea and air pressures.[158]

Subsequent French voyages had stopovers in Australia in the 1820s and 1830s. Between 1824 and 1826, Hyacinthe de Bougainville in the *Thétis* and *Espérance* led a Pacific expedition that aimed to restore France's trade with Indo-China. A visit to Australia was included in the itinerary.[159] The vessels anchored at Van Diemen's Land in June 1825 and then spent nearly three months at Port Jackson. Bougainville set up a monument to Lapérouse at Botany Bay, but had little to report back to France about Australia. D'Urville's voyage in the *Coquille-Astrolabe* visited Jervis Bay and Port Jackson in November and December 1826. Cyrille Pierre Théodore Laplace's voyage in *La Favorite* called at Van Diemen's Land and Sydney in September 1831. In a later voyage in the *Artémise*, Laplace returned to the same locations in Australia in January 1839. But while interesting accounts of the localities, personalities and commercial life of these places are recorded in contemporary records, none of them added anything significant to Australian maritime exploration.[160]

Conclusion

Baudin's expedition was the foremost French voyage of discovery to Australia. Occurring simultaneously with the *Investigator* expedition, the two voyages were conducted in a spirit of national rivalry. However, they were neither a race nor expeditions with ulterior political intentions. Though they largely overlapped in time and examined many of the same bays, coves and coastal locations independently, the French and British expeditions both resulted in significant advances in geographical knowledge of Australia. Baudin examined more of the northwest coast and offshore islands and islets than Flinders, but he did not explore the east coast and Gulf of Carpentaria. Overall the *Investigator*'s voyage claimed more coastal discoveries than the French apart from a discrete part of the modern coast of South Australia and Victoria that the French named Terre Napoléon. The French scientists garnered an impressive haul of botanical specimens. The artists produced significant paintings and sketches of landscape features. Charting and mapmaking were undertaken to a high professional standard. Ethnographical observations of Aborigines, concentrating on Van Diemen's Land, were more probing and enlightening than the British expedition achieved.

Unfortunately, Baudin's expedition was fraught with disagreements between Baudin himself and his scientists. Tensions arose on numerous occasions that were not dissipated. Changes of route were frequent during the traversal of Australia's coasts as the two main vessels were often separated by poor weather and inadequate coordination. Baudin died before the voyage ended. The botanist Péron, who had clashed frequently with Baudin, wrote up the first volume of an official account of the voyage after the expedition returned to France, but this was a subjective narrative driven by his dislike for his commander and his desire to denigrate his actions during the voyage. Péron never produced a detailed catalogue of his botanical specimens, and he died before a second volume of the voyage account could be written. Many scientific specimens were brought back to France, but delays occurred in their systematic study. After these failures, the French were reluctant to organize and equip further voyages to Australia. Subsequent French expeditions to the Pacific after 1815 only focused in an incidental way on Australia. It was left to Britain to complete the hydrographic surveying of Australia thereafter.

Phillip Parker King's Australian Surveys

Flinders's ambitious circumnavigation of Australia was curtailed by the unseaworthiness of HMS *Investigator*. Most of the remaining coastline of Australia was surveyed a few years after Flinders's death by the hydrographer and naval officer Phillip Parker King (1791–1856). He undertook four voyages (December 1817–April 1822) to survey Australian coasts that had not been investigated and charted by Flinders or his predecessors.[1] The first three voyages were made in the *Mermaid*; the last expedition was undertaken in the *Bathurst*. These were the first large-scale expeditions of Australia's coasts made from Port Jackson with an Australian-born commander, but they came under the auspices of the British Admiralty. King eventually provided a detailed two-volume voyage account of his expeditions – a *Narrative of a Survey of the Intertropical and Western Coasts of Australia Performed between the Years 1818 and 1822 …*, published by John Murray in 1827.

King was the son of the naval officer Philip Gidley King, sometime commandant at Norfolk Island and later governor of New South Wales. Brought up partly in England and partly in New South Wales, Phillip Parker King had studied nautical astronomy and maritime surveying at Portsmouth Naval Academy. He became a midshipman in the Royal Navy, and served for six years in the Baltic, the Bay of Biscay and the Mediterranean before being promoted to lieutenant in 1814. He had a long naval career. His surveys of Australia's coastline, examined in this chapter, established his reputation as a maritime explorer. He later charted the coasts of Chile, Peru and Patagonia in HMS *Beagle* (1826–30), carried out field surveys in New South Wales, and became commissioner of the Australian Agricultural Company and a member of the New South Wales Legislative Council.[2]

King's surveys of Australia's coasts arose through initiatives made by Thomas Hurd, the head of the Admiralty's Hydrographic Office. Between 1814 and 1816, Hurd sought to establish a hydrographic service that would survey the world's oceans and coasts. He liaised with Sir Joseph Banks to finish Flinders's work via a thorough survey of the north and northwest sides of Australia. Hurd thought this survey would contribute significantly to identifying the rocks, shoals and reefs that presented a great danger to Royal Naval ships.[3] On 7 January 1817, Hurd set up what later became the Royal Navy Surveying Service, and soon afterwards received approval from the Admiralty and the Colonial Office for an expedition to Australia. King was appointed to command the expedition.[4]

Hurd selected two midshipmen, John Septimus Roe and Frederick Bedwell, to accompany King. Roe had trained in the arts of navigation in the Mathematical School at Christ's Hospital. Bedwell was a sailor who had participated in the Peninsular War and the War of 1812, and a member of the guard who escorted Napoleon Bonaparte to exile in Saint Helena. Allan Cunningham, recommended by Banks, joined the voyage as botanical collector. He had worked at Kew Gardens, and had received botanical information about Australia from Robert Brown, the botanist on Flinders's circumnavigatory voyage.[5] The Admiralty provided King with published accounts of voyages in Australian waters written by Flinders, Péron and Freycinet. The extent of surveying to be undertaken meant that King would need to complete his expedition via a series of seasonal cruises from Port Jackson.[6]

The Admiralty's instructions to King were as follows:

> The principal object of your mission is to examine the hitherto unexplored coasts of New South Wales, from Arnhem Bay, near the western entrance of the Gulf of Carpentaria, westward and southward as far as the North-West Cape; including the opening, or deep bay called Van Diemen's Bay, and the Rosemary Islands and adjacent inlets, which should be minutely examined; and, indeed, all gulfs and openings should be the objects of particular attention; as the chief motive or your survey is to discover whether there be any river on that part of the coast likely to lead to an interior navigation into this great continent.[7]

The Admiralty added that King should examine the coast between Cape Leeuwin and Cape Gosselin, marked on Freycinet's chart, along with the sections of the west coast that French navigators had not seen or were at too great a distance to chart accurately.[8] King was to continue surveying until he had 'examined all parts of the coast which have not been laid down by captain Flinders M[onsieur] Freycinet or preceding navigators or until you shall receive further orders.'[9]

The Colonial Office and the Admiralty oversaw King's Australian expedition, which was intended to gather far more than hydrographic information.[10] Earl Bathurst, the head of the Colonial Office, advised King that the most important subjects for the voyage to cover were the nature of the climate; the direction and shape of mountains; vegetables that might be useful for practical purposes such as in medicine, dyeing or carpentry; minerals; and the characteristics of the Aborigines encountered. King was instructed to find out whether Australia, like other continents, had at least one large river. He was also requested to record a vocabulary of each Aboriginal tribe encountered, noting down the equivalent English words.[11]

The Colonial Office rather than the Admiralty assumed responsibility for providing a vessel, crew and provisions. King regretted the omission of a surgeon but, after arriving at Port Jackson, was unable to find anyone willing to take on this role.[12] To determine longitude at the fixed points of his surveys, King was provided with three Arnold chronometers – no. 413 (box) and nos. 394 and 2054 (both pocket). By the end of the fourth year, no. 394 had stopped and a fourth chronometer, box no. 287 made by Parkinson & Frodsham, was used.[13] Other scientific instruments supplied to King included a pocket sextant, a beam compass, a theodolite, two thermometers, a reflecting telescope, a marine barometer, an azimuth compass and a case of drawing instruments.[14] King took with him copies of Flinders's Admiralty charts along with journals of previous explorers.[15]

The *Mermaid*'s first voyage, December 1817–July 1818

King was instructed to proceed to Port Jackson expeditiously to carry out his survey before a rival French expedition in the *Uranie* began. He arrived at Sydney Cove on 3 September 1817. He had to wait for a seaworthy vessel to arrive from India at the end of September. This was the *Mermaid*, a small ship of 84 tons burden and 56 feet in length that could draw 9 feet of water. King persuaded Governor Lachlan Macquarie of New South Wales to purchase this ship for £2,200. King was allocated a crew numbering eighteen along with Bedwell and Roe as midshipmen; Cunningham as botanist; and Bongaree, the native chief of the Broken Bay tribe, as an Aboriginal assistant. Two whale boats were taken on board the *Mermaid*.[16] The main focus of the voyage was to examine the largely unexplored northwestern Australian coast from North West Cape on the Indian Ocean to the eastern end of Arnhem Land, a distance of 1,500 miles.[17] The voyage began on 21 December 1817. To avoid the westerly monsoon between Timor and New Guinea, the route followed was through Bass Strait in a westerly direction as far as King George Sound and then up the west coast of Australia to begin the survey at North West Cape.[18]

The *Mermaid* struggled in the first fortnight of the voyage against gales and hard westerlies. It was forced to beat to windward while sailing under the Great Australian Bight. On reaching Seal Island, Bedwell and Roe were sent in a whaleboat on what proved a fruitless search to find the bottle Flinders had left there. They left a sealed bottle, giving details of their arrival, in a safe and secure place on the island.[19] King stopped at King George Sound, partly to overhaul the ship's rigging and replenish supplies but also to survey Oyster and Princess Royal harbours. Roe assisted King with this work. They found that vessels drawing more than 12 feet of water could not cross the bar. Cunningham made many new discoveries of plants and seeds at this location. He dried them, placed them in specimen boxes, and began to catalogue them.[20]

On reaching North West Cape in February 1818, King recalculated its position. This is where serious surveying began. He located the cape at 21°48'S, about 11½ miles from the position given by Baudin (21°36'S). King's survey showed that North West Cape was the western head of Exmouth Gulf, which was 25 miles wide and 43 miles deep with about 1,000 square miles of water.[21] The *Mermaid* examined Exmouth Gulf for eight days. The barren flat shores, comprising sand dunes, were unsuitable for landing.[22] Flinders had noted only a small inlet here, while Freycinet had not been aware of a large gulf.[23] King charted the area but lost one anchor and the fluke of a second anchor. He was worried about surveying a previously unknown coast with only one remaining anchor. He was unimpressed with the arid, reddish coloured sand and mangroves. 'The coast about Exmouths Gulf is truly deplorable,' King wrote, adding 'worse than any description I have seen of the deserts of Arabia.'[24]

King found there was no river opening on this stretch of coast, and concluded that it was 'a country entirely unprofitable in every respect for the visitation of any Europeans.'[25] The entire north and northwest coast seemed unsuitable for settlement.[26] King sailed on to the Dampier archipelago where he checked his chart against Baudin's chart of the same area. King accepted many French names bestowed on this area but corrected the inaccurate French longitudes.[27] Many acceptable places for anchoring ships were found among the islands of Dampier's archipelago.[28] Roe was the main support for King in undertaking surveys on shore. The other midshipman, Bedwell, failed to undertake his proper share of the duties. Roe noted the great heat and humidity of the climate on Australia's northwest coast and the regular presence of thunder and lightning. He remarked on the extensive line of breakers among a maze of islands and reflected on the number of ships that had been wrecked in the vicinity.[29]

King's instructions enjoined him to examine the Dampier archipelago closely, and to determine whether a river system was contained within them. The survey could only be accomplished in a small vessel such as the *Mermaid*, which could sail through channels full of shoal between each island.[30] King compared his chart on board ship with Dampier's description of the Rosemary Islands, and concluded that Freycinet, sailing with Baudin, was correct in his conjecture that the Romarin and Malus islands named by the French were those seen by Dampier. During March 1818, the *Mermaid* headed east towards an intended landfall at Cape Arnhem, where King intended to chart Arnhem Land. The only available chart of this section of the coast was a rough outline by Tasman from his voyage of 1644. This plan was frustrated, however, by the sudden ending of the westerly monsoon.[31]

While sailing along Australia's northwest coast, King identified New Year's Island as part of a group, which he surveyed and named. Malay trepangers were sighted, and King became annoyed because they anchored at places he wanted to explore.[32] The *Mermaid* kept away from the numerous praus to avoid friction with the trepangers.[33] King discovered and explored Croker Island, Raffles Bay and Port Essington, a safe anchorage on the Cobourg peninsula, with shelter from prevailing winds. King was impressed with the harbour.[34] He identified Port Essington as a location of potential future shipping and commerce 'from its proximity to the Moluccas and New Guinea and its being in the direct line of communication between Port Jackson and India, as well as from its commanding position with respect to the passage through Torres Strait.'[35] Cunningham, however, noted that Port Essington was surrounded by land deeply overrun by mangroves, it lacked fresh water, and it appeared to be a useless site for agricultural purposes.[36] King's recommendation was eventually followed up, but Cunningham's reservations were later confirmed. Thus, the Colonial Office established a settlement at Port Essington in 1838, but the problems of living there in the wet season led to it being abandoned in 1849.[37]

In late April and early May 1818, King explored Van Diemen Bay in Arnhem Land. The bay's gulf had been discovered by Dutch ships in 1705, but King's voyage was the first to survey the vicinity in detail. It was hoped that this location might lead to an inland sea. Hindered by powerful tides, however, King was disappointed that no waterway leading into the heart of the continent was located there. King renamed the bay Van Diemen Gulf.[38] He then demonstrated the insularity of Bathurst Island and proved that Melville Island was separated from the mainland. Today these two islands are known as the Tiwi islands. This was followed by exploration of a deep inlet that appeared to be a river but turned out not to be so, as it terminated at a distance of 70 miles from its mouth. King named it Cambridge Gulf. The examination of the northern part of De Witt's Land found several bays, inlets and harbours and also Prince Regent River, which penetrated inland in a south-south-easterly direction for 55 miles.[39]

At the south entrance of Apsley Inlet, King decided to return to Port Jackson via the west and south coasts of Australia. The survey of the northwest coast had revealed that it was 'an arid line of low Desert, extending generally some Miles inland and altogether useless for any purpose in Agriculture.'[40] Between 24 and 26 June 1818, the ship passed the Tryal Rocks without seeing them, but King discovered Barrow Island, situated 30 miles off Western Australia's Pilbara coast. The rest of the voyage was conducted in stormy seas, with many crew members suffering from dysentery. King administered medical assistance owing to the absence of a surgeon. He himself was 'dangerously ill,' partly through 'excessive fatigue and anxiety.' The ship's rigging and planking took a battering. On 29 July, the *Mermaid* anchored in Sydney Cove, where she remained for eighteen weeks.[41]

King had frequent recourse during the voyage to Flinders's charts and observations, which he found helpful and accurate.[42] Roe informed his father that the weather had been so hot in northern Australia that 'we were more like blackfellows than Europeans,' and he looked forward to several months' recuperation at Sydney.[43] King had only explored part of Australia's northwest coast; his survey 'was yet not so complete as to reduce to absolute despair the advocates of a great Australian river discharging itself into the ocean.'[44]

King put the *Mermaid* to productive use while waiting to set out again to northern Australian coasts. On 24 December 1818, the *Mermaid* left Port Jackson on a voyage to survey the entrance to Macquarie Harbour on the west coast of Van Diemen's Land. The harbour had been discovered but not properly examined two years previously by James Kelly, a whaling captain. King charted the harbour in detail, identifying the soundings of the channels and the shoals at the harbour's entrance. Cunningham examined the Huon Pine, a native tree only found in the wet, temperate rainforest of southwest Van Diemen's Land. After completing this task, the *Mermaid* returned to Sydney Cove. The voyage ended on 14 February 1819.[45] Four days later, King forwarded to England his journal and charts up to 28 July 1818.[46]

The *Mermaid*'s second voyage, May 1819–January 1820

The *Mermaid*'s second voyage was intended to survey parts of Australia's northern coast, notably Arnhem Land, that previous navigators had not explored. King was resuming the investigations made on the *Mermaid*'s first cruise. On that expedition, the extent of coasts and their sinuous character had left large portions of northern Australia's shores unexamined despite King's meticulous surveying.[47] For this second voyage in the *Mermaid*, an anti-clockwise route was followed. King noted that a passage via Torres Strait would shorten the voyage and enable him to spend enough time on his survey of the northwestern coast.[48]

Lieutenant John Oxley, the Surveyor-General of New South Wales, accompanied King in the *Lady Nelson*. Bongaree was omitted from the crew, having proved of little use on the first voyage. The *Mermaid* and the *Lady Nelson* left Sydney on 8 May 1819 and reached Port Macquarie two days later. King, Oxley and Roe examined and charted the Hastings River in a whaleboat.[49] Oxley sent a report of the survey to the governor of New South Wales, with recommendations about the suitability of Port Macquarie for settlers.[50] The *Lady Nelson* then returned to Port Jackson. King and Oxley were favourably impressed with the area around Port Macquarie, and thought (as did Roe) that it could be the site of a future settlement.[51]

The *Mermaid* left Port Jackson to sail north past the northern rivers district of New South Wales. But as with the previous voyages made by Cook and Flinders, King did not see any of the eight rivers flowing to the coast within a

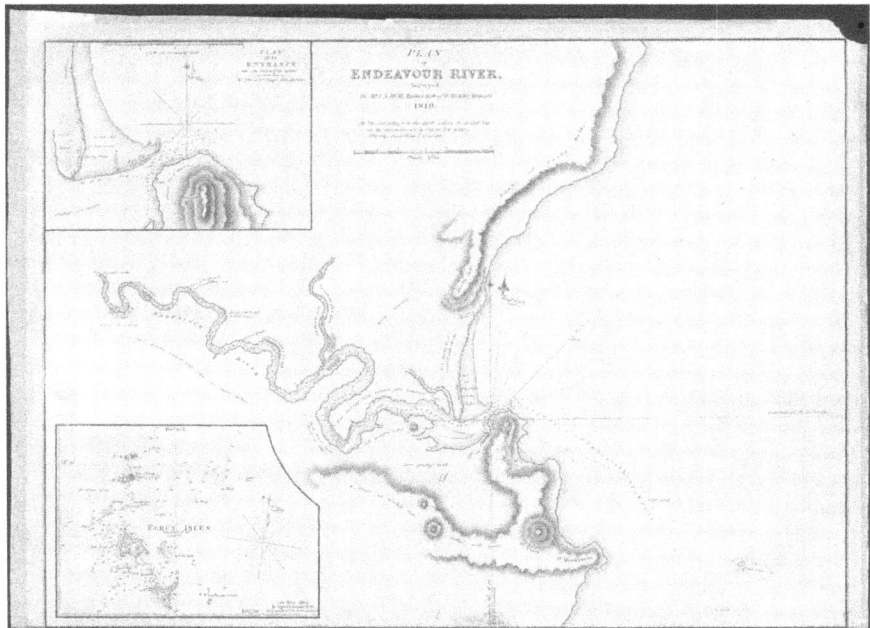

Map 21 John Septimus Roe, *Plan of Endeavour River, 1819* (London: Hydrographical Office of the Admiralty, 1860) MAP RM 693 Bib ID 3535834

distance of 200 miles north of Port Macquarie. He added to Flinders's chart of this coast. Sailing through the Great Barrier Reef, he steered a course closer to the mainland than either Cook or Flinders. King wanted to establish the best route for shipping through this labyrinth of coral rock.[52] An Outer Route beyond the reef was more susceptible to storms than an Inner Route inside the reef, where the waters were generally calmer and anchorages were available. In 1815, Captain Charles Jeffreys sailed via the Inner Route in the *Kangaroo* en route to Ceylon, but devoted little time to charting the reef. Many more shipwrecks occurred on the Outer Route than on the Inner Route so King prepared a proper chart of the latter for future voyages. He later became a staunch advocate of the Inner Route, and produced sailing directions for this course. The Inner Route soon became the standard way of approaching Torres Strait.[53]

King's only landings on the east coast were investigations seeking rivers or openings between the latitude of 22° and Torres Strait, a distance of more than 700 miles.[54] The voyage was uneventful until a whaleboat was lost at sea near Endeavour River, where Cook had been forced to repair his ship after hitting reefs in 1770. King decided to stop in this vicinity. A new whaleboat was constructed from local

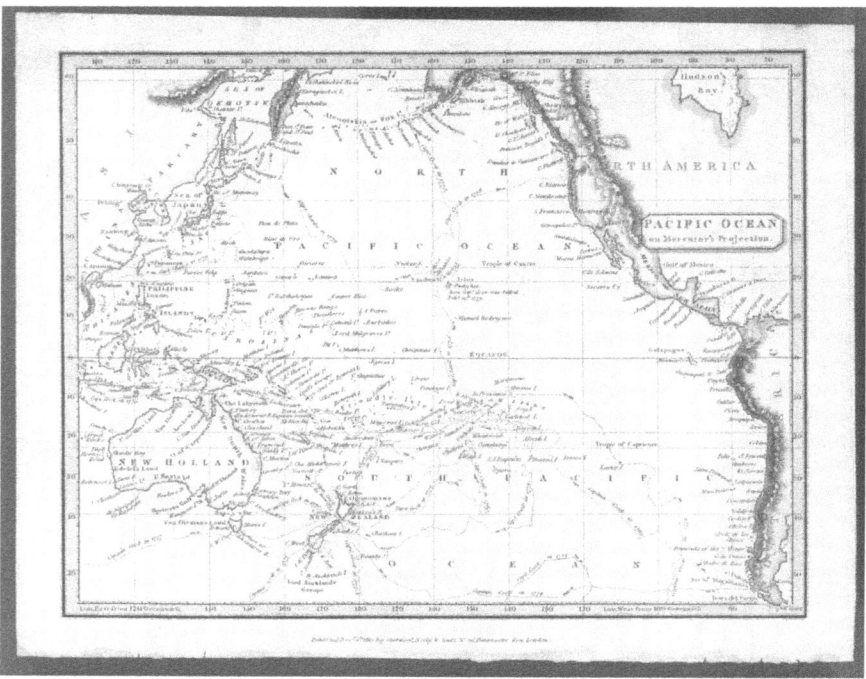

Map 22 Samuel John Neele, *Pacific Ocean on Mercator's Projection* (London: Sherwood, Neely & Jones, 1821) MAP NK 10631 Bib ID 1253172

timber and prefabricated frames, and the *Mermaid* was repaired at exactly the same location that Cook had overhauled the *Endeavour*. Roe explored and charted the river as far as he could venture upstream and produced a detailed, skilled chart showing the shallows, banks, depths and landscape features near Endeavour River.[55] The *Mermaid* passed through Torres Strait to the Gulf of Carpentaria, but nothing of significance was noted. Proceeding westward along Australia's northern coast, King occasionally corrected the coordinates recorded by Flinders and Baudin.[56]

On 27 August, King resumed his survey south of Bathurst Island, where he had curtailed his previous examination of Australia's northern coast in 1818. Owing to shoals, large tidal flows and strong winds, he was unable to bring the *Mermaid* close enough to the shore to identify the Victoria River which empties into the head of Joseph Bonaparte Gulf. But he found and named Encounter Cove, Vansittart Bay and Port Warrender, and corrected Freycinet's plan of the archipelago that included Cassini Island. A survey of the newly discovered Cambridge Gulf took thirteen days. Sailing westwards through passages between many small islands, King named the area Admiralty Gulf, which Baudin had missed.[57] Cunningham observed that the rivers and ports they came across on the northwest coast were valuable as places of shelter for shipping, but the shore was uniformly flat, arid and unsuitable for settlement.[58]

With the crew reduced to two pints of water per day, King headed for Kupang to replenish the ship's supplies and fresh water.[59] The *Mermaid* anchored there on 1 November 1819. King then headed back to Port Jackson, arriving there on 12 January 1820 after a voyage of thirty-five weeks and four days. The Freycinet expedition in the *Uranie* had left Sydney only a few days earlier. The achievements of the voyage in the *Mermaid* were the charting of Port Macquarie, a running survey of Australia's east coast from the Percy Islands to Torres Strait, a further survey of 900 miles inside the Great Barrier Reef, and an examination of 540 miles of Australia's north and northwestern shores.[60] King was gratified to hear that the Admiralty was pleased with his surveying efforts and wanted him to complete an examination of the west coast so that his survey 'will unite with that of Captain Flinders.'[61]

The *Mermaid's* third voyage, June–December 1820

Six months after the return of the *Mermaid* to Port Jackson, King was ready to embark on a third surveying voyage. A surgeon was now included on board ship. King was determined to complete his survey of Australia's north and northwest coasts from Cape Voltaire in Freycinet's chart to Depuch Island, which he had reached in March 1818.[62] The Admiralty hoped that King could finish his survey of Australia's north and western coasts on this voyage, but Cunningham noted that the relatively small complement of men and stores on the *Mermaid*, only allowing a maximum period of one year for the voyage, made it 'exceedingly doubtful' that this could be achieved without a fourth voyage.[63]

The third voyage of the *Mermaid* began on 14 June 1820, but the ship ran into a violent storm which broke her bowsprit and set adrift one of her boats. King was forced to return to Port Jackson. He was concerned that the *Mermaid* was not robust enough to withstand bad weather.[64] King left Port Jackson again on 14 July, heading north, but navigation proved difficult off the Queensland coast and the ship was grounded off Port Bowen after coming across shoals. After setting out again, the ship sprang a leak and had to stop at Endeavour River for repairs.[65] During this part of the voyage, King did not delay by landing anywhere but concentrated on amending the chart made on his last voyage, which he improved and extended.[66]

The *Mermaid* took the Inner Route through the Great Barrier Reef that King had previously followed. Where possible, he sailed closer to the mainland than he had done before.[67] From Port Jackson to Torres Strait, Roe wrote, 'we had the satisfaction of fixing the positions of 40 or 50 reefs or shoals that had no previous existence in any former charts.'[68] King hoped his survey on this voyage would identify geographical features of the coast left in 'a questionable state' on his last voyage. The *Mermaid* passed through Torres Strait via Endeavour Strait. King praised the navigational track Flinders had followed between the Prince of Wales islands and Northwest reef.[69]

The third voyage of the *Mermaid* was cut short by the ship's deficiencies. The survey was resumed at Cape Voltaire, but the ship started to leak badly. Repairs were carried out at Careening Bay, on the Kimberley Coast, in September 1820. An investigation of the ship revealed that iron nails had disintegrated, leaving holes in timbers on the vessel's hull. In addition, the keel and sternpost were damaged. The repair of the *Mermaid* took three weeks.[70] The crew carved the words 'HBMC Mermaid 1820' into the bark of a large boab tree, characterized by a swollen trunk. King attached an inscribed copper plate there. The tree and the carved words are still visible today in what is known as the 'Mermaid Tree.'[71]

After leaving Careening Bay on 9 October, King discovered St George's Basin, which penetrated inland from the coast for 21 miles. A large river emptied into the bay. King named this the Prince Regent River after Britain's heir to the throne. This river was tidal for 40 or 50 miles, and was navigable further up river for boats. The northwest monsoon was about to start. The *Mermaid* reached King George Sound, but repairs to the ship were urgently needed.[72] For these reasons, King decided to head back to Sydney via the west and south Australian coasts. During this return voyage, the ship still leaked badly and water had to be pumped out every two hours. The crew's health was deteriorating.[73] A further search for the Tryal Rocks proved fruitless.[74] Cunningham noted that the return to Port Jackson at this point of the voyage was a necessity 'rather than attempt to make the Coast again in a crazy Vessel whereby the lives of all on board would have been endangered.'[75] The *Mermaid* reached Sydney on 9 December 1820 after a difficult voyage made with stormy winds and lightning.[76]

The *Bathurst's* voyage, May 1821–April 1822

The *Mermaid* needed extensive repairs that would take several months to undertake, so King's final voyage to northwest Australia was undertaken in the *Bathurst*, a brig of 170 tons that was purchased and fitted out for the voyage. This vessel had more capacity than the *Mermaid* to load water and provisions. The *Bathurst* had thirty-two men, including King, on board.[77] The *Bathurst* sailed in company with the hired transport *Dick* north from Sydney on 26 May 1821, heading up the east coast and to the Gulf of Carpentaria. A surgeon was present on the voyage. King revisited some places he had examined in the *Mermaid*. The main focus of the *Bathurst's* voyage was to chart the northwest coast from Prince Regent River, where King had terminated his survey in the previous year.[78]

In August 1821, the *Bathurst* explored the rugged, treacherous Kimberley coast, in northwest Australia. King was particularly interested in places examined by previous explorers in this region. He visited Brunswick Bay, Collier Bay and the Buccaneer archipelago.[79] He thought Cape Lévêque was the point where Dampier anchored on his buccaneering voyage in the *Cygnet* in 1688. Nearby Cape Villaret Bay, named by Baudin, appeared to be where Dampier remarked in 1699 that the tide rose and fell five fathoms. Dampier had used this observation to postulate the existence of either a strait or an opening between this location and the Rosemary Islands. King was sceptical of this claim, thinking it 'more probable that these great tides are occasioned by the numerous inlets that intersect the coast between this and Cape Voltaire.'[80] Tides of up to 36 feet, reefs, misty conditions and dangerous currents hampered the progress of the survey. King found weather and navigational conditions were too treacherous to explore Roebuck Bay.[81]

On 27 August 1821, the *Bathurst* sailed for Mauritius, a British colony, the nearest and healthiest place outside Australia from which necessary sea stores could be obtained. The voyage took thirty days.[82] Returning from this excursion three months later, King reached King George Sound by 23 December. He visited Oyster Harbour, which Flinders had explored in the *Investigator*. He also spent time at King George Sound gathering information on local Aboriginal groups. Instead of proceeding back to Sydney, King sailed north from Cape Leeuwin. He knew the French had carefully examined the coast between Capes Leeuwin and Péron as well as the Swan River and Rottnest Island, but from there up to North-West Cape, with the exception of Shark's Bay on Dirk Hartog Island, they had seen little of the coast and had followed the outline assigned to it by van Keulen.[83]

King did not land on this section of the coast from Rottnest Island northwards because it was mainly unsheltered, unprotected and full of offshore reefs disguised by breaking surf.[84] He named the passage between the Houtman Abrolhos and the mainland the Geelvink Channel in honour of de Vlamingh's ship, which in 1697 was the first European vessel to sail through that passage.[85] King later noted that the west coast, extending for nearly 800 miles between North West Cape and Cape Leeuwin, was fronted by a rocky shore that was largely inaccessible to ships. This coast had only two openings – the Swan River and Shark Bay.[86]

Visiting Dirk Hartog Island, King saw the posts placed by the French and the Dutch, but there were no signs of the Dutch plate left there by de Vlamingh. It was later found that Freycinet had taken it back to France. Roe replanted a post at Cape Inscription with carved letters and a vellum note placed in a hole on the post to record their visit. A stone cairn was erected on an adjacent cliff.[87] King's impressions of this location were favourable except for the vital lack of fresh water. The *Bathurst* continued her voyage to North West Cape and Cygnet Bay in King Sound, which was surveyed.[88]

King made no major discoveries in northwest Australia. Sultry summer weather, difficult currents and regular evening storms made small boat exploration difficult and exhausting among many islets. King hoped he would find the mouth of an inland river system, but without success.[89] Cunningham had anticipated the voyage might be underwhelming: the previous three voyages had shown Australia's northwest and north coasts to be 'generally a desert Waste' and that it was expected that 'the intermediate spaces yet to be examined will be found equally sterile and useless.' He thought the shores in question would never be visited again in his lifetime.[90] During the *Bathurst's* voyage, Cunningham reflected that 'long Exposure to a burning vertical Sun' on his voyages with King had had deleterious effects on his health.[91]

In March and April 1822, the *Bathurst* headed back from Western Australia to Sydney, with depleted water supplies. The damp, humid weather affected King's health, and made his constitution, as he put it, a little older than his teeth. He was laid up in his cabin for the voyage back to Port Jackson. The brig arrived there on 25 April after a voyage of 344 days.[92] King found he had been promoted to commander but also ordered to return to England.[93] He did this in the *Bathurst* in late 1822. King never again set out to Australia on an exploratory mission. His voyages in the *Mermaid* and *Bathurst* had enabled him to survey parts of the northwest and west coasts of Australia ahead of French rivals. He had charted many stretches of coastline, but had found no major river systems. He had significantly advanced knowledge of the Inner Route through the Great Barrier Reef, which was of great advantage to future shipping.[94]

King later wrote a pamphlet on this topic entitled *Sailing Directions for the Inner Route to Torres Strait from Break-Sea Spit to Booby Island* (1843). He thought he had completed the examination of Australia's coasts for the general purposes of navigation, though he drew attention to many blank spaces on charts that would be interesting for others to examine.[95] King's greatest disappointment on his surveying voyages of 1817–22 was the failure to detect 'any opening, rivulet, or creek, running twenty miles in an inland direction from the sea.'[96] This was not the paradox it first appeared to be, however, because the mountain streams of the coast 'generally empty themselves into large lagoons of water, which are formed at the back of the beaches, and communicate with the sea by shoal channels of from three to seven or eight feet in depth, through which the stream of tide usually runs out with great rapidity.'[97]

Botanical achievements

Banks, who played an important role in supporting King's voyages, hoped the botanical collector Cunningham would have 'an opportunity of collecting plants which could by no other means be obtained, & of enriching the Royal Gardens at Kew.'[98] Banks described King's first voyage to north and northwest Australia (which he still named New Holland) as one that would explore 'a Country hitherto utterly unknown to Europeans' where he hoped Cunningham would collect plants 'entirely new to European botanists.'[99] Cunningham was the botanist on all of King's voyages around coastal Australia. On the second voyage, his copy of Robert Brown's *Prodromus* helped him identify Australian flora and fauna. He noted that this would be of 'most essential service' to him in attempting to identify many difficult genera and species.[100]

The *Mermaid* lacked a plant cabin, owing to the need to allow space for two whale boats, and it had only a small space available to store specimens.[101] Cunningham therefore found it difficult to preserve any living plants that could be transported from the north or northwest coasts, and, as a consequence, confined himself mainly to specimens and seeds.[102] To help with his botanizing, Cunningham persuaded King to let him have the help of one or two crew members to accompany him on shore and to assist him on board ship when handling and drying the specimens.[103]

Cunningham was disappointed with his botanical haul from the *Mermaid*'s first voyage.[104] At King George Sound, he was pleased to find specimens of Proteaceae, but was conscious that he was following in the steps of Brown and Bauer. In accordance with his instructions, Cunningham planted peach, apricot, loquat and lemon seeds there to provide evidence of his visit.[105] At Exmouth Gulf, Cunningham discovered some new Proteaceae and Mimoseae, but drought had affected this region 'and the whole proved to be a sterile condemned unprofitable Waste.' Fortunately, a more interesting haul of plants was found on Goulburn Island, including genera peculiar to Australia, such as Grevillea and Pleurandra, but also East India plants such as Justicia, Strychnos, Dioscorea, Ficus and Hibiscus.[106] Cunningham added to his seed collection but the sterility of the northwest coast produced limited vegetation and a sparse haul of specimens. Altogether he collected 300 species of plants and seeds from the first voyage of the *Mermaid*, fewer than he had anticipated.[107]

During the brief excursion to Van Diemen's Land in early 1819, Cunningham was most impressed by the fallen trees of the Huon Pine. He took samples of this wood to take back to Port Jackson for planting there.[108] The Huon Pine was already used in the timber industry but it had not yet been described botanically because its flower and fruit were extremely small. Plant specimens were collected from this excursion to Van Diemen's Land.[109] From time to time, Cunningham sent back to Kew Gardens consignments of living plants, specimens and seeds in cases soldered down with tin for safe packaging.[110]

Cunningham hoped the *Mermaid*'s second voyage would yield more 'flowering and fruiting specimens of plants' than was the case on his first voyage.[111] A stopover of ten days at Port Macquarie, on the east coast, led to the inspection of many plants but they were mainly duplicates of those already identified.[112] Sailing up the east coast a Bossiaea plant not observed elsewhere was seen in Repulse Bay, while on islands in Rockingham Bay a beautiful purple-flowering Melastoma, not previously identified in Australia, was found. Cunningham hoped his botanical journals and specimens from Port Jackson to Kew Gardens would enable botanists in Britain 'to trace the whole diffusion or Geographical Distribution of many Remarkable Intertropical Genera.'[113] On the *Mermaid*'s second voyage Cunningham gathered more than 400 plant specimens, 260 ripened seeds and 50 bulbs. The most significant finds were several new species of Acaciae and some intertropical Grevilliae.[114] Cunningham used the detention of nearly five months at the end of the voyage to prepare his collections and journals for their passage to England.[115]

Cunningham gathered valuable botanical specimens on his remaining voyages with King. On the *Mermaid*'s third voyage, a stopover at Endeavour River enabled Cunningham to take daily walks in pursuit of flora, tracing the steps of Banks and Solander in that area in 1770.[116] He gathered a species of Calamus and a further supply of the bulbs of *Crinum angustifolium* in this vicinity. At South Goulburn Island, more Crina were added to the bulb collections. Some 'curious plants' of the genus Acacia were found in islands situated in Montagu Sound. On the northwest coast, the most remarkable finds were a species of Callitris, with a pyramidal picturesque form, the *Myristica inspida*, known to Brown, and *Cryptocarya triplinervis*. Overall Cunningham's collections formed in this third voyage were not extensive but he hoped 'they may be found important, & together with the seeds and bulbs prove in some measure desirable.'[117]

The *Mermaid*'s fourth voyage yielded relatively fewer novel botanical specimens, but it was expected that the *Bathurst*'s voyage would be more successful in this regard.[118] William Townsend Aiton, the Director of Kew Gardens, urged Cunningham to collect specimens already brought back to England from Western Australia to replace those that had already deteriorated. Genera from different Banksia tribes were particularly wanted, notably *Chorizema, Adenauthus, Telopea, Eucalypts, Dryanthes*, in order to ensure that the Kew collection did not 'fall from that Eminent rank it holds in the Estimation of the World.'[119]

Cunningham's seed collection on the east coast mainly comprised items he had previously transmitted to Kew Gardens. The voyage was disappointing in terms of botanizing.[120] At King George Sound, Cunningham found difficulty in obtaining ripened fruit and could not keep living plants such as *Simsia* and *Franklandia* because of the ship's small size. At the end of the voyage, Cunningham reflected on the termination of his work 'upon Coasts whose diversified floral riches had almost wedded me to their arid shore' while expressing relief that he could not possibly attempt another voyage in such 'solar heat' to complete the survey of Australia's coasts.[121]

At the end of the *Bathurst*'s voyage, Cunningham devoted much time in Port Jackson to the examination, arrangement and packing of his last collections from Australian shores. He acknowledged that many plants he had discovered on the northwest coast would be the same as those found by Brown on the south coast.[122] Cunningham considered that some of his collections on the northwest coast would augment knowledge of their respective genera, particularly among Grevillea, an evergreen flowering plant in the family Proteaceae.[123] He summarized his botanical findings in Australia in an appendix to King's published voyage account.[124]

Encounters with Aborigines

King's instructions enjoined him to record his encounters with Aborigines; to summarize their characteristics and the state of their arts and manufactures; and to note the vocabulary of each Aboriginal tribe met, providing the equivalent English words.[125] King conscientiously followed these instructions on his relatively few encounters with Aborigines. As ever, problems of linguistic communication abounded. On the first voyage of the *Mermaid*, King and his associates came across Aborigines on islands off Dampier's archipelago and tried to get Bongaree to talk to them. Bongaree removed his shirt to display his scarification marks, whereupon the Aborigines jumped for joy. But Bongaree did not understand a word spoken by the Jaburara people there; he himself spoke to them in broken English. King's offer of an English hatchet, chisels and files was refused by the natives, who expressed no interest in English ornaments.[126] A further encounter with Aborigines in Arnhem Land in May 1818 was marked by mutual suspicion and incomprehension, with natives assailing King and his associates with stones and spears, which were quickly returned with a volley of muskets. The Aborigines later returned to the beach and exchanged baskets of fresh water and sago palm fruit for a few chisels and files.[127]

In 1821, on his voyage in the *Bathurst*, King gathered detailed information about the Minang people in the King George Sound area. He compiled a list of sixty-eight words or phrases and noted down fifteen Minang names. He also wrote a long account of their appearance, boomerangs, fishing spears, shields, weapons and tribal structure.[128] King and his associates had several meetings with Aborigines in Oyster Bay. The native people assisted with wooding and watering. One Aboriginal man was fed biscuit, yams and pudding by the crew, and they shaved his beard and gave him a pair of trousers. The men christened him 'Jack,' and he answered to this name. 'Jack' and some fellow Aborigines were allowed on board the *Bathurst* on subsequent days. Some natives seem to have interpreted the gestures of King and his crew accurately, and King himself recognized the word *badoo* as the Port Jackson Aboriginal word for water. This suggests that, despite the gulf between the language of the British crew and the Aborigines, there were ways in which they were learning to communicate.[129]

King felt culturally superior to the Aborigines, whom he described as 'simple savages.' He noted that they smeared their bodies with whale or seal oil, mixed with a red or white pigment, giving them 'not only a hideous appearance, but a very disagreeable smell.'[130] Cunningham reached similar conclusions. 'Some of their faces were covered with fish oil,' he remarked about one group of Aborigines, 'over which they had sprinkled the dust of powdered charcoal, rendering them still more disgusting than they naturally are.'[131] King was fascinated by different groups of Aborigines – the different tribal languages, the variety in the construction of canoes, the use of spears and throwing-sticks, their carelessness and indifference about presents except in areas where they were used to visits by Europeans. King George Sound was the only vicinity where King saw the Aborigines clothed, with a mantle of kangaroo skin over their bodies and only their right arms left bare.[132]

King's charts

After returning from Australia, King worked on his charts from his four surveying voyages. The Admiralty paid him a full salary while he prepared charts, sailing directions for Australia's coasts and his voyage account for publication. King recalculated the timekeeper rates to reconstruct charts of the east and northwest coasts. He had no clerk to assist him as a copyist, but he proceeded swiftly and efficiently to complete this laborious task.[133] King finished his cartographic work by July 1825, having produced thirty-two charts and plans. His sailing directions included observations on ports, islands, winds, tides and currents; a discussion of shoals and reefs; and instructions for taking the Inner Route through the Great Barrier Reef to Torres Strait. King's Australian atlas, with eight coastal sheets, was published by the Admiralty in 1825 along with seven larger-scale plans of important sections of the coast. Roe's charts of Endeavour River and Port Jackson were included. This was the first time that navigators had access to charts of the entire Australian coast.[134] King was a highly proficient maritime surveyor whose work completed the gaps left by d'Entrecasteaux, Flinders and others.[135]

Conclusion

Phillip Parker King's four exploratory voyages between 1817 and 1822 were the first major British expeditions solely based in Australia. Setting out on each occasion from Sydney as a base for equipping and provisioning his vessels, King mainly explored parts of Australia's northwest coast. He undertook meticulous, highly professional surveying among numerous bays, gulfs, islands and islets in difficult conditions where the weather was mainly humid and stormy. He corrected previous charts of the northwest coast and its offshore islands made by Dampier and French explorers, but added a great deal of new geographical knowledge to the mapping of Australia. He was disappointed to find most of the northwest coast was barren, arid and devoid of any main river system into the interior. King carried out an investigation of the Inner Route through the Great Barrier Reef that improved the route through the coral rocks for navigators. After his voyages ended, he promptly and methodically produced highly professional charts of his discoveries. King's voyages also gathered additional information on Aboriginal groups, especially in and around King George Sound, and useful botanical specimens were collected and transferred to Kew Gardens.

The hydrographic surveyors

After Phillip Parker King had completed his surveying voyages most, but not all, of Australia's coastline had been explored and charted. There still remained some loose ends. Between King's departure from Australia in 1823 and the arrival of the *Beagle* in 1837, several Royal Navy ships undertook minor survey tasks around Australia's coasts. In 1822–3, Mark Currie, commander of the *Satellite*, undertook surveys on the New South Wales coast, including an examination of the penal colony at Newcastle. In 1824, Captain James Bremer sailed from Sydney to Melville Island to establish a colony, but this was abandoned four years later because the site was unhealthy, expensive to upkeep, and lacking in trading opportunities. In 1827, James Stirling took the *Success* from Sydney to examine and chart the Swan River, Western Australia, which he recommended as a site for settlement. In 1828, Captain Henry Rous in the *Rainbow* explored northeastern New South Wales, notably the Port Stephens area. In 1830, Robert Beecroft, master of the *Crocodile*, made a sketch of Jervis Bay. In 1836, Lieutenants T. M. Symonds and H. R. Henry, in the *Rattlesnake*, surveyed and oversaw the first nautical chart of Port Phillip and William Hobson investigated and produced a report on Port Phillip Bay. This was followed up by a further survey of Port Phillip's waters by John Clements Wickham in HMS *Beagle* in 1838. Finally, in 1839 Lieutenant Owen Stanley in the brig *Britomart* explored the Cobourg Peninsula.[1]

Surveys of the remaining parts of Australia's coasts and offshore islands were the focus of Royal Navy hydrographic voyages between the mid-1830s and the mid-1850s. In the period 1837–43, successive commanders of the *Beagle*, John Clements Wickham and John Lort Stokes, surveyed Torres Strait, Bass Strait and the west and northwest Australian coasts not yet charted. From 1842 to 1845, this was followed up by a detailed survey of the Great Barrier Reef and Torres Strait by Captain Francis Blackwood in HMS *Fly*. Between 1847 and 1850, some of this work was extended by Captain Owen Stanley in the frigate

HMS *Rattlesnake*, which had a particular remit for charting Torres Strait, the Louisiade Archipelago and eastern New Guinea. Finally, in the period 1853–61 Henry Mangles Denham in HMS *Herald* undertook hydrographic surveys of Bass Strait, Shark Bay, King George Sound, Sydney Harbour, Norfolk Island, Lord Howe Island and several Pacific islands beyond Australian waters.[2]

The *Beagle*'s voyages, 1836–43

In 1829, the Irish naval officer Francis Beaufort was appointed Admiralty hydrographer, the post he held for a quarter of a century. Beaufort promoted voyages that undertook detailed hydrographical surveying and scientific expeditions to increase knowledge of the natural world. He encouraged contributions to natural history from civilian naturalists, naval surgeons and the men on his survey vessels.[3] Beaufort wanted to complete the work of surveying the blank spaces on charts of Australia's coasts.[4] Accordingly, in 1831 he played a major role in preparing an ambitious voyage in the *Beagle* under the command of Robert Fitzroy, a 26-year-old graduate of the Royal Naval College, Portsmouth. The *Beagle* had visited South America in 1828. For its second voyage, it was converted from a two-masted, ten-gun brig to a barque to make her more suitable for surveying.[5]

Beaufort's detailed plan for the *Beagle*'s voyage ranged much more widely than Australian waters. The aim was for Fitzroy to track meridian distances around the world by sailing through the Indian and Pacific oceans and the China Sea; to chart the longitude of every port called with chronometers; and to concentrate on scientific endeavours mainly in the disciplines of botany, geology and meteorology. This voyage of the *Beagle* included Charles Darwin as one of the scientists. He was appointed as a gentleman naturalist through connections made by Beaufort with the University of Cambridge.[6] Fitzroy's choice for his assistant in the *Beagle* was John Lort Stokes, who served as mate, assistant surgeon and surveyor from 5 August 1831 to 17 November 1836.[7]

The *Beagle* made only two, fairly brief stops, in Australia on this voyage. She remained at Sydney for two weeks in January 1836, and called at King George Sound for eight days from 6 March 1836.[8] Though little surveying was attempted, these short stays in Australia were important for Darwin's scientific interests. He compiled copious notes on geological sites in King George Sound. His observation of the duckbill platypus was important for developing his evolutionary theories because he was able to explore the creature's resemblances to both reptiles and mammals – it laid eggs yet suckled its young. Darwin also worked in Australia and elsewhere on the voyage on instructions for the preservation of specimens.[9]

Darwin was unimpressed with Australia's landscapes, but he recorded observations of Aborigines. When in the Sydney area, he observed that 'their countenances were good-humoured & pleasant & they appeared far from such utterly degraded beings as usually represented...they appear to me to stand some few degrees higher in civilization, or more correctly a few lower in barbarism, than the Fuegians.'[10] Darwin feared for the survival of these Aborigines because of inter-tribal conflicts, high infant mortality, and exposure to alcohol and diseases from Europe.[11] He had mixed feelings about other Aboriginal groups. Thus he referred to Western Australian Aborigines as 'true savages,' thought it 'abominable' that they were so filthy, but admired their physical strength and their quiet, cooperative nature.[12] Nevertheless, Darwin had no inclination to linger in Australia, and he left its shores at King George Sound 'without sorrow or regret.'[13]

On subsequent voyages between 1837 and 1843, the *Beagle* conducted significant maritime surveys. Beaufort and the Admiralty jointly provided instructions for these cruises. The focus was on the remaining uncharted portions of Australia's north and northwest coasts. The men on the *Beagle* were expected to explore any likely opening until they had satisfied themselves about the existence or extent of rivers. A detailed survey of Bass Strait was needed, taking account of the tides, the depth of water, and the passages on either side of King Island. Such a survey had become a pressing necessity on account of the number of ships sailing through Bass Strait and the accidents that occurred on a treacherous sailing route. The instructions also requested a thorough survey of Endeavour Strait to determine which of its channels was the safest for ships passing through Torres Strait.[14]

The *Beagle's* instructions omitted any mention, however, of the need for further exploration of the Great Barrier Reef. This may be because Sir John Barrow, the Permanent Secretary of the Admiralty, was concentrating on a settlement in northern Australia. He was convinced that the strategic and commercial importance of the sea routes around Australia's north coast would increase in the near future. He also thought that a large inland sea would be found in the middle of Australia after further maritime exploration. These objectives led to a focus on the shipping routes through Australia's northern waters rather than a focus on charting the Great Barrier Reef.[15]

The Scottish explorer and naval officer John Clements Wickham, recently promoted from lieutenant to captain, was the commander of the voyage, with

Lieutenant John Lort Stokes as first officer and assistant surveyor; they had sailed together while undertaking the *Beagle*'s survey of the Patagonian coastline in the early 1830s.[16] Wickham and Stokes availed themselves of the main surveys undertaken by previous navigators to Australia's northern coasts, including those carried out by d'Entrecasteaux, Flinders, Baudin and King. The *Beagle* also conveyed another expedition, led by George Grey, that was intended to explore the Prince Regent River and to move overland southwards to the Swan River looking for any significant rivers in between. Grey and his associates, however, left the *Beagle* at the Cape of Good Hope to take a schooner to Australia's north coast.[17]

The *Beagle* had four decks. The azimuth compass was placed in its binnacle on the poop deck so that bearings could be taken all around the ship with an uninterrupted view. A modest complement of armaments included a 6-pound carronade, four 6-pound cannon and two 9-pounders. Six smaller boats were stored in the *Beagle* for examining shallow coastal waters and rivers – a yawl, a cutter, two 25-foot whalers, the captain's gig and a 14-foot dinghy.[18]

It was intended that the *Beagle* should undertake successive annual surveys while cruising in Australian waters. She left Plymouth for Australia on 5 July 1837 and anchored off the Swan River, Western Australia, on 15 November later that year. Wickham and Stokes consulted John Septimus Roe, who had sailed on King's voyages to west and northwest Australia between 1817 and 1822. Roe was now Surveyor-General of Western Australia. He advised expertly on what surveying and charting still needed to be accomplished. While Wickham was confined to bed with dysentery in December 1837, Stokes began to chart the coast near the mouth of the Swan River and to survey Rottnest Island.[19]

Roe provided detailed information to Wickham and Stokes about the kind of work they could expect and the nature of the northwest coast. He handed over the logbooks of his own expeditions to that vicinity so that the *Beagle* could be thoroughly prepared in joining up its exploratory work with that of Phillip Parker King's voyages.[20] Roe advised Wickham not to sail to the north coast during the wet season to avoid the blistering heat, humidity, damp weather and lack of fresh water common there late in the year, but Wickham was determined to settle down to his initial main task immediately on the north coast.[21]

The first important surveying activity of the *Beagle* was Roebuck Bay, the site of modern Broome in northwest Australia, where the Admiralty wanted to determine, following Dampier's suggestion, whether it was part of an archipelago of islands or whether it led to a strait. During very hot weather, Wickham and Stokes searched thoroughly to find a large river or inlet, but without success.[22]

According to a notice in the *Nautical Magazine*, this set 'at rest the question respecting Dampier Land being an island'.[23] Stokes was nevertheless convinced that the northwest Australian coastline had not been fully explored by Dampier, Baudin or King and that it 'still offered the lure of discovery'.[24]

On this first phase of the survey, the *Beagle*'s experienced master, Alexander Usborne, was accidentally shot in the back when one of his men's musket discharged after becoming tangled up in a branch. It took over eight hours to help him back through tidal mud to the *Beagle*. Friendly relations characterized meetings with Aborigines on this first stage of the expedition. The natives came to beaches and beckoned the Europeans to land. Wickham reported that the Aborigines were naked, and had the two front teeth of their upper jaw extracted.[25]

In February 1838, the *Beagle* reached Disaster Bay and Valentine Island, where King had abandoned his survey. Wickham completed the survey in this vicinity and prepared a chart of the bay. Beagle Bay was found and named after the ship, but it had arid shores and no fresh water. A special search of the Fitzroy River was made. Unfortunately, the entrance to the Fitzroy River held out no indication of leading to an inland lake, sea or strait; at low water, its mouth was nothing more than a wide expanse of mud drained by a small rivulet.[26] The river was distant from the sea and difficult to approach owing to the strong tides among the islands of Buccaneer's archipelago. The Fitzroy River terminated in low flat land, thickly studded with mangroves. As Robert Tiley has aptly put it, 'Here was no Australian Nile'.[27]

The *Beagle* examined many bays, islands, reefs and shores on this first cruise. The sterility of Australia's northern coast was apparent everywhere. Surveying work was tedious owing to the number of islands to be explored and charted.[28] Stokes surveyed coasts and inlets between Collier Bay and Brunswick Bay in a boat, while Wickham examined Brunswick Bay and the Regent River area. The first cruise ended in late April 1838. The *Beagle* had surveyed 300 miles of new land, and had discovered a river. It seemed very unlikely that any river of consequence emptied into the sea either side of Collier Bay.[29]

Insufficient provisions at Swan River led to a decision to abandon the idea of examining Shark's Bay and Houtman's Abrolhos.[30] In June and July 1838, the *Beagle* sailed from Perth to Sydney via Van Diemen's Land, and remained at Sydney from August to November. In the latter part of that month, the *Beagle* called at Port Phillip to establish a base for surveying the Kent Group of islands and the western part of Bass Strait. The *Beagle* marked soundings with accuracy in the strait. The coast between Port Phillip and Cape Otway was free from 'outlying dangers, but with no place for a vessel to anchor excepting with the wind off the land.'[31] Wickham found good anchorages among Hunter's Isles but advised that a ship should carefully avoid crossing that part of Bass Strait at night-time because of the strong tide. Reid's Rocks, it was discovered, created a line of heavy breakers from 5 to 6 miles in a north-south direction.[32]

The great number of vessels trading through Bass Strait since the formation of Melbourne as a city in 1837 pointed to the need for a re-survey of the entire strait. Wickham found Flinders's soundings ample for the purpose of taking a passage through the strait but correct positions for new soundings were required. Hydrographical work in Bass Strait was time-consuming. Its eastern entrance needed careful examination because most islands there appeared to be considerably out of their true positions in the Admiralty chart.[33] When the *Beagle* returned to Sydney in April 1839, Stokes noted that they employed the time 'in completing our charts, sending home tracings of them, and preparing for our cruise on the northern coast.'[34]

On 22 May 1839, the *Beagle* left Sydney to explore northwestern Australia where a number of openings on the coast still needed examination. The intention was to resume the survey where the last cruise ended for about five or six months. The section of the New South Wales coast between Port Stephens and Breaksea Spit was examined carefully because it was inaccurately laid down in existing charts.[35] Stokes weighed up the pros and cons of sailing through the Great Barrier Reef via the Inner and Outer routes. He concluded that each passage had advantages and disadvantages: the Outer Route was quicker but presented risks in finding safe anchorages each evening, while the Inner Route took longer but had still waters where anchoring was easier.[36] He decided to take the inner passage between Australia's north-east coast and the Great Barrier Reef. Stokes undertook scientific investigations at Cape Upstart to test Darwin's theory that the levels of the earth's crusts were continually changing. Port Essington was also briefly visited.[37]

The survey of the northern coast in 1839 led to the charting of Van Diemen's Gulf, between Melville Island and the mainland, and Clarence Strait and to the discovery and charting of the Adelaide and Victoria rivers. Port Darwin (named by Stokes after the scientist) and Bynoe Harbour were discovered and surveyed. The *Beagle* was the first known ship to enter Port Darwin. Stokes was unimpressed with the location, drawing attention to its shoals, mosquitoes and sandflies.[38] The Adelaide River was a more promising find: it was found to be navigable for vessels of 400 or 500 tons up to 50 miles from its mouth.[39] Crawford Pasco, who served on this voyage, noted the discovery of the Adelaide River but added generally that 'the rivers in tropical Australia, meandering to the ocean through a mangrove-clad shore, are scarcely visible to a ship on the coast.'[40]

Wickham and his men examined Shoal Bay, unseen by King. Stokes set down his impressions of the Aborigines here, and some indigenous words were recorded. In November and December 1839, much time was spent exploring the Victoria River.[41] It was hoped that this river would lead to a great inland sea. Stokes and Wickham followed it upstream for 135 miles in extreme heat (on average 43°C) before abandoning the search after many crew members were exhausted and one was suffering from sunstroke. They found the river had salt water for more than 60 miles from its entrance.[42] During the rest of December, Stokes continued his surveying. He narrowly escaped being attacked by a crocodile, and was wounded in the lung by an Aboriginal spear thrown at him. His condition became critical and so Wickham abandoned the survey and headed back to Swan River.[43]

The *Beagle*'s surveys in 1840 covered the west coast, King George Sound and Bass Strait. In April and May, Stokes and his men explored the three groups of islands of the Houtman Abrolhos. This surveying cruise was made at the suggestion of Governor John Hutt of Western Australia.[44] Stokes noted that the Abrolhos was 'a coral group that had very rarely been visited, since the Dutch ships were lost on them, one 120 and the other 220 years ago, and of which next to nothing was known.'[45] Wickham and Stokes failed to locate the position of Turtle Dove Reef, charted by the Dutch.[46] They spent six weeks among the Abrolhos, carrying out meticulous surveying. They grouped a set of reefs under the heading of the Southern Group of the Abrolhos.[47]

Sailing northwards, the *Beagle* visited Depuch Island, seen by Baudin but not by King. Important samples of Aboriginal rock art were found there. The coast between Depuch Island and Cape Villaret was the one remaining area where they hoped to find a large river or anything that led to an interior navigation. On surveying that area, however, they found neither.[48] To counteract this disappointment, the Aboriginal rock art found was a positive outcome of the cruise. Wickham sent ninety-four sketches to the Admiralty's Hydrographic Office. Beaufort arranged for them to be published in the *Journal of the Royal Geographic Society* in 1841. These were a substantial addition to knowledge of Aboriginal art.[49]

By late August 1840, the *Beagle* was searching for the position of Ritchie's reef and for the long-lost Tryal rocks. Nine days of searching proved fruitless.[50] Wickham charted the Montebello Islands, seen by Baudin in 1801, for the first time. By early October, the *Beagle* had returned to Rottnest Island and the Swan River. Surveying the west coast was now almost complete. The *Beagle* returned to Sydney at the end of this cruise. Wickham, suffering from poor health, decided to retire from naval duties. He wanted Stokes to become his successor, and hoped the *Beagle* could be retained in Australian waters 'with the work in its present unfinished state.' Stokes, who had served in the *Beagle* since 1824, took over command of the vessel from Wickham in March 1841.[51]

The next voyage to the northwest coast included an examination of Exmouth Gulf to examine whether a river reported there existed or not.[52] The *Beagle* reached Sweers Island on 7 July. There Stokes found an old mangrove tree with 'Investigator' and '1802' carved in large letters.[53] To demonstrate his connections with Flinders, Stokes had the word 'beagle' carved on the opposite side of the trunk. He named the location Point Inscription. By the end of July, a river was discovered that Stokes named Flinders after 'our scientific predecessor.'[54]

Beaufort hoped that surveying in the Gulf of Carpentaria would locate a great river flowing into it.[55] In August 1841, Stokes and his crew completed an examination of the south coast of the Gulf of Carpentaria. Almost 200 miles were closely examined in boats. Twenty-six inlets were found, two of which were rivers. But no major river was found. Stokes's chart of the southern shores of the Gulf of Carpentaria remained in use for a century.[56] Having surveyed the area carefully, Stokes concluded that Investigator Road, discovered and named by Flinders, was the only anchorage for ships of all sizes at the head of the Gulf. This cruise also examined Endeavour Strait and found it to be a safe channel for large ships.[57] Stokes thought a settlement could be established on the Albert River in the Gulf of Carpentaria.[58]

The survey resumed in October 1841 at latitude 19°S where the previous year's survey had ended.[59] The *Beagle* explored the northwest coast between Roebuck Bay and North Turtle Island. In December 1841, Stokes summarized the negative findings of this survey of the northwest coast: 'we had now completed the examination of this hitherto unexplored part of the coast which had been the field of many years of speculation. We had proved that no river or other interesting feature existed within it, and that it was a barren tract of country without anything to save it from the reproach of utter sterility.'[60]

Beaufort thought the *Beagle* should now prioritize a full survey of the shores and soundings of Bass Strait after which surveys of Port Dalrymple and other safe anchorages in Van Diemen's Land should be undertaken.[61] The Admiralty Board desired to remove 'from the public mind a certain degree of alarm respecting the danger there and the only way of doing, which is by giving the world a complete chart of it.'[62] By spring 1842, the *Beagle* was back surveying Bass Strait with the assistance of the *Vansittart*, a seventy-ton cutter supplied by Sir John Franklin, governor of Van Diemen's Land and a former associate of Flinders in the *Investigator*. This was used to survey most of the east coast of Van Diemen's Land. The *Vansittart* encountered poor weather, and could only survey a small portion of the unfinished 40 miles of the northern shore of Van Diemen's Land.[63]

Stokes completed this survey at Port Dalrymple in December 1842, by which time he was finishing his chart of Bass Strait. The *Beagle* ended her Australian surveying voyages at Sydney towards the end of January 1843. The planned surveys of Torres Strait and the New Guinea shore never occurred because the *Beagle* was ordered back to England. King wrote a detailed account of the *Beagle's* achievements in Australia that was published in the *Sydney Morning Herald* on 10 February 1843. This pointed out that two of the cruises had navigated the Inner Route towards Torres Strait, making important additions and corrections to the charts then in use. King drew attention to the discovery of several rivers: the Albert and Flinders rivers in the Gulf of Carpentaria and the Adelaide and Victoria rivers in Van Diemen Gulf. He also emphasized the work undertaken by the colonial cutter *Vansittart* in surveying the southern portion of the eastern entrance to Bass Strait.[64]

The *Fly*'s expedition, 1842–5

Beaufort was determined that the next surveying expedition would grapple with the need to chart safe routes through the Great Barrier Reef, the most dangerous part of Australia's waters for shipping.[65] Such a voyage was organized soon after the *Beagle* was recalled to England. Between 1842 and 1845, Captain Francis Price Blackwood led a comprehensive survey of the Reef and Torres Strait in HMS *Fly*. On board, he had John Beete Jukes, a geologist; John MacGillivray, a zoologist; and Harden Melville, an artist. The *Fly* was accompanied by the *Bramble*, a cutter commanded by Lieutenant Charles Yule.[66] Beaufort urged Blackwood to take time and care to negotiate his passages through coral reef. The intention was to find a good opening in the Reef for merchant vessels.[67]

The *Mermaid* had examined the Inner Route through the Great Barrier Reef twenty years earlier, but it had not had time to chart all of the manifold hazards on that route: this was the demanding challenge to be met by the *Fly*. In particular, there was a need to find out how ships could transfer from the Inner Route to the Outer Route, should they wish to sail continuously rather than anchoring at night. The Great Barrier Reef stretched from Breaksea Spit (24°30′S, 153°20′E) to Bristow Island, near the coast of New Guinea (9°15′S,

143°20′E).[68] Blackwood was expected to survey nearly 500 miles (about half) of the outer reef. As for Torres Strait, an examination of the western entrance needed to be made as only one ship had ever sailed from west to east through the strait.[69] The need for safer, more precisely charted shipping routes was sorely needed because of the recorded loss of ships in the region of the Great Barrier Reef, Torres Strait and Coral Sea.[70]

Blackwood was instructed to survey the eastern edge of the entire chain of reefs; to make detailed plans for all safe routes through them; to devise a practical way of marking them with beacons; to determine the position and dimensions of several detached reefs stretching towards Lord Howe Island; to examine and chart reefs to the westward of New Caledonia to define the eastern and western limits of that channel; to collate the evidence amassed by Bligh, Flinders, King and other navigators about a safe entrance to Torres Strait and to improve upon their findings; and to carry out a full survey of Endeavour Strait, with details on its soundings, tides and channels.[71] Blackwood's orders counselled against him undertaking running surveys 'in which much work is apparently executed but no accurate knowledge obtained useful either to mariner or geographer.'[72]

Blackwood thought it wiser to work gradually along the whole length of the Reef, in order to leave no part unexamined, than to undertake the survey in patches. This tedious *modus operandi* was the only method that would yield satisfactory results.[73] The *Fly's* survey cruise in 1843 was mainly devoted to locating a safe route through the Great Barrier Reef to Torres Strait. This was a difficult undertaking, for many rocks, reefs and shoals needed to be avoided. Blackwood surveyed the Reef from Sandy Cape. He began his examination outside of the reefs but because the *Fly* had lost wood on its starboard side Blackwood sailed to Port Bowen where it took three weeks to repair the vessel. Blackwood surveyed Port Bowen, and concluded that Flinders had been too sanguine about its merits as a place of anchorage.[74]

Resuming the survey of the Great Barrier Reef, Blackwood examined the Capricorn group of islands over six days in January. By late March 1843, the *Fly* began to survey the Whitsunday Passage, which Cook and Flinders had passed by.[75] A fortnight in late May and early June involved surveying Rockingham Bay. Blackwood then examined the outer edge of the Great Barrier Reef between Lizard Island and Cape Melville. In early July, Blackwood provided a boat for Jukes to explore the Wickham (now Burdekin) River which flowed into the Coral Sea near Ayr in modern Queensland. Jukes and three companions explored the river for 6 miles, before shoals prevented them from venturing further.[76]

On 1 August 1843, the *Fly* anchored in the Pandora entrance where HMS *Pandora* was lost in 1791 on her return from Tahiti. From this location Blackwood had to decide the best way of approaching Torres Strait safely. He opted for a passage from Raine Island, situated about 375 miles northwest of the modern city of Cairns. He wanted a beacon to be built there as a marker easily spotted by ships, and this structure was erected in 1844 with the use of convict labour. It was visible for 13 nautical miles. This was the first offshore infrastructure built to aid vessels sailing in the vicinity.[77] The low-lying Raine Island, surrounded by coral reef, lay at the entrance to one of the widest and clearest openings through the Great Barrier Reef. From Raine Island, located on the Outer Route, ships could proceed to the Inner Route and Torres Strait. Blackwood thought a ship proceeding cautiously could pass through this passage in forty-eight hours provided it took the precaution of anchoring during the night.[78]

Subsequent cruises made by the *Fly* continued survey work covering the Great Barrier Reef, Torres Strait and Australia's north coast. In 1844, the *Bramble* was detached from the *Fly* to make a complete survey of Endeavour Strait. Port Essington was visited in 1843, 1844 and 1845.[79] Examination of the southern section of the Great Barrier Reef found a clear and safe channel, about 45 miles wide, that was suitable for ships proceeding towards the mainland. However, the outer anchorages located in the vicinity were difficult to access 'as a very strong undercurrent and foul rocky ground make them highly dangerous.'[80] More generally, the officers on the *Fly* found many channels through the Reef were less than a quarter of a mile in width and slightly more than that in length, with a rapid tide, making it 'an affair of some anxiety steering a ship through them.' Care was needed when sailing near the Reef when the sun was gleaming in summertime because the glare made it difficult to make out various sunken patches.[81]

On the *Fly*'s third cruise, the north-east entrance into Torres Strait was surveyed. This discovered a new track called the Great North East Channel that became the main channel in the future for ships sailing from the northern end of the Reef to Endeavour Strait. The Great North East Channel passed between Bampton Island, near New Guinea, and Darnley Island, on the Great Barrier Reef. Blackwood surveyed this area trigonometrically and charted it. This 16-mile wide passage was clear of sunken dangers, averaged 9–12 fathoms in depth, and had good anchorages. This course could be followed during the monsoon season.[82] Blackwood considered this route from Cape York to Portlock's Reef the safest channel through Torres Strait.[83] It soon superseded the passage from Raine Island to Torres Strait, which mariners found difficult to locate and navigate despite the erection of the beacon, especially in difficult weather.[84]

The *Fly* and the *Bramble* negotiated many islets, detached reefs and shoals in shallow waters between the Great Barrier Reef and the eastern entrance to Torres Strait. This was one of the world's most challenging navigational routes for mariners. Blackwood compiled charts of the Great Reef and a pamphlet summarizing his views on the Outer Route to Torres Strait. This advanced maritime knowledge of the possible routes through the reef.[85] Blackwood recommended that the remaining part of the Great Barrier Reef between 17° and 21°S still to be surveyed would be best carried out by a steam vessel 'in this intricate & coral studded sea.'[86]

Blackwood's pamphlet weighed up the merits and demerits of the two main routes through the Great Barrier Reef towards Torres Strait. Recognizing opinions were divided on which was the preferred passage, Blackwood noted that the Inner Route was the safest, navigating between Australia's east coast and the reefs while the Outer Route, which involved sailing between the eastern edge of the reefs and New Caledonia, offered the faster passage. Blackwood advised navigators taking the Inner Route to follow Phillip Parker King's instructions on

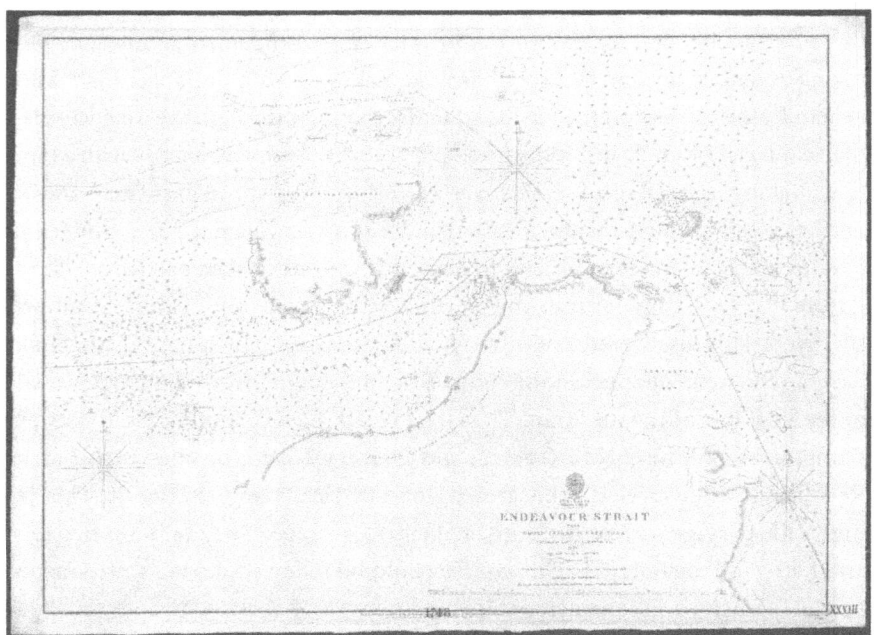

Map 23 *Australia, Torres Strait, Endeavour Strait from Booby Island to Cape York: surveyed by Captn. F. P. Blackwood, R.N., 1844* (London: Admiralty Hydrographic Office, 1846) MAP British Admiralty Special Map Col./87 Bib ID 3791403

this passage precisely in order to avoid numerous shoals. For the Outer Route, he warned mariners about the impact of the trade winds on the ebb tides in the northern reaches of the reef.[87]

Jukes also published his views about the routes through Torres Strait. He noted that the Inner Route identified by King was intricate, narrow but safe, with good anchorages all along its course, while the voyage in the *Fly* was the first serious survey of the Outer Route. Along that route Jukes had discovered there was a passage between 60 and 100 miles in width where there were many detached reefs, some known but many others unknown, and no anchorages. Jukes divided coral reefs into three types: linear reefs, forming the outer edge or barrier; detached reefs, lying outside the barrier; and inner reefs, lying between the barrier and the shore.[88] After the voyage ended, Jukes produced the first published record of the Great Barrier Reef. This included detailed evidence from observations made as the *Fly* moved from reef to reef. Its conclusions supported Darwin's hypothesis about the formation of coral reefs, presented in a published paper in 1842.[89]

Jukes's narrative of the *Fly*'s cruises candidly pointed out the problems of sailing through Torres Strait despite the advances in knowledge of the channels to be followed that its surveying had established. 'However complete and accurate may be the surveys of Torres Strait and the Coral Sea,' he argued, 'it must always remain a dangerous navigation. Slight accidents, such as hazy weather, mistakes in the reckoning, unknown errors in the chronometer or sextant, or want of completeness or soundness in the rigging or finding of the vessel (to say nothing of carelessness or incapacity in the navigator), will always cause a pretty high average of wrecks in the vessels passing through Torres Strait.'[90]

The *Fly* charted part of the southern coastline of New Guinea, but this was a secondary achievement to the charting of the Great Barrier Reef. By 1845, Blackwood and his associates had tired of their work among the labyrinthine maze of the reefs. 'My zeal after three such years as I have had is evaporated,' he wrote to Beaufort, adding 'all on board have had enough of the Coral Reef.'[91] Nevertheless, Blackwood hoped his remark books in combination with his charts would assist mariners following the Outer Route through Torres Strait.[92] Beaufort recalled Blackwood and immediately organized another expedition to complete surveying of the Great Barrier Reef. After Blackwood returned to England in 1846, this work was continued in the *Bramble* under Charles Yule, but Beaufort intended to advance this work with a completely new voyage commanded by an experienced hydrographer.[93]

The surveys of the *Rattlesnake*, 1847–50

A new surveying voyage was organized soon after the *Fly's* expedition had ended. This time the main vessel was the *Rattlesnake*, commanded by Captain Owen Stanley, accompanied by the tender *Bramble*, still under Yule's command. Stanley had sailed on a number of surveying expeditions, and had had experience in assisting the settlement at Port Essington. Between 1837 and 1843, he had surveyed portions of Australia's north coast as captain of HMS *Britomart*. Despite his navigational experience, Stanley was the second choice to command the *Rattlesnake*, and only assumed the position when the first choice pulled out of the voyage owing to pressing family responsibilities.[94]

John MacGillivray was appointed naturalist for the voyage. He was an experienced naturalist who had published articles in his specialist field of study. His brief was to collect flora and fauna from Australia and New Guinea for the Royal Botanic Gardens, Kew and the British Museum. One of the two assistant surgeons on the voyage was the famous future biologist Thomas Huxley, who assumed the role of marine naturalist.[95] Oswald Brierly was the marine painter on the voyage. He accompanied the survey on two cruises and sketched cloud studies, coastal profiles, flora and fauna and indigenous people and artefacts.[96]

Built as a small frigate in 1822, the *Rattlesnake* was an old vessel when it began its expedition under Stanley.[97] It was not in the best state of repair but it was given a thorough refit before the voyage's start. Thirty-four metres in length and 503 tonnes in weight, the *Rattlesnake* carried 180 officers and men. Specially built surveying vessels did not exist, so the selection of a ship for an expedition depended on estimations of how suitable it would be. Beaufort was impressed with the capacity of the *Rattlesnake* to accommodate a large crew and stores. He noted that the ship had plenty of open space on the upper and main decks where cabins and storage rooms could be placed.[98]

Stanley received two sets of instructions for the *Rattlesnake's* voyage – one from the Admiralty, the other from its Hydrographic Office. The former emphasized the need for further examination of the eastern entrance to Torres Strait from the Great Barrier Reef. The *Fly* had surveyed Raine Island Passage, but treacherous waters in that vicinity needed further investigation and it was desirable to locate a further, more northerly entrance to the strait. The Admiralty wanted the *Rattlesnake* to search for an opening to help ships taking the Outer Route around the Great Barrier Reef. Though these vessels benefited from sailing in deep water, the reef's openings were narrow and needed further examination. Stanley was to base his operations at Sydney for refreshment of the crew and refitment. He was directed to take the *Bramble* and the *Castlereagh* as tenders for use in more shallow waters than were suitable for the *Fly*.[99]

The hydrographic instructions, drawn up by Beaufort, were more detailed. They also differed from the Admiralty directives by emphasizing the need for further surveying of the Inner Route through the Great Barrier Reef.[100] Stanley was enjoined to use the detailed charts of Phillip Parker King to improve soundings in all coastal areas visited. He was to survey the Inner Route between Hervey Bay and the Great Barrier Reef with a view to this passage becoming more frequently used when regular shipping lanes were established between Sydney and Singapore – a prime focus of the meetings held in Sydney in 1846 by the Select Committee on Steam Navigation with England. King had laid down a feasible passage near the coast but the whole space occupied by the Inner Route needed to be 'carefully examined and triangulated' to avoid the need for frequent anchoring. The *Rattlesnake* was given the more extensive task of improving the hydrography of the Coral Sea to help ships heading towards Torres Strait. This great expanse of sea stretched from Lord Howe Island to New Caledonia and the Louisiade Archipelago. The surveying was to continue in Torres Strait and along the southeastern shores of New Guinea, with particular attention given to Bligh's Farewell at the western end of the strait.[101]

After arriving at Sydney in the summer of 1847, two lieutenants in the *Rattlesnake* surveyed the inner entrance to Port Jackson, where a reef in the middle of the passage left only a narrow available channel on either side. Stanley re-surveyed Twofold Bay in the *Bramble* to determine where the custom house should be built.[102] Moreton Bay was re-surveyed and Port Curtis (near modern Gladstone) was surveyed at the request of the New South Wales government. The Inner Route through the Great Barrier Reef was examined between Rockingham Bay and Jarvis Island. This coastline was meticulously recorded on eleven sheets. In December 1847 and January 1848, the *Rattlesnake* found it difficult to find fresh water during a period of drought and so Stanley directed the ship back to Sydney, which was reached on 14 January 1848.[103]

After a brief stay in Sydney, in late January 1848 the *Rattlesnake* sailed south to inspect lighthouses in Bass Strait over the summer months. This was again at the wish of the New South Wales government. The lighthouses were situated at Cape Otway, on Victoria's south coast, and on several rocky islands between Wilson's Promontory, also on the Victorian coast, and Cape Portland in Van Diemen's Land; they included lighthouses on Goose Island and Swan Island. These were important markers to aid the safety of intercolonial shipping.[104] Stanley compiled sailing instructions for the following locations in Bass Strait: Port Phillip, Port

Dalrymple, Goose Island, Swan Island and the Kent Group of islands (six granite islands north of the Furneaux Group near Van Diemen's Land).[105]

On 29 April 1848, the *Rattlesnake* and the *Bramble* left Sydney on a ten months' cruise in order to complete the survey of the Inner Route through the Great Barrier Reef.[106] This was now deemed a necessity owing to the rapid growth of steam navigation. The smooth waters of the Inner Route were considered better suited to steamships than the unbroken surge of the Pacific Ocean on the Outer Passage. The surveying of the Inner Route required careful triangulation and soundings laid down for a safe course to be charted.[107]

The survey off the Queensland coast began on 26 May. At various islands, astronomical readings were noted down. Angles were measured from fixed points, usually on islands. In June 1848, the *Rattlesnake* and *Bramble* assisted Edward Kennedy's expedition in the Cape York peninsula, which was intended to find an overland route from Rockingham Bay northwards. Kennedy, the assistant surveyor of New South Wales, was on his third overland expedition. The venture endured great privations and ended in disaster.[108] Kennedy, encountering very difficult terrain, failed to rendezvous with the *Bramble* at Princess Charlotte Bay in early August. Kennedy died from Aboriginal spear wounds in November.[109]

The *Rattlesnake* reached Cape York on 7 October. Meanwhile the *Bramble*, *Asp* and a second cutter were engaged in a survey of Endeavour Strait and the Prince of Wales Channel, completing the survey of the Inner Route between Dunk and Booby islands. The ships arrived back at Sydney on 24 January 1849 after a nine months' absence.[110] Stanley informed Beaufort at the Hydrographic Office that a settlement at Cape York would be helpful as a harbour of refuge for vessels approaching Torres Strait in difficult weather – an idea that was never followed up.[111]

In 1849, the *Rattlesnake* continued the work of the *Beagle*, *Fly* and *Bramble* in Torres Strait by charting eight channels, including five previously unknown.[112] One of Stanley's charts of Torres Strait contained more than 40,000 depth soundings on drawing paper that measured 30 feet in length.[113] The work needed to record these readings was such that Stanley hardly ever left the chart room. The *Rattlesnake* and the *Bramble* then undertook a running survey of the southern coast of New Guinea to the Louisiades, a string of islands encircled by reefs that stretched for 25 miles to the east of New Guinea.[114] Beaufort wanted these waters surveyed in detail because they provided an important passage via Torres Strait between the Pacific and Indian oceans.[115]

Stanley experienced considerable stress while undertaking his duties in the *Rattlesnake* in difficult surveying conditions. Gaunt and haggard, he became petulant, bad tempered and discourteous towards his crew.[116] Soon after leaving the Louisiade Archipelago, he had a paralytic seizure. On arrival at Sydney, he was very ill.[117] He was found dead in his cabin on 13 March 1850 while the ship lay at anchor in Sydney harbour. He was thirty-eight years old. Some writers later suggested that he had committed suicide, but there is no supporting evidence for this conjecture. It seems, on the contrary, that he had fallen on his head. He had received news of the deaths of his father and brother, which had distressed him.[118] Stanley's death led to the abandonment of the *Rattlesnake*'s expedition. Yule took command of the vessel, and sailed in her back to England. No immediate positive results for shipping arose from the *Rattlesnake*'s surveys. A much-anticipated steamship mail contract through Torres Strait never came to fruition, a Torres Strait outpost was not established until 1864, and little attention was given by Britain to navigation in the vicinity of New Guinea.[119]

Nevertheless, the *Rattlesnake*'s detailed surveys had made the Inner Route much safer for ships sailing up Australia's east coast and the charts produced were essential for further surveys in Australian waters over the next century. Jordan Goodman has succinctly summed up the achievements of the *Rattlesnake*'s voyage: 'With accurate charts, the inner passage of the Great Barrier Reef could now be used more safely than ever before…and this route could attract steam shipping, the technology of the future. The Indian Ocean, the Coral Sea and the rest of the Pacific Ocean were now connected; trade and imperial ambitions could flow freely from the one ocean to the other.'[120] Huxley noted that the *Rattlesnake*'s voyage concluded the investigation of the 'the last remaining portion of the globe into which European cruisers and European manufacturers had not penetrated. The great series of ocean explorations for the discovery of new and untrodden lands, within the habitable globe, was thus finished and completed by the voyage of the *Rattlesnake*. Henceforward, those who covet the laurels of discoverers must betake themselves within the limits of Arctic or Antarctic circles.'[121]

The *Herald*'s surveys, 1853–61

A postlude to these efforts to identify and chart remote parts of Australia came with the voyage of H.M.S. *Herald* to Australia between 1852 and 1861 under the command of Captain Henry Mangles Denham, an experienced hydrographic surveyor who had undertaken surveys of coastal Britain. The *Herald* was a copper-sheathed vessel with seventeen officers, twenty-three petty officers, forty-one seamen, thirteen marines and six boys. H.M.S. *Torch*, an iron paddle steamer of 300 tons, was provided as a tender, with forty-nine officers and men. John MacGillivray, who had sailed in the *Fly* and the *Rattlesnake*, was appointed as naturalist for the expedition. William Milne was employed as a botanical collector. The surgeon and assistant surgeon, Frederick Rayner and John MacDonald, were also both trained in natural history.[122] Denham was instructed to explore clusters of islands and reefs between Australia's east coast and the eastern end of New Caledonia. The aim was to chart these waters to help mariners involved in the 'increasing traffic between our Australian colonies & the western coast of America.' The voyage was expected to be more extensive than most naval surveys because the Admiralty also wanted to obtain information on the physical character and mineral and vegetable production of places visited.[123]

The *Herald*'s voyage began on 18 May 1852, reaching at Sydney on 18 February 1853. The first significant hydrographical achievement on the voyage was a survey of tiny Lord Howe Island – 6 miles long and 1½ miles wide – in May and June 1853. Situated just over 400 miles northeast of Sydney, Lord Howe Island had never been properly surveyed. After surveying the island using a triangulation scheme, Denham reported to the Colonial Secretary that the island had no security for ships but would be suitable, owing to its remote location, 375 miles directly east of the Australian mainland, for a convict settlement. He forwarded his survey expeditiously to the Hydrographic Office in London. In spite of his report, Lord Howe Island was never used as a convict settlement.[124]

Between 1854 and 1861, the *Herald* undertook surveys in Norfolk Island, Bass Strait, Shark Bay, Sydney Harbour, King George Sound and the Great Barrier Reef, as well as making three cruises in the Coral Sea and three visits to Fiji.[125] In 1857, the surveying initially concentrated on the Outer Route from Sydney to Torres Strait via the Coral Sea. Denham intended to follow his instructions to search for all possible dangers on this route and to pinpoint the positions of the reefs bordering the tracks of vessels using this passage. This voyage was only begun after damaged rigging of the *Herald* was repaired, but it was forced to turn back to Sydney because of gale-force winds. In July 1857, Denham surveyed Port Jackson so that the Hydrographic Office could publish a new chart of the harbour. Denham took soundings in the harbour and sketched in much topographical material on his chart.[126]

Between 21 December 1857 and 29 June 1858, the *Herald* surveyed Bass Strait, King George Sound and Shark Bay. Denham's survey of King George Sound extended the small-scale survey of the vicinity by Flinders in 1802 and the chart of Princess Royal Harbour by Stokes. Denham undertook a detailed investigation of Shark Bay in March and April 1858. He considered this should more properly be named Shark Gulf: it was about 150 miles long in a north-south direction and between 30 and 85 miles wide from east to west. Numerous shoals and guano islets intersected this bay or gulf.[127] Denham found Herald Bay was the best anchorage in Shark Bay in summer months. Owing to lack of fresh water, timber and vegetation, Denham failed to find any suitable sites for a settlement in Shark Bay, but his associates collected a number of natural history specimens, including mammals, birds and reptiles. Fantailed flycatchers, finches and larks were among the birds gathered.[128]

In 1858–9, Denham undertook two cruises in the Coral Sea, beginning about midway between Australia and New Caledonia. The first cruise lasted from June to December 1858; the second covered the period between April and October 1859. Specific locations covered were Bellona Shoals, South Bellona Reefs, the Chesterfield Archipelago – stretching for almost 200 miles – as well as Bird Islet and its surrounding reef, Cato Island and its nearby reefs. The second cruise followed the Outer Route from Sydney to Torres Strait, and included examinations of Long Island and its area, Kern Reef and the Percy Isles. The survey of the outer edge of the Great Barrier Reef was carried out slowly because the sun needed to be in a suitable position for sighting shoal patches. These voyages took chronometer and tidal readings as well as soundings. Meteorological information was also gathered. All perceived dangers to mariners were noted. Most of the survey dealt with uncharted areas.[129]

Denham's third cruise of the Coral Sea began in January 1860. This was planned to last four months so that the crew would not be disheartened at the possibility of a longer stay in the tropical heat.[130] The cruise examined reefs adjacent to the Outer Route of the Great Barrier Reef, covering 300 miles of the outer edge of the Reef. After charting this treacherous stretch of coral rocks, Denham claimed that a ship could reach Singapore from Sydney in twenty-four days by following the Outer Route rather than the thirty-two days it took following a route to the south and west of Australia.[131] However, he concluded that mail steamers would find the Inner Route preferable as a ship's position could be fixed from coastal features or nearby islands. With the coming of mail steamers using Torres Strait in 1866, the Inner Route became the preferred passage through the intricacies associated with the Great Barrier Reef. As Andrew David has noted, 'it was uneconomical to erect navigational marks on more than one route.'[132]

The *Herald*'s cruises included natural history collecting. The naturalist MacGillivray took the lead on many excursions. He had expertise in zoology, botany and geology. Most of his collections focused on the different Pacific islands that H.M.S. *Herald* visited. He spent a month on Raine Islet, on Australia's northeast coast, where he collected twenty plant species and eighteen bird species.[133] His most significant Australian natural history findings were on Lord Howe Island, situated in the Tasman Sea between Australia and New Zealand. At this location, visited in September 1853, MacGillivray identified thirty-six plant species (exclusive of lichens and mosses); one-third were ferns. He also came across thirty-two species of birds, including golden plovers, bitterns, parakeets and flycatchers. He collected shells, crustacea and insects and spent time cleaning the shells, pinning the insects and skinning birds. He identified the rare and little known *sala personata*, a gannet previously found only on Raine Islet.[134] Lord Howe Island had abundant ferns such as Asplinium, Grammitis, Ptoris and Prynaria.[135] MacGillivray's work as a naturalist on the voyage came to a premature end, however, because he clashed with Denham. MacGillivray was in financial difficulty and wrongly implicated Denham. This led to the naturalist's dismissal from the expedition in 1855.[136]

Denham's surveys in H.M.S. *Herald* took nine years; they produced 200 sheets of charts, plans and drawings.[137] The hydrographical findings were transmitted annually back to the Admiralty. In 1862, the full extent of the surveying carried out on these voyages was laid before the Royal Geographical Society in London. The bare statistics were impressive. The *Herald* had made 163 determinations of

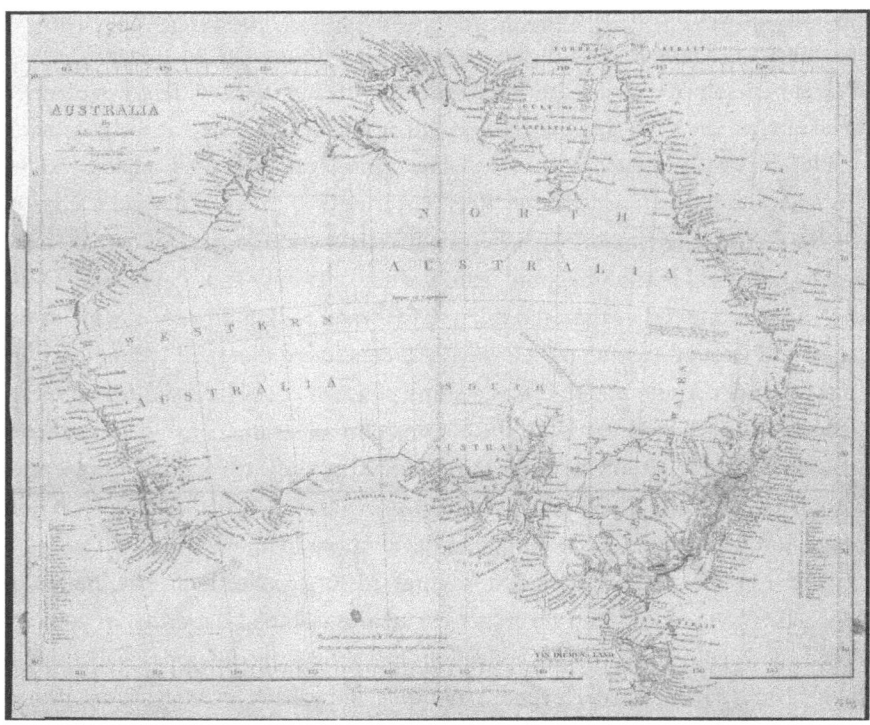

Map 24 John Arrowsmith, *Australia* (London: John Arrowsmith, 1846)
MAP RM 805 Bib ID 3544659

latitude and longitude, 2601 magnetic results, identifications of 41 islands and 42 reefs and shoals, and surveys of 450 miles of Australian coastline.[138] Denham's surveying cruises, however, had only limited contact with Aborigines. Brief encounters with indigenous people occurred in King George Sound, but in April 1858 greater interaction with natives took place in Shark Bay while Denham and his associates were surveying that area. These encounters were cordial. Denham gave the Aborigines presents, including a looking glass, some books, an axe and some biscuits. He named the location Salutation Island, situated on one of the inner gulfs of Freycinet estuary, in recognition of these meetings.[139]

Conclusion

Hydrographic surveys carried out on more remote parts of Australia's shores and offshore islands in the mid-Victorian period concluded the main task of exploring the last continent of the world to be inhabited. Leaving aside unproven voyages to Australia by the Chinese in the fifteenth century and the Portuguese in the early sixteenth century, the long gestation of Australian maritime exploration had taken over three-and-a-half centuries from the first known landfall by a European navigator, a Dutchman, in 1606 until the hydrographical surveys of HMS *Herald* in the 1850s. During that long period, perceptions of the landmass we call Australia had changed considerably from the theoretical geography of Terra Australis Incognita to the designations of New Holland and New South Wales and finally to Australia itself. Until Flinders's circumnavigation of 1801–3, navigators explored and identified only widely separated parts of Australia without realizing that they had come across parts of a vast continent. Indeed, it was not until Flinders's voyage that the supposition that a strait might divide Australia in two, from north to south, was put to rest.

The Netherlands, England and France were more prominent in the maritime exploration of Australia than Spain or Portugal. Though the Spanish and Portuguese pioneered oceanic voyaging in the sixteenth century, they had more interest in the Atlantic and Pacific coasts of South America than any motivation to locate Terra Australis. The Spanish sent out voyages into the Pacific from Chile and Peru in the later sixteenth century, but although there was some motivation to locate Terra Australis, their captains and vessels were directed more to finding safe sea routes to the Philippines and a market for South American bullion in the South Pacific. An Iberian navigator sailed through Torres Strait in 1606 but this was not followed up by further Spanish exploration of either New Guinea or northern Australia. As for the Portuguese, if they had maintained a base in the East Indies beyond 1620, they might have been tempted to despatch exploratory vessels southward towards northwest

Australia, but they were driven out of their Indonesian stronghold by the Dutch and never regained their commercial or military strength in the East Indies.

The Dutch played a much more important role in the maritime exploration of Australia than the Spanish and the Portuguese. Nearly all Dutch voyages to Australia set out from the headquarters of the Dutch East India Company in Batavia. Seeking to extend their commercial strength from that base, the Dutch had the ships, navigators and cartographers with sufficient expertise to carry out voyages of exploration. Some Dutch voyages came across parts of Australia's coasts by accident rather than design; others, such as Tasman's two voyages, were intended to identify new locations for trade. The Dutch were the first Europeans to discover parts of northern Australia, notably the Gulf of Carpentaria; parts of Australia's west and northwest coasts; and the southwest coast from Cape Leeuwin to the St Peter and St Francis Islands. The Dutch named the parts of Terra Australis that they discovered New Holland, and they gave Dutch names to capes, bays and other landscape features. These were identified and illustrated on numerous maps and globes. But despite these advances in geographical knowledge, the Dutch never found sufficient natural resources in New Holland to consider making any settlements there and they lost interest in further exploration of Terra Australis after de Vlamingh's voyage in the 1690s.

French interest in Terra Australis first arose in the 1660s after the publication of details associated with a putative voyage made by Gonneville in the first decade of the sixteenth century. Initially, French interest in following up this voyage was based on an imaginative conception of Terres Australes that had little foundation in actual geography. Apart from a voyage by Bouvet de Lozier in the late 1730s, French voyages to Terra Australis mainly occurred after the end of the Seven Years' War. Even then, the focus of French maritime exploration, as demonstrated by de Bougainville's voyage, lay more in exotic regions of the Pacific, such as Tahiti, rather than in Australia. French voyages of the 1770s and 1780s touched at discrete sections of Australia's coasts. Saint Aloüarn reached Shark Bay in Western Australia after his fellow navigator, Kerguélen, in an accompanying ship, had missed him in fog near the Ile de France. Marion Dufresne surveyed parts of Van Diemen's Land before continuing his voyage to New Zealand, where he was killed. Lapérouse, instructed in mid-voyage to inspect the new English convict settlement at Botany Bay, sojourned at Port Jackson before sailing out into Pacific waters and disappearing. D'Entrecasteaux's voyage in search of Lapérouse undertook significant surveying and charting along with scientific and ethnographic work in the King George Sound area of Western Australia and Van Diemen's Land.

English voyaging towards Australia began with Dampier's two expeditions – one in 1688, the other in 1699 – in which parts of the northwest Australian coast were visited. But although these voyages were publicized in best-selling books, British Pacific expeditions did not become regular ventures until after the Seven Years' War. The major British exploratory voyage to Australia in the late eighteenth century was Cook's in the *Endeavour*, which was the first expedition to identify, survey and chart Australia's east coast. Cook named many locations he saw or visited, he described his interactions with Aborigines, and he claimed what he called New South Wales as a British territory in 1770. Cook's voyage also, of course, sailed further afield to circumnavigate New Zealand and to discover numerous Pacific islands. Cook brought back to Europe rich hauls of plants, seeds, flora and fauna, a veritable cornucopia of scientific samples for dissemination to libraries, museums, herbaria and the Royal Botanic Gardens, Kew. Several British voyages in the 1790s improved knowledge of Torres Strait and Flinders and Bass circumnavigated and charted the coasts of Van Diemen's Land.

At the turn of the nineteenth century, the two largest exploratory voyages to Australia were undertaken by British and French vessels. Flinders, in the *Investigator*, led an expedition between 1801 and 1803 that circumnavigated the Australian continent, surveying and charting coastlines, bays, offshore islands, gulfs and harbours in meticulous detail. Baudin, sailing with the *Géographe* and the *Naturaliste*, commanded a contemporaneous expedition that also sailed around most of Australia, surveying and charting in many locations. These notable voyages vastly increased geographical knowledge of Australia's coasts. Though they were national rivals, it would be stretching a point to argue that Flinders and Baudin were involved in a race to discover Australia. Both voyages produced accurate hydrographical charts, maps and an atlas along with detailed voyage accounts. Scientific observation and collection lay at the heart of these ventures. The British and the French scientists brought back to London and Paris respectively a grand haul of botanical specimens from plants, ferns, shrubs, flowers and trees as well as zoological and geological samples. The French produced more systematic ethnological work than the British, but Flinders and his associates were, for the most part, able to discover more parts of Australia before Baudin and his team reached the same coasts.

Australian maritime exploration continued into the mid-Victorian era. After the difficulties and vicissitudes that beset Baudin's voyage, the French lost interest in sustained further exploration of Australia. They refocused their attention on ventures to the Pacific instead. Some of these expeditions stopped at Australian destinations, especially Western Australia and Van Diemen's Land, but they made only limited contributions to geographical knowledge in those areas. Britain instigated the main exploratory voyages in Australian waters after the end of the Napoleonic wars. Between 1817 and 1822, the English naval officer Phillip Parker King led four cruises from Sydney that explored in minute detail the rocky, indented, lightly inhabited shores of north and northwest Australia. The voyages explored Australian coastal areas that Flinders had been unable to survey and chart owing to the unseaworthiness of the *Investigator* in the latter part of her voyage. Parker King produced very professional charts of the coastlines he had visited. Noteworthy contributions to Australian maritime exploration after the 1820s were made in a succession of vessels commanded by naval officers with professional hydrographical expertise. In the quarter century after 1836, the *Beagle*, the *Fly*, the *Rattlesnake* and the *Herald* made cruises to explore the remaining areas of Australian waters yet to receive surveying and charting – the Great Barrier Reef, the different shipping routes through Torres Strait, the Louisiade Archipelago and the Coral Sea.

Notes

Introduction

1   Martin Woods, 'The Southern Cross Revealed' in *Mapping Our World*, p. 57.
2   E. Dekker, 'Early Explorations of the Southern Celestial Sky,' *Annals of Science*, 44/5 (1987), pp. 440, 469.
3   Jim Bennett, *Navigation: A Very Short Introduction* (Oxford, 2017), p. 6.
4   For recent emphasis upon such intelligence gathering, see Paul Moon, 'From Tasman to Cook: The Proto-Intelligence Phase of New Zealand's Colonisation,' *Journal of Intelligence History*, 18/2 (2019), pp. 253–68.
5   Richard Drayton, 'Knowledge and Empire' in P. J. Marshall, ed., *The Oxford History of the British Empire. Volume 2. The Eighteenth Century* (Oxford, 1998), p. 236.

Chapter 1

1   Alfred Hiatt, '*Terra Australis* and the Idea of the Antipodes' in Anne M. Scott, Alfred Hiatt, Claire McIlroy and Christopher Wortham, eds., *European Perceptions of Terra Australis* (Farnham, 2012), pp. 20, 25, 27, 30, 36–7; Avan Judd Stallard, *Antipodes: In Search of the Southern Continent* (Clayton, VIC, 2016), pp. 232–5.
2   Pearson, *Great Southern Land*, p. 6; Wood, *The Discovery of Australia*, p. 62; Lawrence C. Wroth, *The Early Cartography of the Pacific* (New York, 1944), p. 117; Raleigh A. Skelton, 'Map Compilation, Production, and Research in Relation to Geographical Exploration' in Herman R. Friis, ed., *The Pacific Basin: A History of its Geographical Exploration* (New York, 1967), p. 41.
3   Stallard, *Antipodes*, p. 27; Alfred Hiatt, *Terra Incognita: Mapping the Antipodes before 1600* (London, 2008), p. 6; Granville Allen Mawer, 'The Habitable World' in *Mapping our World*, p. 17.
4   T. M. Perry, *The Discovery of Australia: The Charts and Maps of the Navigators and Explorers* (Melbourne, 1982), p. 12; Mawer, 'The Habitable World,' p. 17; Helen Wallis, 'Visions of Terra Australis in the Middle Ages and Renaissance' in William Eisler and Bernard Smith, eds., *Terra Australis: The Furthest Shore* (Sydney, 1988), p. 36.
5   Glyndwr Williams and Alan Frost, '*Terra Australis*: Theory and Speculation' in Glyndwr Williams and Alan Frost, eds., *Terra Australis to Australia* (Melbourne, 1988), pp. 1, 4.

6   T. M. Knight, 'From Terra Incognita to New Holland', *Cartography*, 6/2 (1967), pp. 82–4; Hiatt, *Terra Incognita*, pp. 149–50; Mawer, *Incognita*, pp. 5, 8.

7   Felipe Fernández-Armesto, *Pathfinders: A Global History of Exploration* (Oxford, 2006), p. 253.

8   Edward Luther Stevenson, *Terrestrial and Celestial Globes: Their History and Construction Including a Consideration of Their Value as Aids in the Study of Geography and Astronomy*, 2 vols. (New Haven, CT, 1921), I, pp. 96–103.

9   Rodney W. Shirley, *The Mapping of the World: Early Printed World Maps 1472–1700* (London, 1983), pp. 61, 72–3; Hiatt, *Terra Incognita*, pp. 186, 209–10.

10 Robert J. King, 'Terra Australis Not Yet Known' in *Mapping our World*, p. 83.

11 Patricia Gilmartin, 'The Austral Continent on 16th-Century Maps: An Iconological Interpretation', *Cartographica*, 21/4 (1984), p. 46.

12 Hiatt, *Terra Incognita*, p. 7.

13 Ibid., pp. 225–6, 228; Stallard, *Antipodes*, pp. 97–102.

14 Andrew Taylor, *The World of Gerald Mercator: The Mapmaker Who Revolutionised Geography* (London, 2004), pp. 89–90.

15 Robert J. King, 'The Mercator Projection' in *Mapping Our World*, p. 90; Armand Rainaud, *Le Continent Austral: Hypothèses et Découvertes* (Paris, 1893), pp. 311–15; Stallard, *Antipodes*, p. 77.

16 Whether Marco Polo spent an extended time in China is open to doubt: see Frances Wood, *Did Marco Polo Go to China?* (London, 1995).

17 Nicholas Crane, *Mercator: The Man Who Mapped the Planet* (London, 2002), pp. 119, 121; William Eisler, *The Furthest Shore: Images of Terra Australis from the Middle Ages to Captain Cook* (Cambridge, 1995), p. 11; William A. R. Richardson, *Was Australia Charted before 1606? The Jave la Grande Inscriptions* (Canberra, 2006), p. 21. Beach was a sixteenth-century mistranscription of Locach. For the doubling of these toponyms because of a clerical error, see Hiatt, *Terra Incognita*, p. 265.

18 Hiatt, *Terra Incognita*, p. 226; Robert J. King, 'Marco Polo's Java and Locach on Mercator's World Maps of 1538 and 1569, and Globe of 1541', *The Globe*, 81 (2016), pp. 41, 45 (quotation).

19 Perry, *The Discovery of Australia*, pp. 20–1; Miriam Estensen, *Discovery: The Quest for the Great South Land* (St Leonards, NSW, 1998), pp. 8–9; Crane, *Mercator*, pp. 305–6. See also Robert J. King, 'Finding Marco Polo's Locach', *Terrae Incognitae*, 50/1 (2018), pp. 35–52.

20 Mike A. Zuber, 'The Armchair Discovery of the Unknown Southern Continent: Gerardus Mercator, Philosophical Pretensions and a Competitive Trade', *Early Science and Medicine*, 16/6 (2011), pp. 505–41.

21 W. A. R. Richardson, 'Mercator's Southern Continent: Its Origins, Influence and Gradual Demise', *Terrae Incognitae*, 25/1 (1993), p. 68.

22 Taylor, *The World of Gerald Mercator*, pp. 214, 217; Martin Woods, 'The First Modern Atlas' in *Mapping our World*, p. 96; Estensen, *Discovery*, p. 12.

23 Michael Richards and Maura O'Connor, eds., *Changing Coastlines: Putting Australia on the World Map 1493–1993* (Canberra, 1993), p. 10; Andrew Sharp, *The Discovery of Australia* (London, 1963), p. 14.

24 Estensen, *Discovery*, pp. 8, 38, 42, 44.

25 Richardson, *Was Australia Charted before 1606?*, p. 97.

26 Gavin Menzies, *1421: The Year China Discovered the World* (London, 2002), pp. 189, 200.

27 W. A. R. (Bill) Richardson, 'Gavin Menzies' Cartographic Fiction: The Case of the Chinese "Discovery" of Australia,' *The Globe*, 56 (2004), pp. 1–11; Robert Finlay, 'How Not to (Re)write World History: Gavin Menzies and the Chinese Discovery of America,' *Journal of World History*, 15/2 (2004), pp. 229–42.

28 Avan Judd Stallard, 'Better than *The Da Vinci Code*: The Theological Edifice That Is Gavin Menzies' *1421*,' *History Australia*, 5/3 (2008), pp. 77. 1–77.12.

29 Eisler, *The Furthest Shore*, pp. 13, 17; Ian Nicholson, *Via Torres Strait: A Maritime History of the Torres Strait Route and the Ships' Post Office at Booby Island* (Nambour, QLD, 1996), p. 8.

30 For a brief account of these voyages, see C. R. *Boxer: The Portuguese Seaborne Empire 1415–1825* (London, 1969), pp. 33, 36–7, and J. H. Parry, *The Spanish Seaborne Empire* (London, 1966), pp. 29–30, 116.

31 Howard Worth, 'An Alternative View of Java la Grande: Approaches to Cartographic History and Their Impact on the Interpretation of the Dieppe Maps,' *The Great Circle*, 33/1 (2011), pp. 33–4. For a forerunner to the Dieppe maps, see John Hewitt, 'Jean Mallard's World Map (ca. 1538–39),' *The Globe*, 79 (2016), pp. 1–12. Some obscure features of the Dieppe maps are investigated in Andrew J. Eliason, 'A Pacific Prospectus: The Origins and Identities of the Islands Depicted in the South Sea on the Dieppe Maps,' *The Globe*, 79 (2016), pp. 13–30, and Robert J. King, 'Cartographic Drift: Pulo Condor and the Ysles de Magna and Ye de Saill on the Dieppe Maps,' *The Globe*, 87 (2020), pp. 1–21.

32 Pearson, *Great Southern Land*, pp. 15–16. A list of the Dieppe maps depicting Jave-la-Grande and their location in libraries and archives is given in Richardson, *Was Australia Charted before 1606?*, p. 96.

33 Richardson, *Was Australia Charted before 1606?*, p. 39. On the controversies surrounding Jave-la-Grande, see also Sharp, *The Discovery of Australia*, pp. 4–6, 9–14.

34 Eisler, *The Furthest Shore*, p. 31; Estensen, *Discovery*, pp. 68–9.

35 Worth, 'An Alternative View of Java la Grande,' p. 38. For the positioning of Jave-la-Grande on the maps of the Dieppe school, see King, 'Marco Polo's Java and Locach,' p. 42.

36 Richardson, *Was Australia Charted before 1606?*, p. 37. For an argument that equates Jave-la-Grande with Australia, see R. Hervé, 'Australia: In French Geographical Documents of the Renaissance,' *JPRAHS*, 41/1 (1956), pp. 23–38.

37 Wallis, 'Visions of Terra Australis', p. 38; Michael Wintroub, 'The Translations of a Humanist Ship Captain: Jean Parmentier's 1529 Voyage to Sumatra,' *Renaissance Quarterly*, 68/1 (2015), pp. 98–132.

38 Estensen, *Discovery*, pp. 53–8, 75, 79–80; Williams and Frost, '*Terra Australis*,' p. 9.

39 Wallis, 'Visions of Terra Australis,' p. 37; W. A. R. (Bill) Richardson, 'Terra Australis, Jave la Grande and Australia: Identity Problems and Fiction' in Scott, Hiatt, McIlroy and Wortham, eds., *European Perceptions of Terra Australis*, pp. 83–109.

40 Robert J. King, 'The "Jagiellonian Globe," Utopia and "Jave la Grande", *Globe Studies*, 55/56 (2009), p. 51.

41 Stallard, *Antipodes*, p. 79. This chart is preserved at the BL, Add. MS 24,065.

42 Chet Van Duzer, *The World for a King: Pierre Desceliers's World Map of 1550* (London, 2015), p. 72.

43 W. A. R. Richardson, 'Jave-la-Grande: A Place Name Chart of Its East Coast,' *The Great Circle*, 6/1 (1984), p. 1; Des Cowley, 'European Voyages of Discovery,' *La Trobe Journal*, 41 (1988), p. 15.

44 Alexander Dalrymple, *Memoir Concerning the Chagos and Adjacent Islands. With a Memoir of the Chart of the Islands N.E. of Madagacar by Jean Baptiste d'Après* (London, 1786), p. 4. Dalrymple's conclusions were supported in R. H. Major, ed., *Early Voyages to Terra Australis* (London, 1859), pp. xxi–lxiv.

45 Richardson, *Was Australia Charted before 1606?*, p. 33; Helen Wallis, 'The Challenge That Is an Australian Map,' *The Globe*, 37 (1992), pp. 4–5. The Harleian manuscript cited is deposited at the BL, Add. MS 5413.

46 Flinders, *A Voyage to Terra Australis*, i, p. 6; Robert J. King, 'The Mysterious Jave la Grande' in *Mapping Our World*, p. 80.

47 Helen Wallis, 'The Dieppe Maps – The First Representation of Australia?' *The Globe*, 17 (1982), pp. 23, 41. See also three other publications by Helen Wallis, 'The Enigma of Java-La-Grande' in *Australia and the European Imagination: Papers from a Conference Held at the Humanities Research Centre, Australian National University, May 1981* (Canberra, 1982), pp. 1–40; 'Did the Portuguese Discover Australia? The Map Evidence' in *Technical Papers of the 12th Conference of the International Cartographic Association, Perth, Western Australia*, 2 vols. (Perth, 1984), II, pp. 203–20, and 'Java la Grande: The Enigma of the Dieppe Maps' in Glyndwr Williams and Alan Frost, eds., *Terra Australis to Australia* (Melbourne, 1988), pp. 39–81.

48 Among many publications by W. A. R. Richardson, who has researched the linguistic evidence painstakingly, are: 'Is Java-la-Grande Australia? The Linguistic Evidence Concerning the West Coast,' *The Globe*, 19 (1983), pp. 9–46; 'Java-la-Grande: A Case Study of Place-Name Corruption,' *The Globe*, 22 (1984), pp. 9–32; and *Was Australia Charted before 1606?* See also Robert J. King, 'Havre de Sylla on Jave La Grande,' *Terrae Incognitae*, 45/1 (2013), pp. 30–61.

49 Richardson, 'Java-la-Grande,' p. 26. For the further argument that the landmass depicted on these maps was based on Marco Polo's two Javas, see Robert J. King,

'The Jagiellonian Globe, a Key to the Puzzle of Jave la Grande,' *The Globe*, 62 (2009), pp. 1–50.

50 C. C. Macknight, 'On the Non-"discovery" of "Australia", *Canberra Historical Journal*, 12 (1983), pp. 34–6.

51 Sharp, *The Discovery of Australia*, pp. 10–11.

52 Sarah Toulouse, 'Marine Cartography and Navigation in Renaissance France' in David Woodward, ed., *The History of Cartography. Volume Three. Cartography in the European Renaissance, part 2* (Chicago, 2007), pp. 1555–6.

53 Frank Lestringant, ed., *Cosmographie Universelle selon les navigateurs tant anciens que modernes par Guillaume le Testu pillotte en la mer du Ponent, de la ville françoyse de Grace* (Paris, 2012), p. 60.

54 Mawer, *Incognita*, p. 47.

55 Andrew Eliason, 'Guillaume le Testu's Opinion of Java la Grande,' *The Globe*, 81 (2016), pp. 89–100.

56 Quoted in C. Jack Hinton, *The Search for the Islands of Solomon* (Oxford, 1969), p. 19.

57 K. G. McIntyre, *The Secret Discovery of Australia: Portuguese Ventures 250 Years before Captain Cook* (Sydney, 1982). See also K. G. McIntyre, 'Portuguese Discoverers on the Australian Coast,' *Journal of the Royal Historical Society of Victoria*, 45/4 (1974), pp. 201–28; Ian McKiggan, 'The Portuguese Expedition to Bass Strait in A.D. 1522,' *Journal of Australian Studies*, 1 (1977), pp. 2–32, and 'Jave-la-Grande: An Apologia,' ibid., 19 (1986), pp. 96–101; and P. Trickett, *Beyond Capricorn: How Portuguese Adventurers Discovered and Mapped Australia and New Zealand 250 Years before Captain Cook* (Adelaide, 2007). An older study suggesting that the Portuguese discovered Australia is George Collingridge, *The Discovery of Australia: A Critical, Documentary and Historic Investigation Concerning the Priority of Discovery in Australasia by Europeans before the Arrival of Lieut. James Cook, in the 'Endeavour', in the year 1770* (Sydney, 1895).

58 McIntyre, *Secret Discovery*, pp. 81–2; Jeremy N. Green, 'The Carronade Island Guns and Australia's Early Visitors,' *The Great Circle*, 4/2 (1982), pp. 73–83.

59 McIntyre, *Secret Discovery*, pp. 270–5, 294.

60 Pearson, *Great Southern Land*, p. 17; W. J. Pinton, 'Some Mahogany Ship Relics Examined' in B. Potter, ed., *The Mahogany Ship: Relic or Legend? Proceedings of the Second Australian Symposium on the Mahogany Ship* (Warrnambool, VIC, 1987), p. 70. See also S. Duncan, 'Shaving with Ockham's Razor: A Reappraisal of the Portuguese Priority Hypothesis,' *The Globe*, 39 (1993), pp. 1–9, and A. Ariel, 'Navigating with Kenneth McIntyre: A Professional Critique,' *The Great Circle*, 6/2 (1984), pp. 135–9.

61 Lawrence Fitzgerald, *Java la Grande: The Portuguese Discovery of Australia* (Hobart, 1985).

62 Richardson, *Was Australia Charted before 1606?*, pp. 44, 47.

63 Robert J. King, 'Regio Patalis: Australia on the Map in 1531? (Early South Sea Voyages, or Merely Cartographic Evolution?)' *The Portolan*, 82 (2011), pp. 8–17.

64 Stallard, *Antipodes*, p. 80; Williams and Frost, '*Terra Australis*,' p. 9.

65 Carlos Martinez Shaw, 'Terra Australis: The Spanish Quest' in John Hardy and Alan Frost, eds., *Studies from Terra Australis to Australia* (Canberra, 1989), pp. 60–2; Stallard, *Antipodes*, p. 120.

66 For the possible routes of Mendana's two voyages, see Helen Wallis, 'The Exploration of the South Sea, 1519 to 1644. A study of the influence of physical factors, with a reconstruction of the routes of the explorers' (University of Oxford D.Phil., 1954). A copy is available at the BL.

67 David Fausett, *Writing the New World: Imaginary Voyages and Utopias of the Great Southern Land* (Syracuse, 1993), p. 21. Mendana's pilots recorded incorrect longitudes: see Skelton, 'Map Compilation,' p. 48.

68 Miriam Estensen, *Terra Australis Incognita: The Spanish Quest for the Mysterious Great South Land* (Crows Nest, NSW, 2006), p. 60.

69 Eisler, *The Furthest Shore*, pp. 44–6; Estensen, *Discovery*, pp. 99–100. Both voyages are discussed in Estensen, *Terra Australis Incognita*, pp. 16–90, and Stallard, *Antipodes*, pp. 120–4. See also Celsus Kelly, ed., *Calendar of Documents: Spanish Voyages in the South Pacific from Alvaro de Mendaña to Alejandro Malaspina 1567–1794 and to Franciscan Missionary Plans for the Peoples of the Austral Lands 1617–1634* (Madrid, 1965), pp. 93–224.

70 Glyndwr Williams, *The Great South Sea: English Voyages and Encounters 1570–1750* (New Haven, CT, 1997), p. 56.

71 In their writings and on maps, Prado and Quiros sometimes used the word 'Austrialia' and on other occasions wrote 'Australia': see Rupert Gerritsen, 'A Note on "Australia" or "Austrialia",' *The Globe*, 72 (2013), pp. 23–30.

72 Eisler, *The Furthest Shore*, p. 47; Wood, *The Discovery of Australia*, pp. 121–6; Stallard, *Antipodes*, pp. 124–9; Clements Markham, ed., *The Voyages of Pedro Fernandez de Quiros 1595 to 1606*, 2 vols. (London, 1904), II, p. 462; Henry N. Stevens and George F. Barwick, eds., *New Light on the Discovery of Australia as Revealed by the Journal of Captain Don Diego de Prado Y Tovar* (London, 1930), p. xiii.

73 Estensen, *Discovery*, p. 104; Stevens and Barwick, eds., *New Light on the Discovery of Australia*, pp. 46–7.

74 Estensen, *Terra Australis Incognita*, pp. 196–7.

75 Stuart B. Kaye, *The Torres Strait* (The Hague, 1997), pp. 1, 4, 5; Markham, ed., *The Voyages of Pedro Fernandez de Quiros*, II, p. 463.

76 Fernández-Armesto, *Pathfinders*, p. 208.

77 Differing accounts of Torres's voyage include F. J. Bayldon, 'Voyage of Luis Vaez de Torres from the New Hebrides to the Moluccas, June to November 1606,' *JRAHS*, 11/3 (1925), pp. 158–94; Brett Hilder, 'The First Navigation of Torres Strait,' *Journal of Navigation*, 30/3 (1977), pp. 459–66, and *The Voyage of Torres: The Discovery of*

the Coastline of New Guinea and Torres Strait by Captain Luis Baéz de Torres in 1606 (St Lucia, QLD, 1980).

78 Estensen, *Terra Australis Incognita*, p. 188; Wallis, 'The Exploration of the South Sea,' pp. 322–3. See also F. J. Bayldon, 'Voyage of Torres,' *JRAHS*, 16/2 (1930), pp. 133–46.

79 Torres's report and Prado's more detailed narrative are published in Stevens, ed., *New Light on the Discovery of Australia*, pp. 86–205.

80 Hilder, the Voyage of Torres, pp. 87, 90. This interpretation is accepted by O. H. K. Spate, *The Spanish Lake: The Pacific since Magellan*, vol. 1 (London, 1979), p. 139.

81 Geoffrey C. Ingleton, '"The First Navigation of Torres Strait": Some Comments,' *Journal of Navigation*, 31/2 (1978), pp. 232–43.

82 Howard T. Fry, *Alexander Dalrymple (1737–1808) and the Expansion of British Trade* (Toronto, 1970), p. 122.

83 Hilder, *The Voyage of Torres*, p. 135; Williams and Frost, 'Terra Australis,' p. 10.

84 Estensen, *Discovery*, p. 108.

85 O. H. K. Spate, *Let Me Enjoy: Essays, Partly Geographical* (Canberra, 1965), p. 267.

Chapter 2

1 C. R. Boxer, *The Dutch Seaborne Empire, 1600–1800* (New York, 1965), p. 26; J. R. Bruijn, F. S. Gaastra and I. Schöffer, *Dutch-Asiatic Shipping in the 17th and 18th Centuries*, 3 vols. (The Hague, 1987), i, p. 119; Felipe Fernández-Armesto, *Pathfinders: A Global History of Exploration* (Oxford, 2006), p. 211.

2 See two studies by Robert Parthesius: *Dutch Ships in Tropical Waters: The Development of the Dutch East India Company (VOC) Network in Asia, 1595–1660* (Amsterdam, 2010) and 'Encounters of the Third Kind – Dutch Shipping in Asia and the Search for the South Land' in Lindsey Shaw and Wendy Wilkins, eds., *Dutch Connections: 400 Years of Australian-Dutch Maritime Links 1606–2006* (Sydney, 2006), pp. 59–60.

3 T. D. Mutch, 'The First Discovery of Australia with Account of the Voyage of the Duyfken, and Career of Willem Jansz,' *JRAHS*, XXVIII/V (1942), p. 305.

4 Femme S. Gaastra, 'The Dutch East India Company: A Reluctant Discoverer,' *The Great Circle*, 19 (1997), pp. 109–23.

5 Colin Sheehan, 'Strangers and Servants of the Company: The United East India Company and Dutch Voyages to Australia' in Peter Veth, Peter Sutton and Margo Neale, eds., *Strangers on the Shore: Early Coastal Contacts in Australia* (Canberra, 2008), p. 21.

6 R. A. Skelton, *Explorers' Maps. Chapters in the Cartographic Record of Geographical Discovery* (London, 1958), pp. 209–10.

7 Günter Schilder, 'From Secret to Common Knowledge: The Dutch Discoveries' in John Hardy and Alan Frost, eds., *Studies from Terra Australis to Australia* (Canberra, 1989), p. 73.

8   James Henderson, *Sent Forth a Dove: Discovery of the Duyfken* (Nedlands, WA, 1999), pp. 23–7; Marit van Huystee, *On the Yacht Duyfken (1601): The First European Ship to Explore the Australian Coast, Report*, Maritime Archaeology Department, Western Australian Maritime Museum no. 105 (1995), pp. 5–12.

9   Eisler, *The Furthest Shore*, p. 69.

10 Pearson, *Great Southern Land*, p. 31; Schilder, 'From Secret to Common Knowledge,' p. 72.

11 J. E. Heeres, *The Part Borne by the Dutch in the Discovery of Australia 1606–1765* (London, 1899), p. v.

12 Jan Tent, 'Geographic and Linguistic Reflections on Moente and Dubbelde Ree: Two of Australia's First Recorded Placenames,' *Geographical Research*, 44/4 (2006), p. 373.

13 Henderson, *Sent Forth a Dove*, pp. 29, 35; Robert Garvey, *To Build a Ship: The VOC Replica Ship Duyfken* (Crawley, WA, 2001), p. 81; Andrew Sharp, *The Discovery of Australia* (Oxford, 1963), p. 18.

14 Byron Heath, *Discovering the Great South Land* (Dural, NSW, 2005), p. 79.

15 Bruce Donaldson. 'The Dutch Contribution to the European Discovery of Australia' in Nonja Peters, ed., *The Dutch Down Under 1606–2006* (Crawley, WA, 2006), p. 5; Sharp, *The Discovery of Australia*, p. 18. The quotation is taken from Eisler, *The Furthest Shore*, p. 69.

16 Mutch, 'The First Discovery of Australia,' p. 325. The chart is reproduced in Frederick Casper Wieder, ed., *Monumenta Cartographica: Reproductions of Unique and Rare Maps, Plans and Views in the Actual Size of the Originals: Accompanied by Cartographical Monographs* (The Hague, 1925–33), V, plate 125.

17 Nick Burningham, 'The Australische Compagnie and the Other *Eendracht* of 1616,' *The Great Circle*, 38/1 (2016), p. 38.

18 Henderson, *Sent Forth a Dove*, pp. 36–45.

19 Nigel Erskine, 'Dutch Encounters and the Australasian Shore' in Shaw and Wilkins, eds., *Dutch Connections*, p. 12.

20 Garvey, *To Build a Ship*, pp. 5–6; Howard Worth, 'The *Duyfken*: An Exploration of the Roles of a Replica Ship,' *The Great Circle*, 35/1 (2013), pp. 75–95.

21 Parthesius, 'Encounters of the Third Kind,' p. 65.

22 Eisler, *The Furthest Shore*, pp. 69–73; Burningham, 'The Australische Compagnie,' pp. 32–44; Wood, *The Discovery of Australia*, pp. 152–3.

23 Wendy van Duivenvoorde, 'Dutch Seaman Dirk Hartog (1583–1621) and His Ship *Eendracht*,' *The Great Circle*, 38/1 (2016), pp. 3, 6–8.

24 Günter Schilder, ed., *Voyage to the Great South Land: Willem de Vlamingh, 1696–7* (Sydney, 1985), p. 49; Wendy van Duivenvoorde, 'Dirk Hartog Was Here! His 1616 Inscription Plate and Dutch Ship Communications' in Nonja Peters, ed., *A Touch of Dutch: Maritime, Military, Migration and Mercantile Connections on the Western Third 1616–2016* (Perth, 2016), p. 18.

25 Extract from Brouwer's letter to managers of the VOC, 17 December 1611, in Willem C. H. Robert, *The Explorations, 1696–1697, of Australia by Willem de Vlamingh* (Amsterdam, 1972), pp. 147, 149.

26 van Duivenvoorde, 'Dutch Seaman Dirk Hartog,' p. 9; Richard Dunn and Rebekah Higgitt, *Ships, Clocks & Stars: The Quest for Longitude* (Glasgow, 2014), pp. 22, 25; R. T. Appleyard and Toby Manford, *The Beginning: European Discovery and Early Settlement of Swan River, Western Australia* (Nedlands, WA, 1979), p. 15.

27 Schilder, ed., *Voyage to the Great South Land*, pp. 49–50; van Duivenvoorde, 'Dirk Hartog Was Here!' p. 18.

28 Günter Schilder, *Monumenta Cartographica Neerlandica, IX: Hessel Gerritsz (1580/81–1632) Master Engraver and Map Maker, Who 'Ruled' the Seas* (Amsterdam, 2013), p. 429.

29 van Duivenvoorde, 'Dutch Seaman Dirk Hartog,' pp. 10–11, 13; Phillip Playford, 'Aboriginal and European Discoveries of Australia,' *Early Days*, 13/1 (2007), p. 57.

30 van Duivenvoorde, 'Dutch Seaman Dirk Hartog,' pp. 10–11, 13; Evan McHugh, *1606: An Epic Adventure* (Sydney, 2006), p. 38.

31 Pearson, *Great Southern Land*, p. 32; Sharp, *The Discovery*, p. 34; van Duivenvoorde, 'Dutch Seaman Dirk Hartog,' pp. 14–15, 19.

32 See two articles by Robert J. King: 'Dirk Hartog Lands on Beach, the Gold-Bearing Province,' *The Globe*, 77 (2015), pp. 12–52, and 'From Beach to Western Australia: Dirk Hartog and the Transition from Speculative to Actual Geography,' *The Great Circle*, 38/1 (2016), pp. 45–71.

33 J. C. Beaglehole, *The Exploration of the Pacific*, 3rd edn. (London, 1966), p. 114.

34 Schilder, ed., *Voyage to the Great South Land*, p. 50; Schilder, ed., *Monumenta Cartographica Neerlandica, IX*, p. 427.

35 Schilder, ed., *Monumenta Cartographica Neerlandica, IX*, p. 429.

36 Avan Judd Stallard, *Antipodes: In search of the Southern Continent* (Clayton, VIC, 2016), p. 142.

37 Sharp, *Discovery*, p. 36; Pearson, *Great Southern Land*, pp. 32–3.

38 J. P. Sigmond and L. H. Zuiderbaan, *Dutch Discoveries of Australia: Shipwrecks, Treasures and Early Voyages off the West Coast* (Adelaide, 1978), p. 37. A recent Biography of de Houtman Is Howard Gray, *Spice at Any Price: The Life and Times of Frederick de Houtman, 1571–1627* (Geraldton, WA, 2019).

39 Schilder, ed., *Voyage to the Great South Land*, pp. 50–1; Beaglehole, *The Exploration of the Pacific*, p. 122. 'Abrolhos' is a Portuguese phrase meaning 'keep awake.'

40 Quoted in Schilder, ed., *Voyage to the Great South Land*, pp. 51–2 (quotation on p. 51).

41 P. A Leupe, *De Reizen der Nederlanders naar het Zuidland of Nieuw-Holland in de 17e en 18e eeuw* (Amsterdam, 1868), p. 32; Mawer, *Incognita*, p. 109.

42 Quoted in Schilder, 'From Secret to Common Knowledge,' p. 75.

43 Schilder, ed., *Voyage to the Great South Land*, p. 52. No original sources from this voyage exist: see Schilder, *Monumenta Cartographica Neerlandica, IX*, p. 430.

44   Heeres, *The Part Borne by the Dutch*, p. 9.

45   Ida Lee, 'The First Sighting of Australia by the English,' *JPRAHS*, 20/5 (1934), pp. 273–80; J. N. Green, 'The Survey and Identification of the English East India Company Ship, Trial (1622),' *International Journal of Nautical Archaeology*, 15/3 (1986), pp. 195–202.

46   Sharp, *Discovery*, p. 43; James A. Henderson, *Phantoms of the Tryall: A Documented Account of Australia's First Shipwreck, the East India Company's Vessel Tryall in 1622 Off the Monte Bello Islands in Western Australia's North-West* (Perth, 1993); Graeme Henderson, *Swallowed by the Sea: The Story of Australia's Shipwrecks* (Canberra, 2016), p. 15.

47   Mawer, *Incognita*, pp. 109–10; Heeres, *The Part Borne by the Dutch*, pp. 18–21.

48   Schilder, 'From Secret to Common Knowledge,' p. 75.

49   Heath, *Discovering the Great South Land*, p. 99; Pearson, *Great Southern Land*, p. 33.

50   Günter Schilder, *Australia Unveiled: The Share of the Dutch Navigators in the Discovery of Australia* (Amsterdam, 1976), p. 84.

51   Mawer, *Incognita*, p. 110; Pearson, *Great Southern Land*, pp. 33, 35. For Carstenszoon's encounters with Aborigines, see Susan Broomhall, 'Emotional Encounters: Indigenous Peoples in the Dutch East India Company's Interactions with the South Lands,' *Australian Historical Studies*, 45/3 (2014), pp. 360–3.

52   Pearson, *Great Southern Land*, p. 34.

53   Quoted in Schilder, 'From Secret to Common Knowledge,' p. 77.

54   Quoted in Pearson, *Great Southern Land*, p. 34.

55   Ibid., p. 35.

56   Donaldson, 'The Dutch Contribution,' p. 12; Sigmond and Zuiderbaan, *Dutch Discoveries of Australia*, p. 49.

57   Schilder, 'From Secret to Common Knowledge,' p. 77. The delay in disseminating findings from the *Arnhem*'s voyage arose from the fact that the ship's journal and original chart were not preserved: see Schilder, *Australia Unveiled*, pp. 94, 318–19.

58   Schilder, ed., *Voyage to the Great South Land*, pp. 53–4; Pearson, *Great Southern Land*, p. 35.

59   Sigmond and Zuiderbaan, *Dutch Discoveries of Australia*, p. 53; Heeres, *The Part Borne by the Dutch*, p. xi.

60   Quoted in Graham Seal, *The Savage Shore: Extraordinary Stories of Survival and Tragedy from the Early Voyages of Discovery* (New Haven, CT, 2016), p. 59.

61   Donaldson, 'The Dutch Contribution,' p. 14.

62   Günter Schilder, *Monumenta Cartographica Neerlandica, IX*, pp. 397, 411 (quotation on p. 411).

63   G. A. Mawer, 'The Mysterious Absence of North West Cape,' *The Globe*, 81 (2016), pp. 105–8.

64   Avan Judd Stallard, 'Antipodes to Terra Australis' (University of Queensland PhD, 2010), p. 202; Mawer, *Incognita*, pp. 111–12.

65 Sharp, *The Discovery of Australia*, p. 55.

66 Pearson, *Great Southern Land*, p. 36; Jean Fornasiero, Peter Monteath and John West-Sooby, *Encountering Terra Australis: The Australian Voyages of Nicolas Baudin and Matthew Flinders*, rev. edn. (Kent Town, SA, 2010), p. 42.

67 For a detailed study of the *Batavia*'s construction and wooden hull, see Wendy van Duivenvoorde, *Dutch East India Company Shipbuilding: The Archaeological Study of Batavia and Other Seventeenth-Century VOC Ships* (College Station, TX, 2015).

68 Jeremy Green, 'The Dutch Down Under: Sailing Blunders' in Peters, ed., *The Dutch Down Under*, pp. 17–19; Sigmond and Zuiderbaan, *Dutch Discoveries of Australia*, p. 66; Henderson, *Swallowed by the Sea*, pp. 18–22. For extended accounts of the *Batavia*'s wreck, see Philippe Godard, *The First and Last Voyage of the Batavia* (Perth, 1993); Henrietta Drake-Brockman, *Voyage to Disaster*, new edn. (Crawley, WA, 1995); Mike Dash, *Batavia's Graveyard* (London, 2002); Michael Sturma, 'Mutiny and Narrative: Francisco Pelsaert's Journals and the Wreck of the *Batavia*', *The Great Circle*, 24/1 (2002), pp. 14–24; and Rupert Gerritsen, 'The First Naval Confrontations in Australian Waters – in 1629?' *Journal of Australian Naval History*, 9/1 (2012), pp. 110–19.

69 Pearson, *Great Southern Land*, p. 38; Sharp, *The Discovery of Australia*, p. 58.

70 See two publications by J. N. Green: 'The VOC Ship *Batavia* Wrecked in 1629 on the Houtman Abrolhos, Western Australia,' *International Journal of Nautical Archaeology*, 4/1 (1975), pp. 43–63, and 'The AVOC Retourschip *Batavia*, Wrecked Western Australia, 1629: An Excavation Report and Catalogue of Artefacts,' *British Archaeological Reports International Series* (489) (1989).

71 John Forsyth, 'The Visit of the Yacht Grootenbroeck to the Coast of the South-land in 1631,' *Journal and Proceedings of the Western Australian Historical Society*, V/1 (1955), pp. 17–26.

Chapter 3

1 Günter Schilder, 'From Secret to Common Knowledge – The Dutch Discoveries' in John Hardy and Alan Frost, eds., *Studies from Terra Australis to Australia* (Canberra, 1989), pp. 72–84, 250–3.

2 Grahame Anderson, *The Merchant of the Zeehaen: Isaac Gilsemans and the Voyages of Abel Tasman* (Wellington, 2001), pp. 39–41.

3 B. J. Slot, *Abel Tasman and the Discovery of New Zealand* (Amsterdam, 1992), pp. 46–7.

4 Ibid., pp. 47–56; Andrew Sharp, *The Voyages of Abel Janszoon Tasman* (Oxford, 1968), pp. 5–10.

5 James Backhouse Walker, *Abel Janszoon Tasman: His Life and Voyages* (Hobart, 1896), p. 17; Anderson, *The Merchant of the Zeehaen*, pp. 42–52.

6   For Van Diemen's career, see Holden Furber, *Rival Empires of Trade in the Orient,*
    1600–1800 (Minneapolis, 1976), pp. 50–2, 54, 59, 62–3, and two articles by Alfons
    van der Kraan: 'Anthony Van Diemen: From Bankrupt to Governor-General, 1593–
    1636 (Part 1),' *The Great Circle,* 26/2 (2004), pp. 3–23, and 'Anthony Van Diemen:
    Patron of Discovery and Exploration, 1636–1645 (Part 2),' *The Great Circle,* 27/1
    (2005), pp. 3–33.

7   *The Tasman Map of 1644: Historical Note and Description of the Manuscript Map*
    in the Mitchell Library, Sydney (Sydney, 1948), p. 12; Kees Zandvliet, 'Golden
    Opportunities in Geopolitics: Cartography and the Dutch East India Company
    during the Lifetime of Abel Tasman' in William Eisler and Bernard Smith, eds.,
    Terra Australis: The Furthest Shore (Sydney, 1988), pp. 67–84.

8   Paul Brunton, 'Abel Janszoon Tasman – The Australian Voyages, Missing Journals
    and Perplexing Charts' in Lindsey Shaw and Wendy Wilkins, eds., *Dutch*
    Connections: 400 Years of Australian-Dutch Maritime Links 1606–2006 (Sydney,
    2006), p. 41.

9   G. R. Crone, 'The Discovery of Tasmania and New Zealand,' *The Geographical*
    Journal, 111/4–6 (1948), p. 257.

10 Eisler, *The Furthest Shore,* p. 78.

11 Paul Brunton, 'The Voyages of Abel Tasman,' *Launceston Historical Society Papers*
    and Proceedings, 16 (2004), p. 2; Schilder, 'From Secret to Common Knowledge,'
    p. 79; Günter Schilder, 'A Continent Takes Shape: The Dutch Mapping of Australia'
    in Michael Richards and Maura O'Connor, eds., *Changing Coastlines: Putting*
    Australia on the World Map 1493–1993 (Canberra, 1993), p. 13.

12 Michael Bennett, 'Van Diemen, Tasman, and the Dutch Reconnaissance,'
    Tasmanian Historical Research Association Papers and Proceedings, 39/2 (1992),
    pp. 75–6.

13 Arnhem Land was named after the Dutch ship that explored the area in 1623.
    Speult Land was named after Herman van Speult, the Dutch Governor of Ambon
    between 1618 and 1625.

14 Mawer, *Incognita,* p. 113; Nigel Erskine, 'Dutch Encounters and the Australasian
    Shore' in Shaw and Wilkins, eds., *Dutch Connections,* p. 15.

15 Bennett, 'Van Diemen, Tasman, and the Dutch Reconnaissance,' p. 77; Mawer,
    Incognita, p. 114.

16 Slot, *Abel Tasman,* p. 41; J. E. Heeres, ed., *The Journal of Abel Janszoon Tasman*
    (Amsterdam, 1898), p. 100 (quotation dated 1634 from the office of the Firando
    factory, Japan).

17 Eisler, *The Furthest Shore,* p. 80.

18 Brunton, 'The Voyages of Abel Tasman,' p. 2; Heeres, ed., *The Journal of Abel*
    Janszoon Tasman, p. 108; Slot, *Abel Tasman,* p. 40.

19 Walker, *Abel Janszoon Tasman,* pp. 26–7. Visscher's ambitious scheme is
    summarized in Wood, *The Discovery of Australia,* pp. 179–80.

20 Flinders, *A Voyage to Terra Australis*, I, p. lxxv.

21 Schilder, 'From Secret to Common Knowledge', p. 79.

22 Frank Broeze, *Island Nation: A History of Australians and the Sea* (St Leonards, NSW, 1998), p. 19; Miriam Estensen, *Discovery: The Quest for the Great South Land* (St Leonards, NSW, 1998), p. 174.

23 Graham Seal, *The Savage Shore: Extraordinary Stories of Survival and Tragedy from the Early Voyages of Discovery* (New Haven, CT, 2016), p. 95.

24 The features of these ships are described in Ab Hoving and Cor Emke, *The Ships of Abel Tasman* (Hilversum, 2000), pp. 25–54.

25 Sharp, *The Voyages of Abel Janszoon Tasman*, p. 30.

26 Brian N. Hooker, 'Towards the Identification of the Terrestrial Globe Carried on the *Heemskerck* by Abel Tasman in 1642–43', *The Globe*, 79/1 (2016), pp. 31–7. Cf. Michael Ross, 'The Mysterious Eastland Revealed', *The Globe*, 53 (2002), pp. 1–22, and Avan Judd Stallard, 'Navigating Tasman's 1642 Voyage of Exploration: Cartographic Instruments and Navigational Decisions', *The Portolan*, 69 (2007), pp. 24–43.

27 Sharp, *The Voyages of Abel Janszoon Tasman*, pp. 30–2.

28 Ibid., pp. 22, 33–9.

29 Heeres, ed., *The Journal of Abel Janszoon Tasman*, pp. 134–5.

30 Slot, *Abel Tasman*, p. 59. See also Vibeke Roeper and Diederick Wildeman, eds., *Het Journaal van Abel Tasman 1642–1643* (The Hague, 2006).

31 Helen Wallis, 'The Exploration of the South Sea, 1519 to 1644. A Study of the Influence of Physical Factors, with a Reconstruction of the Routes of the Explorers' (University of Oxford D.Phil., 1954), p. 372.

32 Heeres, ed., *The Journal of Abel Janszoon Tasman*, p. 106.

33 Brunton, 'The Voyages of Abel Tasman', p. 3; Wood, *The Discovery of Australia*, p. 187; Anderson, *The Merchant of the Zeehaen*, p. 122.

34 Evan McHugh, *1606: An Epic Adventure* (Sydney, 2006), p. 84; Wood, *The Discovery of Australia*, p. 188; Slot, *Abel Tasman*, p. 61.

35 Sharp, *The Voyages of Abel Janszoon Tasman*, p. 88; Pearson, *Great Southern Land*, p. 39.

36 Byron Heath, *Discovering the Great South Land* (Dural, NSW, 2005), p. 112.

37 Sharp, *The Voyages of Abel Janszoon Tasman*, p. 90.

38 Wood, *The Discovery of Australia*, p. 188; Brunton, 'Abel Janszoon Tasman', p. 43; Peter Chapman, 'Tasman and a Dutch Discovery', *Australian Natural History*, 20/2 (1980), p. 41.

39 Sharp, *The Voyages of Abel Janszoon Tasman*, pp. 98–9, 110–12; McHugh, *1606*, p. 85; Lloyd Robson, *A History of Tasmania: Van Diemen's Land from the Earliest Times to 1855. Volume 1* (Melbourne, 1983), p. 5; Philip John Tardif, *John Bowen's Hobart: The Beginning of European Settlement in Tasmania* (Hobart, 2003), p. 6.

40 Heath, *Discovering the Great South Land*, p. 113; Robson, A *History of Tasmania*, I, p. 5. The Dutch claim to possession was never followed up.

41 Heeres, ed., *The Journal of Abel Janszoon Tasman*, p. 112.

42 McHugh, *1606*, p. 88.

43 Wood, *The Discovery of Australia*, p. 191; Heeres, ed., *The Journal of Abel Janszoon Tasman*, p. 112.

44 Schilder, 'A Continent Takes Shape,' (quotation), p. 13.

45 Broeze, *Island Nation*, p. 21.

46 T. M. Knight, 'From Terra Incognita to New Holland,' *Cartography*, 6/2 (1967), p. 87.

47 For details see Eisler, *The Furthest Shore*, pp. 84–90.

48 Wood, *The Discovery of Australia*, p. 311; Brunton, 'The Voyages of Abel Tasman,' pp. 4–5.

49 Anderson, *The Merchant of the Zeehaen*, p. 123; Mawer, *Incognita*, p. 124; Estensen, *Discovery*, pp. 181, 184.

50 *The Tasman Map of 1644*, p. 14.

51 Günter Schilder and Hans Kok, *Sailing for the East: History & Catalogue of Manuscript Charts on Vellum of the Dutch East India Company (VOC) 1602–1799* (Houten, 2010), p. 118.

52 Glyndwr Williams and Alan Frost, 'Terra Australis: Theory and Speculation' in Glyndwr Williams and Alan Frost, eds., *Terra Australis to Australia* (Melbourne, 1988), p. 19.

53 Morgan, ed., *Australia Circumnavigated*, II, p. 405.

54 Sharp, *The Voyages of Abel Janszoon Tasman*, p. 311; Brunton, 'The Voyages of Abel Tasman,' p. 5; Wood, *The Discovery of Australia*, p. 191.

55 Heeres, ed., *The Journal of Abel Janszoon Tasman*, p. 114.

56 Wallis, 'The Exploration of the South Sea,' p. 438.

57 Schilder, 'From Secret to Common Knowledge,' p. 80.

58 Slot, *Abel Tasman*, p. 72.

59 Sharp, *The Voyages of Abel Janszoon Tasman*, pp. 312–13.

60 Letter of the Governor-General and Councillors, 23 December 1644, in Heeres, ed., *The Journal of Abel Janszoon Tasman*, p. 156.

61 Sharp, *The Voyages of Abel Janszoon Tasman*, pp. 314–15; Mawer, *Incognita*, p. 126.

62 Sharp, *The Voyages of Abel Janszoon Tasman*, pp. 314–15; Mawer, *Incognita*, p. 127. The orders are printed in R. H. Major, ed., *Early Voyages to Terra Australis, Now Called Australia* (London, 1859), pp. 43–58.

63 McHugh, *1606*, pp. 93–4; Schilder and Kok, *Sailing for the East*, p. 119; T. M. Perry, *The Discovery of Australia: The Charts and Maps of the Navigators and Explorers* (Melbourne, 1982), p. 41.

64 Anderson, *The Merchant of the Zeehaen*, p. 132. For suggestions about Tasman's route in the Gulf of Carpentaria, see Carsten Berg Høgenhoff, *Sweers Islands Unveiled: Details from Abel Tasman and Matthew Flinders' Explorations of Australia* (Oslo, 2006), pp. 25–33.

65   J. P. Sigmond and L. H. Zuiderbaan, *Dutch Discoveries of Australia: Shipwrecks, Treasures and Early Voyages off the West Coast* (Adelaide, 1976), p. 82.

66   Wood, *The Discovery of Australia*, p. 202; Sharp, *The Voyages of Abel Janszoon Tasman*, p. 329; Robert Logan Jack, *Northmost Australia: Three Centuries of Exploration, Discovery, and Adventure in and around the Cape York Peninsula, Queensland ...*, 2 vols. (London, 1921), I, p. 73.

67   Entry for 26 December 1802 in Morgan, ed., *Australia Circumnavigated*, II, p. 120; Kenneth Morgan, *Matthew Flinders, Maritime Explorer of Australia* (London, 2016), p. 61.

68   Matthew Flinders, 'The "Memoir"' in Morgan, ed., *Australia Circumnavigated, II*, pp. 406–7.

69   Entry for 8 December 1802, Ibid., II, pp. 197–8.

70   Sharp, *The Voyages of Abel Janszoon Tasman*, pp. 316–17 (quotations); Wallis, 'The Exploration of the South Sea,' pp. 439, 443.

71   Jack, *Northmost Australia*, I, p. 64.

72   Campbell Macknight, 'A Useless Discovery: Australia and Its People in the Eyes of Others from Tasman to Cook,' *The Globe*, 61 (2008), pp. 1–10.

73   For a critical view of Tasman's voyages, see Bennett, 'Van Diemen, Tasman, and the Dutch Reconnaissance,' p. 18. For remembrance of Tasman's voyage, see Stefan Petrow, 'Godfather of Tasmania: Commemorating Abel Tasman 1838 to 2012,' *Journal of Australian Studies*, 38/2 (2014), pp. 157–74.

74   Mawer, *Incognita*, p. 129.

75   Kees Zandvliet, 'Mapping the Dutch World Overseas in the Seventeenth Century' in David Woodward, ed., *The History of Cartography. Volume Three. Cartography in the European Renaissance. Part 2* (Chicago, 2007), p. 1443.

76   Wood, *The Discovery of Australia*, pp. 205–6.

77   Jan O. M. Broek, 'Geographical Exploration by the Dutch' in Herman R. Friis, ed., *The Pacific Basin: A History of Its Geographic Exploration* (New York, 1967), p. 164.

78   Slot, *Abel Tasman*, p. 85.

79   Günter Schilder, 'New Cartographical Contributions to the Coastal Exploration of Australia in the Course of the Seventeenth Century,' *Imago Mundi*, 26/1 (1972), p. 43; McHugh, *1606*, p. 91.

80   Daniel A. Baugh, 'Seapower and Science: The Motives for Pacific Exploration' in Derek Howse, ed., *Background to Discovery: Pacific Exploration from Dampier to Cook* (Berkeley and Los Angeles, 1990), p. 11.

81   Brian Hooker, 'Two Sets of Tasman Longitudes in Seventeenth and Eighteenth Century Maps,' *Geographical Journal*, 156/1 (1990), p. 24; Paul Moon, 'From Tasman to Cook: The Proto-intelligence Phase of New Zealand's Colonisation,' *Journal of Intelligence History*, 18/2 (2019), p. 256.

82 Brunton, 'The Voyages of Abel Tasman,' p. 6; Maggie Patton, 'Tasman's Journal' in *Mapping Our World*, p. 137. For useful comparative remarks on these two journals, see Slot, *Abel Tasman*, pp. 90–2.

83 Slot, *Abel Tasman*, p. 89.

84 John Ogilby, *The Unknown South-land in America, Being the Latest and Most Accurate Description of the New World* (London, 1671), pp. 653–61; Glyndwr Williams, 'New Holland to New South Wales: The English Approaches' in Williams and Frost, eds., *Terra Australis to Australia*, p. 119; Eisler, *The Furthest Shore*, p. 83.

85 Crone, 'The Discovery of Tasmania and New Zealand,' p. 258. For the translation, see Robert Hooke, 'A Relation of a Voyage Made towards the South Terra Incognita; Extracted from the Journal of Captain Abel Tasman …' in Robert Hooke, ed., *Philosophical Collections*, 6 (London, 1682), pp. 179–86.

86 Flinders, *A Voyage to Terra Australis*, I, p. xiii.

87 This is reproduced in Frederick Casper Wieder, ed., *Monumenta Cartographica: Reproductions of Unique and Rare Maps, Plans and Views in the Actual Size of the Originals: Accompanied by Cartographical Monographs*, 5 vols. (The Hague, 1925–33), IV, plate 97.

88 Sharp, *The Voyages of Abel Janszoon Tasman*, p. 343.

89 William Foster, 'An Early Chart of Tasmania,' *The Geographical Journal*, 37/5 (1911), pp. 550–1. For information on the other charts and maps of Tasman's voyage of 1642 to Van Diemen's Land, see Sharp, *The Voyages of Abel Janszoon Tasman*, pp. 100–1.

90 Heeres, ed., *The Journal of Abel Janszoon Tasman*, pp. 69–73.

91 Williams, 'New Holland to New South Wales,' p. 117; Eisler, *The Furthest Shore*, pp. 82–3.

92 For the library's acquisition of the map, see Brunton, 'The Voyages of Abel Tasman,' pp. 6–7.

93 Schilder, 'From Secret to Common Knowledge,' p. 81. The origins of the map have elicited different explanations. Schilder considers that the map was made around 1695. The origins of the Bonaparte map are discussed in Anderson, *The Merchant of the Zeehaen*, pp. 155–8, and Brian N. Hooker, 'New Light on the Origin of the Tasman-Bonaparte Map,' *The Globe*, 78 (2015), pp. 1–8. See also *The Tasman Map of 1644*, pp. 17–18, and Maggie Patton, 'Tasman's Legacy' in *Mapping Our World*, pp. 140–1. The construction of the map and its subsequent history are discussed in Ian Burnet, *The Tasman Map: The Biography of a Map* (Kenthurst: NSW, 2019).

94 Perry, *The Discovery of Australia*, pp. 39–41.

95 Schilder, 'New Cartographical Contributions,' p. 42.

96 Helen Wallis, 'The Challenge That Is an Australian Map,' *The Globe*, 37 (1992), pp. 1–5; Zandvliet, 'Golden Opportunities in Geopolitics,' p. 80.

97 Martin Woods, 'New Holland's Birth Certificate' in *Mapping Our World*, p. 139.

98   Ibid.

99   Günter Schilder, *Australia Unveiled: The Share of the Dutch Navigators in the Discovery of Australia* (Amsterdam, 1976), p. 197; Schilder, 'A Continent Takes Shape,' p. 14; *Australia in Maps: Great Maps in Australia's History from the National Library's Collection* (Canberra, 2007), pp. 30–3.

100 Hooker, 'New Light,' p. 3.

Chapter 4

1   Andrew Sharp, *The Voyages of Abel Janszoon Tasman* (Oxford, 1968), p. 25.

2   Campbell Macknight, 'A Useless Discovery? Australia and Its People in the Eyes of Others from Tasman to Cook,' *The Globe*, 61 (2008), pp. 2–3.

3   Pearson, *Great Southern Land*, pp. 40–2. For a detailed account of the wreck, see James Henderson, *Marooned* (Perth, 1982).

4   Pearson, *Great Southern Land*, pp. 40–2; Rupert Gerritsen, 'The Arrival of the *Immenhorn*: Insights into a Little-Known Voyage to the West Coast of Australia in 1659,' *The Great Circle*, 34/1 (2014), p. 40. See also Jeremy N. Green, *The Loss of the Verenigde Oostindische Compagnie Jacht VERGULDE DRAECK, Western Australia 1656*, British Archaeological Reports Supplementary Series 36, Part 1 (1977), pp. 1–60.

5   Phillip Playford, *Carpet of Silver: The Wreck of the Zuytdorp* (Crawley, WA, 1996), p. 24.

6   Phillip E. Playford, *Voyage of Discovery to Terra Australis: By Willem De Vlamingh, 1696–1697* (Perth, 1998), p. 4.

7   Günter Schilder, ed., *Voyage to the Great South Land: Willem de Vlamingh, 1696–7* (Sydney, 1985), pp. 165–7. The charts and instruments taken on the voyage are listed on pp. 16–17 of this book.

8   Phillip E. Playford, 'Discoveries and Disasters – Early Dutch, French and British Exploration and Shipwrecks on the Coast of Western Australia' in Lindsey Shaw and Wendy Wilkins, eds., *Dutch Connections: 400 Years of Australian-Dutch Maritime Links 1606–2006* (Sydney, 2006), p. 31.

9   Playford, *Carpet of Silver*, pp. 25–6; Schilder, ed., *Voyage to the Great South Land*, pp. 60–3, 66 (quotation).

10 Playford, *Carpet of Silver*, p. 26; Peter Sigmond, 'Two Pewter Plates' in Leo Akveld, Frank Broeze, Femme Gaastra, Gordon Jackson and Willem Mörzer Bruyns, eds., *In het kielzog: Maritiem-historisches studies aangeboden aan Jaap R. Bruijn bijzijn vertrek als hoogleraar zeegeschiedenis aande Universiteit Leiden* (Amsterdam, 2003), pp. 248, 250, 254–5; and Jeremy Green, 'Proof of the Daring Spirit of His Ancestors' in *Mapping Our World*, p. 161.

11 Schilder, ed., *Voyage to the Great South Land*, p. 101.

12 Ibid., p. 99; Johannes Heniger, 'Dutch Contributions to the Study of Exotic Natural History in the Seventeenth and Eighteenth Centuries' in William Eisler and Bernard Smith, eds., *Terra Australis: The Furthest Shore* (Sydney, 1988), p. 27; Willem C. H. Robert, *The Explorations, 1696–1697, of Australia by Willem de Vlamingh* (Amsterdam, 1972), p. 22.

13 Martin Terry, 'Early Mapping of the Pacific,' *The Globe*, 37 (1992), p. 22.

14 Extract from a letter of the Governor General and Councillors of the East Indies to the Managers of the Dutch East India Company at the Chamber Amsterdam, 30 November 1697, in Robert, *The Explorations, 1696–1697, of Australia*, p. 163.

15 Martin Woods, 'The Last Great Dutch Voyage to Australia' in *Mapping Our World*, p. 163.

16 Eric Ketelaar, 'Exploration of the Archived World: From de Vlamingh's Plate to Digital Realities,' *Archives and Manuscripts*, 36/2 (2008), p. 17; Günter Schilder, 'New Holland: The Dutch Discoveries' in Glyndwr Williams and Alan Frost, eds., *Terra Australis to Australia* (Melbourne, 1988), p. 110.

17 Jan Tent and Helen Slatyer, 'Naming Places on the "South Land": European Naming Practices from 1606 to 1803,' *Australian Historical Studies*, 40/1 (2009), p. 9.

18 Glyndwr Williams, *The Great South Sea: English Voyages and Encounters 1570–1750* (New Haven, CT, 1997), p. 131.

19 Macknight, 'A Useless Discovery?' p. 3; J. E. Heeres, *The Part Borne by the Dutch in the Discovery of Australia 1606–1765* (London, 1899), pp. 87–9; Flinders, *A Voyage to Terra Australis*, I, pp. xiii–xiv.

20 Playford, *Carpet of Silver*; Phillip Playford, 'The Wreck of the *Zuytdorp*,' *Journal and Proceedings of the Western Australian Historical Society*, 5/5 (1959), pp. 5–41; Jeremy Green, 'The Dutch Down Under: Sailing Blunders' in Nonja Peters, ed., *The Dutch Down Under: 1606–2006* (Crawley, WA, 2006), pp. 66–7; Michael McCarthy, 'The Dutch on Australian Shores: The *Zuytdorp* Tragedy – An Unfinished Business' in Shaw and Wilkins, eds., *Dutch Connections*, pp. 94–108. Items from the wreck were discovered in the late 1950s and salvage attempts have been in progress since 1963.

21 Green, 'The Dutch Down Under,' pp. 68–70. Several expeditions to the *Zeewijk's* wreck site have been undertaken since 1976.

22 Macknight, 'A Useless Discovery?' p. 4; Arlin Migliazzo, ed., *Lands of True and Certain Bounty: The Geographical Theories and Colonisation Strategies of John Pierre Purry* (London, 2002), pp. 14–17.

23 Schilder, 'From Secret to Common Knowledge,' p. 84.

24 Glyn Williams, *Naturalists at Sea: From Dampier to Darwin* (New Haven, CT, 2013), pp. 8–9; Leslie R. Marchant, *An Island unto Itself: The Life of William Dampier, Naturalist and Buccaneer* (Perth, 1988), p. 11.

25 Jan Kociumbas, *The Oxford History of Australia: Volume 2: Possessions, 1770–1860* (Oxford, 1992), p. 72.

26 BL, Sloane MS 3236, Voyages of W. Dampier through the South Seas, 1681–91, f. 222.

27 Williams, *The Great South Sea*, pp. 106–7. This coloured chart can be seen at
    https://archive.org/details/atlasmaritimusor00sell

28 William Dampier, *A New Voyage Round the World: The Journal of an English
    Buccaneer* (orig. pub. 1697; reprinted London, 1998), p. 216.

29 Ibid., p. 217.

30 Trevor Tuckfield, 'William Dampier – Where Did He Land?' *Journal and
    Proceedings of the Western Australian Historical Society*, V/I (1955), pp. 9, 11. The
    best-informed discussions of the location of the landfall are two studies by Leslie R.
    Marchant, 'William Dampier's Significance in Australia's Maritime Discovery,' *Early
    Days*, 9/4 (1986), pp. 54–9, and *An Island unto Itself*, pp. 110–21.

31 Marchant, *An Island unto Itself*, p. 64.

32 Quoted in Diana Preston and Michael Preston, *A Pirate of Exquisite Mind: The Life
    of William Dampier: Explorer, Naturalist and Buccaneer* (London, 2005), p. 244.

33 Williams, *Naturalists at Sea*, p. 11.

34 Ibid., pp. 14, 20–1 (quotation on p. 21).

35 Glyndwr Williams, 'The Pacific: Exploration and Exploitation' in P. J. Marshall, ed.,
    The Oxford History of the British Empire. Volume 2. The Eighteenth Century (Oxford,
    1998), p. 553.

36 Robert Sexton, 'Dampier's Roebuck,' *Bulletin of the Australasian Institute for
    Maritime Archaeology*, 35/1 (2011), pp. 28–38. Admiralty instructions for the
    voyage are found in TNA, ADM1/1692.

37 Ernest Scott, 'The Maritime Exploration of Western Australia, with Especial
    Reference to the Voyages of Dampier and D'Entrecasteaux,' *Report of the Eighteenth
    Meeting of the Australasian Association for the Advancement of Science* (Perth,
    1928), p. 412.

38 John M. Ward, 'British Policy in the Exploration of the South Pacific, 1699–1793,'
    JPRAHS, XXXIII/1 (1947), pp. 27–8; John Kemp, 'William Dampier: Navigator
    Extraordinary,' *Journal of Navigation*, 67/4 (2014), pp. 549, 555, 557.

39 Williams, *Naturalists at Sea*, pp. 21–2; Glyndwr Williams, 'New Holland – The
    English Approach' in John Hardy and Alan Frost, eds., *Studies from Terra Australis
    to Australia* (Canberra, 1988), pp. 86–7.

40 Williams, *The Great South Sea*, p. 123; Tuckfield, 'William Dampier,' p. 11.

41 The most thorough discussion of Dampier's route is in Marchant, *An Island unto
    Itself*, pp. 122–47. See also Alex George, 'William Dampier as a Natural Historian,'
    The Great Circle, 37/1 (2016), p. 37, and Kemp, 'William Dampier,' pp. 563–4.

42 See two studies by Gary C. Williams: 'William Dampier: Science, Exploration,
    and Literary Influence, Including His *Hydrographical Treatise* of 1699,' *Proceedings
    of the California Academy of Sciences* (Fourth Series), 59/14 (2008), pp. 592–602,
    and 'The Historical Context and Influence of William Dampier's Hydrographic
    Science,' *The Great Circle*, 37/1 (2016), p. 72.

43 William Dampier, ed., James A. Williamson, *A Voyage to New Holland* (London, 1939), p. 94.

44 Preston and Preston, *A Pirate of Exquisite Mind*, p. 252; T. M. Perry, 'British Charting of Australian Waters' in Michael Richards and Maura O'Connor, eds., *Changing Coastlines: Putting Australia on the World Map 1493–1993* (Canberra, 1993), p. 20.

45 Glyndwr Williams, 'New Holland to New South Wales: The English Approaches' in Williams and Frost, eds., *Terra Australis to Australia*, p. 133.

46 Williams, 'New Holland', p. 87; Williams, *The Great South Sea* (quotation), p. 131.

47 Marchant, *An Island unto Itself*, p. 124.

48 Ward, 'British Policy', p. 29.

49 Joseph C. Shipman, *William Dampier: Seaman-Scientist* (Lawrence, KS, 1962), p. 47; Dennis Reinhartz, 'William Dampier and the Wreck of the *Roebuck* off Ascension Island in 1701', *Terrae Incognitae*, 47/2 (2015), pp. 97–105.

50 See two articles by M. McCarthy, 'HM Ship *Roebuck* (1690–1701): Global Maritime Heritage?' *International Journal of Nautical Archaeology*, 33/2 (2004), pp. 330–7, and '300 Years on: The Search for William Dampier and His Elusive Ship', *The Great Circle*, 37/1 (2015), pp. 1–15.

51 Details of his court martial are available in TNA, ADM 1/5262/237, ff. 287–351.

52 Williams, *Naturalists at Sea*, pp. 21–2; George, 'William Dampier as a Natural Historian', p. 39.

53 Glyndwr Williams, 'Buccaneers, Castaways, and Satirists: The South Seas in English Consciousness before 1750', *Eighteenth-Century Life*, 18/3 (1994), p. 118.

54 Williams, *The Great South Sea*, p. 113; Philip Edwards, *Sea-Narratives in Eighteenth-Century England* (Cambridge, 1994), pp. 21–5; Michael McCarthy, 'Who Do You Trust? Discrepancies between the "Official and Unofficial" Sources Recording Explorers' Perceptions of Places and Their People' in Anne M. Scott, Alfred Hiatt, Claire McIlroy and Christopher Wortham, eds., *European Perceptions of Terra Australis* (Farnham, 2011), p. 192.

55 Williams, *Naturalists at Sea*, pp. 14, 25; Edwards, *Sea-Narratives*, p. 17; Marchant, 'William Dampier's Significance', p. 40.

56 Anton Gill, *The Devil's Mariner: A Life of William Dampier, Pirate and Explorer, 1651–1715* (London, 1997), pp. 11, 239.

57 Dampier, *A New Voyage Round the World*, p. 218; Dampier, *A Voyage to New Holland*, pp. 105–7.

58 Quoted in Gill, *The Devil's Mariner*, p. 252.

59 Adrian Mitchell, *Dampier's Monkey: The South Seas Voyages of William Dampier Including William Dampier's Unpublished Journal* (Kent Town, SA, 2010), p. 73.

60 George, 'William Dampier as a Natural Historian', p. 37; Williams, 'William Dampier', p. 567.

61 Dampier, *A Voyage to New Holland*, pp. 98–9, 106–7; Williams, *The Great South Sea*, p. 130. See also George, 'William Dampier as a Natural Historian', pp. 43–8.

62 Marchant, 'William Dampier's Significance,' p. 46.

63 Ibid., p. 49; Dampier, *A Voyage to New Holland*, pp. 108–11.

64 George, 'William Dampier as a Natural Historian,' p. 40.

65 Alex S. George, *William Dampier in New Holland: Australia's First Natural Historian* (Hawthorn, VIC, 1999), pp. 2, 21; Serena K. Marner, 'William Dampier and His Botanical Collections' in Howard Morphy and Elizabeth Edwards, eds., *Australia in Oxford* (Oxford, 1988), pp. 1–2. George's book provides a detailed description of Dampier's Australian plant specimens (pp. 61–95) and the birds, sea life and land animals he saw and recorded in west Australia (pp. 99–133). See also T. G. B. Osborn and C. A. Gardner, 'Dampier's Australian Plants,' *Proceedings of the Linnean Society of London*, 151/2 (1939), pp. 44–50.

66 Shino Konishi, *The Aboriginal Male in the Enlightenment World* (London, 2012), pp. 54, 64.

67 Dampier, *A New Voyage Round the World*, pp. 218–19. See also Preston and Preston, *A Pirate of Exquisite Mind*, p. 247. Dampier's manuscript account is in BL, Sloane MS 3236, Voyages of W. Dampier through the South Seas, 1681–91. This was probably written after Dampier returned from the East Indies to England in 1691: see Williams, *The Great South Sea*, pp. 112–13.

68 Dampier, *A Voyage to New Holland*, p. 102.

69 Pauline Turner Strong, 'Fathoming the Primitive: Australian Aborigines in Four Explorers' Journals, 1697–1845,' *Ethnohistory*, 33/2 (1986), p. 177.

70 Geraldine Barnes, 'Traditions of the Monstrous in William Dampier's *New Holland*' in Judy A. Hayden, ed., *Travel Narratives, the New Science, and Literary Discourse, 1569–1750* (Farnham, 2012), pp. 91–6.

71 Williams, 'New Holland,' p. 87.

72 Martin Crotty and Erik Eklund, eds., *Australia to 1901: Selected Readings in the Making of a Nation* (Croydon, VIC, 2003), p. 34; Macknight, 'A Useless Discovery?' p. 3.

73 Williams, 'New Holland,' p. 88. For Dampier's influence on *Gulliver's Travels*, see Williams, 'William Dampier,' pp. 576, 579–83.

74 Wood, *The Discovery of Australia*, pp. 239–40; Glyndwr Williams and Alan Frost, 'Terra Australis: Theory and Speculation' in Williams and Frost, eds., *Terra Australis to Australia*, p. 28.

75 John Campbell, ed., *Navigantium atque Itinerantium Bibliotheca: Or, a Compleat Collection of Voyages and Travels*, 2 vols. (London, 1774–8), I, p. 272.

76 See above, pp. 48, 50. On these maps, see also Günter Schilder, *Australia Unveiled: The Share of the Dutch Navigators in the Discovery of Australia* (Amsterdam, 1976), pp. 196, 198, 374–7, and Margaret Cameron Ash, 'French Mischief: A Foxy Map of New Holland,' *The Globe*, 68 (2011), pp. 1–14.

77 Schilder, *Australia Unveiled*, p. 203; Martin Woods, '"Terre Australe," East of New Holland' in *Mapping Our World*, p. 143; Terry, 'Early Mapping of the Pacific,' p. 22.

Chapter 5

1   Detailed treatments of these broad themes include Wood, *The Discovery of Australia;* Eisler, *The Furthest Shore*; Miriam Estensen, *Discovery: The Quest for the Great South Land* (Sydney, 1998); and Alan Powell, *Northern Voyagers: Australia's Monsoon Coast in Maritime History* (Melbourne, 2010).

2   Jan Kociumbas, *The Oxford History of Australia: Volume 2: Possessions 1770–1860* (Oxford, 1992), p. 72.

3   John Gascoigne, 'Motives for European Exploration of the Pacific in the Age of Enlightenment', *Pacific Science*, 54/3 (2000), pp. 227–37.

4   P. J. Marshall and Glyndwr Williams, *The Great Map of Mankind: British Perceptions of the World in the Age of Enlightenment* (London, 1982), pp. 258–60.

5   Glyndwr Williams, 'The Achievement of the English Voyages, 1650–1800' in Derek Howse, ed., *Background to Discovery: Pacific Exploration from Dampier to Cook* (Berkeley and Los Angeles, CA, 1990), p. 62.

6   David Mackay, 'The Burden of Terra Australis: Experiences of Real and Imagined Lands' in Robin Fisher and Hugh Johnston, eds., *From Maps to Metaphors: The Pacific World of George Vancouver* (Vancouver, 1993), pp. 269, 272.

7   Alexander Dalrymple, *An Account of Discoveries Made in the South Pacifick Ocean* (London, 1767), p. 96.

8   Daniel A. Baugh, 'Seapower and Science: The Motives for Pacific Exploration' in Howse, ed., *Background to Discovery*, pp. 5, 32.

9   Alan Frost, *The Voyage of the Endeavour: Captain Cook and the Discovery of the Pacific* (St Leonards, NSW, 1998), pp. 11–13; Robert E. Gallagher, ed., *Byron's Journal of His Circumnavigation, 1764–1766* (Cambridge, 1964).

10 Helen Wallis, ed., *Carteret's Voyage Round the World, 1766–1769*, 2 vols. (Cambridge, 1965), II, p. 302.

11 Alan Frost, 'Science for Political Purposes: European Explorations of the Pacific Ocean, 1764–1806' in Roy MacLeod and Philip H. Rehbock, eds., *Nature in Its Greatest Extent: Western Science in the Pacific* (Honolulu, 1988), p. 30; Stuart Murray, '"Notwithstanding Our Signs to the Contrary": Textuality and Authority at the Endeavour River, June to August 1771' in Glyndwr Williams, ed., *Captain Cook: Explorations and Reassessments* (Woodbridge, 2004), p. 71. The correct date in this article's title should be 1770.

12 Glyndwr Williams, 'The Pacific: Exploration and Exploitation' in P. J. Marshall, ed., *The Oxford History of the British Empire. Volume 2. The Eighteenth Century* (Oxford, 1998), p. 556.

13 Hugh Carrington, ed., *The Discovery of Tahiti: A Journal of the Second voyage of H.M.S. Dolphin round the World by George Robertson 1766–1768* (London, 1948), p. 135. It should be noted, however, that Robertson's was the only one of

the eighteen surviving journals from the voyage that referred to the sighting of a southern continent: see Glyndwr Williams, 'The *Endeavour* Voyage: A Coincidence of Motives' in Margarette Lincoln, ed., *Science and Exploration: European Voyages to the Southern Oceans in the Eighteenth Century* (Woodbridge, 1998), pp. 9–10.

14   John Dunmore, *Storms and Dreams: The Life of Louis de Bougainville: Soldier, Explorer, Statesman* (Auckland, 2005), pp. 187–90. For further discussion of this voyage, see p. 89.

15   Martin Terry, 'Early Mapping of the Pacific,' *The Globe*, 37 (1992), p. 23.

16   Mel Gooding, David Mabberley and Joe Studholme, *Joseph Banks' Florilegium: Botanical Treasures from Cook's First Voyage* (London, 2017), p. 19.

17   Carrington, ed., *The Discovery of Tahiti*, p. xxv.

18   Mawer, *Incognita*, p. 170; Simon Schaffer, 'In Transit: European Cosmologies in the Pacific' in Kate Fullagar, ed., *The Atlantic World in the Antipodes: Effects and Transformations since the Eighteenth Century* (Newcastle upon Tyne, 2012), pp. 74–5.

19   J. C. Beaglehole, ed., *The Journals of Captain James Cook on his Voyages of Discovery*, vol. 1. *The Voyage of the Endeavour 1768-1771* (Cambridge, 1955), p. cclxxxii; Paul Moon, 'From Tasman to Cook: The Proto-Intelligence Phase of New Zealand's Colonisation,' *Journal of Intelligence History*, 18/2 (2019), p. 262.

20   Geoffrey Blainey, *Sea of Dangers: Captain Cook and His Rivals* (Camberwell, VIC, 2009), p. 4.

21   Frost, 'Science for Political Purposes,' p. 33.

22   Mawer, *Incognita*, p. 171; John Gascoigne, *Captain Cook: Voyager between Worlds* (London, 2007), pp. 17–24.

23   John Robson, *Captain Cook's World: Maps of the Life and Voyages of James Cook R.N.* (London, 2000), p. 45; Wood, *The Discovery of Australia*, p. 273.

24   Blainey, *Sea of Dangers*, p. ix.

25   J. C. Beaglehole, *The Life of Captain James Cook* (Stanford, CA, 1974), pp. 137, 142–6; J. C. Beaglehole, 'Eighteenth-Century Science and the Voyages of Discovery,' *New Zealand Journal of History*, 3/2 (1969), pp. 107–23.

26   Terry, 'Early Mapping of the Pacific,' p. 23; D. J. Carr, 'The Books That Sailed with the *Endeavour*,' *Endeavour*, 7/4 (1983), pp. 194–201.

27   Richard Dunn and Rebekah Higgitt, *Ships, Clocks and Stars: The Quest for Longitude* (Glasgow, 2014), p. 129.

28   Robson, *Captain Cook's World*, map 1.10 (n.p.).

29   Ibid., pp. 46–53 and maps 1.11–1.21 (n.p.); Mawer, *Incognita*, pp. 174–5; Wood, *The Discovery of Australia*, p. 275.

30   J. C. Beaglehole, ed., *The Endeavour Journal of Joseph Banks 1768–1771*, 2 vols. (Sydney, 1962), II, p. 38.

31   Ibid., II, p. 38.

32   Wood, *The Discovery of Australia*, pp. 283–4.

33 Ibid., pp. 287–8; Beaglehole, *The Life of Captain James Cook*, p. 226.

34 Margaret Cameron Ash, *Lying for the Admiralty: Captain Cook's Endeavour Voyage* (Dural Delivery Centre, NSW, 2018), pp. 148–9.

35 For what to me seems an unconvincing argument that Cook deliberately recorded Point Hicks incorrectly, see Margaret Cameron-Ash, 'Captain Cook Invented Point Hicks to Hide Bass Strait', *The Globe*, 84 (2018), pp. 39–45. Another sceptical view can be found in Trevor Lipscombe, 'Cook Conspiracy at Point Hicks?' *The Globe*, 87 (2020), pp. 51–6.

36 Entry for 19 April 1770 in Beaglehole, ed., *The Journals of Captain James Cook*, I, p. 299. Whether Cook saw Point Hicks, or another landmark, is discussed in Thomas W. Fowler, 'Captain Cook's Australian Landfall', *Victorian Geographical Journal*, 25 (1907), pp. 7–12, and Trevor J. Lipscombe, 'The Point Hicks Controversy – The Clouded Facts', *Victorian Historical Journal*, 85 (2014), pp. 232–53. See also two further articles by Trevor Lipscombe: 'Lt. James Cook on the Coast of Victoria 1770', *Victorian Historical Journal*, 89/1 (2018), pp. 137–51, and 'Lt James Cook's Misplaced Landmarks on the Coasts of Victoria and NSW', *The Globe*, 87 (2020), pp. 33–7.

37 Ernest Scott, 'English and French Navigators on the Victorian Coast', *Victorian Historical Magazine*, II, no. 4 (1912), p. 151.

38 Whether the land features he named were given the correct location is discussed in two articles by Trevor J. Lipscombe, 'Cook's Cape Dromedary – Is It Montague Island?' and 'Is Cook's Cape Howe Really Telegraph Point?' *Map Matters*, 32 (2017), pp. 2–11. Additional articles correcting Cook's named land features in Australia can be found in back issues of *Map Matters* (www.australiaonthemap.org.au) and *Placenames Australia* (www.anps.org.au).

39 Wood, *The Discovery of Australia*, p. 289; Edgar Beale, 'Cook's First Landing Attempt in New South Wales', *JPRAHS*, 50/3 (1964), pp. 191–204.

40 Entry for 6 May 1770 in Beaglehole, ed., *Journals of Captain James Cook*, I, p. 312. Cook originally named the location Stingray Bay: see Wood, *The Discovery of Australia*, pp. 292–4.

41 Maria Nugent, *Captain Cook Was Here* (Cambridge, 2009), p. 35.

42 Robson, *Captain Cook's World*, map 1.23; entry for 6 May 1770 in Beaglehole, ed., *Journals of Captain James Cook*, I, pp. 312–13.

43 Commentary on the voyage up the east coast, accompanied by maps, is available in Robson, *Captain Cook's World*, pp. 53–6, and maps 1.22–1.32 (n.p.). Cook's place names are listed in David Blair, *James Cook's Toponyms: Placenames of Eastern Australia April–August 1770*, ANPS Placenames report no. 1 (South Turramurra, NSW, 2015).

44 Clem Lack, 'The Achievements of James Cook: Navigator, Humanist, and Anthropologist', *Journal of the Royal Historical Society of Queensland*, 9/1 (1970), p. 25.

45 Alan Villiers, *Captain Cook, the Seamen's Seaman* (London, 1967), p. 171.

46 Entry for 11 June 1770 in Beaglehole, ed., *Journals of Captain James Cook*, I, p. 344.

47 Blainey, *Sea of Dangers*, p. 245.

48 Beaglehole, *The Life of Captain James Cook*, p. 238; Nicholas Thomas, *Discoveries: The Voyages of Captain Cook* (London, 2003), p. 115.

49 Entry for 10 June 1770 in Beaglehole, ed., *The Endeavour Journal*, II, p. 77.

50 Quoted in Wood, *The Discovery of Australia*, pp. 299–300.

51 Thomas, *Discoveries*, pp. 122–5. For the type of kangaroo seen by Cook, see H. C. Raven, 'The Identity of Captain Cook's Kangaroo,' *Journal of Mammalogy*, 20/1 (1939), pp. 50–7; T. C. S. Morrison-Scott and F. C. Sawyer, 'The Identity of Captain Cook's Kangaroo,' *Bulletin of the British Museum (Natural History), Zoology*, 1/3 (1950), pp. 43–50; and Denis J. Carr, 'The Identity of Captain Cook's Kangaroo' in D. J. Carr, ed., *Sydney Parkinson: Artist of Cook's Endeavour Voyage* (London, 1983), pp. 242–9.

52 Entries for 22 June, 14 July 1770 in Beaglehole, ed., *The Endeavour Journal*, II, pp. 50, 94 (quotation); Danielle Clode, *Continent of Curiosities: A Journey through Australian Natural History* (Cambridge, 2006), p. 14.

53 Lack, 'The Achievements of James Cook,' p. 32.

54 Entry for 16 August 1770 in Beaglehole, ed., *Journals of Captain James Cook*, I, p. 378.

55 Beaglehole, *The Life of Captain James Cook*, pp. 241–2.

56 Entry for 14 August 1770, in Beaglehole, ed., *Journals of Captain James Cook*, I, p. 375. 360 nautical leagues = 1,243 miles.

57 Entry for 17 August 1770, ibid., p. 380. For a descriptive account of Cook's passage through the coral rocks, see Iain McCalman, *The Reef: A Passionate History: The Great Barrier Reef from Captain Cook to Climate Change* (New York, 2014), pp. 13–33.

58 Beaglehole, *The Life of Captain James Cook*, pp. 242–4; Villiers, *Captain Cook*, p. 175.

59 Entry for 17 August 1770 in Beaglehole, ed., *Journals of Captain James Cook*, I, p. 380.

60 Lack, 'The Achievements of James Cook,' p. 29.

61 Entry for 22 August 1770, in Beaglehole, ed., *Journals of Captain James Cook*, I, pp. 387–8. The process of ritual and naming of the island is examined in Suvendrini Perera, *Australia and the Insular Imagination: Beaches, Borders, Boats, and Bodies* (New York, 2009), pp. 20–1. For scepticism about whether a possession ceremony occurred, see Cameron Ash, *Lying for the Admiralty*, p. 183.

62 Robert J. King, 'Terra Australis, New Holland and New South Wales: The Treaty of Tordesillas and Australia,' *The Globe*, 47 (1998), p. 44.

63 Entry for 21 August 1770 in Beaglehole, ed., *The Endeavour Journal*, II, p. 110.

64 Entry for 23 August 1770 in Beagehole, ed., *Journals of Captain James Cook*, I, p. 390.

65 Entry for 13 August 1770, ibid., p. 370; Blainey, *Sea of Dangers*, p. 303.

66 For commentary on Endeavour Strait, see C. B. Yule, *The Australia Directory: Volume 2, East Coast, Torres Strait and Coral Sea* ... (London, 1859), pp. 202, 208.

67 Entry for 26 August 1770 in Beaglehole, ed., *The Endeavour Journal*, II, p. 111; Cook to the Admiralty Secretary, 23 October 1770, in Beaglehole, ed., *Journals of Captain James Cook*, I, pp. 410 (quotation), 500–1.

68 Alexander Dalrymple, *A Letter from Mr Dalrymple to Dr Hawkesworth* ... (London, 1773), p. 29.

69 Wood, *Discovery of Australia*, pp. 306, 338 (quotation). See also Kenneth Morgan, 'From Cook to Flinders: The Navigation of Torres Strait', *IJMH*, 27/1 (2015), pp. 44–6.

70 Joan Druett, *Tupaia: The Remarkable Story of Captain Cook's Polynesian Navigator* (Santa Barbara, CA, 2011), pp. 211–13; Gascoigne, *Captain Cook*, p. 33.

71 Cook to Philip Stephens, 23 October 1770, in Beaglehole, ed., *The Journals of Captain James Cook*, I, p. 501.

72 Robson, *Captain Cook's World*, maps 1.32–1.38 (n.p.).

73 Quoted in Wood, *The Discovery of Australia*, p. 313.

74 Gascoigne, *Captain Cook*, p. 35.

75 Lack, 'The Achievements of James Cook', p. 41.

76 Williams, 'The Pacific', pp. 560–1.

77 Glyn Williams, *Voyages of Delusion: The Quest for the Northwest Passage* (New Haven, CT, 2003).

78 Williams, 'The Pacific', pp. 561–2.

79 Andrew C. F. David, *The Charts and Coastal Views of Captain Cook's Voyages*, vol. 2. The Voyage of the *Resolution* and *Adventure 1772–1775*, Hakluyt Society, extra series, 44 (London, 1992), pp. 80–96.

80 Dan Sprod, 'Tobias Furneaux, RN, and His Pacific Voyaging', *Tasmanian Historical Research Association, Papers and Proceedings*, 51/3 (2004), p. 148; J. C. Beaglehole, ed., *The Journals of Captain James Cook*, II, p. 736; Cameron Ash, *Lying for the Admiralty*, pp. 157–8.

81 See below, p. 114.

82 Solander to James Lind, 27 July 1774, in Edward Duyker and Per Tingbrand, eds., *Daniel Solander: Collected Correspondence 1753–1782* (Melbourne, 1995), p. 326.

83 Nugent, *Captain Cook Was Here*, p. 19; Doreen Mellor, 'Cook, His Mission and Indigenous Australia' in Michelle Hetherington and Howard Morphy, eds., *Discovering Cook's Collections* (Canberra, 2009), pp. 115–16.

84 Beaglehole, ed., *Journals of Captain Cook* ... *The Voyage of the Endeavour*, p. cclxxxiii.

85 Bronwen Douglas, 'Voyages, Encounters, and Agency in Oceania: Captain Cook and Indigenous People', *History Compass*, 6/3 (2008), pp. 712–37.

86 Nugent, *Captain Cook Was Here*, pp. 19–20, 73.

87 Entry for 27 April 1770 in Beaglehole, ed., *The Endeavour Journal*, II, p. 54.

88 Pauline Turner Strong, 'Fathoming the Primitive: Australian Aborigines in Four Explorers' Journals, 1697–1845', *Ethnohistory*, 33/2 (1986), p. 179.

89 Nugent, *Captain Cook Was Here*, pp. 12, 19, 53, 87; Sydney Parkinson, *A Journal of a Voyage to the South Seas in His Majesty's Ship, The Endeavour* (London, 1773), p. 135.

90 Entry for 2 May 1770 in Beaglehole, ed., *Journals of Captain Cook*, I, p. 308.

91 Nugent, *Captain Cook Was Here*, p. vii.

92 Thomas, *Discoveries*, pp. 114, 122; Nugent, *Captain Cook Was Here*, pp. 72, 87.

93 Thomas, *Discoveries*, p. 121. Similarities and differences in the interaction between Cook, his associates and Aborigines at Endeavour River are analysed in Murray, 'Notwithstanding Our Signs to the Contrary', pp. 59–76.

94 See above, pp. 62–3.

95 Nugent, *Captain Cook Was Here*, p. 8; Strong, 'Fathoming the Primitive', p. 179.

96 Entry for 22 April 1770 in Beaglehole, ed., *The Endeavour Journal*, II, p. 50.

97 Ibid., ii, pp. 53, 55–6, 91–3, 111–37; Beaglehole, ed., *Journals of Captain Cook*, I, pp. 309, 312, 357–8, 360–2, 393–7, 399.

98 Gascoigne, *Captain Cook*, p. 33; Shino Konishi, *The Aboriginal Male in the Enlightenment World* (London, 2012), p. 110; Parkinson, *A Journal of a Voyage to the South Seas*, pp. 148–52.

99 Beaglehole, ed., *The Endeavour Journal*, II, p. 130.

100 Beaglehole, ed., *Journals of Captain Cook*, I, p. 399.

101 Ibid., p. clxiii; Beaglehole, ed., *The Endeavour Journal*, II, p. 44; Beaglehole, *The Life of Captain James Cook*, p. 251.

102 Glyndwr Williams, '"Far More Happier than We Europeans": Reactions to the Australian Aborigines on Cook's Voyage', *Historical Studies*, 19/77 (1981), pp. 499–512.

103 Thomas, *Discoveries*, pp. 129–30.

104 Deborah Bird Rose, 'The Saga of Captain Cook: Morality in Aboriginal and European Law', *Aboriginal Studies*, 2 (1984), pp. 24–39.

105 Williams, 'The Pacific', pp. 560, 564.

106 Bernard Smith, 'The Intellectual and Artistic Framework of Pacific Exploration in the Eighteenth Century' in William Eisler and Bernard Smith, eds., *Terra Australis: The Furthest Shore* (Sydney, 1988), p. 123; John McAleer and Nigel Rigby, *Captain Cook and the Pacific: Art, Exploration and Empire* (New Haven, CT, 2017), p. 72. For Cook's determination of longitude, see Richard Dunn, 'James Cook and the New Navigation' in James K. Barnett and David L. Nicandri, eds., *Arctic Ambitions: Captain Cook and the Northwest Passage* (Seattle, 2015), pp. 89–107. The lunar distance method of calculating longitude is explained in David Waters, 'Navigational Problems in Captain Cook's Day' in Antoinette Shalkop, ed., *Exploration in Alaska:*

Captain Cook Commemorative Lectures June–November 1978 (Anchorage, AK, 1980), pp. 52–3, and Seymour L. Chapin, 'A Survey of the Efforts to Determine Longitude at Sea, 1660–1760. Part II: The Use of Celestial Bodies,' *Navigation*, 3/7 (1953), pp. 244–8.

107 Andrew C. F. David, 'Cook and the Cartography of Australia,' *The Globe*, 22 (1984), p. 47.

108 Andrew David, *The Charts and Coastal Views of Captain Cook's Voyages: The Voyage of the Endeavour 1768–1771* (London: The Hakluyt Society, 1988), p. 11.

109 David, 'Cook and the Cartography of Australia,' pp. 50–1. Cook's tidal measurements were accurate in general to about 15 cm in height and 0.5 hours in time: see Philip L. Woodworth and Glen H. Rowe, 'The Tidal Measurements of James Cook during the Voyage of the Endeavour,' *History of Geo- and Space Sciences*, 9 (2018), pp. 85–103.

110 These are preserved in an atlas in BL, Add. MS 7085. Modern reproduction of Cook's charts of Australia can be found in two volumes edited by Andrew C. F. David: *The Charts and Coastal Views of Captain Cook's Voyages. Volume 1. The Voyage of the Endeavour 1768–1771* (London, 1988), pp. 260–312, and *The Charts and Coastal Views of Captain Cook's Voyages*, vol. 2. The Voyage of the *Resolution* and *Adventure* 1772–1775 (London, 1992), pp. 80–96.

111 David, 'Cook and the Cartography of Australia,' pp. 55–6.

112 H. G. Taylor, *The Discovery of Tasmania* (Hobart, 1973), pp. 6–7.

113 Beverley Hooper, ed., *With Captain James Cook in the Antarctic and Pacific: The Private Journal of James Burney, Second Lieutenant of the Adventure on Cook's Second Voyage 1772–1773* (Canberra, 1975), pp. 37, 42 n. 2.

114 Gooding, Mabberley and Studholme, *Joseph Banks' Florilegium*, p. 166; R. J. Henderson, 'Plants of Australia' in Carr, ed., *Sydney Parkinson*, p. 131.

115 Glyn Williams, *Naturalists at Sea: From Dampier to Darwin* (New Haven, CT, 2013), p. 86.

116 Ibid., p. 75.

117 See two publications by William T. Stearn: 'The Botanical Explorations of Banks and Solander on Captain Cook's 1768–71 Voyage in the *Endeavour*' in *Captain Cook's Florilegium*, n.p. and 'The Botanical Results of the Endeavour Voyage,' *Endeavour*, 27 (1968), pp. 3–10. Parkinson's original botanical paintings are deposited at the NHM in eighteen folio volumes. Reproductions of plants collected in Australia can be found in Gooding, Mabberley and Studholme, *Joseph Banks's Florilegium*, plates 77–140 (n.p.) and *Captain Cook's Florilegium* (London, 1973), plates 16–27 (n.p.).

118 Alwyne Wheeler, 'Animals' in Carr, ed., *Sydney Parkinson*, p. 195; Williams, *Naturalists at Sea*, p. 91; Bernard Smith, *European Vision and the South Pacific*, 2nd edn. (New Haven, CT, 1985), p. 18.

119 P. J. P. Whitehead, 'Zoological Specimens from Captain Cook's Voyages,' *Journal of the Society for the Bibliography of Natural History*, 5/3 (1969), pp. 161–2.

120 Parkinson, *A Journal of a Voyage to the South Seas*, pp. 144–6.

121 Wheeler, 'Animals,' pp. 201, 203; A. M. Lysaght, 'Banks's Artists and His *Endeavour* Collections' in *The British Museum Yearbook*, 3 (London, 1979), p. 26.

122 Alan Frost, *Mutiny, Mayhem, Mythology: Bounty's Enigmatic Voyage* (Sydney, 2018), p. 219.

Chapter 6

1 Margaret Sankey has written several overlapping essays on this theme, including 'Nationalism and Identity in Seventeenth-Century France: The Abbé Paulmier and the *Terres australes*,' *AJFS*, 44/3 (2007), pp. 195–206; 'The Abbé Jean Paulmier and the French Missions in the *Terres australes*: Myth and History,' *AJFS*, 50/1 (2013), pp. 3–15; 'Mapping *Terra Australis* in the French Seventeenth Century: The Mémoires of the Abbé Jean Paulmier' in Anne M. Scott, Alfred Hiatt, Claire McIlroy and Christopher Wortham, eds., *European Perceptions of Terra Australis* (Farnham, 2011), pp. 111–34; 'The Abbé Paulmier's Mémoires and Early French Voyages in Search of Terra Australis,' (quotation) in John West-Sooby, ed., *Discovery and Empire: The French in the South Seas* (Adelaide, 2013), pp. 42–66; and 'Est ou Ouest: le mythe des terres australes en France aux XVII et XVIII siècles' in Kumari R. Issur and Vinesh Y. Hookoomsing, eds., *L'Océan Indien dans les littératures francophones* (Paris, 2001), pp. 13–26. See also Elizabeth Bonner, 'Did the French Discover Australia? The First French Scientific Voyage of Discovery, 1503–1505' in David W. Lovell, ed., *Revolution, Politics, and Society: Elements in the Making of Modern France* (Canberra, 1994), pp. 40–8, and William Jennings, 'Self and Other: Gonneville's Encounters in Terra Australis and Brazil,' *Viator: Medieval and Renaissance Studies*, 39/2 (2008), pp. 215–26.

2 Leyla Perrone Moisés, *Vinte Luas: Viagem de Paulmier de Gonneville ao Brasil, 1503–1505* (São Paulo, 1992). It is now argued that Gonneville landed in Brazil rather than Australia.

3 John Dunmore, *French Explorers of the Pacific.1. The Eighteenth Century* (Oxford, 1965), pp. 4–6. The original copy of this document has never been located.

4 William Jennings, 'Gonneville's *Terra Australis*: Too Good to Be True?' *AJFS*, 50/1 (2013), pp. 75–86.

5 Sankey, 'The Abbé Jean Paulmier,' p. 6.

6 Lynne Withey, *Voyages of Discovery: Captain Cook and the Exploration of the Pacific* (Berkeley and Los Angeles, CA, 1987), pp. 199–200; John Gascoigne, 'The Globe Encompassed: France and Pacific Convergences in the Age of Enlightenment' in

West-Sooby, ed., *Discovery and Empire*, pp. 24–6. See also two studies by O. H. K. Spate: 'De Lozier Bouvet and Mercantilist Expansion in the Pacific in 1740' in John Parker, ed., *Merchants and Scholars: Essays in the History of Exploration and Trade* (Minneapolis, MN, 1965), pp. 221–37, and 'Between Tasman and Cook: Bouvet's Place in the History of Exploration' in J. Andrews, ed., *Frontiers and Men: A Volume in Memory of Griffith Taylor (1880–1963)* (Melbourne: Cheshire, 1966), pp. 174–86.

7 Dunmore, *French Explorers of the Pacific*, I, p. 201.

8 Noelene Bloomfield, *Almost a French Australia: French British Rivalry in the Southern Oceans* (Braddon, 2012), p. 34.

9 Jean Garagnon, 'French Imaginary Voyages to the Austral Lands in the Seventeenth and Eighteenth Centuries' in *Australia and the European Imagination: Papers from a Conference Held at the Humanities Research Centre*, Australian National University, May 1981 (Canberra, 1982), p. 91; Tom Ryan, 'Le Président des Terres Australes: Charles de Brosses and the French Enlightenment Beginnings of Oceanic Anthropology,' *Journal of Pacific History*, 37/2 (2002), p. 157.

10 John Dunmore, *Visions & Realities: France in the Pacific 1695–1995* (Waikanae, 1997), p. 39.

11 *Maps in Australia: Great Maps in Australia's History from the National Library's Collections* (Canberra: National Library of Australia, 2008), pp. 46–7.

12 For this voyage, see p. 68.

13 Gascoigne, 'The Globe Encompassed,' p. 29; Pearson, *Great Southern Land*, pp. 71–2.

14 A. Carey Taylor, 'Charles de Brosses, the Man behind Cook' in Basil Greenhill, ed., *The Opening of the Pacific – Image and Reality* (Greenwich, 1971), pp. 5, 8. See also A. Carey Taylor, *Le Président de Brosses et l'Australie* (Paris, 1937), pp. 148–51.

15 Anne Salmond, *Aphrodite's Island: The European Discovery of Tahiti* (Berkeley and Los Angeles, CA, 2009); Wood, *The Discovery of Australia*, p. 260.

16 Elliott Forsyth, 'French Exploration in the Pacific in the Eighteenth Century' in John Hardy and Alan Frost, eds., *Studies from Terra Australis to Australis* (Canberra, 1989), p. 94; Dunmore, *French Explorers of the Pacific*, I, p. 97. For a detailed account of Bougainville's voyage, see John Dunmore, *Storms and Dreams: The Life of Louis de Bougainville* (Fairbanks, AK, 2007), pp. 141–213.

17 Dunmore, *Visions & Realities*, p. 56; Dunmore, *French Explorers of the Pacific*, I, pp. 99, 109, 112.

18 Jean Fornasiero and John West-Sooby, 'The Acquisitive Eye? French Observations in the Pacific from Bougainville to Baudin' in West-Sooby, ed., *Discovery and Empire*, p. 74.

19 Myra Stanbury, 'Louis Aleno de Saint Aloüarn (1738–1772): A Forgotten 18th-Century French Explorer,' *The Great Circle*, 39/2 (2017), p. 27.

20 Jennings, 'Gonneville's *Terra Australis*,' p. 78; Jonathan Lamb, 'Inchoate Possession: How Captain Kerguelen Claimed an Island,' *Journal for Maritime Research*, 7/1 (2005), pp. 1–15.

21 Stanbury, 'Louis Aleno de Saint Aloüarn,' p. 32.

22 Philippe Godard, 'The Saint Allouarn Discoveries,' *Quarterly Newsletter: The Australian Association for Maritime History*, 77 (1999), p. 8; Dunmore, *French Explorers of the Pacific*, I, pp. 205, 212.

23 Stanbury, 'Louis Aleno de Saint Aloüarn,' p. 35.

24 Ibid., pp. 35–7; Pearson, *Great Southern Land*, p. 74; Nicolas Bigourdan, 'The French Connection with New Holland: An Overview of Research Studies,' *The Great Circle*, 37/2 (2015), p. 80.

25 Dunmore, *Visions & Realities*, pp. 63–4; Dunmore, *French Explorers of the Pacific*, I, pp. 220–35, 239–44.

26 Pearson, *Great Southern Land*, p. 74.

27 Ibid., p. 72. On the St Aloüarn expedition, see also Maurice Raymond de Brossard, *Kerguelen: Le Découvreur et Ses Îles* (Paris, 1970), pp. 230–57 and Philippe Godard, Tugdual de Kerros, Sue Baxter, Odette Margot and Myra Stanbury, *1772 – The French Annexation of New Holland – The Tale of Louis de Saint Aloüarn* (Fremantle, 2009).

28 Seymour Chapin, 'The Men from across La Manche: French Voyages, 1660–1790' in Derek W. Howse, ed., *Background to Discovery: Pacific Exploration from Dampier to Cook* (Berkeley and Los Angeles, CA, 1990), p. 111; Dunmore, *French Explorers of the Pacific*, I, p. 167.

29 Dunmore, *French Explorers of the Pacific*, I, p. 171.

30 Edward Duyker, *An Officer of the Blue: Marc-Joseph Marion Dufresne 1724–1772* (Melbourne, 1994), pp. 122–4; Edward Duyker, ed., *The Discovery of Tasmania: Journal Extracts from the Expeditions of Abel Janszoon Tasman and Marc-Joseph Marion Dufresne 1642 & 1772* (Hobart, 1992), p. 39 (quotations).

31 *Crozet's Voyage to Tasmania, New Zealand, the Ladrone Islands, and the Philippines in the Years 1771–1772* (London, 1891), p. 19.

32 Pearson, *Great Southern Land*, p. 73.

33 Duyker, ed., *The Discovery of Tasmania*, pp. 4–5, 15, 28; Mault, 'Notes on Charts,' p. 110.

34 Dunmore, *French Explorers of the Pacific*, I, p. 179.

35 Duyker, ed., *The Discovery of Tasmania*, pp. 25 (quotations), 26, 31–3; Pearson, *Great Southern Land*, p. 73.

36 Duyker, ed., *The Discovery of Tasmania*, pp. 22 (quotation), 33.

37 See above, pp. 78–81.

38 Dunmore, *Visions & Realities*, pp. 84–5; Dunmore, *French Explorers of the Pacific*, I, p. 195.

39 John Dunmore, *Where Fate Beckons: The Life of Jean-François de la Pérouse* (Wollombi, NSW, 2006), pp. 180–2.

40 Robert J. King, 'William Bolts and the Austrian Origins of the Lapérouse Expedition,' *Terrae Incognitae*, 40/1 (2008), pp. 1–28.

41 Dunmore, *French Explorers of the Pacific*, I, pp. 254–7; Ernest Scott, *Lapérouse* (Sydney, 1913), p. 48; Carol E. Harrison, 'Projections of the Revolutionary Nation: French Expeditions in the Pacific, 1791–1803' in Carol E. Harrison and Ann Johnson, eds., *National Identity: The Role of Science and Technology* (Chicago, IL, 2009), p. 34.

42 Alan Frost, *The Global Reach of Empire: Britain's Maritime Expansion in the Indian and Pacific Oceans, 1764–1815* (Carlton, VIC, 2003), pp. 82–5; John Dunmore, 'Dream and Reality: French Voyages and Their Vision of Australia' in *Australia and the European Imagination: Papers from a Conference Held at the Humanities Research Centre*, Australian National University, *May 1981* (Canberra, 1982), p. 113.

43 Dunmore, *Where Fate Beckons*, pp. 182, 188–90; Dunmore, *Visions & Realities*, pp. 91–2.

44 Scott, *Lapérouse*, p. 47; Robert J. King, 'What Brought Lapérouse to Botany Bay?' *JRAHS*, 85/2 (1999), pp. 140–7; Dunmore, *French Explorers of the Pacific*, I, p. 275.

45 Dunmore, *French Explorers of the Pacific*, II, pp. 395–6, 399–403; Dunmore, *Where Fate Beckons*, pp. 245, 247.

46 David Collins, *An Account of the English Colony in New South Wales* (1798; reprinted Sydney, 1975), p. 16 (quotation); Glyn Williams, *Naturalists at Sea: From Dampier to Darwin* (New Haven, CT, 2013), p. 163.

47 Frost, *The Global Reach of Empire*, p. 6; John Dunmore, ed., *The Journal of Jean-François de Galaup de la Pérouse, 1785–1788*, 2 vols. (London, 1994–5), I, p. cxcvii.

48 Dunmore, *Where Fate Beckons*, pp. 249, 261–2; King, 'What Brought Lapérouse to Botany Bay?' p. 144.

49 Alan Frost, 'From the Hills of Provence to the Coast of Van Diemen's Land: The Expedition of Antoine Raymond-Joseph Bruny d'Entrecasteaux, 1791–1793/4' in John Mulvaney and Hugh Tyndale-Biscoe, eds., *Rediscovering Recherche Bay* (Canberra, 2007), p. 13.

50 Dunmore, *Visions & Realities*, p. 101; Dunmore, *French Explorers of the Pacific*, I, p. 284 (quotation).

51 Dunmore, ed., *The Journal of Jean-François de Galaup de la Pérouse*, II, pp. ccviii–ccxiii.

52 Leslie R. Marchant, 'Hyperion and the Satyrs: French Monarchist and Revolutionary Scientists and Australian Discovery 1791–1795: The Accomplishments of the D'Entrecasteaux Expedition,' *Early Days*, 11/1 (1995), p. 26.

53 Ibid., pp. 20–1.

54 Dunmore, *Visions & Realities*, p. 102; Dunmore, *French Explorers of the Pacific*, I, p. 285.

55 Marchant, 'Hyperion and the Satyrs,' pp. 11–32.

56 Harrison, 'Projections of the Revolutionary Nation,' p. 42; Williams, *Naturalists at Sea*, p. 165.

57 Dunmore, ed., *The Journal of Jean-François de Galaup de la Pérouse*, I, p. ccviii.

58 Marchant, 'Hyperion and the Satyrs,' p. 27.

59 See below, p. 109.

60 Marchant, 'Hyperion and the Satyrs,' p.27; Edward Duyker and Maryse Duyker, eds., *Bruny D'Entrecasteaux, Voyage to Australia & the Pacific 1791–1793* (Carlton, VIC, 2001), pp. 27, 135; Edward Duyker, *Citizen Labillardière: A Naturalist's Life in Revolution and Exploration (1755–1834)* (Melbourne, 2003), p. 128.

61 Dunmore, *French Explorers of the Pacific*, I, p. 290.

62 Duyker and Duyker, eds., *Bruny D'Entrecasteaux*, pp. 133 (first quotation), 135 (second quotation).

63 Frank Horner, *Looking for La Pérouse: D'Entrecasteaux in Australia and the South Pacific 1792–1793* (Carlton, VIC, 1995), pp. 113, 122.

64 Duyker and Duyker, eds., *Bruny D'Entrecasteaux*, pp. 129, 132 (quotation).

65 Edward Duyker, 'Jacques-Julien Houtou de Labillardière (1755–1834): Explorer and Botanist' in Eric Berti and Ivan Barko, eds., *French Lives in Australia* (Melbourne, 2015), p. 27.

66 Horner, *Looking for La Pérouse*, pp. 63, 139, 143; Duyker, *Citizen Labillardière*, pp. 106–8.

67 Duyker and Duyker, eds., *Bruny D'Entrecasteaux*, pp. 60, 152–3, 159.

68 Ibid., p. 161 (quotation); Horner, *Looking for La Perouse*, p. 71; Michael Pearson, '"Nothing Left Undone": The Hydrographic Surveys of Beautemps-Beaupré' in Mulvaney and Tyndale-Biscoe, eds., *Rediscovering Recherche Bay*, pp. 21, 29.

69 Duyker, *Citizen Labillardière*, pp. 98, 103–5, 142–5. See also D. J. Galloway, 'Labillardiere's Tasmanian lichens,' *Papers and Proceedings of the Royal Society of Tasmania*, 122/2 (1988), pp. 97–108.

70 Gintaras Kantvilas, 'Labillardière and the Beginnings of Botanical Exploration in Tasmania' in Mulvaney and Tyndale-Biscoe, eds., *Rediscovering Recherche Bay*, p. 38; Williams, *Naturalists at Sea*, p. 167.

71 Hélène Richard, *Le Voyage de Dentrecasteaux à la recherché de Lapérouse*, 2 vols. (Paris, 1986), I, p. xli; Colin Dyer, 'From Happiness to Havoc: The Aboriginal Bruny Islanders before Settlement by the British, as Witnessed by French Explorers, 1792–1802,' *JRAHS*, 102/1 (2016), p. 32.

72 Duyker, *Citizen Labillardière*, p. 148. See also Claudia Grant, 'Revolution and the Noble Savage: The Observations of La Billardière' in Maurice Blackman, ed., *Australian Aborigines and the French* (Kensington, NSW, 1990), pp. 81–97, and Stephanie Anderson, 'French Anthropology in Australia, a Prelude: The Encounters between Aboriginal Tasmanians and the Expedition of Bruny d'Entrecasteaux, 1793,' *Aboriginal History*, 24 (2000), pp. 212–23.

73 Dyer, 'From Happiness to Havoc,' pp. 33–4.

74   Nicole Starbuck, 'Exploration, Observation and Regeneration: Voyagers'
     Perceptions of French and Tasmanian Families during the French Revolution,'
     Annales Historiques de la Révolution Française, no. 385 (2016), pp. 175–98.

75   Williams, *Naturalists at Sea*, p. 171; Martin Terry, 'The French and the Aborigines:
     A Decade of Depiction' in Blackman, ed., *Australian Aborigines and the French*,
     p. 101; Edward Duyker, 'Uncovering Jean Piron: In Search of D'Entrecasteaux's
     Artist,' *Explorations: A bulletin devoted to the study of Franco-Australian links*, 39
     (2005), pp. 37–45.

76   Duyker and Duyker, eds., *Bruny D'Entrecasteaux*, pp. 45 (first quotation), 140
     (second quotation), 142–8.

77   Dunmore, *French Explorers of the Pacific*, I, p. 331; Leslie R. Marchant, 'Bruny
     D'Entrecasteaux, Joseph-Antoine Raymond (1739–1793)' in Douglas Pike,
     ed., *ADB*, I (Melbourne, 1966), pp. 171–2.

78   Gavin de Beer, *The Sciences Were Never at War* (London, 1960), pp. 45, 47, 49,
     58–9; Harrison, 'Projections of the Revolutionary Nation,' p. 48; Frost, 'From the
     Hills of Provence,' p. 14.

79   Horner, *Looking for La Pérouse*, p. 245.

80   Kantvilas, 'Labillardière and the Beginnings of Botanical Exploration,' pp. 40–1;
     Williams, *Naturalists at Sea*, p. 167.

81   Duyker, 'Jacques-Julien Houtou de Labillardière,' pp. 30–1.

82   Kantvilas, 'Labillardière and the Beginnings of Botanical Exploration,' pp. 40–1.

83   Ibid., p. 42. For one example of this dispersal, see Joan Apfelbaum, 'Australian
     Collections of Labillardière in the Herbarium of the Academy of Natural Sciences
     of Philadelphia,' *Taxon*, 26/5–6 (1977), pp. 541–8.

84   Harrison, 'Projection of the Revolutionary Nation,' p. 49; Danielle Clode and
     Carol E. Harrison, 'Precedence and Posterity: Patterns of Publishing from French
     Scientific Expeditions to the Pacific (1785–1840),' *AJFS*, 50/3 (2013), p. 367.

Chapter 7

1   Pearson, *Great Southern Land*, p. 69; R. W. Giblin, *The Early History of Tasmania:
     The Geographical Era 1642–1804* (London, 1928), pp. 86–9.

2   A. R. Williamson, *Eastern Traders: Some Men and Ships of Jardine, Matheson &
     Company and Their Contemporaries in the East India Company's Maritime Service*
     (Ipswich, 1976), pp. 20, 25.

3   For a contemporary account of the voyage, see George Mortimer, *Observations and
     Remarks Made during a Voyage to the North West Coast of America* (London, 1791).
     See also H. G. Taylor, *The Discovery of Tasmania* (Hobart, 1973), pp. 16–19.

4   Kenneth Morgan, *Matthew Flinders, Maritime Explorer of Australia* (London, 2016), p. 42.

5   Kenneth Morgan, 'From Cook to Flinders: The Navigation of Torres Strait,' *IJMH*, 27/1 (2015), p. 43.

6   Alan Powell, *Northern Voyagers: Australia's Monsoon Coast in Maritime History* (Melbourne, 2010), p. 37. The First Fleet ships that took convicts to New South Wales in 1788 did not return to England via Torres Strait: see A. K. Cavenagh, 'The Return of the First Fleet Ships,' *The Great Circle*, 2/2 (1989), pp. 1–16.

7   Anne Salmond, *Bligh: William Bligh in the South Seas* (Berkeley and Los Angeles, CA, 2011), pp. 222–3; Jennifer Gall, ed., *In Bligh's Hand: Surviving the Mutiny on the Bounty* (Canberra, 2010), p. 85.

8   Flinders, *A Voyage to Terra Australis*, I, p. xvi.

9   Owen Rutter, ed., *The Voyage of the Bounty's Launch as Related in William Bligh's Despatch to the Admiralty and the Journal of John Fryer* (London, 1934), p. 41; C. B. Yule, *The Australia Directory. Volume 2: East Coast, Torres Strait and Coral Sea* ... (London, 1859), p. 232.

10 William Bligh, *A Voyage to the South Sea, Undertaken by Command of His Majesty, for the Purpose of Conveying the Bread-Fruit Tree to the West Indies, in His Majesty's Ship the Bounty* ... (London, 1792), p. 221.

11 Gall, ed., *In Bligh's Hand*, pp. 87–9, 151. Bligh's chart is reproduced in John Blake, *The Sea Chart: The Illustrated History of Nautical Maps and Navigational Charts* (London, 2004), 88. See also ML, William Bligh, 'A Survey of the Straits between New Holland and New Guinea' (SAFE/F79/5).

12 A.C.F. David, 'The Surveyors of the Bounty: A Preliminary Study of the Hydrographic Surveys of William Bligh, Thomas Hayward and Peter Heywood and the Charts Published from Them' (unpublished typescript, UKHO, Ministry of Defence Archives, Taunton, 1982), p. 23. Cook's and Bligh's surveys are illustrated in Hawkesworth, *An Account of the Voyages Undertaken by the Order of His Present Majesty for Making Discoveries in the Southern Hemisphere*, 3 vols. (London, 1773), III, p. 589, and Bligh, *A Voyage to the South Sea*, p. 220.

13 Salmond, *Bligh*, pp. 289–307; Peter Gesner, 'Pandora Project Stage 2: Four More Seasons of Excavation at the Pandora Historic Shipwreck,' *Memoirs of the Queensland Museum/Culture*, 9 (2016), pp. 26–46; Flinders, *A Voyage to Terra Australis*, I, p. xvii.

14 National Museum of the Royal Navy, Portsmouth, MS 180/16, Copy of statement by Captain Edwards as to the loss of the ship *Pandora*, n.d. A map showing the route of the open boats through Torres Strait can be seen at http://www.fatefulvoyage.com/pandora/pandoraHome.html and P. Gesner, 'HMS *Pandora* Project – A Report on Stage 1: Five Seasons of Excavation,' *Memoirs of the Queensland Museum, Cultural Heritage Series*, 2/1 (2000), p. 16.

15 Salmond, *Bligh*, pp. 309–11.

16 Gesner, 'Pandora Project Stage 2,' p. 33.

17 David Thomas Renouard, quoted in H. E. Maude, 'The Voyage of the *Pandora*'s Tender,' *MM*, 50/3 (1964), p. 228.

18 Roy Schreiber, ed., *Captain Bligh's Second Chance: An Eyewitness Account of His Return to the South Seas by Lt George Tobin* (London, 2007), pp. 154–6.

19 TNA, MPI 1/96, 'A Survey of the Straits between New Holland and New Guinea by Wm. Bligh' (*c*.1793), reproduced in Ida Lee, *Captain Bligh's Second Voyage to the South Sea* (London, 1920), facing p. 178, and in the facsimile edition of *The Log of the Bounty* (Guildford, 1975).

20 Powell, *Northern Voyagers*, p. 37. Contracts for the voyages led by Alt and Bampton are printed in Watson, ed., *HRA*, series 1, I, pp. 421–6.

21 Flinders, *A Voyage to Terra Australis*, I, p. xxx; Blainey, *The Tyranny of Distance*, pp. 57–8; J. C. Garran, 'William Wright Bampton and the Australian Merino,' *JRAHS*, 58/1 (1972), pp. 1–12.

22 James Horsbrugh, *The India Directory, or, Directions for Sailing to and from the East Indies, China, Australia, and the Interjacent Ports of Africa and South America ...*, 2 vols., 5th edn. (London, 1841), I, p. 734.

23 Reginald Appleyard, 'Vancouver's Discovery and Exploration of King George's Sound' *Early Days*, 9/4 (1982), pp. 86–8.

24 Ibid., pp. 86–7; W. Kaye Lamb, ed., *George Vancouver: A Voyage of Discovery to the North Pacific Ocean and Round the World 1791–1795*, 4 vols. (Cambridge, 1984), I, p. 325. See also Glyn Williams, *Naturalists at Sea: Scientific Travellers from Dampier to Darwin* (New Haven, CT, 2013), pp. 137–9.

25 Stephen Bown, *Madness, Betrayal and the Lash: The Epic Voyage of Captain George Vancouver* (Vancouver, 2008), p. 106.

26 Quoted in George Godwin, *Vancouver: A Life 1757–1798* (Vancouver, 1931), pp. 41, 204–5.

27 Kaye Lamb, ed., *George Vancouver*, I, pp. 59 (quotation), 330, 331 (quotation).

28 Ibid., pp. 331–2.

29 Bown, *Madness, Betrayal and the Lash*, p. 107; John M. Naish, *The Interwoven Lives of George Vancouver, Archibald Menzies, Joseph Whidbey, and Peter Puget: Exploring the Pacific Northwest Coast* (Lewiston, NY, 1996), p. 105.

30 TNA, ADM 55/13, Logbook of the *Chatham* (1791), f. 20; Kaye Lamb, ed., *George Vancouver*, I, pp. 59, 337, 341.

31 Appleyard, 'Vancouver's Discovery,' pp. 89–91.

32 Kaye Lamb, ed., *George Vancouver*, I, pp. 333–5, 337, 344.

33 Ibid., I, pp. 342, 345 (quotation), 358.

34 James K. Barnett, *Captain George Vancouver in Alaska and the North Pacific* (Anchorage, AK, 2017), p. 10.

35 BL, Add. MS 32,641, A. Menzies, Journal of Vancouver's Voyage, 1790–4, f. 60.

36 Kaye Lamb, ed., *George Vancouver*, I, p. 353.

37 Appleyard, 'Vancouver's Discovery,' p. 95; Sylvia J. Hallam, *Fire and Hearth: A Study of Aboriginal Usage and European Usurpation in South-western Australia* (Canberra, 1975), p. 158.

38 Naish, *The Interwoven Lives*, pp. 103–4.

39 E. W. Groves, 'Archibald Menzies's Visit to King George Sound, Western Australia, September–October 1791,' *Archives of Natural History*, 40/1 (2013), pp. 139–48.

40 Naish, *The Interwoven Lives*, p. 103; James McCarthy, *Monkey Puzzle Man: Archibald Menzies, Plant Hunter* (Dunbeath, Caithness, 2008), pp. 87, 91 n.20.

41 Appleyard, 'Vancouver's Discovery,' p. 96.

42 McCarthy, *Monkey Puzzle Man*, p. 87.

43 Morgan, *Matthew Flinders*, p. 35.

44 Taylor, *The Discovery of Tasmania*, pp. 49–50; Mault, 'Notes on Charts,' p. 112; Ida Lee, 'Captain John Hayes – An Early Tasmanian Explorer,' *The Tasmanian Mail*, 11 December 1909, p. 45; Margriet Roe, 'Hayes, Sir John (1768–1831)' in Pike, ed., *ADB*, I, p. 527.

45 Hélène Richard, 'L'Expédition de D'Entrecasteaux (1791–1794) et les origins de L'Implantation Anglaise en Tasmanie,' *Revue française d'histoire d'outre-mer*, LXIX/257 (1982), pp. 296–7.

46 This paragraph is based on two articles by Andrew C. F. David, 'Peter Heywood and Northwest Australia,' *The Great Circle*, 1/1 (1979), pp. 4–14, and 'From Mutineer to Hydrographer: The Surveying Career of Peter Heywood,' *International Hydrographic Review*, 3/2 (2002), pp. 6–11.

47 Rhys Richards, 'The Cruise of the *Kingston* and the *Elligood* in 1800 and the Wreck Found on King Island in 1802,' *The Great Circle*, 13/1 (1991), pp. 35–53.

48 Josephine Bastian, *'A Passion for Exploring New Countries': Matthew Flinders & George Bass* (Melbourne, 2016).

49 Estensen, *The Life of Matthew Flinders*, p. 39.

50 Miriam Estensen, *The Life of George Bass, Surgeon and Sailor of the Enlightenment* (Crows Nest, NSW, 2005); Michael Roe, 'New Light on George Bass, Entrepreneur and Intellectual,' *JRAHS*, 72/4 (1987), pp. 251–72.

51 Geoffrey C. Ingleton, 'Flinders as Cartographer' in R. W. Russell, ed., *Matthew Flinders – The Ifs of History* (Bedford Park, SA, 1979), p. 64. Manuscript charts of Sydney harbour and Botany Bay compiled by an assistant to Hunter are included in Australian National Maritime Museum, William Bradley, Logbook on H.M.S. *Sirius* (1787–92).

52 Flinders, *A Voyage to Terra Australis*, I, pp. xcvi–xcvii.

53 Hunter to Banks, 1 August 1797, in Chambers, ed., *The Indian and Pacific Correspondence*, IV, p. 459.

54 Estensen, *The Life of Matthew Flinders*, pp. 52–3; R.J.B. Knight and Alan Frost, eds., *The Journal of Daniel Paine 1794–1797, Together with Documents Illustrating the Beginning of Government Boat-building and Timber-gathering in New South Wales, 1795–1805* (Sydney, 1983), p. 39.

55 Dan Sprod, ed., *Van Diemen's Land Revealed: Flinders and Bass and Their Circumnavigation of the Island in the Colonial Sloop Norfolk 1798–1799* (Hobart, 2009), p. 7.

56 Keith Bowden, ed., *Matthew Flinders' Narrative of Tom Thumb's Cruise to Canoe Rivulet* (Brighton, VIC, 1985), pp. 4–6, 9–10, 12–13, 18–19.

57 Estensen, *The Life of Matthew Flinders*, pp. 60–1. Arrowsmith's publication was entitled *A Topographical Plan of the Settlement of New South Wales, Including Port Jackson, Botany Bay and Broken Bay. Surveyed by Messrs Grimes and Flinders – Communicated by Lt. Col. Paterson of the New South Wales Corps* (London, 1799).

58 Estensen, *The Life of George Bass*, pp. 115–16; R. V. Tooley, *The Mapping of Australia* (London, 1979), p. xiii; Scott, *The Life of Matthew Flinders*, pp. 68–9.

59 There are many descriptions of this voyage, including Estensen, *The Life of George Bass*, pp. 79–91; Harry and Valda Cole, *Mr Bass's Western Port. The Whaleboat Voyage* (Hastings, VIC, 1997); and Valda Cole, 'George Bass and the Whaleboat Voyage,' *Victorian Historical Journal*, 69/2 (1998), pp. 77–97. Bass's journal of the voyage is published in Bladen, ed., *HRNSW*, II, pp. 312–33.

60 Ernest Scott, 'English and French Navigators on the Victorian Coast,' *Victorian Historical Magazine*, 2/4 (1912), p. 158; T. M. Perry, *Australia's First Frontier: The Spread of Settlement in New South Wales, 1788–1829* (Melbourne, 1963), p. 111.

61 Flinders, *A Voyage to Terra Australis*, I, pp. cxiii, cxix (quotation).

62 Matthew Flinders, 'Narrative of an expedition to Furneauxs Islands on the Coast of New South Wales, in the Port Jackson Colonial Schooner *Francis*. By Matthew Flinders 2 Lieutenant of HMS *Reliance* March 1798,' *La Trobe Library Journal*, 13 (1974), pp. 12–13; M. Aurosseau, 'Flinders' Voyage in the *Francis*, 1798,' *The Geographical Journal*, 111/1-3 (1948), pp. 111–13.

63 Estensen, *The Life of Matthew Flinders*, pp. 70–1.

64 UKHO, Matthew Flinders, 'Sketch of the Parts between Van Diemen's Land and New South Wales. Seen in the *Francis* schooner 1798. By M. Flinders 2 Lieut. of H.M. Ship *Reliance*. The Part of New South Wales was coasted by Mr. Bass, Surgeon of the *Reliance* in a whale boat & where not seen in the *Francis* is taken from him,' chart y65, shelf X. Bass reported the sketch in a letter to Lt.-Col. Paterson, 20 August 1797, in Bladen, ed., *HRNSW*, III, p. 289. The sketch is reproduced in Cole and Cole, *Mr Bass's Western Port*, pp. 63, 65.

65 Hunter to Evan Nepean, 3 September 1798, in Watson, ed., *HRA*, II, p. 221; Hunter to Banks, 12 March, 25 July 1798, in Chambers, ed., *The Indian and Pacific Correspondence*, IV pp. 489–93.

66 Estensen, *The Life of Matthew Flinders*, pp. 72–3; Flinders, *A Voyage to Terra Australis*, I, p. cxxxviii.

67 Annotated excerpts from Flinders's and Bass's notes on the voyage appear in C. C. Macknight, ed., *Low Head to Launceston: The Earliest Reports of Port Dalrymple and the Tamar* (Launceston, 1998), pp. 1–53.

68 Flinders, 'Narrative of the Expedition of the Colonial Sloop *Norfolk*,' pp. 59–62.

69 Michael Roe, ed., *The Journal and Letters of Captain Charles Bishop on the North-West Coast of America, in the Pacific and in New South Wales 1794–1799* (London, 1967), pp. xliii–xliv.

70 Estensen, *The Life of Matthew Flinders*, pp. 91–2; Hunter to Banks, 1 June 1799, in Chambers, ed., *The Indian and Pacific Correspondence*, V, pp. 85–8.

71 Flinders, *A Voyage to Terra Australis*, I, p. cxciii. Descriptive accounts of Flinders's voyage to northern New South Wales in August 1799 are provided in Collins, ed. Fletcher, *An Account of the English Colony in New South Wales*, I, pp. 161–88, and Bastian, 'A Passion for Exploring New Countries,' pp. 53–60.

72 ML, Matthew Flinders, Journal in the *Norfolk* sloop, 1799, MS C211/2; Robert James Smith, 'Matthew Flinders and the North Coast of New South Wales, 1799,' *JRAHS*, 89/2 (1999), pp. 163–8.

73 NMM, Matthew Flinders, Journal kept on board the *Reliance* (1798–9), entry for 21 August 1799, ADM/L/R/79B; Flinders, *A Voyage to Terra Australis*, I, p. ccii. There are several rivers along this coast, but Flinders probably missed them because of the absence of estuaries: see T. M. Perry, 'Seasons for Exploration. The Second Daniel Brock Memorial Lecture, 1975,' *Proceedings of the Royal Geographical Society Australasia, South Australian Branch*, 76 (1975), p. 54.

74 Hunter to Banks, 1 June 1799, in Chambers, ed., *The Indian and Pacific Correspondence*, V, pp. 85–8.

75 Hunter to Nepean, 15 August 1799, in Watson, ed., *HRA*, II, p. 381.

76 Hunter to Banks, 20 February 1800, in Chambers, ed., *The Indian and Pacific Correspondence*, V, pp. 159–60.

77 Lincolnshire Archives, Flinders to Dr Matthew Flinders, 19 November 1800, Flinders Correspondence, 3/2.

78 Geoffrey C. Ingleton, *Matthew Flinders: Navigator and Chartmaker* (Guildford, 1986), p. 52. Arrowsmith's chart had a few errors which Flinders corrected, leading to publication of a revised version on 20 February 1801: see Morgan, *Matthew Flinders*, p. 42.

79 Flinders provided material from his own chart to aid Arrowsmith: that chart is in TNA, ADM 352/489, Original Surveys: Australia, east coast: Queensland: Port Stephens to Northumberland islands.

80 R. V. Tooley, *The Printed Maps of New South Wales 1773–1873* (London, 1968), pp. 10–11; Kenneth Morgan, 'Matthew Flinders and the Charting of Australia's Coasts, 1798–1814,' *Terrae Incognitae*, 50/2 (2018), pp. 15–20. For commentary

on the details included in these charts, see Ruth Gooch, 'Puzzling over the Early Flinders Charts,' *Victorian Historical Journal*, 78/1 (2007), pp. 5–22.

81 NMM, Flinders to Pulteney Malcolm, 17 January 1800, Flinders Papers, FLI/8a.

82 James Wiles to Banks, 16 March 1793, and Flinders to Banks, 21 October 1793, in Chambers, ed., *The Indian and Pacific Correspondence*, IV, pp. 96, 158.

83 Banks to John King, 15 May 1798, ibid., IV, p. 502. The first part of the quotation reflects the fact that Banks and Flinders had strong attachments to Lincolnshire – Banks by inheritance and Flinders by birth.

84 Philip Gidley King to Banks, 20 March 1799, in Chambers, ed., *The Indian and Pacific Correspondence*, V, p. 60.

85 NMM, Flinders to Pulteney Malcolm, 17 January 1800, Flinders Papers, FLI/8a.

86 'Notes regarding the *Lady Nelson*' [1800] in Chambers, ed., *The Indian and Pacific Correspondence*, V, pp. 142–6.

87 David Mackay, 'In the Shadow of Cook: The Ambition of Matthew Flinders' in John Hardy and Alan Frost, eds., *European Voyaging towards Australia* (Canberra, 1990), pp. 105–6.

88 Estensen, *The Life of Matthew Flinders*, pp. 110–11.

89 Charles H. Bertie, 'Matthew Flinders, Australia's Navigator,' *JPAHS*, 3/7 (1915–17), p. 303.

90 Rüdiger Joppien and Neil Chambers, 'The Scholarly Library and Collections of Knowledge of Sir Joseph Banks' in Giles Mandelbrote and Barry Taylor, eds., *Libraries within the Library: The Origins of the British Library's Printed Collections* (London, 2009), pp. 222–43; Neil Chambers, 'Joseph Banks, the British Museum and Collections in the Age of Empire' in R.G.W. Anderson, M. L. Caygill, A. G. MacGregor and L. Syson, eds., *Enlightening the British: Knowledge, Discovery and the Museum in the Eighteenth Century* (London, 2003), pp. 99–113.

91 Nigel Rigby, '"The Whole of the Surveying Department Rested on Me": Matthew Flinders, Hydrography and the Navy' in Marc Serge Rivière and Kumari R. Issur, eds., *Baudin-Flinders dans L'Océan: Voyages, Découvertes, Rencontre: Voyages, Discoveries, Encounter* (Paris, 2006), p. 263.

92 Flinders to Banks, 6 September 1800, in Paul Brunton, ed., *Matthew Flinders: Personal Letters from an Extraordinary Life* (Sydney, 2002), p. 51.

93 Ibid.

94 G. S. Ritchie, *The Admiralty Chart: British Naval Hydrography in the Nineteenth Century* (London, 1967), p. 81. For different interpretations of the eventual search for this strait, see Rupert Gerritsen, 'Getting the Strait Facts Straight,' *The Globe*, 72 (2013), pp. 11–21, and Kenneth Morgan, 'A Historical Myth? Matthew Flinders and the Quest for a Strait,' *Australian Historical Studies*, 48/1 (2017), pp. 52–67.

95 Kenneth Morgan, 'Sir Joseph Banks as Patron of the *Investigator* Expedition: Natural History, Geographical Knowledge and Australian Exploration,' *IJMH*, 26/2 (2014), pp. 235–64.

96   Banks to Flinders, 16 November 1800, in Chambers, ed., *The Indian and Pacific Correspondence*, V, p. 217.

Chapter 8

1   Banks to Flinders, 16 November 1800, in Ian Chambers, ed., *The Indian and Pacific Correspondence of Sir Joseph Banks, 1768–1820*, vol. V (London, 2012), p. 159.

2   John Gascoigne, 'Joseph Banks and the Expansion of Empire' in Margarette Lincoln, ed., *Science and Exploration: European Voyages to the Southern Oceans in the Eighteenth Century* (Woodbridge, 1998), pp. 39–40.

3   TNA, ADM 2/293, Admiralty to the Navy Board, 21 November 1800.

4   TNA, ADM 2/294/51, Admiralty to the Navy Board, 10 December 1800.

5   Flinders, *A Voyage to Terra Australis*, I, p. cciv.

6   Peter Ashley, 'HMS Investigator – A "Copper-Bottomed" Ship?' in Marc Serge Rivière and Kumari R. Issur, eds., *Baudin-Flinders dans l'Océan Indien: Voyages, Découvertes, Rencontre: Travels, Discoveries, Encounter* (Paris, 2006), pp. 271–88.

7   TNA, ADM 8/81, Admiralty List Book.

8   N. T. Geeson and R. T Sexton, 'H.M. Sloop *Investigator*,' *MM*, 56/3 (1970), pp. 291–2; Peter Ashley, *The Indomitable Captain Matthew Flinders, Royal Navy* (Clanfield, Hants, 2005), p. 21.

9   Banks to George John Spencer [December 1800] in Neil Chambers, ed., *The Letters of Sir Joseph Banks: A Selection, 1768–1820* (London, 2000), pp. 219–20.

10   Kenneth Morgan, *Matthew Flinders, Maritime Explorer of Australia* (London, 2016), p. 51.

11   NHM, Banks to Marquis Cornwallis, 23 February 1801, Robert Brown Correspondence, 3, f. 114.

12   Bernard Smith, *European Vision and the South Pacific*, 2nd edn. (New Haven, CT, 1985), p. 197.

13   D. J. Mabberley, *Jupiter Botanicus: Robert Brown of the British Museum* (London, 1985), p. 62; Mark Webb, 'Peter Good: Gardener on a Voyage of Discovery' in Juliet Wege, Alex George, Jan Gathe, Kris Lemson and Kath Napier, eds., *Matthew Flinders and His Scientific Gentlemen: The Expedition of H.M.S. Investigator to Australia 1801–1805* (Welshpool, WA, 2005), pp. 97–103.

14   David T. Moore, 'Robert Brown on H.M.S. Investigator 1801–1805: An Overview of the Natural History Collecting Localities' in Wege, George, Gathe, Lemson and Napier, eds., *Matthew Flinders and His Scientific Gentlemen*, p. 50; Phyllis I. Edwards, 'Robert Brown (1773–1858) and the Natural History of Matthew Flinders' Voyage in H.M.S. *Investigator*, 1801–1805,' *Journal of the Society for the Bibliography of Natural History*, 7 (1976), p. 388.

15 Elizabeth Findlay, *Arcadian Quest: William Westall's Australian Sketches* (Canberra, 1998), pp. xii–xiii.

16 Maskelyne to Banks, 23 and 24 December 1800, in Chambers, ed., *The Indian and Pacific Correspondence*, V, pp. 229–31; Cambridge University Library, RGO 35/55, Maskelyne to Banks, 23 January 1801, Board of Longitude Papers.

17 BL, Add. MS 32439, ff. 30-1, Navy Board to Robert Brown, William Daniel, Ferdinand Bauer, Peter Good and John Allen, 15 April 1801, Robert Brown Papers.

18 S. R. Band, 'John Allen, Miner: On board H.M.S. Investigator 1801-1804,' *Bulletin of the Peak District Mines Historical Society*, 10 (1987), pp. 67–78.

19 Blane to Banks, 17 January and 14 February 1801, in Chambers, ed., *The Indian and Pacific Correspondence*, V, pp. 252-3, 276-7; ML, Bell to Blane, 12 January 1801, Banks Papers, series 63.17, 63.32.

20 Lincolnshire Archives, Flinders to Dr Flinders, 10 July 1801, Flinders Correspondence, 3/8.

21 Flinders to Banks, 29 April 1801, in Bladen, ed., *HRNSW*, IV, pp. 352-3.

22 John McAleer and Nigel Rigby, *Captain Cook and the Pacific: Art, Exploration & Empire* (New Haven, 2017), p. 194.

23 Flinders to Banks, 6 June 1801, in Bladen, ed., *HRNSW*, IV, p. 387.

24 Banks to Flinders, June 1801, ibid., IV, pp. 388-9.

25 Flinders to Banks, 29 October 1801, ibid., IV, p. 601.

26 Morgan, *Matthew Flinders*, pp. 67–75; entry for 9 December 1801 in Morgan, ed., *Australia Circumnavigated*, I, p. 242.

27 Entry for 8 December 1801 in Morgan, ed., *Australia Circumnavigated*, I, p. 238.

28 Morgan, *Matthew Flinders*, pp. 79-81. The British Admiralty had copied French charts captured from D'Entrecasteaux's expedition: see Gavin de Beer, *The Sciences Were Never at War* (London, 1960), p. 50.

29 T. G. Vallance, D. T. Moore and E. W. Groves, eds., *Nature's Investigator: The Diary of Robert Brown in Australia, 1801-1805* (Canberra, 2001), pp. 116-17; Morgan, *Matthew Flinders*, p. 81.

30 Morgan, *Matthew Flinders*, pp. 78-9; Greg Keighery and Neil Gibson, 'The Flinders Expedition in Western Australia: Robert Brown, the Plants and Their Influence on W.A. Botany' in Wege, George, Gathe, Lemson and Napier, eds., *Matthew Flinders and His Scientific Gentlemen*, pp. 106-13.

31 See above, pp. 30-1.

32 Entry for 3 February 1802 in Morgan, ed., *Australia Circumnavigated*, I, p. 292.

33 Morgan, *Matthew Flinders*, pp. 83-8; Paul Carter, *The Road to Botany Bay: An Exploration of Landscape and History* (London, 1988), pp. 180, 184-5.

34 Flinders, *A Voyage to Terra Australis*, I, p. 195.

35 For this expedition see below, pp. 148-9.

36 Nicole Starbuck, 'Sir Joseph Banks and the Baudin Expedition: Exploring the Politics of the Republic of Letters', *French History and Civilisation: Papers from the George Rudé Seminar*, 3 (2009), pp. 59–60.

37 Morgan, *Matthew Flinders*, pp. 89–96; Jean Fornasiero and John West-Sooby, 'A Contested Coast? Revisiting the Baudin-Flinders Encounter of April 1802' in Carolyn Collins and Paul Sendziuk, eds., *Foundational Fictions in South Australian History* (Adelaide, 2018), pp. 16–19.

38 Morgan, *Matthew Flinders*, p. 98.

39 Ibid., pp. 96–102; Peter Hambly, ed., *Pierre Bernard Milius, Last Commander of the Baudin Expedition: The Journal 1800–1804* (Canberra, 2013), p. 168.

40 Miriam Estensen, *The Life of Matthew Flinders* (Sydney, 2002), p. 239.

41 Trevor J. Lipscombe, 'Cook's Cape Dromedary – Is It Montague island?' *Map Matters*, 32 (2017), p. 2; McAleer and Rigby, *Captain Cook and the Pacific*, p. 196.

42 Morgan, *Matthew Flinders*, pp. 105–9; Flinders, *A Voyage to Terra Australis*, II, p. 83.

43 James Bowen and Margarita Bowen, *The Great Barrier Reef: History, Science, Heritage* (Cambridge, 2002), p. 64; Flinders, *A Voyage to Terra Australis*, I, pp. 99–102.

44 Bowen and Bowen, *The Great Barrier Reef*, p. 65; Flinders, *A Voyage to Terra Australis*, II, pp. 99–100.

45 TNA, ADM 352/487, Chart of Terra Australis by Matthew Flinders, Commander of HMS *Investigator*, 1802, Sheet 8, Australia: East Coast: Queensland: Bustard Bay to Cape Sandwich.'

46 Flinders, *A Voyage to Terra Australis*, II, pp. 104, 112, 116–18; Kenneth Morgan, 'From Cook to Flinders: The Navigation of Torres Strait', *IJMH*, 27/1 (2015), pp. 55–8.

47 Entry for 8 April 1803 in Morgan, ed., *Australia Circumnavigated*, II, p. 149.

48 Flinders to Banks, 28 March 1803, in Bladen, ed., *HRNSW*, V, p. 78.

49 Estensen, *The Life of Matthew Flinders*, pp. 246–7.

50 Carsten Berg Høgenhoff, *Sweers Islands Unveiled: Details from Abel Tasman and Matthew Flinders' Explorations of Australia* (Oslo, 2006), p. 25.

51 Flinders, *A Voyage to Terra Australis*, II, p. 135.

52 T. M. Perry, 'Seasons for Exploration. The Second Daniel Brock Memorial Lecture, 1975', *Proceedings of the Royal Geographical Society Australasia, South Australian Branch*, 76 (1975), p. 55; Morgan, ed., *Australia Circumnavigated*, I, p. 35.

53 Morgan, ed., *Australia Circumnavigated*, ii, pp. 139–40, 146, 162; Flinders, *A Voyage to Terra Australis*, II, pp. 133–5.

54 Morgan, ed., *Australia Circumnavigated*, I, p. 37, II, pp. 179–84.

55 Ibid., I, pp. 38–9; entry for 23 December 1802 in Vallance, Moore and Groves, eds., *Nature's Investigator*, p. 331.

56 Morgan, ed., *Australia Circumnavigated*, II, pp. 212, 220; C. C. Macknight, *The Voyage to Marege': Macassan Trepangers in Northern Australia* (Melbourne, 1976), p. 52.

57 Morgan, ed., *Australia Circumnavigated*, II, pp. 241, 243; Flinders, *A Voyage to Terra Australis*, II, p. 189.

58 Nos. 100 and 101 in T. M. Perry and D. H. Simpson, eds., *Drawings by William Westall; Landscape Artist on Board HMS Investigator during the Circumnavigation of Australia by Captain Matthew Flinders R. N. in 1801–1803* (London, 1962); Findlay, *Arcadian Quest*, pp. 14–15, 39; F. D. McCarthy, 'The Cave Paintings of Groote Eylandt and Chasm Island' in C. P. Mountford, ed., *Records of the American-Australian Scientific Expedition to Arnhem Land* (Melbourne, 1960), pp. 297–414.

59 Morgan, ed., *Australia Circumnavigated*, I, p. 39.

60 Ibid., II, p. 288; entry for 17 February 1803 in Vallance, Moore and Groves, eds., *Nature's Investigator*, p. 368. Trepang were also known as sea cucumbers.

61 D. J. Mulvaney, *The Prehistory of Australia* (London, 1969), p. 17.

62 Morgan, ed., *Australia Circumnavigated*, I, p. 63.

63 Entry for 18 February 1803 in Vallance, Moore and Groves, eds., *Nature's Investigator*, p. 372.

64 John Gascoigne, *Encountering the Pacific in the Age of Enlightenment* (Cambridge, 2014), p. 350.

65 Entry for 5 March 1803 in Vallance, Moore and Groves, eds., *Nature's Investigator*, p. 382.

66 Morgan, ed., *Australia Circumnavigated*, I, p. 40.

67 Ibid., I, pp. 41–2; ML, Flinders to Bell, 27, 29, 30 May 1803, Matthew Flinders letterbook (1801–6). Bell's replies are not extant.

68 Morgan, ed., *Australia Circumnavigated*, I, p. 43.

69 Flinders, *A Voyage to Terra Australis*, II, p. 272; Geoffrey C. Ingleton, *Matthew Flinders: Navigator and Chartmaker* (Guildford, 1986), pp. 228, 236.

70 Flinders to King, 10 June 1803 in Watson, ed., *HRA*, first series, IV, pp. 370–1.

71 Flinders, *A Voyage to Terra Australis*, II, pp. 274–5.

72 Morgan, ed., *Australia Circumnavigated*, I, pp. 44–5.

73 Morgan, *Matthew Flinders*, pp. 143–8.

74 Ibid., pp. 148–66, 179–95.

75 Ibid., pp. 167–75; Phyllis I. Edwards, 'Robert Brown (1773–1858) and the Natural History of Matthew Flinders' Voyage in H.M.S. *Investigator*, 1801–1805,' *Journal of the Society for the Bibliography of Natural History*, 7/4 (1976), pp. 385–407; Marlene J. Norst, *Ferdinand Bauer: The Australian Natural History Drawings* (London, 1989).

76 Morgan, ed., *Australia Circumnavigated*, I, p. 59. Flinders did not know about Cook's reflections on the Aborigines as his remarks were not published until long after his death.

77 Bronwen Douglas, 'Slippery Word, Ambiguous Praxis: "Race" and late 18th-Century Voyagers in Oceania,' *Journal of Pacific History*, XLI/1 (2006), p. 22.

78 Morgan, ed., *Australia Circumnavigated*, I, pp. 257–8, II, p. 273; Scott, *The Life of Matthew Flinders*, p. 148.

79 Morgan, ed., *Australia Circumnavigated*, II, p. 23.

80 Ibid., I, pp. 249–51, 257–8, II, p. 23; Flinders, *A Voyage to Terra Australis*, I, pp. 58–9, 66–7.

81   Entry for 5 August 1802 in Vallance, Moore and Groves, eds., *Nature's Investigator*, p. 238.

82   Flinders, *A Voyage to Terra Australis*, II, pp. 209–10.

83   Morgan, ed., *Australia Circumnavigated*, I, p. 61.

84   Paul Carter, *Living in a New Country: History, Travelling and Language* (London, 1992), pp. 161–2; Isobel White, 'Birth and Death of a Ceremony,' *Aboriginal History*, 4/1 (1980), pp. 33–42.

85   Banks to William Marsden, 3 January 1806, in Bladen, ed., *HRNSW*, V, p. 181.

86   Peter Watts, Jo Ann Pomfrett and David Mabberley, *An Exquisite Eye: The Australian Flora & Fauna Drawings 1801–1820 of Ferdinand Bauer* (Glebe, NSW, 1997), p. 22; N. B. Kinnear, 'Robert Brown's Zoological Collections Made during the Voyage of the "Investigator,"' *Proceedings of the Linnean Society of London*, 144 (1931), pp. 36–8; Alwyne Wheeler, 'The Zoological Manuscripts of Robert Brown,' *Archives of Natural History*, 20/3 (1993), pp. 417–24. The ornithological results of the voyage are described in Hubert Massey Whittell, *The Literature of Australian Birds: A History and a Bibliography of Australian Ornithology* (Perth, 1954), pp. 49–55.

87   TNA, ADM 1/4379, [Banks] to Marsden, January 1806, Admiralty Correspondence and Papers.

88   Morgan, ed., *Australia Circumnavigated*, I, pp. 68–9.

89   Brown to Banks, 18 June 1807, in Chambers, ed., *The Indian and Pacific Correspondence*, VII, pp. 265–6.

90   Brown to Banks, 2 June 1809, ibid., VII, p. 453. A prodromus was the Latin name for a preliminary publication intended as a forerunner to a later, comprehensive publication.

91   BL, Add. MS 32439, ff. 288–91, n.d. but 1809, Robert Brown Papers; Marlene J. Norst, 'Recognition and Renaissance: Ferdinand Lucas Bauer 1760–1826,' *Australian Natural History*, 23/4 (1990), p. 299.

92   D. J. Mabberley, 'The Legacy of Flinders' Naturalist [the Life and Work of Pioneering Botanist Robert Brown],' *Australian Geographic*, 60 (2000), pp. 54–5, 58, 63.

93   K. A. Austin, *The Voyage of the Investigator 1801–1803: Commander Matthew Flinders, R.N.* (Adelaide, 1964), p. 199.

94   Margaret Steven, *First Impressions: The British Discovery of Australia* (London, 1988), p. 74.

95   Ann Moyal, *'A Bright & Savage Land': Scientists in Colonial Australia* (Sydney, 1986), p. 25.

96   D. J. Mabberley, *Jupiter Botanicus: Robert Brown of the British Museum* (London, 1985), pp. 161, 164; Edwards, 'Botany of the Flinders Voyage,' pp. 152–3.

97   Jim Endersby, *Imperial Nature: Joseph Hooker and the Practices of Victorian Science* (Chicago, 2008), pp. 215, 236.

98   Mabberley, 'The Legacy of Flinders' Naturalist,' p. 57.

99 Watts, Pomfrett and Mabberley, *An Exquisite Eye*, pp. 27–8; Norst, 'Recognition and Renaissance,' pp. 300, 304; James Taylor, *Picturing the Pacific: Joseph Banks and the Shipboard Artists of Cook and Flinders* (London, 2018), pp. 60–3.

100 R. M. Barker, 'The Botanical Legacy of 1802: South Australian Plants Collected by Robert Brown and Peter Good on Matthew Flinders' Investigator and by the French Scientists on Baudin's Geographe and Naturaliste,' *Journal of the Adelaide Botanic Gardens*, 21 (2007), p. 9.

101 Norst, *Ferdinand Bauer*, pp. 84–7. Twenty-five of Bauer's finished plant drawings are reproduced in W. T. Stearn, *The Australian Flower Paintings of Ferdinand Bauer* (London, 1976).

102 Westall to Banks, 31 January 1804, in Chambers, ed., *The Indian and Pacific Correspondence*, VI, pp. 310–11.

103 Bowen and Bowen, *The Great Barrier Reef*, p. 71.

104 Findlay, *Arcadian Quest*, pp. 14–16; Bernard Smith, *European Vision and the South Pacific*, 2nd edn. (New Haven, CT, 1985), pp. 196–7.

105 Findlay, *Arcadian Quest*, pp. 14–16; Kay Stehn and Alex George, 'Artist in a New Land: William Westall in New Holland' in Wege, George, Gathe, Lemson and Napier, eds., *Matthew Flinders and His Scientific Gentlemen*, pp. 87–8.

106 For an analysis of one Westall oil painting, see John J. Bradley and Amanda Kearney, '"He Painted the Law": William Westall, "Stone Monuments" and Remembrance of Things Past,' *Journal of Material Culture*, 16/1 (2011), pp. 25–45.

107 Peter Monteath, 'Contradictory Encounters: William Westall in Australia' in Anne Chittleborough, Gillian Dooley, Brenda Glover and Rick Hosking, eds., *Alas, for the Pelicans! Flinders, Baudin & Beyond* (Kent Town, SA, 2003), pp. 50–3; Tim Bonyhady, *Images in Opposition: Australian Landscape Painting 1801–1890* (Melbourne, 1985), p. 87.

108 Smith, *European Vision and the South Pacific*, pp. 191, 197. Detailed appraisal of Westall can be found in two studies by James M. S. Taylor: 'The Creation and Reception of William Westall's Admiralty Oil Paintings, Derived from His Voyage in H.M.S. Investigator, 1801–3' (University of Sussex D.Phil., 2015) and *Picturing the Pacific*, pp. 59, 155, 163, 176–83, 188–231.

109 Morgan, ed., *Australia Circumnavigated*, I, pp. 76–7, II, p. 410; Jim Bennett, *Navigation: A Very Short Introduction* (Oxford, 2017), pp. 78–9, 89.

110 Morgan, ed., *Australia Circumnavigated*, I, pp. 80, 211–12. For an appraisal of Flinders's survey methods and findings, see M. K. Barritt, 'Matthew Flinders's Survey Practices and Records,' *Journal of the Hakluyt Society* (2014), pp. 1–15.

111 T. M. Perry, 'Matthew Flinders and the Charting of the Australian Coast,' *The Globe*, 23 (1985), p. 2; Morgan, ed., *Australia Circumnavigated*, II, p. 414.

112 The text of the 'Memoir' is presented in Morgan, ed., *Australia Circumnavigated*, II, pp. 402–505, and discussed in Dany Bréelle, 'Matthew Flinders et la mise

en cartes d'un nouvel espace indo-pacifique,' *Cybergeo: European Journal of Geography*, n.p.

113 Morgan, ed., *Australia Circumnavigated*, I, pp. 77–8; Flinders, *A Voyage to Terra Australis*, I, p. 255. Cambridge University Library, RGO 14/68, f. 67r, Crosley to the Commissioners of Longitude, 3 March 1814. See also Kenneth Morgan, 'Finding Longitude: The *Investigator* expedition, 1801–1803,' *IJMH*, 29/4 (2017), pp. 771–87.

114 Morgan, ed., *Australia Circumnavigated*, I, p. 82; Anthony Payne, 'The Publication and Readership of Voyage Journals in the Age of Vancouver, 1730–1830' in Stephen Haycox, James Barnett and Caedman Liburd, eds., *Enlightenment and Exploration in the North Pacific 1741–1805* (Seattle, 1997), pp. 176–7.

115 Greg Wood, 'Successive States: Aaron Arrowsmith's Chart of the Pacific Ocean, 1798–1832,' *The Globe*, 70 (2012), p. 7; entries for 22 and 26 January 1811 in Brown and Dooley, eds., *Matthew Flinders Private Journal*, p. 343.

116 For details, see Dany Bréelle, 'Matthew Flinders's Australian Toponomy and Its British Connections,' *Journal of the Hakluyt Society* (2013), pp. 1–41.

117 Gillian Dooley, 'The Library of Soho Square: Matthew Flinders, Sir Joseph Banks and the publication of "A Voyage to Terra Australis" (1814),' *Script & Print*, 41/3 (2017), p. 172.

118 Morgan, ed., *Australia Circumnavigated*, I, p. 84; ML, Flinders to Banks, 17 August 1813, Matthew Flinders letterbook (1810–14); A. Lodewyckx, 'The Name of Australia: Its Origin and Early Use,' *Victorian Historical Magazine*, XIII/3 (1929), p. 100. For a detailed discussion of Flinders's charts and atlas, see Kenneth Morgan, 'Matthew Flinders and the Charting of Australia's Coasts, 1798–1814,' *Terrae Incognitae*, 50/2 (2018), pp. 115–45.

119 Jan Tent and Helen Slatyer, 'Naming Places on the "Southland": European Place-Naming Practices from 1606 to 1803,' *Australian Historical Studies*, 40/1 (2009), p. 6; David Taylor, *The States of a Nation: The Politics and Surveys of the Australian State Borders* (Bathurst, NSW, 2006), p. 21.

120 Scott Polar Research Institute, University of Cambridge, Franklin to Robert Brown, 9 June 1815, MS 248/296/5, Sir John Franklin Collection.

121 Brown, 'The Late Captain Flinders,' *The Nautical Magazine and Naval Chronicle*, January 1854, p. 30.

122 Morgan, *Matthew Flinders*, p. 199.

Chapter 9

1   Jean Fornasiero, Peter Monteath and John West-Sooby, *Encountering Terra Australis: The Australian Voyages of Nicolas Baudin and Matthew Flinders* (Kent Town, SA, 2004), pp. 17–20; Jean Bourgoin and Etienne Taillemite, 'The Baudin Expedition

to Australia 1800–1804,' *International Hydrographic Review*, 3/1 (2002), pp. 6–7; Jean Fornasiero and John West-Sooby, 'Voyages et déplacements des savoirs. Les expéditions de Nicolas Baudin entre Révolution et Empire,' *Annales Historiques de la Révolution Française*, no. 385 (2016), pp. 23–46. French voyages of scientific discovery in the era of Baudin are the subject of Jean Fornasiero and John West-Sooby, 'The French Revolution and the Politics of Sea Voyaging,' *The French Australian Review*, 62 (2017), pp. 3–18. Baudin's proposals for the voyage are available at the Archives Nationales, Paris, BB4995. The instructions from the Ministry of Marine and the Institut are published in Jacqueline Bonnemains, ed., *Mon voyage aux Terres Australes: journal personnel du commandant Baudin* (Paris, 2000), pp. 29–120.

2 John West-Sooby, Jean Fornasiero and Margaret Sankey, 'Nicolas Baudin (1754–1803), from Seafarer to Philosophical Voyager' in Eric Berti and Ivan Barko, eds., *French Lives in Australia* (Melbourne, 2015), p. 51.

3 For the historiography of the Baudin expedition, see Peter Cowley, Jean Fornasiero and Margaret Sankey, 'The Baudin Expedition in Review: Old Quarrels and New Approaches,' *AJFS*, XLI/2 (2004), pp. 4–14.

4 Christine Cornell, ed., *The Journal of Post Captain Nicolas Baudin Commander-in-Chief of the Corvettes Géographe and Naturaliste Assigned by Order of the Government to a Voyage of Discovery* (Adelaide, 1974), p. 1.

5 John Dunmore, *French Explorers in the Pacific. II. The Nineteenth Century* (Oxford, 1969), p. 10.

6 Cornell, ed., *The Journal of Post Captain Nicolas Baudin*, pp. 2–4.

7 William P. Helling, 'Redistributing the Blame: Baudin's Voyage to the Australian Seas,' *The Great Circle*, 15/2 (1993), p. 108.

8 Bourgoin and Taillemite, 'The Baudin Expedition,' pp. 8–9; Anthony J. Brown, *Ill-Starred Captains: Flinders and Baudin* (London, 2001), pp. 32 (quotation), 36. See also Michel Jangoux, 'Les Zoologistes et Botanistes qui Accompagnerent le Capitaine Baudin aux Terres Australes,' *AJFS*, 41/2 (2004), pp. 55–78.

9 Hilary King, 'The Marine Chronometers of the Baudin Expedition to Australia, 1800–1804,' *Antiquarian Horology*, 23/6 (1997), pp. 508–21; Patrick Llewellyn, 'Baudin's Chronometer' in Jean Fornasiero, Lindl Lawton and John West-Sooby, eds., *The Art of Science: Nicolas Baudin's Voyagers 1800–1804* (Adelaide, 2016), p. 115.

10 Nicole Starbuck, 'Sir Joseph Banks and the Baudin Expedition: Exploring the Politics of the Republic of Letters,' *French History and Civilization: Papers from the George Rudé Seminar*, 3 (2009), pp. 56–68.

11 A popular book, emphasizing such a race, is Klaus Toft, *The Navigators: Flinders vs. Baudin: The Race between Matthew Flinders and Nicolas Baudin to Discover the Fabled Passage through the Middle of Australia* (Potts Point, NSW, 2002). For the view expressed here, see Kenneth Morgan, *Matthew Flinders, Maritime Explorer of Australia* (London, 2016), p. 92.

12 This was effectively demonstrated long ago in Ernest Scott, *Terre Napoléon: A History of French Explorations and Projects in Australia* (London, 1910).

13 Dunmore, *French Explorers in the Pacific*, II, p. 11; Jean Fornasiero and John West-Sooby, 'The Acquisitive Eye? French Observations in the Pacific from Bougainville to Baudin' in John West-Sooby, ed., *Discovery and Empire: The French in the South Seas* (Adelaide, 2013), p. 76.

14 Paul Carter, 'Looking for Baudin' in Susan Hunt and Paul Carter, eds., *Terre Napoléon: Australia through French Eyes 1800–1804* (Sydney, 1999), p. 23.

15 Frank Horner, *The French Reconnaissance: Baudin in Australia 1801–1803* (Melbourne, 1987), pp. 57, 60.

16 Archives nationales, Paris, Baudin to Hamelin, 9 October 1800, Marine 5JJ 35, 40 B-D.

17 Helling, 'Redistributing the Blame,' pp. 110–11.

18 Horner, *The French Reconnaissance*, pp. 83–4.

19 Bourgoin and Taillemite, 'The Baudin Expedition,' pp. 9–10; Fornasiero, Monteath and West-Sooby, *Encountering Terra Australis*, pp. 23, 26–7; O. H. K. Spate, 'Baudin and Flinders' in R. W. Russell, ed., *Matthew Flinders – The Ifs of History* (Bedford Park, SA, 1979), p. 91.

20 Fornasiero, Monteath and West-Sooby, *Encountering Terra Australis*, pp. 28, 41; Bourgoin and Taillemite, 'The Baudin Expedition,' pp. 10–11; Horner, *The French Reconnaissance*, pp. 151, 154; Edward Duyker, *Francois Péron: An Impetuous Life: Naturalist and Voyager* (Melbourne, 2006), p. 84.

21 Helling, 'Redistributing the Blame,' p. 112; Colin Wallace, *The Lost Australia of François Péron* (London, 1984), p. 45.

22 Helling, 'Redistributing the Blame,' pp. 113–15; Duyker, *Francois Péron*, p. 84; Fornasiero, Monteath and West-Sooby, *Encountering Terra Australis*, p. 51.

23 Dunmore, *French Explorers in the Pacific*, II, p. 17; François Péron, *Voyage of Discovery to the Southern Lands Continued by Louis de Freycinet, Books I to III, Second Edition 1824* (Adelaide, 2006), p. 151.

24 Entry for 23 June 1801 in Cornell, ed., *The Journal of Post Captain Nicolas Baudin*, p. 201.

25 Horner, *The French Reconnaissance*, pp. 143, 174; Duyker, *François Péron*, pp. 85–6.

26 Fornasiero, Monteath and West-Sooby, *Encountering Terra Australis*, pp. 53–5; entry for 26 June 1801 in Cornell, ed., *The Journal of Post Captain Nicolas Baudin*, p. 206 (quotation).

27 Peron, *Voyage of Discovery*, books I–III, p. 160; entry for 14 July 1801 in Cornell, ed., *The Journal of Post Captain Nicolas Baudin*, p. 220; Helling, 'Redistributing the Blame,' p. 115.

28 Horner, *The French Reconnaissance*, p. 164; Brown, *Ill-Starred Captains*, p. 136.

29 Leslie R. Marchant, 'The French Discovery and Survey of the Legendary North-West Cape and Willem River in Western New Holland,' *Imago Mundi*, 40 (1988), p. 48.

30 Fornasiero, Monteath and West-Sooby, *Encountering Terra Australis*, pp. 65, 67; entry for 19 August 1801 in Cornell, ed., *The Journal of Post Captain Nicolas Baudin*, p. 252; Brown, *Ill-Starred Captains*, p. 138.

31 Fornasiero and West-Sooby, 'Taming the Unknown,' p. 62.

32 Entries for 23 July and 21 August 1801 in Cornell, ed., *The Journal of Post Captain Nicolas Baudin*, pp. 227, 254.

33 François Péron, *Voyage of Discovery to the Southern Lands, Continued by Louis de Freycinet, Second Edition 1824, Book IV* (Adelaide, 2003), p. 152.

34 Horner, *The French Reconnaissance*, pp. 179, 181, 190; Fornasiero, Monteath and West-Sooby, *Encountering Terra Australis*, p. 62; Bourgoin and Taillemite, 'The Baudin Expedition,' p. 12.

35 Entry for 13 January 1802 in Cornell, ed., *The Journal of Post Captain Nicolas Baudin*, p. 300.

36 Fornasiero and West-Sooby, 'Taming the Unknown,' p. 64; Fornasiero, Monteath and West-Sooby, *Encountering Terra Australis*, pp. 88, 97, 109.

37 Carol E. Harrison, 'Projections of the Revolutionary Nation: French Expeditions in the Pacific, 1791–1803,' *Osiris*, 24/1 (2009), p. 44.

38 Duyker, *François Péron*, p. 114; Brown, *Ill-Starred Captains*, pp. 201–2.

39 Horner, *The French Reconnaissance*, p. 191; Duyker, *François Péron*, p. 124; Péron, *Voyage of Discovery*, books I–III, pp. 191, 203–4, 228.

40 Brown, *Ill-Starred Captains*, p. 210.

41 Péron, *Voyage of Discovery*, books I–III, pp. 229 (quotation), 243–4.

42 Entry for 26 February 1802 in Cornell, ed., *The Journal of Post-Captain Nicolas Baudin*, p. 343.

43 Duyker, *François Péron*, pp. 118–20; Fornasiero, Monteath and West-Sooby, *Encountering Terra Australis*, p. 189.

44 Peter Hambly, ed., *Pierre Bernard Milius, Last Commander of the Baudin Expedition: The Journal 1800–1804* (Canberra, 2013), pp. 118–21 (quotations on pp. 118–20).

45 Horner, *The French Reconnaissance*, p. 204.

46 Ibid., pp. 182, 196; entry for 15 January 1802 in Cornell, ed., *The Journal of Post-Captain Nicolas Baudin*, p. 304 (quotation).

47 Entries for 29–30 January and 1 February 1802, in Cornell, ed., *The Journal of Post-Captain Nicolas Baudin*, pp. 318, 321, 323.

48 Fornasiero, Monteath and West-Sooby, *Encountering Terra Australis*, p. 112.

49 Duyker, *François Péron*, p. 121. For the daily proceedings between members of Baudin's expedition and the Aborigines, see N.J.B. Plomley, *The Baudin Expedition and the Tasmanian Aborigines 1802* (Hobart, 1983), pp. 38–54, 76–9. For artistic representation, see Jane Southwood, 'The Artwork of the Baudin Expedition to Australia (1800–1804): Nicolas-Martin Petit's 1802 Portrait of an Aboriginal Woman and Child from Van Diemen's Land' in Natalie Edwards, Ben McCann and Peter Poiana, eds., *Framing French Culture* (Adelaide, 2015), pp. 103–26.

50 Entry for 26 January 1802 in Cornell, ed., *The Journal of Post-Captain Nicolas Baudin*, p. 318; Duyker, *François Péron*, p. 120.

51 Glyn Williams, *Naturalists at Sea: From Dampier to Darwin* (New Haven, CT, 2013), p. 211.

52 Entry for 2 March 1802 in Cornell, ed., *The Journal of Post-Captain Nicolas Baudin*, p. 353.

53 Fornasiero, Monteath and West-Sooby, *Encountering Terra Australis*, p. 121.

54 Horner, *The French Reconnaissance*, pp. 208, 241, 244, 246; Helling, 'Redistributing the Blame,' p. 119.

55 Gregory C. Eccleston, 'The Neglect of Baudin's Manuscript Charts of the Victorian Coastline,' *The Globe*, 66 (2010), pp. 27–58.

56 Duyker, *François Péron*, pp. 126, 131; entry for 12 March 1802 in Cornell, ed., *The Journal of Post-Captain Nicolas Baudin*, p. 359.

57 Starbuck, *Baudin, Napoleon and the Exploration of Australia*, p. 127.

58 Williams, *Naturalists at Sea*, pp. 212–13; Helling, 'Redistributing the Blame,' p. 120.

59 Flinders, *A Voyage to Terra Australis*, I, pp. 192–3.

60 Horner, *The French Reconnaissance*, p. 220.

61 John West-Sooby and Jean Fornasiero, 'Matthew Flinders through French Eyes: Nicolas Baudin's Lessons from Encounter Bay,' *Journal of Pacific History*, 52/1 (2017), pp. 1–14.

62 Jean Fornasiero and John West-Sooby, 'The Baudin Expedition: Glory, Disgrace and Redemption' in Fornasiero, Lawton and West-Sooby, eds., *The Art of Science*, p. 44.

63 Fornasiero, Monteath and West-Sooby, *Encountering Terra Australis*, p. 177; Péron, *Voyage of Discovery*, books I–III, p. 260; Horner, *The French Reconnaissance*, p. 228.

64 Péron, *Voyage of Discovery*, books I–III, p. 251.

65 Entry for 8 May 1802 in Cornell, ed., *The Journal of Post-Captain Nicolas Baudin*, p. 401.

66 Péron, *Voyage of Discovery*, books I–III, p. 267.

67 Ibid., book IV, p. 25.

68 John Dunmore, 'Dream and Reality: French Voyages and Their Vision of Australia' in *Australia and the European Imagination: Papers from a Conference Held at the Humanities Research Centre, Australian National University, May 1981* (Canberra, 1982), p. 114.

69 Fornasiero, Monteath and West-Sooby, *Encountering Terra Australis*, pp. 183, 185, 188, 195, 203; entry for 4 June 1802 in Cornell, ed., *The Journal of Post-Captain Nicolas Baudin*, p. 416; Bourgoin and Taillemite, 'The Baudin Expedition,' p. 13.

70 ML, Banks to King, 1 January 1801, King family correspondence, A 1980/2; Jean Fornasiero and John West-Sooby, eds., *French Designs on Colonial New South Wales: François Péron's Memoir on the English Settlements in New Holland, Van Diemen's Land and the Archipelagos of the Great Pacific Ocean* (Adelaide, 2014), pp. 60–1.

71   Joan Webb, *George Caley, Nineteenth Century Naturalist* (Chipping Norton, NSW, 1995), p. 41.

72   Fornasiero and West-Sooby, eds., *French Designs on Colonial New South Wales*, pp. 63–4; Michel Jangoux, 'La Première relâche du *Naturaliste* au Port Jackson (26 April–18 May 1802): le témoignage du capitaine Hamelin,' *AJFS*, XLI/2 (2004), pp. 126–51.

73   Williams, *Naturalists at Sea*, p. 213; Fornasiero, Monteath and West-Sooby, *Encountering Terra Australis*, pp. 202–3. For a detailed account of the Baudin expedition at Port Jackson, see two studies by Nicole Starbuck: 'Nicolas Baudin: La relâche a Sydney et la deuxième campagne du *Géographe*' in Michel Jangoux, ed., *Portés par L'Air du Temps les Voyages du Capitaine Baudin* (Brussels, 2010), pp. 133–42, and *Baudin, Napoléon and the Exploration of Australia* (London, 2013).

74   Fornasiero, Monteath and West-Sooby, *Encountering Terra Australis*, pp. 200–1; Fornasiero and West-Sooby, 'Taming the Unknown,' p. 66. See also Margaret Sankey, 'The Baudin Expedition in Port Jackson, 1802: Cultural Encounters and Enlightenment Politics,' *Explorations*, 31 (2001), pp. 5–36.

75   Jean Fornasiero, 'Framing New Holland or Framing a Narrative? A Representation of Sydney According to Charles-Alexandre Lesueur' in Edwards, McCann and Poiana, eds., *Framing French Culture*, p. 95.

76   Fornasiero and West-Sooby, eds., *French Designs on Colonial New South Wales*; Bruce Bennett, 'Exploration or Espionage? Flinders and the French,' *Journal of the European Association of Studies on Australia*, 2/1 (2011), p. 17; Macquarie to Earl Bathurst, 30 April 1814, in Watson, ed., *HRA*, series 1, VIII, p. 241.

77   Fornasiero and West-Sooby, eds., *French Designs on Colonial New South Wales*, pp. 68, 73, 76, 80, 82.

78   Nicole Starbuck, 'Colonial Vision: French Voyager-artists, Aboriginal Subjects and the British Colony at Port Jackson' and Fornasiero, 'Framing New Holland,' pp. 29–52, 81–102.

79   Jean Fornasiero, 'Deux observateurs de l'homme aux antipodes: Nicolas Baudin et François Péron' in M. Jangoux, ed., *Portes par l'air du temps: les voyages du Capitaine Baudin*, special issue of *Etudes sur le 18ème siècle*, 38 (2010), pp. 157–70. On French perceptions of Aborigines at Port Jackson, see also two papers by Nicole Starbuck: 'Neither Civilized nor Savage: The Aborigines of Colonial Port Jackson, through French Eyes, 1802' in Alexander Cook, Ned Curthoys and Shino Konishi, eds., *Representing Humanity in the Age of Enlightenment* (London, 2013), pp. 123–33, 212–15, and 'The Baudin Expedition and the Aborigines of "Botany Bay": Colonial Ethnography in the Era of Bonaparte,' *Zeitschrift für Australienstudien/Australian Studies Journal*, 32 (2018), pp. 29–43.

80   West-Sooby, Fornasiero and Sankey, 'Nicolas Baudin,' p. 54.

81   Hambly, ed., *Pierre Bernard Milius*, p. 168.

82   West-Sooby, Fornasiero and Sankey, 'Nicolas Baudin,' p. 53; Duyker, *François Péron*, p. 143.

83 Entries for 9 and 10 December 1802 in Cornell, ed., *The Journal of Post-Captain Nicolas Baudin*, p. 442.

84 Horner, *The French Reconnaissance*, pp. 251, 261, 266–8; Duyker, *François Péron*, pp. 135, 152. An English naval officer thought the French were more interested in settling in New Zealand than in Van Diemen's Land and the Bass Strait islands: see G. A. Mawer, ed., *Captain James Colnett, A Voyage to New Holland and Round the World* (Dural Delivery Centre, NSW, 2016), pp. 64–5.

85 Entry for 14 December 1802 in Cornell, ed., *The Journal of Post-Captain Nicolas Baudin*, p. 446.

86 Duyker, *François Péron*, p. 159; Horner, *The French Reconnaissance*, p. 176.

87 Peron, *Voyage of Discovery*, book IV, p. 20; Fornasiero, Monteath and West-Sooby, *Encountering Terra Australis*, p. 229.

88 Pearson, *Great Southern Land*, p. 91; Horner, *The French Reconnaissance*, p. 277; Duyker, *François Péron*, p. 162.

89 Fornasiero, Monteath and West-Sooby, *Encountering Terra Australis*, pp. 239, 241; Péron, *Voyage of Discovery*, book IV, p. 65.

90 Fornasiero, Monteath and West-Sooby, *Encountering Terra Australis*, p. 246.

91 Dujker, *François Péron*, p. 168; Péron, *Voyage of Discovery*, book IV, p. 84.

92 Entry for 11 February 1803 in Cornell, ed., *The Journal of Post-Captain Nicolas Baudin*, p. 479.

93 Horner, *The French Reconnaissance*, pp. 278, 280–1, 285–6, 288, 291; entry for 20 February 1803 in Cornell, ed., *The Journal of Post-Captain Nicolas Baudin*, p. 484.

94 Duyker, *François Péron*, p. 181.

95 Horner, *The French Reconnaissance*, p. 293; Pearson, *Great Southern Land*, p. 91.

96 Entry for 22 March 1803 in Cornell, ed., *The Journal of Post-Captain Nicolas Baudin*, pp. 511–12 (quotation on p. 512).

97 Horner, *The French Reconnaissance*, p. 296.

98 Ibid., pp. 300–1, 305–6.

99 Williams, *Naturalists at Sea*, pp. 216–17; Fornasiero, Monteath and West-Sooby, *Encountering Terra Australis*, pp. 269–70, 273.

100 Jean Fornasiero, 'Of Rivalry and Reputation: Nicolas Baudin and Matthew Flinders' in Serge M. Rivière and Kumari R. Issur, eds., *Baudin-Flinders dans L'Océan Indien: Voyages, Découvertes, Rencontre: Travels, Discoveries, Encounter* (Paris, 2006), p. 175. See also G. Hasenohr, 'Health Factors as They Affected the Attitudes and Decisions on the Voyage of *Le Géographe*,' *South Australian Geographical Journal*, 99 (2000), pp. 16–19.

101 Bourgoin and Taillemite, 'The Baudin Expedition,' p. 14.

102 Martin Terry, 'The French and the Aborigines: A Decade of Depiction' in Maurice Blackman, ed., *Australian Aborigines and the French* (Kensington, 1990), pp. 102–3. For meetings by the expedition's members with Aborigines, see B. Plomley and J. Piord-Bernier, eds., *The General: The Visits of the*

Expedition Led by Bruny d'Entrecasteaux to Tasmanian Waters in 1792 and 1793 (Launceston, 1993), pp. 279–86.

103 Fornasiero, Monteath and West-Sooby, *Encountering Terra Australis*, pp. 358–61; entry for 15 January 1802 in Cornell, ed., *The Journal of Post-Captain Nicolas Baudin*, p. 305. See also entries for 30 January and 1 February 1802, ibid., pp. 321, 323. For a detailed discussion of Baudin's views on Aborigines, see Jean Fornasiero and John West-Sooby, 'Taming the Unknown: Representation of Terra Australis by the Baudin Expedition 1801–1803' in Anne Chittleborough, Gillian Dooley, Brenda Glover and Rick Hosking, eds., *Alas for the Pelicans! Flinders, Baudin and Beyond: Essays and Poems* (Kent Town, SA, 2002), pp. 59–80.

104 Horner, *The French Reconnaissance*, p. 196.

105 Duyker, *François Péron*, p. 121; Fornasiero, Monteath and West-Sooby, *Encountering Terra Australis*, pp. 362–4; and Colin Dyer, 'From Happiness to Havoc: The Aboriginal Bruny Islanders before Settlement by the British, as Witnessed by French explorers, 1792–1801,' *JRAHS*, 102/1 (2016), pp. 35–42.

106 Clare Johnson, 'François Péron and the Passion for Objects' in Chittleborough, Dooley, Glover and Hosking, eds., *Alas, for the Pelicans!*, p. 38.

107 Patty O'Brien, 'Divine Browns and the Mighty Whiteman: Exotic Primitivism and the Baudin Voyage to Tasmania in 1802,' *Journal of Australian Studies*, 23/63 (1999), pp. 13–21.

108 Shino Konishi, 'Early Encounters in Aboriginal Place: The Role of Emotions in French Readings of Indigenous Sites,' *Australian Aboriginal Studies*, issue 2 (2015), pp. 12–23.

109 Frank Horner, 'Anthropology and the Baudin Expedition, 1800–1804' in Blackman, ed., *Australian Aborigines and the French*, pp. 37–46.

110 Miranda Hughes, 'The Dynamometer and the Diemenese' in H. E. Le Grand, ed., *Experimental Inquiries: Historical, Philosophical and Social Studies of Experimentation in Science* (Dordrecht, 1990), pp. 87–98.

111 Shino Konishi, *The Aboriginal Male in the Enlightenment World* (London, 2012), p. 158.

112 Fornasiero, Monteath and West-Sooby, *Encountering Terra Australis*, pp. 365–6; Miranda J. Hughes, 'Philosophical Travellers at the Ends of the Earth: Baudin, Péron and the Tasmanians' in R. W. Horne, ed., *Australian Science in the Making* (Cambridge, 1988), pp. 25, 33–5.

113 Rhys Jones, 'Images of Natural Man' in Jacqueline Bonnemains, Elliott Forsyth and Bernard Smith, eds., *Baudin in Australian Waters: The Artwork of the French Voyage of Discovery to the Southern Lands, 1801–1804* (Melbourne, 1988), pp. 35–64.

114 Horner, *The French Reconnaissance*, p. 260. For perceptions of Aborigines by the members of Baudin's expedition, see Stephanie Anderson, 'French Anthropology in Australia: The First Fieldwork Expedition: François Péron's Anthropological Contributions to Baudin's "Voyage of Discovery to the Southern Hemisphere" (1800–1804),' *Aboriginal History*, 25 (2001), pp. 228–42; Shino Konishi, '"Inhabited by a Race of Formidable Giants": French Explorers, Aborigines,

and the Endurance of the Fantastic in the Great South Land, 1803, *Australian Humanities Review*, 44 (2008), pp. 7–22; Shino Konishi, 'François Péron and the Tasmanians: An Unrequited Romance' in Ingereth Macfarlane and Mark Hannah, eds., *Transgressions: Critical Indigenous Australian Histories* (Canberra, 2007), pp. 1–18; Shino Konishi, ' François Péron: Meditation on Death, Humanity and Savage Society' in Cook, Curthoys and Konishi, eds., *Representing Humanity in the Age of Enlightenment*, pp. 109–21, 209–11; and Miranda J. Hughes, 'Tall Tales or True Stories? Baudin, Péron, and the Tasmanians, 1802' in Roy McLeod and Philip F. Rehbock, eds., *Nature in Its Greatest Extent: Western Science in the Pacific* (Honolulu, 1988), pp. 65–86.

115 Michel Jangoux, ed., *Journal du Voyage aux Antilles de la Belle Angélique (1796–1798)* (Paris, 2009).

116 Ralph Kingston, 'A Not So Pacific Voyage: The "Floating Laboratory" of Nicolas Baudin,' *Endeavour*, 31/4 (2007), p. 146.

117 John West-Sooby, 'Baudin, Flinders and the Scientific Voyage' in Rivière and Issur, eds., *Baudin-Flinders*, pp. 188–90; Michel Jangoux, 'Nicolas Baudin par son contemporain André-Pierre Ledru: une autre perception du capitaine naturaliste' in Sophie Linon-Chipon and Daniela Vaj, eds., *Relations savants, voyages et discours scientifiques* (Paris, 2006), pp. 107–20.

118 Fornasiero and West-Sooby, 'Taming the Unknown,' p. 60 (quotation); Harrison, 'Projections of the Revolutionary Nation,' p. 44.

119 C. Jouanin, 'Nicolas Baudin chargé de réunir une collection pour la future impératrice Joséphine,' *AJFS*, XLI/2 (2004), pp. 43–54.

120 Hughes, 'Philosophical travellers,' p. 41; Noelene Bloomfield, 'Overview: France's Quest for Terra Australis: Strategies, Maladies and Triumphs,' *The Great Circle*, 39/2 (2017), pp. 19–20.

121 Williams, *Naturalists at Sea*, p. 217. For the animals collected, see Stephanie Pfennigwerth, 'New Creatures Made Known: Some Animal Histories of the Baudin Expedition' in West-Sooby, ed., *Discovery and Empire*, pp. 172–213. For the ornithological results of the voyage, see Hubert Massey Whittall, *The Literature of Australian Birds: A History and a Bibliography of Australian Ornithology* (Perth, 1954), pp. 58–69.

122 Sankey, Cowley and Fornasiero, 'The Baudin Expedition,' p. 4; C. Jouanin, 'Les emeus de l'expédition Baudin,' *L'Oiseau et la Revue Française d'Ornithologie*, 29 (1959), pp. 168–201.

123 Wolf Mayer, 'The Geological Work of the Baudin Expedition in Australia (1801–1803): The Mineralogists, the Discoveries and the Legacy,' *Earth Sciences History*, 28/2 (2009), pp. 293–324.

124 Duyker, *François Péron*, pp. 213–14.

125 West-Sooby, 'Baudin, Flinders and the Scientific Voyage,' p. 192. The expedition's scientific achievements are considered in Diana S. Jones, 'A Lasting Legacy: The Baudin Expedition in Australian Waters,' *The Great Circle*, 39/2 (2017), pp. 56–85.

126 Sophie C. Ducker, 'History of Australian Phycology: The Significance of Early French Exploration,' *Brunonia*, 2/1 (1979), p. 33.

127 Jones, 'A Lasting Legacy,' pp. 62–5. The French botanist Jussieu acknowledged the voyage's contributions to natural history in 'Notice sur l'expédition à la Nouvelle-Hollande, enterprise pour des recherches de géographie et d'histoire naturelle,' *Annales du Muséum d'Histoire Naturelle*, 5 (1804), pp. 1–11.

128 Ann Moyal, '*A Bright & Savage Land': Scientists in Colonial Australia* (Sydney, 1986), p. 33.

129 Duyker, *François Péron*, pp. 15–17; Cornell, ed., *The Journal of Post-Captain Nicolas Baudin*, p. 576.

130 Dany Bréelle, 'The Hydrographical Work of the Engineer-Geographers of the Baudin Expedition and the Rise of Louis Freycinet as the Cartographer of the Voyage,' *The Great Circle*, 39/2 (2017), p. 95.

131 Fornasiero, Monteath and West-Sooby, *Encountering Terra Australis*, p. 302; Leslie R. Marchant, 'The Baudin Scientific Mission of Exploration and the French Contribution to the Maritime Discovery of Australia,' *The Globe*, 23 (1985), pp. 22–5; Jean Fornasiero, Lindl Lawton and John West-Sooby, 'Unlocking Mysteries: Charting and Naming the Australian Coasts' in Fornasiero, Lawton and West-Sooby, eds., *The Art of Science*, pp. 106–8.

132 Rupert Gerritsen and Peter Reynders, 'The Freycinet Map of 1811: The First Full Map of Australia?' *The Globe*, 72 (2013), p. 2.

133 Bréelle, 'The Hydrographical Work of the Engineer-Geographers,' p. 105.

134 Bourgoin and Taillemite, 'The Baudin Expedition,' p. 17. For further information on the maps, see Bréelle, 'The Hydrographical Work of the Engineer-Geographers,' pp. 86–119.

135 Gerritsen and Reynders, 'The Freycinet Map of 1811,' p. 2; Morgan, *Matthew Flinders*, p. 184.

136 Jean Fornasiero and John West-Sooby, 'Naming and Shaming: The Baudin Expedition and the Politics of Nomenclature in the Terres Australes' in Anne M. Scott, Alfred Hiatt, Claire McIlroy and Christopher Wortham, eds., *European Perceptions of Terra Australis* (London, 2011), pp. 172, 174–5. See also Jean Fornasiero and John West-Sooby, 'Cartography as Narrative: The Maps of the Baudin Expedition' in Rupert Gerritsen, Robert King and Andrew Eliason, eds., *The Freycinet Map of 1811: Proceedings of the Symposium Commemorating the 200th Anniversary of the Publication of the First Map of Australia* (Canberra, 2012), pp. 20–32.

137 Wallace, *The Lost Australia of François Péron*, pp. 148–9.

138 MM. Lesueur and Petit, *Voyage of Discovery to the Southern Lands: An Historical Record: Atlas, 1824* (Adelaide, 2008), pp. vii–viii.

139 For a comprehensive treatment of their pantings, see Gabrielle Baglione, Cédric Crémière, Jean Fornasiero and John West-Sooby, *Charles-Alexandre Lesueur: Painter and Naturalist: A Forgotten Treasure* (Le Havre, 2016).

140 Elliott Forsyth, 'The Australian Aborigines as Seen by the Artists of the Baudin Expedition of 1800–1804' in Blackman, ed., *Australian Aborigines and the French*, pp. 111–33.

141 Lesueur and Petit, *Voyage of Discovery*, p. ix; Fornasiero, Monteath and West-Sooby, *Encountering Terra Australis*, pp. 310–19, 323, 327; Rhys Jones, 'Images of Natural Man' in Jacqueline Bonnemains, Elliott Forsyth and Bernard Smith, eds., *Baudin in Australian Waters: The Artwork of the French Voyage of Discovery to the Southern Lands 1800–1804* (Melbourne, 1988), pp. 52–7; Konishi, *The Aboriginal Male*, pp. 82–3.

142 Fornasiero, Monteath and West-Sooby, *Encountering Terra Australis*, pp. 326–7; Fornasiero and West-Sooby, 'Taming the Unknown,' pp. 69–70. For a complete descriptive catalogue of the drawings and paintings of Australian subjects by Lesueur and Petit from the Lesueur Collection in this museum, see Bonnemains et al., eds., *Baudin in Australia*.

143 Harrison, 'Projections of the Revolutionary Nation,' pp. 49–50.

144 Williams, *Naturalists at Sea*, pp. 218–19.

145 J. C. Batt and L. A. Triebel, *The French Exploration of Australia, with Special Reference to Tasmania* (Hobart, 1957), p. 54.

146 Entry for 21 March 1803 in Cornell, ed., *The Journal of Post-Captain Nicolas Baudin*, p. 509.

147 Duyker, *François Péron*, pp. 217, 223–4; O. H. K. Spate, 'Amés Damnées,' *Overland*, 58 (1974), pp. 52–7; Carol E. Harrison, 'Projections of the Revolutionary Nation: French Expeditions in the Pacific, 1791–1803' in Carol E. Harrison and Ann Johnson, eds., *National Identity: The Role of Science and Technology* (Chicago, 2009), p. 44.

148 Jean Fornasiero and John West-Sooby, 'Doing It by the Book: Breaking the Reputation of Nicolas Baudin' in Jean Fornasiero and Colette Mrowa-Hopkins, eds., *Explorations and Encounters in French* (Adelaide, 2010), pp. 135–64; Helling, 'Redistributing the Blame,' p. 107.

149 For a modern edition of Baudin's voyage account, see Jacqueline Bonnemains, ed., *Mon Voyages aux Terres Australes: Journal personnel du commandant Baudin* (Paris, 2000).

150 Jean Fornasiero and John West-Sooby, 'The Narrative Interruptions of Science: The Baudin Expedition to Australia (1800–1804),' *Forum for Modern Language Studies*, 49/4 (2013), pp. 457–71.

151 Williams, *Naturalists at Sea*, p. 218; Margaret Sankey, 'The English Translation of the *Voyages de decouvertes aux Terres Australes* of François Péron: The Politics of Discovery in Early Nineteenth century France and England' in Rivière and Issur, eds., *Baudin-Flinders*, pp. 195–216.

152 Danielle Clode and Carol E. Harrison, 'Precedence and Posterity: Patterns of Publishing from French Scientific Expeditions to the Pacific (1785–1840),' *AJFS*, 50/3 (2013), p. 362.

153 Duyker, *François Péron*, p. 324; Sankey, 'The English Translation,' p. 195.

154 Clode and Harrison, 'Precedence and Posterity,' p. 368; Margaret Sankey, 'Writing the Voyage of Scientific Exploration: The Logbooks, Journals and Notes of the Baudin Expedition (1800–1804),' *Intellectual History Review*, 20/3 (2010), pp. 401–13.

155 Clode and Harrison, 'Precedence and Posterity,' p. 368.

156 John Dunmore, *French Explorers in the Pacific. II. The Nineteenth Century* (Oxford, 1969), pp. 63, 65.

157 Ibid., pp. 72, 76, 95–7, 106; Tiley, *The Mermaid Tree*, pp. 46, 48–9, 69–71.

158 Dunmore, *French Explorers in the Pacific*, II, pp. 110–11, 153; Tiley, *The Mermaid Tree*, pp. 95, 99.

159 Tiley, *The Mermaid Tree*, p. 113.

160 Dunmore, *French Explorers in the Pacific*, II, pp. 156, 173, 180, 182, 184, 251–2, 326–9; Maria Nugent, *Botany Bay: Where Histories Meet* (Crows Nest, NSW, 2005), p. 101. The contemporary accounts include Marc-Serge Rivière, ed., *The Governor's Noble Guest: Hyacinthe de Bougainville's Account of Port Jackson, 1825* (Melbourne, 1999).

Chapter 10

1 D. F. Branagan, 'Phillip Parker King: Colonial Anchor Man' in Alwyne Wheeler and James H. Price, eds., *From Linnaeus to Darwin: Commentaries on the History of Biology and Geography* (London, 1985), p. 181.

2 Anon., 'King, Phillip Parker (1791–1856)' in Douglas Pike, ed., *ADB*, II (Melbourne, 1967), pp. 61–4.

3 Denver Beanland, 'Connections in Charting the Great Barrier Reef, 1770–1850,' *Queensland History Journal*, 24/3 (2019), p. 261.

4 Marsden Hordern, *King of the Australian Coast: The Work of Phillip Parker King in the Mermaid and Bathurst 1817–1822* (Melbourne, 1997), pp. 12–14.

5 Ibid., p. 48; Marsden Hordern, 'John Septimus Roe, 1797–1878: Naval Officer, Cartographer and Explorer,' *Journal of Australian Naval History*, 8/2 (2011), p. 52; Felix Driver and Luciana Martins, 'John Septimus Roe and the Art of Navigation, c.1815–1830,' *History Workshop Journal*, 54 (2002), p. 146; W. G. McMinn, *Allan Cunningham: Botanist and Explorer* (Melbourne, 1970), pp. 3, 5, 12. Roe's pencilled jottings on the voyages of the *Mermaid* are available in the John Septimus Roe logbooks (1817–22), ACC 491AD/3-4, ACC 2162AD/1-7, 9–11, at the State Library of Western Australia, Perth.

6 ML, Instructions from the Admiralty, 4 February 1817, in Phillip Parker King letterbook (1817–22), MLMSS 4429. King was only furnished with volume 1 of Péron's account.

7   Phillip Parker King, *Narrative of a Survey of the Intertropical and Western Coasts of Australia Performed between the Years 1818 and 1822 by Captain Phillip P. King*, 2 vols. (London, 1827; repr. Adelaide, 2012), I, p. xxvii.

8   Ibid., I, p. xxviii.

9   ML, Instructions from the Admiralty, 4 February 1817, Phillip Parker King letterbook (1817–22), MLMSS 4429.

10 Brian Douglas Abbott, *Phillip Parker King 1791–1856: A Most Admirable Australian* (Armidale, NSW, 2012), p. 62.

11 King, *Narrative of a Survey*, I, pp. xxxii–xxxiii; McMinn, *Allan Cunningham*, p. 35.

12 Tiley, *The Mermaid Tree*, p. 26; ML, King to J. W. Croker, 11 December 1817, Phillip Parker King letterbook (1817–22), MLMSS 4429.

13 King, *Narrative of a Survey*, II, pp. 404–7.

14 ML, Memorandum to Instructions from the Admiralty, 4 February 1817, Phillip Parker King letterbook (1817–22), MLMSS 4429.

15 Abbott, *Phillip Parker King*, p. 64.

16 King, *Narrative of a Survey*, I, pp. xxxvi–xxxviii; ML, King to Croker, 1 October 1817, MLDOC 920. Banks informed Cunningham that he would be joining the expedition: see ML, Banks to Cunningham, 10 February 1817, Sir Joseph Banks Papers, series 20.18. Bongaree had of course been a member of Flinders's *Investigator* expedition. King's logbooks on the *Mermaid* and *Bathurst* for 1818–22 (MS 72/1-11, 73/2 and MS 79) are deposited at the National Museum of the Royal Navy, Portsmouth.

17 Hordern, *King of the Australian Coast*, p. 68.

18 King, *Narrative of a Survey*, I, p. 2.

19 Ida Lee, *Early Explorers in Australia: From the Log-Books and Journals, Including the Diary of Allan Cunningham, Botanist, from March 1, 1817 to November 19, 1818* (London, 1925), pp. 313, 322.

20 King, *Narrative of a Survey*, I, pp. 10–11, 13–19; Hordern, *King of the Australian Coast*, pp. 59–60, 65. The plants collected are listed in Lee, *Early Explorers*, pp. 313–24.

21 Hordern, *King of the Australian Coast*, pp. 70–2.

22 Allan Cunningham to Banks, 9 June, 25 September 1818, in A. E. Orchard and T. A. Orchard, eds., *Allan Cunningham: Letters of a Botanist/Explorer 1791–1839* (Weston Creek, ACT, 2015), pp. 87, 92.

23 Abbott, *Phillip Parker King*, p. 78.

24 Pearson, *Great Southern Land*, p. 92; ML, King to Croker, 11 June 1818, King Papers, MLMSS 4345.

25 ML, King to Croker, 10 June 1818, Phillip Parker King letterbook (1817–22), MLMSS 4429.

26 ML, King to Croker, 11 June 1818, King Papers, MLMSS 4345.

27 Pearson, *Great Southern Land*, p. 93.

28 Phillip Parker King, 'On the Maritime Geography of Australia' in Barron Field, ed., *Geographical Memoirs, or New South Wales; by Various Hands* ... (London, 1825), p. 287.

29 Hordern, 'John Septimus Roe', pp. 53–4; F. R. Mercer, *Amazing Career: The Story of Western Australia's First Surveyor-General* (Perth, n.d.), p. 79.

30 Cunningham to Banks, 9 June 1818, in Orchard and Orchard, eds., *Allan Cunningham*, p. 88.

31 Tiley, *The Mermaid Tree*, p. 34.

32 Ibid., p. 39; ML, King to Croker, 10 June 1818, Phillip Parker King letterbook (1817–22), MLMSS 4429.

33 Cunningham to Banks, 9 June 1818, in Orchard and Orchard, eds., *Allan Cunningham*, p. 89.

34 Pearson, *Great Southern Land*, p. 93; Hordern, *King of the Australian Coast*, pp. 89, 94–5, 103, 109.

35 King, *Narrative of a Survey*, I, p. 92.

36 Jordan Goodman, 'Making Imperial Space: Settlement, Surveying and Trade in Northern Australia in the Nineteenth Century' in David Killingray, Margarette Lincoln and Nigel Rigby, eds., *Maritime Empires: British Imperial Maritime Trade in the Nineteenth Century* (Woodbridge, 2004), p. 131; Lee, *Early Explorers*, p. 374.

37 Gerald S. Graham, *Great Britain in the Indian Ocean: A Study of Maritime Enterprise, 1810–1850* (Oxford, 1967), pp. 423–43.

38 King, *Narrative of a Survey*, I, p. 106; Hordern, *King of the Australian Coast*, pp. 118–20, 123; William Desborough Cooley, *The History of Maritime and Inland Discovery*, 3 vols. (London, 1831), III, p. 143.

39 Cooley, *The History of Maritime and Inland Discovery*, III, pp. 143–4.

40 Cunningham to Banks, 9 June 1818, in Orchard and Orchard, eds., *Allan Cunningham*, p. 89.

41 King, *Narrative of a Survey*, I, pp. 123, 127, 142, 144; Hordern, *King of the Australian Coast*, pp. 136–8, 142; Tiley, *The Mermaid Tree*, p. 44 ML, John Septimus Roe to his father, 6 August 1818 (quotations), item 147, John Septimus Roe letters, series 04, MLMSS 7964/4.

42 ML, Phillip Parker King Remark Books (1817–18), MLMSS 5277.

43 ML, Roe to his father, 6 August 1818, item 147, John Septimus Roe letters, series 04, MLMSS 7964/4.

44 Cooley, *The History of Maritime and Inland Discovery*, III, p. 145. For a summary of the voyage, see TNA, ADM 1/2030, King to Croker, 22 July 1825.

45 King, *Narrative of a Survey*, I, pp. 151, 153, 159, 163; Hordern, *King of the Australian Coast*, pp. 145, 152–4; McMinn, *Allan Cunningham*, p. 40; ML, Roe to his father, 16 February 1819, item 149, John Septimus Roe letters, series 04, MLMSS 7964/4.

46 ML, King to Croker, 23 February 1819, King Papers, MLMSS 4345.

47 Cunningham to Banks, 29 March 1819, in Orchard and Orchard, eds., *Allan Cunningham*, p. 106.

48 ML, King to Thomas Hurd, 23 February 1819, Phillip Parker King letterbook (1817–22), MLMSS 4429.

49 King, *Narrative of a Survey*, I, pp. 164–73; Hordern, *King of the Australian Coast*, 160–1; Tiley, *The Mermaid Tree*, pp. 50–1; ML, Roe to his father, 19 April and 5 November 1819, items 151–2, John Septimus Roe letters, series 04, MLMSS 7964/4.

50 Richard Johnson, *The Search for the Inland Sea: John Oxley, Explorer, 1783–1828* (Melbourne, 2001), pp. 160–2; Watson, ed., *HRA*, I: 10, pp. 178–82.

51 ML, Roe to his father, 5 November 1819, item 152, John Septimus Roe letters, series 04, MLMSS 7964/4; ML, King to Governor Macquarie, 20 May 1819, Phillip Parker King letterbook (1817–22), MLMSS 4429; Johnson, *The Search for the Inland Sea*, pp. 160–2.

52 In two voyages (in 1810–11), the hydrographic surveyor Samuel Ashmore had sailed through the outer reef. He made further voyages through the Reef in 1827–30: see Stephen Sheaffe, 'Samuel Ashmore and Tracks through the Great Barrier Reef,' *Queensland History Journal*, 24/3 (2019), pp. 268–83.

53 Tiley, *The Mermaid Tree*, pp. 50–1; Pearson, *Great Southern Land*, pp. 94–6; Beanland, 'Connections in Charting the Great Barrier Reef,' p. 261.

54 King, 'On the Maritime Geography of Australia,' p. 277.

55 Pearson, *Great Southern Land*, p. 94; Hordern, *King of the Australian Coast*, pp. 164–6, 179; Hordern, 'John Septimus Roe,' p. 54.

56 King, *Narrative of a Survey*, I, pp. 251, 272.

57 Ibid., I, pp. 320–1, 325, 327; Pearson, *Great Southern Land*, p. 96; Tiley, *The Mermaid Tree*, pp. 61, 63; ML, King to Croker and Henry Goulburn, 9 November 1819, Phillip Parker King letterbook (1817–22), MLMSS 4429.

58 Cunningham to Banks, 8 November 1819, in Orchard and Orchard, eds., *Allan Cunningham*, p. 116.

59 ML, Roe to his father, 5 November 1819, item 152, John Septimus Roe letters, series 04, MLMSS 7964/4.

60 Hordern, *King of the Australian Coast*, pp. 209, 211, 213; ML, Roe to his father, 21 January 1820, item 153, John Septimus Roe letters, series 04, MLMSS 7964/4.

61 ML, Croker to King, 11 December 1819, King Family Papers, MLMSS 7048/3.

62 ML, King to Croker, 26 May 1820, King Papers, MLMSS 4345.

63 Cunningham to William T. Aiton, 12 June 1820, in Orchard and Orchard, eds., *Allan Cunningham*, p. 127.

64 ML, King to the Admiralty, 26 May 1820, Phillip Parker King letterbook (1817–22), MLMSS 4429.

65 Cunningham to Aiton, 1 February 1821, in Orchard and Orchard, eds., *Allan Cunningham*, p. 130.

66 TNA, ADM 1/2980, King to the Admiralty, 1 February 1821.

67 Tiley, *The Mermaid Tree*, p. 75; Hordern, *King of the Australian Coast*, p. 235; ML, Roe to his father, 29 January 1821, item 157, John Septimus Roe letters, series 04, MLMSS 7964/4. King summarized the best passages to follow through the coral reefs off the Queensland coast: see King, *Narrative of a Survey*, I, pp. 386–7.

68 ML, Roe to his father, 29 January 1821, item 157, John Septimus Roe letters, series 04, MLMSS 7964/4.

69 ML, King to Goulburn, 26 May 1820, Phillip Parker King letterbook (1817–22), MLMSS 4429; TNA, ADM 1/2980, King to the Admiralty, 1 February 1821.

70 ML, King, Roe and Bedwell, 'Report of Survey,' 8 October 1820, MLMSS 4429.

71 Pearson, *Great Southern Land*, p. 97; Abbott, *Phillip Parker King*, p. 120.

72 TNA, ADM 1/2980, King to the Admiralty, 1 February 1821.

73 ML, King to Croker and Goulburn, January 1821, Phillip Parker King letterbook (1817–22), MLMSS 4429; Tiley, *The Mermaid Tree*, pp. 76–7, 79–81; ML, Roe to his father, 29 January 1821, item 157, John Septimus Roe letters, series 04, MLMSS 7964/4.

74 King, *Narrative of a Survey*, I, p. 444.

75 Cunningham to Aiton, 1 February 1821, in Orchard and Orchard, eds., *Allan Cunningham*, p. 131.

76 Hordern, *King of the Australian Coast*, p. 261.

77 King, *Narrative of a Survey*, II, pp. 1–2; ML, King to Macquarie, 10 January 1821, Phillip Parker King letterbook (1817–22), MLMSS 4429.

78 Hordern, *King of the Australian Coast*, pp. 277, 295; Lee, *Early Explorers*, p. 459. A teenage girl was a stowaway on this voyage: see Matt Fishburn, 'Phillip Parker King's Stowaway,' *JRAHS*, 103/1 (2017), pp. 80–93.

79 Pearson, *Great Southern Land*, p. 98.

80 King, *Narrative of a Survey*, II, pp. 87–8, 106–7 (quotation on p. 107).

81 McMinn, *Allan Cunningham*, p. 46.

82 ML, King to the Commissioners of the Navy, 14 September 1821, Phillip Parker King letterbook (1817–22), MLMSS 4429; Cunningham to Aiton, 7 July 1821, in Orchard and Orchard, eds., *Allan Cunningham*, p. 141; TNA, ADM 1/2980, King to the Admiralty, 29 September 1821.

83 King, *Narrative of a Survey*, II, pp. 120, 159–60; Hordern, *King of the Australian Coast*, pp. 312, 326; Tiley, *The Mermaid Tree*, p. 90.

84 Cunningham to Aiton, 16 July 1822, in Orchard and Orchard, eds., *Allan Cunningham*, p. 147.

85 Lee, *Early Explorers*, pp. 476–7.

86 King, 'On the Maritime Geography of Australia,' p. 289.

87 Tiley, *The Mermaid Tree*, p. 91; Pearson, *Great Southern Land*, p. 98. The Vlamingh plate was returned by France to Australia after the Second World War, and is now deposited at the Western Australian Maritime Museum. See Marnie Bassett, *Realms*

and Islands: The World Voyage of Rose de Freycinet in the Corvette Uranie 1817–1820 from Her Journal and Letters and the Reports of Louis de Saulces Freycinet Capitaine de Corvette (London, 1962), pp. 251–4.

88 King, *Narrative of a Survey*, II, pp. 180, 188; Pearson, *Great Southern Land*, p. 98.

89 Tiley, *The Mermaid Tree*, pp. 91–2.

90 Cunningham to Aiton, 24 May 1821, in Orchard and Orchard, eds., *Allan Cunningham*, p. 137.

91 Cunningham to George Suttor, 4 November 1821, ibid., p. 159.

92 ML, King to Hurd, 4 May 1822, Phillip Parker King letterbook (1817–22), MLMSS 4429; Hordern, *King of the Australian Coast*, pp. 355–6.

93 ML, John Barrow to King, 9 July 1821, King Family Papers, MLMSS 7048/1-8.

94 Tiley, *The Mermaid Tree*, p. 92.

95 King, *Narrative of a Survey*, II, p. 243. A long appendix to this book (pp. 248–399) comments on places visited by King during his voyages in the *Mermaid* and *Bathurst*.

96 King, 'On the Maritime Geography of Australia,' p. 273.

97 Ibid., pp. 273–4.

98 Banks to Cunningham, 13 February 1817, in Orchard and Orchard, eds., *Allan Cunningham*, p. 74. Daily descriptions of the plants and seeds collected by Cunningham are given in the three volumes of his journals for 1817–19 at the NHM. Extensive extracts from his journals are included in Lee, *Early Explorers*, pp. 310–488.

99 Banks to Cunningham, 10 July 1817, in Orchard and Orchard, eds., *Allan Cunningham*, p. 77.

100 Cunningham to Aiton, 15 October 1818, ibid., p. 97.

101 Cunningham to Banks, 9 June 1818, ibid., p. 90.

102 Cunningham to Aiton, 1 December 1817, ibid., p. 83. For Cunningham's collecting sites, see S. Curry, B. R. Maslin and J. A. Maslin, *Allan Cunningham Australian Collecting Localities*, Flora of Australia Supplementary series, 13 (Canberra, 2002).

103 Royal Botanic Gardens, Kew, Library and Archives, Cunningham to Banks, 1 December 1817, Kew Collectors VIIa, Cunningham Correspondence (1817–31), KCL/8/5.

104 McMinn, *Allan Cunningham*, p. 39.

105 Ibid., p. 37; Cunningham to Banks, 9 June 1818, in Orchard and Orchard, eds., *Allan Cunningham*, p. 87.

106 Cunningham to Banks, 9 June 1818, in Orchard and Orchard, eds., *Allan Cunningham*, pp. 87–8.

107 Cunningham to Banks, 25 September 1818, ibid., p. 92; McMinn, *Allan Cunningham*, p. 39.

108 Cunningham to Banks, 29 March 1819, in Orchard and Orchard, eds., *Allan Cunningham*, p. 105. See also A. E. Orchard and T. A. Orchard, *The Botanist and the Judge: Allan Cunningham in Tasmania 1818–1819* (Weston Creek, ACT, 2014), pp. 69–78.

109 Mc Minn, *Allan Cunningham*, p. 40. The plants collected are listed in Orchard and Orchard, *The Botanist and the Judge*, pp. 117–64.

110 Cunningham to Aiton, 29 March 1819, in Orchard and Orchard, eds., *Allan Cunningham*, p. 107.

111 Cunningham to Banks, 17 April 1819, ibid., p. 109.

112 Cunningham to Banks, 21 May 1819, ibid., p. 110.

113 Cunningham to Banks, 8 November 1819, ibid., pp. 112, 114.

114 Cunningham to Banks, 8 November 1819, and to Aiton, 9 November 1819, ibid., pp. 116–17.

115 Cunningham to Aiton, 12 June 1820, ibid., p. 127.

116 Robert Heward, 'Biographical Sketch of the late Allan Cunningham,' *Journal of Botany*, IV (1842), p. 250.

117 Cunningham to Aiton, 1 February 1821, in Orchard and Orchard, eds., *Allan Cunningham*, pp. 130–1, 133 (quotations on pp. 130, 133).

118 Cunningham to Aiton, 24 May 1821, ibid., p. 138.

119 Royal Botanic Gardens, Kew, Library and Archives, Aiton to Cunningham, 3 July 1821, Kew Collectors VIIa, Cunningham correspondence, 1817–31, KCL/8/5.

120 Orchard and Orchard, eds., *Allan Cunningham*, pp. 141–2.

121 Cunningham to Aiton, 16 July 1822, ibid., pp. 146–7, 150 (quotations on p. 147).

122 Heward, 'Biographical Sketch,' p. 251.

123 Cunningham to Brown, 16 July 1822, in Orchard and Orchard, eds., *Allan Cunningham*, p. 158.

124 King, *Narrative of a Survey*, II, pp. 497–530.

125 Ibid., I, pp. xxxii–xxxiii.

126 Hordern, *King of the Australian Coast*, pp. 82–3, 85; Lee, *Early Explorers*, p. 337; Tiffany Shellam, 'Mediating Encounters through Bodies and Talk' in Shino Konishi, Maria Nugent and Tiffany Shellam, eds., *Indigenous Intermediaries: New Perspectives on Exploration Archives* (Canberra, 2015), pp. 88–90.

127 King, *Narrative of a Survey*, I, pp. 110–11; Lee, *Early Explorers*, p. 373.

128 Hordern, *King of the Australian Coast*, pp. 326–38.

129 See three studies by Tiffany Shellam: *Shaking Hands on the Fringe: Negotiating the Aboriginal World at King George's Sound* (Crawley, WA, 2009), pp. 7–13; '"Thro' the Medium of Biscuits": Phillip Parker King and the Menang, 1821' in Gaye Sculthorpe, ed., *Yurlmun: Mokare Mia Boodjar (Returning to Mokare's Home Country): Encounters and Collections in Menang Country* (Welshpool, 2016), pp. 10–17; and 'Ethnographic Inquiry on Phillip Parker King's Hydrographic Survey' in Martin Thomas and Amanda Harris, eds., *Expeditionary Anthropology: Teamwork, Travel and the 'Science of Man'* (New York, 2018), pp. 205–32.

130 King, 'On the Maritime Geography,' pp. 293–4.

131 Lee, *Early Explorers*, p. 340.

132 King, 'On the Maritime Geography,' pp. 292, 293, 295. King's *Narrative Survey*, II, pp. 632–7, has an appendix that focuses on dissimilarities in the Aboriginal language.

133 ML, King to Croker, 25 January 1823, King Papers, MLMSS 4345.

134 Hordern, *King of the Australian Coast*, pp. 393–4.

135 Abbott, *Phillip Parker King*, p. 149.

Chapter 11

1   Pearson, *Great Southern Land*, p. 108; Geoffrey C. Ingleton, *Charting a Continent: Marine Exploration and Hydrographical Surveying in Australian Waters* (Sydney, 1944), pp. 25–6, 52–3; J.M.R. Cameron, 'Prelude to Colonization: James Stirling's Examination of Swan River, March 1827,' *Australian Geographer*, 12/4 (1973), pp. 309–27; Michael Cannon and Ian MacFarlane, eds., *Historical Records of Victoria. Foundation Series. Volume 4: Communications, Trade and Transport* (Melbourne, 1985), pp. 3, 5–13. For the *Rattlesnake*'s surveys in Port Phillip Bay, see also NLA, John Henry Norcock, Private Journal (1836–7), esp. the entry for 1 December 1836.

2   Pearson, *Great Southern Land*, pp. 108–12.

3   Randolph Cock, 'Sir Francis Beaufort and the co-ordination of British scientific activity, 1829–55' (University of Cambridge PhD, 2003), p. 175.

4   Marsden Hordern, *Mariners Are Warned! John Lort Stokes and H.M.S. Beagle in Australia 1837–1843* (Melbourne, 1989), p. 9; Jordan Goodman, *The Rattlesnake: A Voyage of Discovery to the Coral Sea* (London, 2005), p. 10. Excellent maps in Hordern's book show the *Beagle*'s routes on its cruises in Australian waters.

5   Iain McCalman, *Darwin's Armada: Four Voyages and the Battle for the Theory of Evolution* (New York, 2009), pp. 25–7.

6   Ibid., p. 29; Peter Nichols, *Evolution's Captain: The Tragic Fate of Robert Fitzroy, the Man Who Sailed Charles Darwin around the World* (London, 2003), pp. 96–7.

7   NMM, STK 29, Capt. Robert Fitzroy to Lords Commissioners of the Admiralty, n.d., Papers relating to the voyage of the *Beagle*.

8   Nichols, *Evolution's Captain*, p. 216; McCalman, *Darwin's Armada*, pp. 70, 72.

9   Patrick Armstrong, *Charles Darwin in Western Australia: A Young Scientist's Perception of an Environment* (Nedlands, WA, 1985), pp. 10, 41; John Laurent and Margaret Campbell, *The Eye of Reason: Charles Darwin in Australia* (Wollongong, 1987), pp. 25–73.

10 Entry for 16 January 1836 in Richard Darwin Keynes, ed., *Charles Darwin's Beagle Diary* (Cambridge, 1988), p. 398.

11 McCalman, *Darwin's Armada*, p. 72.

12 Armstrong, *Charles Darwin in Western Australia*, p. 38.

13 Entry for 14 March 1836 in Keynes, ed., *Charles Darwin's Beagle Diary*, p. 413. For a similar comment, expressing his lack of affection for Australia, see Charles Darwin to Catherine Darwin, 29 April 1836, in Frederick Burkhardt, ed., *Charles Darwin, the Beagle Letters* (Cambridge, 2008), p. 386.

14 These are included in Hordern, *Mariners Are Warned!*, pp. 310–20 (quotation on p. 310).

15 Tiley, *The Mermaid Tree*, p. 145; Goodman, *The Rattlesnake*, p. 11.

16 Tiley, *The Mermaid Tree*, p. 151; Pearson, *Great Southern Land*, p. 108; Hordern, *Mariners Are Warned!*, p. 10.

17 Hordern, *Mariners Are Warned!*, p. 157; Tiley, *The Mermaid Tree*, pp. 150, 160.

18 Hordern, *Mariners Are Warned!*, pp. 326–7.

19 Ibid., pp. 34–5.

20 UKHO, SL 24, Wickham to Capt. Beaufort, 3 January 1838, Captain's letters: Wickham 1837–41.

21 Tiley, *The Mermaid Tree*, p. 160.

22 Hordern, *Mariners Are Warned!*, pp. 44, 48; J. Lort Stokes, *Discoveries in Australia; with an Account of the Coasts and Rivers Explored and Surveyed during the Voyage of H.M.S. Beagle, in the Years 1837-38-39-40-41-42-43*, 2 vols. (London, 1846), I, p. 80.

23 'Proceedings of H.M.S. Beagle – Commander J. C. Wickham,' *The Nautical Magazine* (1838), p. 680.

24 Hordern, *Mariners Are Warned!*, p. 49.

25 Tiley, *The Mermaid Tree*, p. 162; UKHO, SL 24, Wickham to Beaufort, 17 April 1838, Captain's letters: Wickham 1837–41.

26 Hordern, *Mariners Are Warned!*, p. 68.

27 UKHO, SL 24, Wickham to Beaufort, 17 April 1838, Captain's letters: Wickham 1837–41; 'Proceedings of H.M.S. Beagle,' p. 682; Tiley, *The Mermaid Tree*, p. 165 (quotation).

28 Stokes, *Discoveries in Australia*, I, p. 168; UKHO, SL 24, Wickham to Beaufort, 7 November 1838, Captain's letters: Wickham 1837–41.

29 Pearson, *Great Southern Land*, p. 108; UKHO, SL 24, Wickham to Beaufort, 17 April 1838, Captain's letters: Wickham 1837–41.

30 UKHO, SL 24, Wickham to Beaufort, 7 November 1838, Captain's letters: Wickham 1837–41.

31 UKHO, SL 24, Wickham to Beaufort, 4 January 1839, ibid.

32 Ibid.

33 UKHO, SL 24, Wickham to Beaufort, 8, 20 May 1839, ibid.

34 Stokes, *Discoveries in Australia*, I, pp. 224, 245, 260, 307 (quotation); Hordern, *Mariners Are Warned!*, pp. 121, 135.

35 UKHO, SL 24, Wickham to Beaufort, 16 August 1838, 10 June 1839, Captain's letters: Wickham 1837–41.

36 Stokes, *Discoveries in Australia*, I, pp. 311, 372–3.

37 Hordern, *Mariners Are Warned!*, pp. 145, 147–8; Tiley, *The Mermaid Tree*, p. 171.

38 Pearson, *Great Southern Land*, p. 108; Alan Powell, *John Stokes and the Men of the Beagle: Discoverers of Port Darwin* (Darwin, 1986), p. 1.

39 UKHO, SL 24, Wickham to Beaufort, 27 August 1839, Captain's letters: Wickham 1837–41.

40 Crawford Pasco, *A Roving Commission: Naval Reminiscences* (London, 1897), p. 104.

41 Stokes, *Discoveries in Australia*, II, pp. 9–13, 23, 112–15.

42 UKHO, SL 24, Wickham to Beaufort, 2 February 1840, Captain's letters: Wickham 1837–41.

43 Tiley, *The Mermaid Tree*, pp. 203–5; UKHO, SL 24, Wickham to Beaufort, 2 February 1840, Captain's letters: Wickham 1837–41.

44 Pearson, *Great Southern Land*, p. 108; Tiley, *The Mermaid Tree*, p. 218.

45 Stokes, *Discoveries in Australia*, II, p. 135.

46 Ibid., II, pp. 143–56, 161–6; Hordern, *Mariners Are Warned!*, p. 214.

47 Tiley, *The Mermaid Tree*, p. 220.

48 Hordern, *Mariners Are Warned!*, pp. 220–1; UKHO, SL 24, Wickham to Beaufort, 22 February 1840, Captain's letters: Wickham 1837–41.

49 Pearson, *Great Southern Land*, p. 108.

50 Hordern, *Mariners Are Warned!*, p. 227; Stokes, *Discoveries in Australia*, II, p. 207.

51 UKHO, SL 24, Wickham to Beaufort, 11 January 1841, Captain's letters: Wickham 1837–41.

52 NMM, Acting Commander to Sir J. J. G. Brewer, 4 May 1841, Letterbook of the *Beagle* (1841–3), Stokes Papers, STK 14.

53 Tiley, *The Mermaid Tree*, pp. 220–1, 223–4; UKHO, SL 30a, Stokes to Beaufort, 21 August 1841, Captain's letters: J. L. Stokes 1841–7.

54 Hordern, *Mariners Are Warned!*, pp. 248, 253–4, 258–9; Stokes, *Discoveries in Australia*, II, pp. 268, 293 (quotation).

55 UKHO, Beaufort to Stokes, 30 September 1841, Letterbook no. 10 (1841–2).

56 Stokes, *Discoveries in Australia*, II, p. 325; Pearson, *Great Southern Land*, p. 110.

57 Stokes, *Discoveries in Australia*, II, p. 272; UKHO, SL 30a, Stokes to Beaufort, 25 August 1841, Captain's letters: J. L. Stokes 1841–7.

58 NMM, Stokes to Sir George Gipps, 21 December 1841, Letterbook of the *Beagle* (1841–3), Stokes Papers, STK 11.

59 Hordern, *Mariners Are Warned!*, p. 270.

60 UKHO, SL 30a, Stokes to Beaufort, 25 December 1841, Captain's letters: J. L. Stokes 1841–7.

61 UKHO, Beaufort to Stokes, 30 September 1841, Letterbook no. 10 (1841–2).

62 UKHO, Beaufort to Wickham, 8 September 1840, Letterbook no. 9 (1839–41).

63 UKHO, SL 30a, Stokes to Beaufort, 22 March 1842, ibid.; Archives Office of Tasmania, Hobart, Stokes to Sir John Franklin, 5 January 1843, NS279/18/26.

64 Hordern, *Mariners Are Warned!*, pp. 283, 294, 297; Goodman, *The Rattlesnake*, p. 12; *Sydney Morning Herald*, 10 February 1843.

65 Goodman, *The Rattlesnake*, p. 12.

66 Pearson, *Great Southern Land*, p. 110; Tiley, *The Mermaid Tree*, p. 234; Robert Ralph, 'John MacGillivray – His Life and Work', *Archives of Natural History*, 20/2 (1993), p. 187.

67 Goodman, *The Rattlesnake*, p. 12.

68 J. Beete Jukes, *Narrative of the Surveying Voyage of H.M.S. Fly, commanded by Captain F. P. Blackwood, R.N ....*, 2 vols. (London, 1847), I, p. 311.

69 Tiley, *The Mermaid Tree*, pp. 232–3. The reefs between Sandy Cape and Torres Strait are described in Jukes, *Narrative of the Surveying Voyage*, I, pp. 318–32.

70 Between 1791 and 1850, more than twenty ships were recorded lost in this region: see Jim Allen and Peter Corris, eds., *The Journal of John Sweatman: A Nineteenth Century Surveying Voyage in North Australia and Torres Strait* (St Lucia, QLD, 1977), p. xvi.

71 Jukes, *Narrative of the Surveying Voyage*, I, pp. 256–8.

72 UKHO, Proposed orders for Capt. Blackwood, 29 March 1842, Minute book no. 3 (1837–42).

73 UKHO, Blackwood to Beaufort, 29 April 1843, Letterbook no. 11 (1842–4).

74 UKHO, SL 29, Blackwood to Beaufort, 20 April 1843, Captain's letters: Blackwood 1841–6. The dangers of navigating the Great Barrier Reef on the *Fly*'s voyage are fully explained in UKHO, OD 79, HMS *Fly* (1842–4), vol. 3: Australia East Coast and Great Barrier Reef.

75 UKHO, SL 29, Blackwood to Beaufort, 29 April 1843, Captain's letters: Blackwood 1841–6.

76 Allan McInnes, 'Dangers and Difficulties of the Torres Strait and Inner Route', *JRHSQ*, 10/4 (1979), pp. 58–60.

77 Jukes, *Narrative of the Surveying Voyage*, I, pp. 9–10, 46, 90, 99, 131; Tiley, *The Mermaid Tree*, pp. 234, 236; *Letters and Extracts from the Addresses and Occasional Writings of J. Beete Jukes* (London, 1871), p. 191.

78 *Letters and Extracts*, p. 226; UKHO, SL 29, Blackwood to Beaufort, 26 October 1844, Captain's letters: Blackwood 1841–6. For detailed consideration of the navigation through Torres Strait, see UKHO, OD 90, Frederick J. Evans, Master's remarks, HMS surveying ship *Fly*, 1845–6.

79 Jukes, *Narrative of the Surveying Voyage*, I, pp. 136, 349–57.

80 UKHO, OD 77, H.M.S. Fly Remark Book, vol. 1 (1842–6), f. 93.

81 UKHO, OD 78, H.M.S. Fly: Australia East Coast Great Barrier Reef, vol. 2 (1843), ff. 13–14 (quotation on f. 13).

82 UKHO, SL 29, Blackwood to Beaufort, 17 April, 8 June and 19 July 1845, Captain's letters: Blackwood 1841–6.

83 UKHO, OD 78, Blackwood to Lt. Yule, 18 October 1845, H.M.S. Fly: Australia East Coast Great Barrier Reef, vol. 2 (1843), f. 50.

84 UKHO, SL 29, Blackwood to Beaufort, 23 July 1845, Captain's Letters: Blackwood 1841–6; Tiley, *The Mermaid Tree*, p. 239; Alexander George Findlay, *A Directory for the Navigation of the South Pacific Ocean, with Descriptions of Its Coasts, Islands Etc. from the Strait of Magalhaens to Panama, and Those of New Zealand, Australia Etc.; Its Winds, Currents, and Passages* (London, 1884), p. 945.

85 J. H. S. Osborn, 'Torres Strait and the Inner Route', *The Journal of Navigation*, 30/1 (1977), p. 21; F. P. Blackwood, *Directions for the Outer Passage from Sydney to Torres Strait to Accompany the Chart of the Barrier Reefs* (London, 1847); Goodman, *The Rattlesnake*, p. 14.

86 UKHO, SL 29, Blackwood to Beaufort, 1 September 1846, Captain's Letters: Blackwood 1841–6.

87 Blackwood, *Directions for the Outer Passage*, pp. 1, 6.

88 Jukes, *Narrative of the Surveying Voyage*, I, pp. 312–17.

89 Ann Moyal, *'A Bright & Savage land': Scientists in Colonial Australia* (Sydney, 1986), p. 76.

90 Jukes, *Narrative of the Surveying Voyage*, I, p. 304.

91 UKHO, Minute Book, 6/3 (1846–9).

92 UKHO, Blackwood to Beaufort, 24 July 1846, Incoming Letters prior to 1857. Blackwood's Remark books are deposited at UKHO, OD 77–9.

93 Goodman, *The Rattlesnake*, p. 14; Tiley, *The Mermaid Tree*, p. 160. One by-product of these cruises was the collection of skulls and skeletons for anatomical investigation: see Paul Turnbull, *Science, Museums and Collecting the Indigenous Dead in Colonial Australia* (London, 2017), pp. 81–2.

94 Pearson, *Great Southern Land*, p. 111; Goodman, *The Rattlesnake*, pp. 16–19.

95 Tiley, *The Mermaid Tree*, p. 249; Goodman, *The Rattlesnake*, p. 30; J. H. Calaby, 'MacGillivray, John (1821–1867)' in Pike, ed., *ADB*, II, pp. 167–8.

96 Ingleton, *Charting a Continent*, p. 69; Warwick Hirst, *Upon a Painted Ocean: Sir Oswald Brierly in the Picture Gallery, State Library of New South Wales* (Sydney, 2004), p. 2.

97 Ingleton, *Charting a Continent*, p. 69.

98 Tiley, *The Mermaid Tree*, p. 250; Goodman, *The Rattlesnake*, pp. 20–1.

99 John MacGillivray, *Narrative of the Voyage of HMS Rattlesnake*, 2 vols. (London 1852), I, pp. 2–3; T. H. Huxley, 'Science at Sea', *Westminster Review*, 61 (January 1854), p. 101.

100 Goodman, *The Rattlesnake*, p. 135.

101 Ibid., p. 136; MacGillivray, *Narrative of the Voyage of HMS Rattlesnake*, I, pp. 6–9; Huxley, 'Science at Sea', p. 102 (quotation).

102 MacGillivray, *Narrative of the Voyage of HMS Rattlesnake*, I, pp. 42–4; Cheshire RO, Owen Stanley to Charles Tyers, 28 August 1847, Correspondence and manuscripts of Owen Stanley, 1837–50.

103 MacGillivray, *Narrative of the Voyage of H.M.S. Rattlesnake*, I, p. 66; Goodman, *The Rattlesnake*, pp. 106–7, 112, 145–7. For a contemporary description of this section

of the voyage, see Leicestershire and Rutland Record Office, Arthur Packe, Private Journal on H. M.'s surveying vessels the *Rattlesnake* and *Bramble*, DE 1672/15.

104 Goodman, *The Rattlesnake*, pp. 149–50; MacGillivray, *Narrative of the Voyage of HMS Rattlesnake*, I, p. 68.

105 UKHO, OD 67, Owen Stanley, 'Bass Strait', ff. 28–34.

106 MacGillivray, *Narrative of the Voyage of HMS Rattlesnake*, I, pp. 68, 76.

107 Adelaide Lubbock, *Owen Stanley R.N. 1811–1850 Captain of the 'Rattlesnake'* (Melbourne, 1968), pp. 196–7.

108 Cheshire RO, Owen Stanley to his family, 7 April 1848, Correspondence and Manuscripts of Owen Stanley, 1837–50.

109 Goodman, *The Rattlesnake*, pp. 149–50, 172. For a detailed discussion of Kennedy's expedition, see Edgar Beale, *Kennedy of Cape York* (Adelaide, 1970), pp. 151–238.

110 MacGillivray, *Narrative of the Voyage of HMS Rattlesnake*, I, pp. 122, 161.

111 UKHO, SL 15c, Stanley to Beaufort, 31 January 1849, Captain's letters: Owen Stanley & Yule 1846–7.

112 For informative accounts of the voyage, see Cheshire RO, Owen Stanley private journal (1849), Correspondence and Manuscripts of Owen Stanley, 1837–50; NLA, MS 3784, George Inskip, Private Journal on board HMS *Bramble* (1849–50); and John Oxley Library, State Library of Queensland, Charles James Card Diaries (1847–50). For nautical details, see NLA, James Thomas Stanton, Log of HMS *Rattlesnake* (1849–50). Rough draft descriptions written during the voyage are available in ML, Z A 501–11, Oswald Brierly, Journals on board HMS *Rattlesnake* (1848–9).

113 Cheshire RO, Owen Stanley to Louisa Stanley, 15 May 1849, Correspondence and Manuscripts of Owen Stanley, 1837–50.

114 Cheshire RO, Owen Stanley to Lord Stanley, 5 October 1849, ibid.

115 Goodman, *The Rattlesnake*, pp. 207, 221, 223; Ingleton, *Charting a Continent*, p. 68; Tiley, *The Mermaid Tree*, pp. 250–7, 266.

116 Cheshire RO, John Thomson to Mary Thomson, [?] February 1850, Correspondence and manuscripts of Owen Stanley, 1837–50.

117 Goodman, *The Rattlesnake*, p. 270; Lubbock, *Owen Stanley*, p. 266.

118 Cheshire RO, John Thomson to Mary Thomson, [?] February 1850, Correspondence and Manuscripts of Owen Stanley, 1837–50.

119 Tiley, *The Mermaid Tree*, pp. 267–8.

120 Goodman, *The Rattlesnake*, pp. 276–7.

121 Huxley, 'Science at Sea', p. 115.

122 Andrew David, *The Voyage of H.M.S. Herald to Australia and the South-West Pacific 1852–1861 under the Command of Captain Henry Mangles Denham* (Melbourne, 1995), pp. 3–7.

123 TNA, ADM 2/1560, Hyde Parker and Alexander Milne to Capt. H. M. Denham, 17 May 1852, ff. 292–307.

124 David, *The Voyage of H.M.S. Herald*, pp. 10, 26, 29–32.

125 Ibid., pp. 165–9, 219; Pearson, *Great Southern Land*, p. 112. For the survey of Bass
Strait, Denham followed the chart drawn up by John Lort Stokes in the *Beagle*: see
UKHO, OD 70, entry for 26 December 1857 in extracts from Denham's Remark
Book, Capt. Denham, H.M.S. Herald: Australia SE Coast Port Jackson to Bass
Strait, f. 11. For the elaborate survey of Norfolk Island, see ML, B 1131, Remarks:
HMS *Herald* from Sydney to the Fiji islands (1855–60), entries during June 1856.

126 David, *The Voyage of H.M.S. Herald*, pp. 265, 268, 271–4. Denham's journals on
the cruise are available at UKHO, OD 88, 90, 94. Detailed remarks on the *Herald*'s
cruises are available in ML, A 4335/item 1, Captain Arthur Onslow Journal
(1857–61), Macarthur Family Papers.

127 UKHO, OD 94, H.M.S. Herald, Capt. Denham: Australia SW coast: King George
Sound to Shark Bay, 1858, f. 33.

128 David, *The Voyage of H.M.S. Herald*, pp. 276, 289–90, 298, 308; TNA, ADM
125/135, f. 79, Denham to Rear Admiral Sir Michael Seymour, 9 July 1858.

129 David, *The Voyage of H.M.S. Herald*, pp. 313, 315, 317, 325, 329, 404.

130 UKHO, OD 88, Captain Denham's Journal of the Exploring Cruise of H.M.S.
Herald, 1860: Australia East Coast and Coral Sea.

131 David, *The Voyage of H.M.S. Herald*, pp. 342, 348, 354, 363, 376, 381, 397, 405;
'Outer Route from Sydney to Torres Strait,' *The Nautical Magazine*, XXIX/4 (1860),
pp. 170–3. For the meteorological results, see National Metereological Archive,
Exeter, Meteorological Journal of H.M.S. *Herald* (1852–8), journal no. 890.

132 David, *The Voyage of H.M.S. Herald*, p. 408.

133 John MacGillivray, 'An Account of Raine's Islet, on the N.E. coast of New Holland,'
The Zoologist: A Popular Miscellany of Natural History, iv (1846), pp. 1473–81.

134 TNA, ADM 7/851, entries for 7, 9, 10, 13 September 1853 in John MacGillivray
Private Journal on the voyage of H.M.S. *Herald*, vol. 1, ff. 61, 63–5. See also John
MacGillivray, 'Notes on Australian Natural History,' *The Zoologist: A Popular
Miscellany of Natural History*, iv (1846), pp. 1485–91.

135 Royal Botanic Gardens Archives, Kew, KCL/9/1, William Grant Milne, vol. 3:
1852–60, f. 109. This manuscript contains a detailed account of the natural history
of Lord Howe Island on ff. 96–112.

136 David, *The Voyage of H.M.S. Herald*, p. 161. For MacGillivray's career as a
naturalist, see Ralph, 'John MacGillivray,' pp. 185–95.

137 Pearson, *Great Southern Land*, p. 112.

138 Henry Mangles Denham, 'The "Herald's" Voyage, 1852–61,' *Proceedings of the Royal
Geographical Society of London*, 6/5 (1861–2), pp. 197–200.

139 David, *The Voyage of H.M.S. Herald*, pp. 288, 303–7.

Bibliography

The British Library, London

Manuscripts Division

Add. MS 5413 The Harleian Mappemonde.
Add. MS 7085 James Cook, Charts from the voyage of H.M.S. *Endeavour*, 1768–71.
Add. MS 24065 Pierre Desceliers, World Map, 1550.
Add. MS 32439 Robert Brown Papers.
Add. MS 32641 Archibald Menzies Journal of Vancouver's voyage, 1790–4.
Sloane MS 3236 Voyages of William Dampier through the South Seas, 1681–91.
Stowe MS 794 Matthew Bowles Alt, Log of the *Chesterfield*, 1793–4.

India Office Records

Ac. 111 No. 389, Chart of the Passage of the *Hormazier*, 1793.

Natural History Museum, London

Library and Archives

Allan Cunningham Journals (1817–19).
Robert Brown Correspondence, vol. 3.

Caird Library & Archive, National Maritime Museum, Greenwich

The Flinders Papers

FLI/5 Matthew Flinders, Service Papers.
FLI/8a Log and portion of Matthew Flinders' Journal in H.M.S. *Providence*, 1791–3.
FLI/15/1 Matthew Flinders, 'A Chart of the Passage between New Holland and New Guinea as Seen in His Majesty's Ship *Providence* in 1792'.
FLI/105 Admiral William Smythe, A Brief Memoir of Captain Flinders, 1845.

Admiralty Papers

ADM/L/R/79B Navy Board: Lieutenants' Logs: Matthew Flinders, Journal kept on
board the *Reliance*, 1798–9.

John Lort Stokes Papers

STK 11 Letterbook of the *Beagle*, 1841–3.
STK 29 Papers relating to the voyage of the *Beagle*, 1831–6.

Royal Botanic Gardens Archives, Kew

KCL/8/5 Kew Collectors VIIa Cunningham Correspondence, 1817–31.
KCL/9/1 William Grant Milne, vol. 3: 1852–60.

The National Archives, Kew

ADM 1/1692, 2030 Admiralty Correspondence and Papers: Letters from Captains.
ADM 1/2980 Admiralty Correspondence and Papers: Letters from Lieutenants.
ADM 1/4379 Admiralty Correspondence and Papers: Letter from Sir Joseph Banks, 1805.
ADM 1/5262/287 Navy Department: Correspondence and Papers: Courts Martial.
ADM 2/141, 293–4, 1560 Admiralty Out-Letters.
ADM 7/851 Private Journal of John MacGillivray on the voyage of H.M.S. *Herald*, vol. 1.
ADM 8/81 Admiralty List Book.
ADM 55/13 Logbook of the *Chatham*, 1791.
ADM 55/151 Logbook by William Bligh in the *Bounty*.
ADM 55/96 Francis Godolphin Bond, Logbook in the *Providence*.
ADM 125/135 Admiralty: China Station. Correspondence. East Indies and Pacific.
Australian Division.
ADM 352/487 Chart of Terra Australis by Matthew Flinders, Commander of HMS
Investigator, 1802, Sheet 8, Australia: East Coast: Queensland: Bustard Bay to Cape
Sandwich.
ADM 352/489 Original Surveys: Australia, East Coast: Queensland: Port Stephens to
Northumberland islands.
ADM 352/119/2 'The Coast of New South Wales from Cape Tribulation to Endeavour
Straits Shewing the Labyrinth & ca on a Larger Scale with the Tracks of Capt. Cook
and Lieut. Bligh.'
MPI 1/96 A Survey of the Straits between New Holland and New Guinea by William
Bligh (*c.* 1793).

National Museum of the Royal Navy, Portsmouth

MS 72/12 Journal of Captain William Bampton Ship *Shaw Hormuzear* towards Batavia, May to September 1793 in company with the *Chesterfield*, whaler.

MS 73/2 Phillip Parker King, Logbooks of HMS *Bathurst*, 1821–2.

MS 79/12 Phillip Parker King, Logbooks of HMS *Mermaid* and HMS *Bathurst*, 1818–21.

MS 180/16 Copy of statement by Captain Edwards as to the loss of the ship Pandora, n.d.

Cheshire Record Office, Chester

Owen Stanley Papers, Series 2 Correspondence and Manuscripts of Owen Stanley, 1837–50. (Digital versions of these papers are available on the National Library of Australia website.)

Lincolnshire Archives, Lincoln

Flinders Papers.

Leicestershire and Rutland Record Office, Leicester

DE 1672/15 Arthur Packe, Private journal on H.M.'s surveying vessels *Rattlesnake* and *Bramble*.

Cambridge University Library

Manuscripts Department

Royal Greenwich Observatory, Board of Longitude Papers

RGO 14/68 Correspondence and related papers regarding Observations made on Voyages of Discovery.

RGO 35/55 Letters from Nevil Maskelyne to Sir Joseph Banks.

Scott Polar Research Institute, University of Cambridge

Thomas H. Manning Polar Archives

MS 248 Sir John Franklin Collection.

National Meteorological Archive, Exeter

Metereological Journal of H.M.S. *Herald*, 1852–8.

United Kingdom Hydrographic Office, Ministry of Defence Archives, Taunton

Incoming letters prior to 1857.

Letterbook nos. 9 (1839–41), 10 (1841–2) and 11 (1842–4).

Matthew Flinders, 'Sketch of the Parts between Van Diemen's Land and New South Wales. Seen in the *Francis* schooner 1798. By M. Flinders 2 Lieut. of H.M. Ship *Reliance*. The Part of New South Wales was coasted by Mr. Bass, Surgeon of the *Reliance* in a whale boat & where not seen in the *Francis* is taken from him', chart y65, shelf X.

Minute Book nos. 3 (1837–42) and 6 (1846–9).

Remark Books, OD 77–9: HMS *Fly*, 1841–6; OD 67: HMS *Rattlesnake*, 1848; OD 70, 88, 90, 94: HMS *Herald,* 1858–60; OD 100: HMS *Beagle*, 1841–2.

Surveyors' letters SL 15c, Captain's letters: Owen Stanley and Yule, 1846–7.

Surveyors' letters SL 24, Captain's letters: Wickham, 1837–41.

Surveyors' letters SL 29, Captain's letters: Blackwood, 1841–6.

Surveyors' Letters SL 30a, Captain's letters: J. L. Stokes, 1841–7.

Archives nationales de France, Paris

Série marine

BB4995, Baudin to Hamelin, 9 October 1800, Marine 5JJ 35, 40 B-D.

Archives Office of Tasmania, Hobart, Australia

NS 279/18/26 John Lort Stokes to Sir John Franklin, 15 January 1843.

John Oxley Library, State Library of Queensland, Brisbane, Australia

Charles James Card Diaries, 1847–50. (A digital version is available on the State Library of Queensland website.)

Australian National Maritime Museum, Sydney

William Bradley, Logbook on H.M.S. *Sirius (1787–92)*.

Mitchell Library, State Library of New South Wales, Sydney, Australia

Sir Joseph Banks Papers, series 20.18, 63.17, 63.32, 72.005.
MS C 211/2 Matthew Flinders, Journal in the *Norfolk* sloop, 1799.
SAFE/F79/5 William Bligh, 'A Survey of the Straits between New Holland and New Guinea'.
Matthew Flinders letterbooks, 1801–6 and 1810–14.
MLDOC 920 Phillip Parker King, Letter to J. W. Croker, 1 October 1817.
MLMSS 4429 Phillip Parker King letterbook, 1817–23.
MLMSS 4345 J. W. Croker, Letters received from Phillip Parker King, 1818–29.
MLMSS 5277 Phillip Parker King Remark books, 1817–18.
MLMSS 7964/4 John Septimus Roe letters, series 04.
MLMSS A 3925 Log of HMS *Rattlesnake*, 1846–8.
ZML MSS 7048/3 King Family Papers: Letters received by Phillip Parker King.
A 1980/2 King Family Correspondence.
B 1131 Francis Hixson Papers, 1848–60.
A 4335/item 1 Macarthur Family Papers: Captain Arthur Onslow Journal, 1857–61.
Z A 501-511 Oswald Brierly, Journals on HMS *Rattlesnake*, 1848–9.

State Library of Victoria, Melbourne, Australia

Manuscripts Department

'A Brief memoir of Captain Matthew Flinders. R. N.,' p. 2, J. J. Shillinglaw Papers, box 81.

National Library of Australia, Canberra

George Inskip, Private Journal kept on board HMS *Bramble*, 1849–50 (MS 3784).
James Thomas Stanton, Log of HMS *Rattlesnake*, 1849–50 (MS 4029).
Private Journal of John Henry Norcock, 1835–7 (MS 5896).

State Library of Western Australia, Perth, Australia

ACC 491AD/3-4, ACC 2162AD/1-7, 9-11 John Septimus Roe logbooks, 1817–22.

Printed Primary Sources

Allen, Jim and Carris, Peter, eds., *The Journal of John Sweatman: A Nineteenth Century Surveying Voyage in North Australia and Torres Strait* (St Lucia: University of Queensland Press, 1977).

Arrowsmith, Aaron, *A Topographical Plan of the Settlement of New South Wales, Including Port Jackson, Botany Bay and Broken Bay. Surveyed by Messrs Grimes and Flinders – Communicated by Lt. Col. Paterson of the New South Wales Corps* (London: A. Arrowsmith, 1799).

Australia in Maps: Great Maps in Australia's History from the National Library's Collection (Canberra: National Library of Australia, 2007).

Beaglehole, J. C., ed., *The Journals of Captain James Cook on His Voyages of Discovery. Volume 1. The Voyage of the Endeavour 1768–1771*, Hakluyt Society's Publications, extra series, 34 (Cambridge: Cambridge University Press, 1955).

Beaglehole, J. C., ed., *The Journals of Captain James Cook on His Voyages of Discovery. Volume 2. The Voyage of the Resolution and Adventure 1772–1775*, Hakluyt Society's Publications, extra series, 35 (Cambridge: Cambridge University Press, 1961).

Beaglehole, J. C., ed., *The Endeavour Journal of Joseph Banks 1768–1771*, 2 vols. (Sydney: The Trustees of the Public Library of New South Wales in Association with Angus and Robertson, 1962).

Blackwood, F. P., *Directions for the Outer Passage from Sydney to Torres Strait to Accompany the Chart of the Barrier Reefs* (London: Hydrographic Office, 1847).

Bladen, F. M., ed., *Historical Records of New South Wales*, 7 vols. (Sydney: Government Printer, 1892–1901).

Blake, John, *The Sea Chart: The Illustrated History of Nautical Maps and Navigational Charts* (London: Conway Maritime Press, 2004).

Bligh, William, *A Voyage to the South Sea, Undertaken by Command of His Majesty, for the Purpose of Conveying the Bread-Fruit Tree to the West Indies, in His Majesty's Ship the Bounty ....* (London: G. Nicol, 1792).

Bonnemains, Jacqueline, ed., *Mon voyage aux Terres Australes: journal personnel du commandant Baudin* (Paris: Imprimerie nationale éditions, 2000).

Bowden, Keith, ed., *Matthew Flinders' Narrative of Tom Thumb's Cruise to Canoe Rivulet* (Brighton, VIC: South-Eastern Historical Association, 1985).

Brown, Anthony J. and Dooley, Gillian, eds., *Matthew Flinders Private Journal 1803–1814* (Adelaide: Friends of the State Library of South Australia, 2008).

Brown, Robert, 'The Late Captain Flinders,' *The Nautical Magazine and Naval Chronicle* (January 1854), pp. 29–30.

Brunton, Paul, ed., *Matthew Flinders: Personal Letters from an Extraordinary Life* (Sydney: Hordern House in association with the State Library of New South Wales, 2002).

Burkhardt, Frederick, ed., *Charles Darwin, The Beagle Letters* (Cambridge: Cambridge University Press, 2008).

Campbell, John, ed., *Navigantium atque Itinerantium Bibliotheca: Or, a Compleat Collection of Voyages and Travels*, 2 vols. (London: Printed for T. Woodward, A. Ward, S. Birt, D. Browne, T. Longman, R. Hett, C. Hitch, H. Whitridge, S. Austen, J. Hodges, J. Robinson, B. Dod, T. Harris, J. Hinton, J. Rivington, J. Ward, 1774–8).

Cannon, Michael and MacFarlane, Ian, eds., *Historical Records of Victoria. Foundation Series. Volume 4: Communications, Trade and Transport* (Melbourne: Victorian Government Printing Office, 1985).

Carrington, Hugh, ed., *The Discovery of Tahiti: A Journal of the Second Voyage of H.M.S. Dolphin Round the World by George Robertson 1766–1768*, Hakluyt Society's Publications, second series, 98 (London: The Hakluyt Society, 1948).

Chambers, Neil, ed., *The Letters of Sir Joseph Banks: A Selection, 1768–1820* (London: Imperial College Press, 2000).

Chambers, Neil, ed., *The Indian and Pacific Correspondence of Sir Joseph Banks, 1768–1820*, vols. 3–8 (London: Pickering & Chatto, 2010–14).

Chambers, Neil, ed., *Endeavouring Banks: Exploring Collections from the Endeavour Voyage 1768–1771* (London: Paul Holberton Publishing, 2016).

Collins, David, ed., Brian H. Fletcher, *An Account of the English Colony in New South Wales: with Remarks on the Dispositions, Customs, Manners & c. of the Native Inhabitants of That Country. To Which Are Added, Some Particulars of New Zealand; Compiled, by Permission, from the Mss. of Lieutenant-Governor King*, 2 vols. 1st edn. (London, 1798, 1802; reprinted Sydney: Reed in association with the Royal Historical Society, 1975).

Cole, Valda, ed., *The Summer Survey: Log of the Lady Nelson 1801–1802 John Murray* (Hastings, VIC: Hastings-Western Port Historical Society, Inc., 2001).

Cooley, William Desborough, *The History of Maritime and Inland Discovery*, 3 vols. (London: Longman, Rees, Orme, Brown, and Green, and John Taylor, 1831).

Cornell, Christine, ed., *The Journal of Post Captain Nicolas Baudin Commander-in-Chief of the Corvettes Géographe and Naturaliste Assigned by Order of the Government to a Voyage of Discovery* (Adelaide: Libraries Board of South Australia, 1974).

Crotty, Martin and Eklund, Erik, eds., *Australia to 1901: Selected Readings in the Making of a Nation* (Croydon, VIC: Tertiary Press, 2003).

Dalrymple, Alexander, *An Account of Discoveries Made in the South Pacifick Ocean* (London: privately printed, 1767).

Dalrymple, Alexander, *A Letter from Mr Dalrymple to Dr Hawkesworth …* (London: Printed for J. Nourse, T. Payne, Brotherton and Sewell, B. White, J. Robson, P. Elmsly, T. Davies and S. Leacroft, 1773).

Dalrymple, Alexander, *Memoir Concerning the Chagos and Adjacent Islands. With a Memoir of the Chart of the Islands N.E. of Madagascar by Jean Baptiste Après* (London: G. Bigg, 1786).

Dalrymple, Alexander, *Chart of the Passage of the Ship Hurmazier Capt. Bampton thro' Torres Strait 1793 Communicated by Philip Dundas esq. Superintendant [sic] at Bombay* (London: A Dalrymple, 1798) (http://acms.sl.nsw.gov.au/album/ItemViewer.aspx?itemid=1070973&suppress=N&imgindex=18).

Dampier, William, ed. James A. Williamson, *a Voyage to New Holland* (London: The Argonaut Press, 1939).

Dampier, William, *A Discourse of Trade Winds, Breezes, Storms, Seasons of the Year and Currents of the Torrid Zone throughout the World* (London: James Knapton, 1699).

Dampier, William, *A New Voyage Round the World: The Journal of an English Buccaneer* (orig. pub. 1697; reprinted London: Hummingbird Press, 1998).

David, Andrew C. F., ed., *The Charts and Coastal Views of Captain Cook's Voyages. Volume 1. The Voyage of the Endeavour 1768-1771*, Hakluyt Society, extra series, 43 (London: The Hakluyt Society in association with the Australian Academy of the Humanities, 1988).

David, Andrew C. F., *The Charts and Coastal Views of Captain Cook's Voyages. Volume 2. The Voyage of the Resolution and Adventure 1772-1775*, Hakluyt Society, extra series, 44 (London: The Hakluyt Society in association with the Australian Academy of the Humanities, 1992).

Denham, Henry Mangles, 'The "Herald's" Voyage, 1852-61,' *Proceedings of the Royal Geographical Society of London*, 6/5 (1861-2), pp. 197-200.

Dunmore, John, ed., *The Journal of Jean-François de Galaup de la Pérouse, 1785-1788*, 2 vols., Hakluyt Society's Publications, second series, 179-80 (London: Hakluyt Society, 1994-5).

Duyker, Edward, ed., *The Discovery of Tasmania: Journal Extracts from the Expeditions of Abel Janszoon Tasman and Marc-Joseph Marion Dufresne 1642 & 1772* (Hobart: St David's Park Publishing, 1992).

Duyker, Edward and Duyker, Maryse, eds., *Bruny D'Entrecasteaux, Voyage to Australia & the Pacific 1791-1793* (Carlton, VIC: Melbourne University Press, 2001).

Duyker, Edward and Tingbrand, Per, eds., *Daniel Solander: Collected Correspondence 1753-1782* (Melbourne: The Miegunyah Press, 1995).

Estensen, Miriam, ed., *The Letters of George & Elizabeth Bass* (Crows Nest, NSW: Allen & Unwin, 2009).

Findlay, Alexander George, *A Directory for the Navigation of the South Pacific Ocean, with Descriptions of Its Coasts, Islands Etc. from the Strait of Magalhaens to Panama, and Those of New Zealand, Australia Etc.; Its Winds, Currents, and Passages* (London: Richard Holmes Laurie, 1884).

Flinders, Matthew, *Observations on the Coasts of Van Diemen's Land, on Bass's Strait and Its Islands, and on Part of the Coasts of New South Wales: Intended to Accompany the Charts of the Late Discoveries in Those Countries* (London: John Nichols, 1801).

Flinders, Matthew, *A Voyage to Terra Australis; Undertaken for the Purpose of Completing the Discovery of That Vast Country, and Prosecuted in the Years 1801, 1802, and 1803, in His Majesty's Ship the Investigator, and Subsequently in the Armed Vessel Porpoise and Cumberland Schooner, with an Account of the Shipwreck of the Porpoise, Arrival of the Cumberland at Mauritius, and Imprisonment of the Commander during Six and a Half Years in That Island*, 2 vols. (London: G. & W. Nicol, 1814).

Flinders, Matthew, 'Narrative of an Expedition to Furneauxs Islands on the Coast of New South Wales, in the Port Jackson Colonial Schooner *Francis*. By Matthew Flinders 2 Lieutenant of HMS *Reliance* March 1798,' *La Trobe Library Journal*, 13 (1974), pp. 4–13.

Flinders, Matthew, 'Narrative of the Expedition of the Colonial Sloop *Norfolk*, from Port Jackson through the Strait Which Separates Van Diemen's Land from New Holland and from Thence Round the South Cape Back to Port Jackson, Completing the Circumnavigation of the Former Island. With Some Remarks on the Coasts and Harbours' reprinted in Dan Sprod, ed., *Van Diemen's Land Revealed: Flinders and Bass and Their Circumnavigation of the Island in the Colonial Sloop Norfolk 1798–1799* (Hobart: Blubber Head Press, 2009), pp. 23–70.

Fornasiero, Jean, ed., *Reflections of a Philosophical Voyager: Nicolas Baudin Letter to Philip Gidley King 24 December 1802* (Adelaide: Friends of the State Library of South Australia, 2016).

Fornasiero, Jean and West-Sooby, John, eds., *French Designs on Colonial New South Wales: François Péron's Memoir on the English Settlements in New Holland, Van Diemen's Land and the Archipelagos of the Great Pacific Ocean* (Adelaide: Friends of the State Library of South Australia, 2014).

Gall, Jennifer, ed., *In Bligh's Hand: Surviving the Mutiny on the Bounty* (Canberra: National Library of Australia, 2010).

Gallagher, Robert E., ed., *Byron's Journal of His Circumnavigation, 1764–1766*, Hakluyt Society's Publications, second series, 122 (Cambridge: Cambridge University Press, 1964).

Hambly, Peter, ed., *Pierre Bernard Milius, Last Commander of the Baudin Expedition: The Journal 1800–1804* (Canberra: National Library of Australia Publishing, 2013).

Hamilton, George, *A Voyage Round the World in His Majesty's Frigate Pandora Performed under the Direction of Captain Edwards in the Years 1790, 1791, and 1792* (London: W. Phorson, B. Law and Son, 1793).

Hawkesworth, John, *An Account of the Voyages Undertaken by Order of His Present Majesty: For Making Discoveries in the Southern Hemisphere and Successively Performed by Commodore Byron, Captain Wallis, Captain Carteret and Captain Cook in the Dolphin, the Swallow and the Endeavour*, 3 vols. (London: W. Strahan and T. Cadell, 1773).

Heward, Robert, 'Biographical Sketch of the late Allan Cunningham,' *Journal of Botany*, IV (1842), pp. 231–320.

Hooke, Robert, ed., 'A Relation of a Voyage Made towards the South Terra Incognita; Extracted from the Journal of Captain Abel Tasman …' in Robert Hooke, ed., *Philosophical Collections*, 6 (London: Richard Chiswell &c., 1682).

Hooker, J. D., *The Botany of the Antarctic Voyage of H.M.S. Erebus and Terror 1839–1843. Volume 3. Flora Tasmania. 1. CXII–CXXVII* (London: Reeve Brothers, 1860).

Hooper, Beverley, ed., *With Captain James Cook in the Antarctic and Pacific: The Private Journal of James Burney Second Lieutenant of the Adventure on Cook's Second Voyage 1772–1773* (Canberra: National Library of Australia, 1975).

Horsbrugh, James, *The India Directory, or, Directions for Sailing to and from the East Indies, China, Australia, and the Interjacent Ports of Africa and South America ...*, 2 vols., 5th edn. (London: W. H. Allen and Co., 1841).

Hunter, John, *An Historical Journal of the Transactions at Port Jackson and Norfolk Island* (London: John Stockdale, 1793).

Huxley, Julian, ed., *T. H. Huxley's Diary on the Voyage of H.M.S. Rattlesnake* (London: Chatto and Windus, 1935).

Huxley, T. H., 'Science at Sea,' *Westminster Review*, 61 (1854), pp. 98–119.

Jangoux, Michel, ed., *Journal du Voyage aux Antilles de la Belle Angélique (1796–1798)* (Paris: Presses de l'Université Paris-Sorbonne, 2009).

Jukes, J. Beete, *Narrative of the Surveying Voyage of H.M.S. Fly, Commanded by Captain F. P. Blackwood. R.N ....*, 2 vols. (London: T. & W. Boone, 1847).

Jussieu, A. L., 'Notice sur l'expédition à la Nouvelle-Hollande, enterprise pour des recherches de géographie et d'histoire naturelle,' *Annales du Muséum d'Histoire Naturelle*, 5 (1804), pp. 1–11.

Kelly, Celsus, ed., *Calendar of Documents: Spanish Voyages in the South Pacific from Alvaro de Mendaña to Alejandro Malaspina 1567–1794 and to Franciscan Missionary Plans for the Peoples of the Austral Lands 1617–1634* (Madrid: Franciscan Historical Studies [Australia] in association with Archivo Ibero-Americano [Madrid], 1965).

King, Phillip Parker, 'On the Maritime Geography of Australia' in Barron Field, ed., *Geographical Memoirs, or New South Wales; by Various Hands ...* (London: John Murray, 1825), pp. 271–96.

King, Phillip Parker, *Narrative of a Survey of the Intertropical and Western Coasts of Australia Performed between the Years 1818 and 1822 by Captain Phillip P. King*, 2 vols. (London: John Murray, 1827; repr. Adelaide: Friends of the State Library of South Australia, 2012).

King, Phillip Parker, *Directions for the Inner Route from Sydney to Torres Strait* (London: Hydrographic Office, 1847).

Knight, R.J.B. and Frost, Alan, eds., *The Journal of Daniel Paine 1794–1797, Together with Documents Illustrating the Beginning of Government Boat-Building and Timber-Gathering in New South Wales, 1795–1805* (Sydney: Library of Australian History in association with the National Maritime Museum, Greenwich, 1983).

Lamb, W. Kaye, ed., *George Vancouver: A Voyage of Discovery to the North Pacific Ocean and round the World 1791–1795*, 4 vols., Hakluyt Society's Publications, second series, 163–6 (Cambridge: Cambridge University Press, 1984).

Lestringant, Frank, ed., *Cosmographie Universelle selon les navigateurs tant anciens que modernes par Guillaume le Testu pillotte en la mer du Ponent, de la ville françoyse de Grace* (Paris: Camets les Tropiques, 2012).

Lesueur, Charles-Alexandre and Petit, Nicolas-Martin, *Voyage of Discovery to the Southern Lands: An Historical Record: Atlas, 1824* (Adelaide: Friends of the State Library of South Australia, 2008).

Letters and Extracts from the Addresses and Occasional Writings of J. Beete Jukes (London: Chapman and Hall, 1871).

The Log of the Bounty (Guildford: Genesis Publications, 1975).

MacGillivray, John, 'An Account of Raine's Islet, on the N.E. Coast of New Holland,' 'Ornithological Excursion to the North Coast of New Holland,' and 'Notes on Australian Natural History,' *The Zoologist*, iv (1846), pp. 1473–91.

MacGillivray, John, *Narrative of the Voyage of H.M.S. Rattlesnake, Commanded by the Late Captain Owen Stanley…*, 2 vols. (London: T. & W. Boone, 1852).

Macknight, C. C., ed., *Low Head to Launceston: The Earliest Reports of Port Dalrymple and the Tamar* (Launceston: Historical Survey of Northern Tasmania, 1998).

Major, R. H., ed., *Early Voyages to Terra Australis, now Called Australia,* Hakluyt Society's Publications, First Series, 25 (London: The Hakluyt Society, 1859).

Markham, Clements, ed., *The Voyages of Pedro Fernandez de Quiros 1595 to 1606,* 2 vols., Hakluyt Society's Publications, second series, 14–15 (London: The Hakluyt Society, 1904).

Mawer, G. A., ed., *Captain James Colnett, a Voyage to New Holland and Round the World* (Dural Delivery Centre, NSW: Rosenberg, 2016).

Migliazzo, Arlin, ed., *Lands of True and Certain Bounty: The Geographical Theories and Colonisation Strategies of John Pierre Purry* (London: Associated University Presses, 2002).

Morgan, Kenneth, ed., *Australia Circumnavigated: The Voyage of Matthew Flinders in HMS Investigator, 1801–1803,* Hakluyt Society, third series, 28–9, 2 vols. (London: Ashgate, 2015).

Mortimer, George, *Observations and Remarks Made during a Voyage to the North West Coast of America* (London: Cadell, 1791).

The Nautical Magazine and Naval Chronicle (1837–8, 1840, 1846–7, 1853).

Ogilby, John, *The Unknown South-land in America, Being the Latest and Most Accurate Description of the New World* (London: Printed by the author, 1671).

Orchard, A. E. and Orchard, T. A., eds., *Allan Cunningham: Letters of a Botanist/ Explorer 1791–1839* (Weston Creek, ACT: privately published, 2015).

'Outer Route from Sydney to Torres Strait,' *The Nautical Magazine*, XXIX/4 (1860), pp. 170–3.

Parkinson, Sydney, *A Journal of a Voyage to the Southern Seas in His Majesty's Ship, The Endeavour* (London: Stanfield Parkinson, 1773).

Péron, Francois, *Voyage of Discovery to the Southern Lands, Continued by Louis de Freycinet, Book IV, Second Edition 1824* (Adelaide: Friends of the State Library of South Australia, 2003).

Péron, François, *Voyage of Discovery to the Southern Lands Continued by Louis de Freycinet, Books I to III, Second Edition 1824* (Adelaide: Friends of the State Library of South Australia, 2006).

Perry, T. M. and Simpson, D. H., eds., *Drawings by William Westall; Landscape Artist on board HMS Investigator during the Circumnavigation of Australia by Captain Matthew Flinders R. N. in 1801–1803* (London: Royal Commonwealth Society, 1962).

Plomley, B. and Piord-Bernier, J., eds., *The General: The Visits of the Expedition Led by Bruny d'Entrecasteaux to Tasmanian Waters in 1792 and 1793* (Launceston: Queen Victoria Museum, 1993), pp. 279–86.

Rivière, Marc-Serge, ed., *A Woman of Courage: The Journal of Rose de Freycinet on Her Voyage around the World 1817–1820* (Canberra: National Library of Australia, 1996).

Rivière, Marc-Serge, ed., *The Governor's Noble Guest: Hyacinthe de Bougainville's Account of Port Jackson, 1825* (Melbourne: Melbourne University Press, 1999).

Roe, Michael, ed., *The Journal and Letters of Captain Charles Bishop on the North-West Coast of America, in the Pacific and in New South Wales 1794–1799*, Hakluyt Society, *Second Series, 131* (London: Hakluyt Society, 1967).

Roeper, Vibeke and Wildeman, Diederick, eds., *Het Journaal van Abel Tasman 1642–1643* (The Hague: Nationaal Archief, 2006).

Rutter, Owen, ed., *The Voyage of the Bounty's Launch as Related in William Bligh's Despatch to the Admiralty and the Journal of John Fryer* (London: Golden Cockerel Press, 1934).

Schilder, Günter, ed., *Voyage to the Great South Land: Willem de Vlamingh, 1696–7* (Sydney: Royal Australian Historical Society in association with the Australian Bank, 1985).

Schreiber, Roy, ed., *Captain Bligh's Second Chance: An Eyewitness Account of His Return to the South Seas by Lt George Tobin* (London: Chatham Publishing, 2007).

Sprod, Dan, ed., *Van Diemen's Land Revealed: Flinders and Bass and Their Circumnavigation of the Island in the Colonial Sloop Norfolk 1798–1799* (Hobart: Blubber Head Press, 2009).

Stevens, Henry N. and Barwick, George F., eds., *New Light on the Discovery of Australia as Revealed by the Journal of Captain Don Diego de Prado Y Tovar*, Hakluyt Society's Publications, Second Series II, *64* (London: The Hakluyt Society, 1930).

Sydney Morning Herald (1843).

Vallance, T. G., Moore, D. T. and Groves, E. W., eds., *Nature's Investigator: The Diary of Robert Brown in Australia, 1801–1805* (Canberra: Australian Biological Resources Study, 2001).

Wallis, Helen, ed., *Carteret's Voyage Round the World, 1766–1769*, 2 vols., Hakluyt Society's Publications, second series, 124–5 (Cambridge: Cambridge University Press, 1965).

Watson, Frederick, ed., *Historical Records of Australia. Series 1. Governor's Despatches to and from England. Volume 1: 1788–1796* (Canberra: Library Committee of the Commonwealth Parliament, 1914).

The Zoologist: A Popular Miscellany of Natural History (London: John Van Voorst), vol. 4 (1846).

Secondary Sources

Anderson, Grahame, *The Merchant of the Zeehaen: Isaac Gilsemans and the Voyages of Abel Tasman* (Wellington: Te Papa Press, 2001).

Anderson, Stephanie, 'French Anthropology in Australia, a Prelude: The Encounters between Aboriginal Tasmanians and the Expedition of Bruny d'Entrecasteaux, 1793,' *Aboriginal History*, 24 (2000), pp. 212–23.

Anderson, Stephanie, 'French Anthropology in Australia: The First Fieldwork Expedition: François Péron's Anthropological Contributions to Baudin's "Voyage of Discovery to the Southern Hemisphere" (1800–1804), '*Aboriginal History*, 25 (2001), pp. 228–42.

Anon., 'King, Phillip Parker (1791–1856)' in Douglas Pike, ed., *Australian Dictionary of Biography*, vol. 2 (Melbourne: Melbourne University Press, 1967), pp. 61–4.

Apfelbaum, Joan, 'Australian Collections of Labillardière in the Herbarium of the Academy of Natural Sciences of Philadelphia,' *Taxon*, 26/5–6 (1977), pp. 541–8.

Appleyard, Reginald, 'Vancouver's Discovery and Exploration of King George's Sound' *Early Days: Journal of the Royal Western Australian Historical Society*, 9/4 (1982), pp. 86–98.

Appleyard, R. T. and Manford, Toby, *The Beginning: European Discovery and Early Settlement of Swan River, Western Australia* (Nedlands, WA: University of Western Australia Press, 1979).

Ariel, A., 'Navigating with Kenneth McIntyre: A Professional Critique,' *The Great Circle*, 6/2 (1984), pp. 135–9.

Ashley, Peter, 'HMS Investigator – A "Copper-Bottomed" Ship?' in Marc Serge Rivière and Kumari R. Issur, eds., *Baudin-Flinders dans l'Océan Indien: Voyages, Découvertes, Rencontre: Travels, Discoveries, Encounter* (Paris: L'Harmattan, 2006), pp. 271–88.

Ashley, Peter, *The Indomitable Captain Matthew Flinders, Royal Navy* (Clanfield, Hants: Pierhead Press, 2005).

Atlas of the World: Gerard Mercator's Map of the World (1569) (Zutphen: Walburg Pers, 2012).

Aurosseau, M., 'Flinders' Voyage in the *Francis*, 1798,' *The Geographical Journal*, 111/1–3 (1948), pp. 111–13.

Austin, K. A., *The Voyage of the Investigator 1801–1803: Commander Matthew Flinders, R.N.* (Adelaide: Rigby, 1964).

Baglione, Gabrielle, Crémière, Cédric, Fornasiero, Jean and West-Sooby, John, *Charles-Alexandre Lesueur: Painter and Naturalist: A Forgotten Treasure* (Le Havre: Museum d'Histoire Naturelle du Havre, 2016).

Band, S. R., 'John Allen, Miner: On Board H.M.S. Investigator 1801–1804,' *Bulletin of the Peak District Mines Historical Society*, 10 (1987), pp. 67–78.

Barker, R. M., 'The Botanical Legacy of 1802: South Australian Plants Collected by Robert Brown and Peter Good on Matthew Flinders' Investigator and by the French Scientists on Baudin's Geographe and Naturaliste,' *Journal of the Adelaide Botanic Gardens*, 21 (2007), pp. 5–44.

Barnes, Geraldine, 'Traditions of the Monstrous in William Dampier's *New Holland*' in Judy A. Hayden, ed., *Travel Narratives, the New Science, and Literary Discourse, 1569–1750* (Farnham: Ashgate, 2012), pp. 87–101.

Barnett, James K., *Captain George Vancouver in Alaska and the North Pacific* (Anchorage, AK: Todd Communications, 2017).

Barritt, M. K., 'Matthew Flinders's Survey Practices and Records,' *Journal of the Hakluyt Society* (2014), pp. 1–15.

Bassett, Marnie, *Realms and Islands: The World Voyage of Rose de Freycinet in the Corvette Uranie 1817–1820 from Her Journal and Letters and the Reports of Louis de Saulces Freycinet Capitaine de Corvette* (London: Oxford University Press, 1962).

Bassett, Marnie, *Behind the Picture: H.M.S. Rattlesnake's Australia-New Guinea Cruise, 1846 to 1850* (Melbourne: Oxford University Press, 1966).

Bastian, Josephine, '*A Passion for Exploring New Countries': Matthew Flinders & George Bass* (Melbourne: Australian Scholarly Publishing, 2016).

Bastock, John, *Ships on the Australia Station* (Frenchs Forest, NSW: Child & Associates, 1988).

Batt, J. C. and Triebel, L. A., *The French Exploration of Australia, with Special Reference to Tasmania* (Hobart: Government Printer, Tasmania, 1957).

Baugh, Daniel A., 'Seapower and Science: The Motives for Pacific Exploration' in Derek Howse, ed., *Background to Discovery: Pacific Exploration from Dampier to Cook* (Berkeley and Los Angeles: University of California Press, 1990), pp. 1–55.

Bayldon, F. J., 'Voyage of Luis Vaez de Torres from the New Hebrides to the Moluccas, June to November 1606,' *Journal and Proceedings of the Royal Australian Historical Society*, 11/3 (1925), pp. 158–94.

Bayldon, F. J., 'Voyage of Torres,' *Journal and Proceedings of the Royal Australian Historical Society*, 16/2 (1930), pp. 133–46.

Beaglehole, J. C., *The Exploration of the Pacific*, 3rd edn. (London: Adam & Charles Black, 1966).

Beaglehole, J. C., 'Eighteenth-Century Science and the Voyages of Discovery,' *New Zealand Journal of History*, 3/2 (1969), pp. 107–23.

Beaglehole, J. C., *The Life of Captain James Cook* (Stanford, CA: Stanford University Press, 1974).

Beale, Edgar, 'Cook's First Landing Attempt in New South Wales,' *Journal and Proceedings of the Royal Australian Historical Society*, 50/3 (1964), pp. 191–204.

Beale, Edgar, *Kennedy of Cape York* (Adelaide: Rigby Limited, 1970).

Beanland, Denver, 'Connections in Charting the Great Barrier Reef, 1770–1850,' *Queensland History Journal*, 24/3 (2019), pp. 251–67.

Beer, Gavin de, *The Sciences Were Never at War* (London: Thomas Nelson and Sons, 1960).

Bennett, Bruce, 'Exploration or Espionage? Flinders and the French,' *Journal of the European Association for Studies on Australia*, 2/1 (2011), pp. 14–23.

Bennett, Jim, *Navigation: A Very Short Introduction* (Oxford: Oxford University Press, 2017).

Bennett, Michael, 'Van Diemen, Tasman, and the Dutch Reconnaissance,' *Tasmanian Historical Research Association Papers and Proceedings*, 39/2 (1992), pp. 68–82.

Bertie, Charles H., 'Matthew Flinders, Australia's Navigator,' *Journal and Proceedings of the Australian Historical Society*, 3/7 (1915–17), pp. 295–326.

Bigourdan, Nicolas, 'The French Connection with New Holland: An Overview of Research Studies,' *The Great Circle*, 37/2 (2015), pp. 76–95.

Blainey, Geoffrey, *The Tyranny of Distance: How Distance Shaped Australia's History* (Melbourne: Sun Books, 1966).

Blainey, Geoffrey, *Sea of Dangers: Captain Cook and His Rivals* (Camberwell, VIC: Viking, 2009).

Blair, David, *James Cook's Toponyms: Placenames of Eastern Australia April–August 1770, ANPS Placenames Report No. 1* (South Turramurra, NSW: Placenames Australia, Inc., 2015).

Bloomfield, Noelene, *Almost a French Australia: French-British Rivalry in the Southern Oceans* (Braddon: Halstead Press, 2012).

Bloomfield, Noelene, 'Overview: France's Quest for Terra Australis: Strategies, Maladies and Triumphs,' *The Great Circle*, 39/2 (2017), pp. 8–24.

Bonner, Elizabeth, 'Did the French Discover Australia? The First French Scientific Voyage of Discovery, 1503–1505' in David W. Lovell, ed., *Revolution, Politics, and Society: Elements in the Making of Modern France* (Canberra: Australian Defence Force Academy, 1994), pp. 40–8.

Bonyhady, Tim, *Images in Opposition: Australian Landscape Painting 1801–1890* (Melbourne: Oxford University Press, 1985).

Bourgoin, Jean and Taillemite, Etienne, 'The Baudin Expedition to Australia 1800–1804,' *International Hydrographic Review*, 3/1 (2002), pp. 6–19.

Bowden, Keith Macrae *George Bass 1771–1803: His Discoveries, Romantic Life, and Tragic Disappearance* (Melbourne: Melbourne University Press, 1952).

Bowen, James and Bowen, Margarita, *The Great Barrier Reef: History, Science, Heritage* (Cambridge: Cambridge University Press, 2002).

Bown, Stephen, *Madness, Betrayal and the Lash: The Epic Voyage of Captain George Vancouver* (Vancouver: Douglas & McIntyre, 2008).

Boxer, C. R., *The Dutch Seaborne Empire, 1600–1800* (New York: Alfred A. Knopf, 1965).

Boxer, C. R., *The Portuguese Seaborne Empire 1415–1825* (London: Hutchinson & Co., 1969).

Bradley, John J. and Kearney, Amanda, '"He Painted the Law": William Westall, "Stone Monuments" and Remembrance of Things Past,' *Journal of Material Culture*, 16/1 (2011), pp. 25–45.

Branagan, D. F., 'Phillip Parker King: Colonial Anchor Man' in Alwyne Wheeler and James H. Price, eds., *From Linnaeus to Darwin: Commentaries on the History of Biology and Geography* (London: British Museum, Natural History, 1985), pp. 179–93.

Bréelle, Dany, 'Matthew Flinders's Australian Toponomy and Its British Connections,' *Journal of the Hakluyt Society* (2013), pp. 1–41.

Bréelle, Dany, 'Matthew Flinders et la mise en cartes d'un nouvel espace indo-pacifique,' *Cybergeo: European Journal of Geography* (2016), n.p.

Bréelle, Dany, 'The Hydrographical Work of the Engineer-Geographers of the Baudin Expedition and the Rise of Louis Freycinet as the Cartographer of the voyage,' *The Great Circle*, 39/2 (2017), pp. 86–119.

Broek, Jan O. and Friis, M., ed., *The Pacific Basin: A History of Its Geographical Exploration* (New York: American Geographical Society, 1967), pp. 151–69.

Broeze, Frank, *Island Nation: A History of Australians and the Sea* (St Leonards, NSW: Allen & Unwin, 1998).

Broomhall, Susan, 'Emotional Encounters: Indigenous Peoples in the Dutch East India Company's Interactions with the South Lands,' *Australian Historical Studies*, 45/3 (2014), pp. 350–67.

Brossard, Maurice Raymond de, *Kerguelen: Le Découvreur et Ses Îles* (Paris: Éditions France-Empire, 1970).

Brown, Anthony J., *Ill-Starred Captains: Flinders and Baudin* (London: Chatham Publishing, 2001).

Bruijn, J. R., Gaastra, F. S. and Schöffer, I., *Dutch-Asiatic Shipping in the 17th and 18th Centuries*, 3 vols. (The Hague: Martinus Nijhoff, 1987).

Brunton, Paul, 'The Voyages of Abel Tasman,' *Launceston Historical Society Papers and Proceedings*, 16 (2004), pp. 1–8.

Brunton, Paul, 'Abel Janszoon Tasman – the Australian Voyages, Missing Journals and Perplexing Charts' in Lindsey Shaw and Wendy Wilkins, eds., *Dutch Connections: 400 Years of Australian-Dutch Maritime Links 1606–2006* (Sydney: Australian Maritime Museum, 2006), pp. 40–57.

Burnet, Ian, *The Tasman Map: The Biography of a Map* (Kenthurst, NSW: Rosenberg Books, 2019).

Burningham, Nick, 'The Australische Compagnie and the Other *Eendracht* of 1616,' *The Great Circle*, 38/1 (2016), pp. 32–44.

Calaby, J. H., 'MacGillvray, John (1821–1867)' in Douglas Pike, ed., *Australian Dictionary of Biography*, vol. 2 (Melbourne: Melbourne University Press, 1967), pp. 167–8.

Cameron, J.M.R., 'Prelude to Colonization: James Stirling's Examination of Swan River, March 1827,' *Australian Geographer*, 12/4 (1973), pp. 309–27.

Cameron-Ash, Margaret, 'French Mischief: A Foxy Map of New Holland,' *The Globe*, 68 (2011), pp. 1–14.

Cameron-Ash, Margaret, 'Juggling "Australia," "Austrialia," and "New Holland",' *The Globe*, 73 (2013), pp. 29–38.

Cameron-Ash, Margaret, 'Captain Cook Invented Point Hicks to Hide Bass Strait,' *The Globe*, 84 (2018), pp. 39–45.

Cameron-Ash, Margaret, *Lying for the Admiralty: Captain Cook's Endeavour Voyage* (Kenthurst, NSW: Rosenberg Publishing, 2018).

Captain Cook's Florilegium (London: Lion and Unicorn Press, 1973).

Carr, D. J., 'The Books That Sailed with the *Endeavour*,' *Endeavour*, 7/4 (1983), pp. 194–201.

Carr, D. J., 'The Identity of Captain Cook's Kangaroo' in D. J. Carr, ed., *Sydney Parkinson: Artist of Cook's Endeavour Voyage* (London and Canberra: Croom Helm, 1983), pp. 242–9.

Carter, Paul, *The Road to Botany Bay: An Exploration of Landscape and History* (London: Faber, 1988).

Carter, Paul, *Living in a New Country: History, Travelling and Language* (London: Faber, 1992).

Carter, Paul, 'Looking for Baudin' in Susan Hunt and Paul Carter, eds., *Terre Napoléon: Australia through French Eyes 1800–1804* (Sydney: Historic Houses Trust of New South Wales in Association with Hordern House, 1999), pp. 21–31.

Cavenagh, A. K., 'The Return of the First Fleet Ships,' *The Great Circle*, 2/2 (1989), pp. 1–16.

Chambers, Neil, 'Joseph Banks, the British Museum and Collections in the Age of Empire' in R. G. W. Anderson, M. L. Caygill, A. G. MacGregor and L. Syson, eds., *Enlightening the British: Knowledge, Discovery and the Museum in the Eighteenth Century* (London: British Museum Press, 2003), pp. 222–43.

Chapin, Seymour, 'The Men from across La Manche: French Voyages, 1660–1790' in Derek Howse, ed., *Background to Discovery: Pacific Exploration from Dampier to Cook* (Berkeley and Los Angeles: University of California Press, 1990), pp. 81–114.

Chapin, Seymour L., 'A Survey of the Efforts to Determine Longitude at Sea, 1660–1760. Part II: The Use of Celestial Bodies,' *Navigation*, 3/7 (1953), pp. 242–9.

Chapman, Peter, 'Tasman and a Dutch Discovery,' *Australian Natural History*, 20/2 (1980), pp. 39–42.

Clode, Danielle, *Continent of Curiosities: A Journey through Australian Natural History* (Cambridge: Cambridge University Press, 2006).

Clode, Danielle and Harrison, Carol E., 'Precedence and Posterity: Patterns of Publishing from French Scientific Expeditions to the Pacific (1785–1840),' *Australian Journal of French Studies*, 50/3 (2013), pp. 361–79.

Cock, Randolph, 'Sir Francis Beaufort and the Co-Ordination of British Scientific Activity, 1829–55' (University of Cambridge PhD, 2003).

Cole, Harry and Valda, *Mr Bass's Western Port. The Whaleboat Voyage* (Hastings, VIC: Hastings-Western Port Historical Society in association with South Eastern Historical Association, 1997).

Cole, Valda, 'George Bass and the Whaleboat Voyage,' *Victorian Historical Journal*, 69/2 (1998), pp. 77–97.

Collingridge, George, *The Discovery of Australia: A Critical, Documentary and Historic Investigation Concerning the Priority of Discovery in Australasia by Europeans before the Arrival of Lieut. James Cook, in the 'Endeavour', in the Year 1770* (Sydney: Hayes Brothers, 1895).

Cowley, Des, 'European Voyages of Discovery,' *La Trobe Library Journal*, 41 (1988), pp. 15–24.

Cowley, Peter, Fornasiero, Jean and Sankey, Margaret, 'The Baudin Expedition in Review: Old Quarrels and New Approaches,' *Australian Journal of French Studies*, XLI/2 (2004), pp. 4–14.

Crane, Nicholas, *Mercator: The Man who Mapped the Planet* (London: Weidenfeld & Nicolson, 2002).

Crone, G. R., 'The Discovery of Tasmania and New Zealand,' *The Geographical Journal*, 111/4–6 (1948), pp. 257–63.

Crozet's Voyage to Tasmania, New Zealand, the Ladrone Islands, and the Philippines in the Years 1771–1772, trans. H. Ling Roth (London: Truslove & Shirley, 1891).

Curry, S., Maslin, B. R. and Maslin, J. A., *Allan Cunningham Australian Collecting Localities*, Flora of Australia Supplementary series, 13 (Canberra: Australian Biological Resources Study, 2002).

Dash, Mike, *Batavia's Graveyard* (London: Weidenfield & Nicolson, 2002).

David, Andrew, *The Voyage of HMS Herald to Australia and the South-West Pacific 1852–1861 under the Command of Captain Henry Mangles Denham* (Melbourne: The Miegunyah Press, 1995).

David, Andrew, *The Charts and Coastal Views of Captain Cook's Voyages: The Voyage of the Endeavour 1768–1771* (London: The Hakluyt Society, 1988).

David, Andrew C. F., 'Peter Heywood and Northwest Australia,' *The Great Circle*, 1/1 (1979), pp. 4–14.

David, Andrew C. F., 'The Surveyors of the Bounty: A Preliminary Study of the Hydrographic Surveys of William Bligh, Thomas Hayward and Peter Heywood and the Charts Published from Them,' unpublished typescript, Royal Navy Hydrographic Department, Ministry of Defence Archives, Taunton (1982).

David, Andrew C. F., 'Cook and the Cartography of Australia,' *The Globe*, 22 (1984), pp. 47–59.

David, Andrew C. F., 'From Mutineer to Hydrographer: The Surveying Career of Peter Heywood,' *International Hydrographic Review*, 3/2 (2002), pp. 6–11.

Dekker, E., 'Early Explorations of the Southern Celestial Sky,' *Annals of Science*, 44/5 (1987), pp. 439–70.

Desmond, Ray, *Kew: The History of the Royal Botanic Gardens* (London: The Harvill Press, 1995).

Diment, J. A., Humphries, C. J., Newington, L. and Shaughnessy, E., 'Catalogue of the Natural History Drawings Commissioned by Joseph Banks on the *Endeavour* Voyage 1768–1771 Held in the British Museum (Natural History). Part 1. Botany: Australia,' *Bulletin of the British Museum (Natural History) Historical Series*, 11 (1984), pp. 1–183.

Donaldson, Bruce, 'The Dutch Contribution to the European Discovery of Australia' in Nonja Peters, ed., *The Dutch Down under 1606–2006* (Crawley, WA: University of Western Australia Press, 2006), pp. 4–25.

Dooley, Gillian, 'The Library of Soho Square: Matthew Flinders, Sir Joseph Banks and the Publication of "A Voyage to Terra Australis" (1814),' *Script & Print*, 41/3 (2017), pp. 169–86.

Douglas, Bronwen, 'Slippery Word, Ambiguous Praxis: "Race" and Late 18th-Century Voyagers in Oceania,' *Journal of Pacific History*, XLI/1 (2006), pp. 1–29.

Douglas, Bronwen, 'Voyages, Encounters, and Agency in Oceania: Captain Cook and Indigenous People', *History Compass*, 6/3 (2008), pp. 712–37.

Drake-Brockman, Henrietta, *Voyage to Disaster*, new edn. (Crawley, WA: University of Western Australia Press, 1995).

Drayton, Richard, 'Knowledge and Empire' in P. J. Marshall, ed., *The Oxford History of the British Empire*, vol. 2. *The Eighteenth Century* (Oxford: Oxford University Press, 1998), pp. 231–52.

Driver, Felix and Martins, Luciana, 'John Septimus Roe and the Art of Navigation, *c*.1815–1830', *History Workshop Journal*, 54 (2002), pp. 144–61.

Druett, Joan, *Tupaia: The Remarkable Story of Captain Cook's Polynesian Navigator* (Santa Barbara, CA: Praeger, 2011).

Ducker, Sophie C., 'History of Australian Phycology: The Significance of Early French Exploration', *Brunonia*, 2/1 (1979), pp. 19–42.

Duncan, S., 'Shaving with Ockham's Razor: A Reappraisal of the Portuguese Priority Hypothesis', *The Globe*, 39 (1993), pp. 1–9.

Dunmore, John, *French Explorers of the Pacific.1. The Eighteenth Century* (Oxford: The Clarendon Press, 1965).

Dunmore, John, *French Explorers in the Pacific. II. The Nineteenth Century* (Oxford: The Clarendon Press, 1969).

Dunmore, John, 'Dream and Reality: French Voyages and Their Vision of Australia' in *Australia and the European Imagination: Papers from a Conference Held at the Humanities Research Centre, Australian National University*, May 1981 (Canberra: Australian National University, 1982), pp. 109–21.

Dunmore, John, *Visions & Realities: France in the Pacific 1695–1995* (Waikanae: Heritage Press, 1997).

Dunmore, John, *Where Fate Beckons: The Life of Jean-François de la Pérouse* (Wollombi, NSW: Exisle Publishing, 2006).

Dunmore, John, *Storms and Dreams: The Life of Louis de Bougainville* (Fairbanks, AK: University of Alaska Press, 2007).

Dunmore, John, *Chasing a Dream: The Exploration of the Imaginary Pacific* (Auckland: Upstart Press, 2016).

Dunn, Richard, 'James Cook and the New Navigation' in James K. Barnett and David L. Nicandri, eds., *Arctic Ambitions: Captain Cook and the Northwest Passage* (Seattle: University of Washington Press, 2015), pp. 89–107.

Dunn, Richard and Higgitt, Rebekah, *Ships, Clocks and Stars: The Quest for Longitude* (Glasgow: Collins, 2014).

Duyker, Edward, *An Officer of the Blue: Marc-Joseph Marion Dufresne 1724–1772* (Melbourne: Melbourne University Press, 1994).

Duyker, Edward, *Citizen Labillardière: A Naturalist's Life in Revolution and Exploration (1755–1834)* (Melbourne: The Miegunyah Press, 2003).

Duyker, Edward, 'Uncovering Jean Piron: In Search of D'Entrecasteaux's Artist', *Explorations: A Bulletin Devoted to the Study of Franco-Australian links*, 39 (2005), pp. 37–45.

Duyker, Edward, *Francois Péron: An Impetuous Life: Naturalist and Voyager* (Melbourne: The Miegunyah Press, 2006).

Duyker, Edward, 'Jacques-Julien Houtou de Labillardière (1755–1834): Explorer and Botanist' in Eric Berti and Ivan Barko, eds., *French Lives in Australia* (Melbourne: Australian Scholarly Publishing, 2015), pp. 20–35.

Dyer, Colin, 'From Happiness to Havoc: The Aboriginal Bruny Islanders before Settlement by the British, as Witnessed by French Explorers, 1792–1802,' *Journal of the Royal Australian Historical Society*, 102/1 (2016), pp. 32–44.

Eccleston, Gregory C., 'The Neglect of Baudin's Manuscript Charts of the Victorian Coastline,' *The Globe*, 66 (2010), pp. 27–58.

Edwards, Philip, *Sea-Narratives in Eighteenth-Century England* (Cambridge: Cambridge University Press, 1994).

Edwards, Phyllis I., 'Robert Brown (1773–1858) and the Natural History of Matthew Flinders' Voyage in H.M.S. *Investigator*, 1801–1805,' *Journal of the Society for the Bibliography of Natural History*, 7 (1976), pp. 385–407.

Eisler, William, *The Furthest Shore: Images of Terra Australis from the Middle Ages to Captain Cook* (Cambridge: Cambridge University Press, 1995).

Eliason, Andrew, 'Guillaume le Testu's Opinion of Java la Grande,' *The Globe*, 81 (2016), pp. 89–100.

Eliason, Andrew J., 'A Pacific Prospectus: The Origins and Identities of the Islands depicted in the South Sea on the Dieppe Maps,' *The Globe*, 79 (2016), pp. 13–30.

Endersby, Jim, *Imperial Nature: Joseph Hooker and the Practices of Victorian Science* (Chicago, IL: University of Chicago Press, 2008).

Erskine, Nigel, 'Dutch Encounters and the Australasian Shore' in Lindsey Shaw and Wendy Wilkins, eds., *Dutch Connections: 400 Years of Australian-Dutch Maritime Links 1606–2006* (Sydney: Australian Maritime Museum, 2006), pp. 10–25.

Erskine, Nigel, 'New Constellations' in *Mapping Our World: Terra Incognita to Australia* (Canberra: National Library of Australia, 2013), pp. 60–1.

Estensen, Miriam, *Discovery: The Quest for the Great South Land* (St Leonards, NSW: Allen & Unwin, 1998).

Estensen, Miriam, *The Life of Matthew Flinders* (Sydney: Allen & Unwin, 2002).

Estensen, Miriam, *The Life of George Bass, Surgeon and Sailor of the Enlightenment* (Crows Nest, NSW: Allen & Unwin, 2005).

Estensen, Miriam, *Terra Australis Incognita: The Spanish Quest for the Mysterious Great South Land* (Crows Nest, NSW: Allen & Unwin, 2006).

Fausett, David, *Writing the New World: Imaginary Voyages and Utopias of the Great Southern Land* (Syracuse: Syracuse University Press, 1993).

Fausett, David, 'Historical and Literary Parallels in the Early Mapping of Australia,' *Terrae Incognitae*, 26/1 (1994), pp. 27–35.

Fernández-Armesto, Felipe, *Pathfinders: A Global History of Exploration* (Oxford: Oxford University Press, 2006).

Findlay, Elizabeth, *Arcadian Quest – William Westall's Australian Sketches* (Canberra: National Library of Australia, 2000).

Finlay, Robert, 'How Not to (Re)write World History: Gavin Menzies and the Chinese Discovery of America,' *Journal of World History*, 15/2 (2004), pp. 229–42.

Fishburn, Matt, 'Phillip Parker King's Stowaway,' *Journal of the Royal Australian Historical Society*, 103/1 (2017), pp. 80–93.

Fitzgerald, Lawrence, *Java la Grande: The Portuguese Discovery of Australia* (Hobart: The Publishers Pty Ltd., 1985).

Fornasiero, Jean, 'Of Rivalry and Reputation: Nicolas Baudin and Matthew Flinders' in Serge M. Rivière and Kumari R. Issur, eds., *Baudin-Flinders dans L'Océan Indien: Voyages, Découvertes, Rencontre: Travels, Discoveries, Encounter* (Paris: L'Harmattan, 2006), pp. 157–77.

Fornasiero, Jean, 'Deux observateurs de l'homme aux antipodes: Nicolas Baudin et François Péron' in M. Jangoux, ed., *Portés par l'air du temps: les voyages du Capitaine Baudin, special issue of Etudes sur le 18ème siècle*, 38 (Brussels: Editions de l'Univérsité de Bruxelles, 2010), pp. 157–70.

Fornasiero, Jean, 'Framing New Holland or Framing a Narrative? A Representation of Sydney According to Charles-Alexandre Lesueur' in Natalie Edwards, Ben McCann and Peter Poiana, eds., *Framing French Culture* (Adelaide: University of Adelaide Press, 2015), pp. 81–102.

Fornasiero, Jean and West-Sooby, John, 'Taming the Unknown: Representation of Terra Australis by the Baudin Expedition 1801–1803' in Anne Chittleborough, Gillian Dooley, Brenda Glover and Rick Hosking, eds., *Alas for the Pelicans! Flinders, Baudin and Beyond: Essays and Poems* (Kent Town, SA: Wakefield Press, 2002), pp. 59–80.

Fornasiero, Jean and West-Sooby, John, 'A Cordial Encounter? The Meeting of Matthew Flinders and Nicolas Baudin' in Ian Coller, Helen Davies and Julie Kalman, eds., *French History and Civilization: Papers from the George Rudé Seminar Volume 1 2005* (Melbourne: Print and Design Centre: University of Melbourne, 2005), pp. 53–61.

Fornasiero, Jean and West-Sooby, John, 'The Acquisitive Eye? French Observations in the Pacific from Bougainville to Baudin' in John West-Sooby, ed., *Discovery and Empire: The French in the South Seas* (Adelaide: University of Adelaide Press, 2009), pp. 69–98.

Fornasiero, Jean and West-Sooby, John, 'Doing It by the Book: Breaking the Reputation of Nicolas Baudin' in Jean Fornasiero and Colette Mrowa-Hopkins, eds., *Explorations and Encounters in French* (Adelaide: University of Adelaide Press, 2010), pp. 135–64.

Fornasiero, Jean and West-Sooby, John, 'Naming and Shaming: The Baudin Expedition and the Politics of Nomenclature in the Terres Australes' in Anne M. Scott, Alfred Hiatt, Claire McIlroy and Christopher Wortham, eds., *European Perceptions of Terra Australis* (London: Ashgate, 2011), pp. 141–58.

Fornasiero, Jean and West-Sooby, John, 'Cartography as Narrative: The Maps of the Baudin Expedition' in Rupert Gerritsen, Robert King and Andrew Eliason, eds., *The Freycinet Map of 1811: Proceedings of the Symposium Commemorating the 200th*

Anniversary of the Publication of the First Map of Australia (Canberra: Australia on the Map Division of the Australasian Hydrographic Society, 2012), pp. 20–32.

Fornasiero, Jean and West-Sooby, John, 'The Narrative Interruptions of Science: The Baudin Expedition to Australia (1800–1804),' *Forum for Modern Language Studies*, 49/4 (2013), pp. 457–71.

Fornasiero, Jean and West-Sooby, John, 'The Baudin Expedition: Glory, Disgrace and Redemption' in Jean Fornasiero, Lindl Lawton and John West-Sooby, eds., *The Art of Science: Nicolas Baudin's Voyagers 1800–1804* (Adelaide: Wakefield Press, 2016), pp. 35–49.

Fornasiero, Jean and West-Sooby, John, 'Voyages et déplacements des savoirs. Les expéditions de Nicolas Baudin entre Révolution et Empire,' *Annales Historique de la Révolution Française*, no. 385 (2016), pp. 23–46.

Fornasiero, Jean and West-Sooby, John, 'The French Revolution and the Politics of Sea Voyaging,' *The French Australian Review*, 62 (2017), pp. 3–18.

Fornasiero, Jean and West-Sooby, John, 'A Contested Coast? Revisiting the Baudin-Flinders Encounter of April 1802' in Carolyn Collins and Paul Sendziuk, eds., *Foundational Fictions in South Australian History* (Adelaide: Wakefield Press, 2018), pp. 13–27, 199–202.

Fornasiero, Jean, Monteath, Peter and West-Sooby, John, *Encountering Terra Australis: The Australian Voyages of Nicolas Baudin and Matthew Flinders*, rev. edn. (Kent Town, SA: Wakefield Press, 2010).

Fornasiero, Jean, Lawton, Lindl and West-Sooby, John, 'Unlocking Mysteries: Charting and Naming the Australian Coasts' in Jean Fornasiero, Lindl Lawton and John West-Sooby, eds., *The Art of Science: Nicolas Baudin's Voyagers 1800–1804* (Adelaide: Wakefield Press, 2016), pp. 102–22.

Forsyth, Elliott, 'French Exploration in the Pacific in the Eighteenth Century' in John Hardy and Alan Frost, eds., *Studies from Terra Australis to Australis* (Canberra: Highland Press in association with the Australian Academy of the Humanities, 1989), pp. 93–7.

Forsyth, Elliott, 'The Australian Aborigines as Seen by the Artists of the Baudin Expedition of 1800–1804' in Maurice Blackman, ed., *Australian Aborigines and the French* (Kensington, NSW: University of New South Wales Press, 1990), pp. 111–33.

Forsyth, John, 'The Visit of the Yacht Grootenbroeck to the Coast of the South-land in 1631,' *Journal and Proceedings of the Western Australian Historical Society*, V/1 (1955), pp. 17–26.

Foster, William, 'An Early Chart of Tasmania,' *The Geographical Journal*, 37/5 (1911), pp. 550–1.

Fowler, Thomas W., 'Captain Cook's Australian Landfall,' *Victorian Geographical Journal*, 25 (1907), pp. 7–12.

Frost, Alan, 'Science for Political Purposes: European Explorations of the Pacific Ocean, 1764–1806' in Roy MacLeod and Philip H. Rehbock, eds., *Nature in Its Greatest*

Extent: Western Science in the Pacific (Honolulu: University of Hawaii Press, 1988), pp. 27–44.

Frost, Alan, *The Voyage of the Endeavour: Captain Cook and the Discovery of the Pacific* (St Leonards, NSW: Allen & Unwin, 1998).

Frost, Alan, *The Global Reach of Empire: Britain's Maritime Expansion in the Indian and Pacific Oceans, 1764–1815* (Carlton, VIC: The Miegunyah Press, 2003).

Frost, Alan, 'From the Hills of Provence to the Coast of Van Diemen's Land: The Expedition of Antoine-Raymond-Joseph Bruny d'Entrecasteaux, 1791–1793/4' in John Mulvaney and Hugh Tyndale-Biscoe, eds., *Rediscovering Recherche Bay* (Canberra: National Academies Forum, 2007), pp. 9–16.

Frost, Alan, *Mutiny, Mayhem, Mythology: Bounty's Enigmatic Voyage* (Sydney: Sydney University Press, 2018).

Fry, Howard T., *Alexander Dalrymple (1737–1808) and the Expansion of British Trade* (Toronto: University of Toronto Press for the Royal Commonwealth Society, 1970).

Furber, Holden, *Rival Empires of Trade in the Orient, 1600–1800* (Minneapolis, MN: University of Minnesota Press, 1976).

Gaastra, Femme S., 'The Dutch East India Company: A Reluctant Discoverer,' *The Great Circle*, 19 (1997), pp. 109–23.

Galloway, D. J., 'Labillardiere's Tasmanian Lichens,' *Papers of the Proceedings of the Royal Society of Tasmania*, 122/2 (1988), pp. 97–108.

Galloway, D. J. and Groves, E. W., 'Archibald Menzies MD, FLS (1754–1842), Aspects of His Life, Travels and Collections,' *Archives of Natural History*, 14/1 (1987), pp. 3–43.

Garagnon, Jean, 'French Imaginary Voyages to the Austral Lands in the Seventeenth and Eighteenth Centuries' in *Australia and the European Imagination: Papers from a Conference Held at the Humanities Research Centre, Australian National University*, May 1981 (Canberra: Australian National University, 1982), pp. 87–107.

Garran, J. C., 'William Wright Bampton and the Australian Merino,' *Journal of the Royal Australian Historical Society* 58/1 (1972), pp. 1–12.

Garvey, Robert, *To Build a Ship: The VOC Replica Ship Duyfken* (Crawley, WA: University of Western Australia Press, 2001).

Gascoigne, John, 'Joseph Banks and the Expansion of Empire' in Margarette Lincoln, ed., *Science and Exploration: European Voyages to the Southern Oceans in the Eighteenth Century* (Woodbridge: The Boydell Press, 1998), pp. 39–51.

Gascoigne, John, 'Motives for European Exploration of the Pacific in the Age of Enlightenment,' *Pacific Science*, 54/3 (2000), pp. 227–37.

Gascoigne, John, *Captain Cook: Voyager between Worlds* (London: Hambledon Continuum, 2007).

Gascoigne, John, 'The Globe Encompassed: France and Pacific Convergences in the Age of Enlightenment' in John West-Sooby, ed., *Discovery and Empire: The French in the South Seas* (Adelaide: University of Adelaide Press, 2009), pp. 17–40.

Gascoigne, John, *Encountering the Pacific in the Age of Enlightenment* (Cambridge: Cambridge University Press, 2014).

Geeson, N. T. and Sexton, R. T., 'H.M. Sloop *Investigator*,' *The Mariner's Mirror*, 56/3 (1970), pp. 275–98.

George, Alex, 'William Dampier as a Natural Historian,' *The Great Circle*, 37/1 (2016), pp. 36–52.

George, Alex S., *William Dampier in New Holland: Australia's First Natural Historian* (Hawthorn, VIC: Bloomings Books, 1999).

Gerritsen, Rupert, 'The First Naval Confrontations in Australian Waters – in 1629?' *Journal of Australian Naval History*, 9/1 (2012), pp. 110–19.

Gerritsen, Rupert, 'A Note on "Australia" or "Austrialia",' *The Globe*, 72 (2013), pp. 23–30.

Gerritsen, Rupert, 'Getting the Strait Facts Straight,' *The Globe*, 72 (2013), pp. 11–21.

Gerritsen, Rupert, 'The Arrival of the *Immenhorn*: Insights into a Little-Known Voyage to the West Coast of Australia in 1659,' *The Great Circle*, 34/1 (2014), pp. 39–48.

Gerritsen, Rupert and Reynders, Peter, 'The Freycinet Map of 1811: The First Full Map of Australia?' *The Globe*, 72 (2013), pp. 1–10.

Gesner, Peter, 'HMS Pandora Project – A Report on Stage 1: Five Seasons of Excavation,' *Memoirs of the Queensland Museum, Cultural Heritage Series*, 2/1 (2000), pp. 1–52.

Gesner, Peter, 'Pandora Project Stage 2: Four More Seasons of Excavation at the Pandora Historic Shipwreck,' *Memoirs of the Queensland Museum/ Culture*, 9 (2016), pp. 23–46.

Gibbs, Martin and McPhee, Ewen, 'The Raine Island Entrance: Wreck Traps and the Search for a Safe Way through the Great Barrier Reef,' *The Great Circle*, 26/2 (2004), pp. 24–54.

Gill, Anton, *The Devil's Mariner: A Life of William Dampier, Pirate and Explorer, 1651–1715* (London: Michael Joseph, 1997).

Gilmartin, Patricia, 'The Austral Continent on 16th-Century Maps: An Iconological Interpretation,' *Cartographica*, 21/4 (1984), pp. 38–52.

Godard, Philippe, *The First and Last Voyage of the Batavia* (Perth: Abrolhos Publishing, 1993).

Godard, Philippe, 'The Saint Aloüarn Discoveries,' *Quarterly Newsletter: The Australian Association for Maritime History*, 77 (1999), pp. 8–9.

Godard, Philippe, de Kerros, Tugdual, Baxter, Sue, Margot, Odette and Stanbury, Myra, *1772 – The French Annexation of New Holland – The Tale of Louis de Saint Aloüarn* (Fremantle: Western Australian Maritime Museum, 2009).

Godwin, George *Vancouver: A Life 1757–1798* (Vancouver: D. Appleton, 1931).

Gooch, Ruth, 'Puzzling over the Early Flinders Charts,' *Victorian Historical Journal*, 78/1 (2007), pp. 5–22.

Gooding, Mel, Mabberley, David and Studholme, Joe, *Joseph Banks' Florilegium: Botanical Treasures from Cook's First Voyage* (London: Thames & Hudson, 2017).

Goodman, Jordan, 'Making Imperial Space: Settlement, Surveying and Trade in Northern Australia in the Nineteenth Century' in David Killingray, Margarette Lincoln and Nigel Rigby, eds., *Maritime Empires: British Imperial Maritime Trade in the Nineteenth Century* (Woodbridge: The Boydell Press, 2004), pp. 128–41.

Goodman, Jordan, *The Rattlesnake: A Voyage of Discovery to the Coral Sea* (London: Faber and Faber, 2005).

Gough, Barry, 'Pacific Exploration in the 1780s and 1790s' in John Hardy and Alan Frost, eds., *Studies from Terra Australis to Australia* (Canberra: Highland Press in association with the Australian Academy of the Humanities, 1989), pp. 99–107, 254–5.

Graham, Gerald S., *Great Britain in the Indian Ocean: A Study of Maritime Enterprise, 1810–1850* (Oxford: Oxford University Press, 1967).

Grant, Claudia, 'Revolution and the Noble Savage: The Observations of La Billardière' in Maurice Blackman, ed., *Australian Aborigines and the French* (Kensington: University of New South Wales Press, 1990), pp. 81–97.

Gray, Howard, *Spice at Any Price: The Life and Times of Frederick de Houtman, 1571–1627* (Geraldton: Westralian Books, 2019).

Green, Jeremy, 'The Dutch Down Under: Sailing Blunders' in Nonja Peters, ed., *The Dutch Down Under 1606–2006* (Crawley, WA: University of Western Australia Press, 2006), pp. 56–71.

Green, Jeremy, 'Proof of the Daring Spirit of His Ancestors' in *Mapping Our World: Terra Australis to Australia* (Canberra: National Library of Australia, 2013), p. 161.

Green, J. N., 'The VOC Ship *Batavia* Wrecked in 1629 on the Houtman Abrolhos, Western Australia,' *International Journal of Nautical Archaeology*, 4/1 (1975), pp. 43–63.

Green, J. N., 'The Loss of the Verenigde Oostindische Compagnie Jacht VERGULDE DRAECK, Western Australia 1656,' *British Archaeological Reports Supplementary Series* 36/1 (1977), pp. 1–60.

Green, J. N., 'The Carronade Island Guns and Australia's Early Visitors,' *The Great Circle*, 4/2 (1982), pp. 73–83.

Green, J. N., 'The Survey and Identification of the English East India Company Ship, Trial (1622),' *International Journal of Nautical Archaeology*, 15/3 (1986), pp. 195–204.

Green, J. N., 'The AVOC Retourschip *Batavia*, Wrecked Western Australia, 1629: An Excavation Report and Catalogue of Artefacts,' *British Archaeological Reports International Series* (489) (1989).

Groves, E. W., 'Archibald Menzies's Visit to King George Sound, Western Australia, September–October 1791,' *Archives of Natural History*, 40/1 (2013), pp. 139–48.

Gurney, Alan, *Below the Convergence: Voyages towards Antarctica, 1699–1839* (New York: W. W. Norton, 1997).

Hallam, Sylvia J., *Fire and Hearth: A Study of Aboriginal Usage and European Usurpation in South-Western Australia* (Canberra: Australian Institute of Aboriginal Affairs, 1975).

Harrison, Carol E., 'Projections of the Revolutionary Nation: French Expeditions in the Pacific, 1791–1803' in Carol E. Harrison and Ann Johnson, eds., *National Identity: The Role of Science and Technology* (Chicago, IL: University of Chicago Press, 2009), pp. 33–52.

Hasenohr, G., 'Health Factors as They Affected the Attitudes and Decisions on the Voyage of *Le Géographe*,' *South Australian Geographical Journal*, 99 (2000), pp. 16–19.

Heath, Byron, *Discovering the Great South Land* (Dural, NSW: Rosenberg Publishing, 2005).

Heeres, J. E., *The Part Borne by the Dutch in the Discovery of Australia 1606–1765* (London: Luzac & Co., 1899).

Helling, William P., 'Redistributing the Blame: Baudin's Voyage to the Australian Seas,' *The Great Circle*, 15/2 (1993), pp. 107–27.

Henderson, Graeme, *Swallowed by the Sea: The Story of Australia's Shipwrecks* (Canberra: NLA Publishing, 2016).

Henderson, James, *Marooned* (Perth: St George Books, 1982).

Henderson, James, *Sent Forth a Dove: Discovery of the Duyfken* (Nedlands, WA: University of Western Australia Press, 1999).

Henderson, James A., *Phantoms of the Tryall: A Documented Account of Australia's First Shipwreck, the East India Company's Vessel Tryall in 1622 off the Monte Bello Islands in Western Australia's North-West* (Perth: St George, 1993).

Henderson, R. J., 'Plants of Australia' in D. J. Carr, ed., *Sydney Parkinson: Artist of Cook's Endeavour Voyage* (London and Canberra: Croom Helm Limited, 1983), pp. 128–77.

Heniger, Johannes, 'Dutch Contributions to the Study of Exotic Natural History in the Seventeenth and Eighteenth Centuries' in William Eisler and Bernard Smith, eds., *Terra Australis: The Furthest Shore* (Sydney: International Cultural Corporation of Australia, 1988), pp. 59–66.

Hervé, R., 'Australia: In French Geographical Documents of the Renaissance,' *Journal and Proceedings of the Royal Australian Historical Society*, 41/1 (1956), pp. 23–38.

Hewitt, John, 'Jean Mallard's World Map (ca. 1538–39),' *The Globe*, 79 (2016), pp. 1–12.

Hewitt, John, 'Beyond Dieppe,' *The Globe*, 86 (2019), pp. 11–18.

Hiatt, Alfred, *Terra Incognita: Mapping the Antipodes before 1600* (London: The British Library, 2008).

Hiatt, Alfred, '*Terra Australis* and the Idea of the Antipodes' in Anne M. Scott, Alfred Hiatt, Claire McIlroy and Christopher Wortham, eds., *European Perceptions of Terra Australis* (Farnham: Ashgate, 2012), pp. 9–43.

Hilder, Brett, 'The First Navigation of Torres Strait,' *Journal of Navigation*, 30/3 (1977), pp. 459–66.

Hilder, Brett, *The Voyage of Torres: The Discovery of the Coastline of New Guinea and Torres Strait by Captain Luis Baéz de Torres in 1606* (St Lucia, QLD: University of Queensland Press, 1980).

Hirst, Warwick, *Upon a Painted Ocean: Sir Oswald Brierly in the Picture Gallery, State Library of New South Wales* (Sydney: State Library of New South Wales, 2004).

Høgenhoff, Carsten Berg, *Sweers Islands Unveiled: Details from Abel Tasman and Matthew Flinders' Explorations of Australia* (Oslo: Høgenhoff Forlag, 2006).

Hooker, Brian N., 'Two Set of Tasman Longitudes in Seventeenth and Eighteenth Century Maps,' *Geographical Journal*, 156/1 (1990), pp. 23–30.

Hooker, Brian N., 'New Light on the Origin of the Tasman-Bonaparte Map,' *The Globe*, 78 (2015), pp. 1–8.

Hooker, Brian N., 'Towards the Identification of the Terrestrial Globe Carried on the *Heemskerck* by Abel Tasman in 1642–43,' *The Globe*, 79/1 (2016), pp. 31–7.

Hordern, Marsden, *Mariners Are Warned! John Lort Stokes and H.M.S. Beagle in Australia 1837–1843* (Melbourne: The Miegunyah Press, 1989).

Hordern, Marsden, *King of the Australian Coast: The Work of Phillip Parker King in the Mermaid and Bathurst 1817–1822* (Melbourne: The Miegunyah Press, 1997).

Hordern, Marsden, 'John Septimus Roe, 1797–1878: Naval Officer, Cartographer and Explorer,' *Journal of Australian Naval History*, 8/2 (2011), pp. 51–65.

Horner, Frank, *The French Reconnaissance: Baudin in Australia 1801–1803* (Melbourne: Melbourne University Press, 1987).

Horner, Frank, 'Anthropology and the Baudin Expedition, 1800–1804' in Maurice Blackman, ed., *Australian Aborigines and the French* (Kensington, NSW: University of New South Wales Press, 1990), pp. 37–46.

Horner, Frank, *Looking for La Pérouse: D'Entrecasteaux in Australia and the South Pacific 1792–1793* (Carlton, VIC: The Miegunyah Press, 1995).

Hoving, Ab and Emke, Cor, *The Ships of Abel Tasman* (Hilversum: Uitgeverij Verloren, 2000).

Howse, Derek and Sanderson, Michael, *The Sea Chart* (Newton Abbot: David & Charles, 1973).

Hughes, Miranda, 'The Dynamometer and the Diemenese' in H. E. Le Grand, ed., *Experimental Inquiries: Historical, Philosophical and Social Studies of Experimentation in Science* (Dordrecht: Kluwer Academic Publishers, 1990), pp. 87–98.

Hughes, Miranda J. 'Philosophical Travellers at the Ends of the Earth: Baudin, Péron and the Tasmanians' in R. W. Horne, ed., *Australian Science in the Making* (Cambridge: Cambridge University Press, 1988), pp. 23–45.

Hughes, Miranda J., 'Tall Tales or True Stories? Baudin, Péron, and the Tasmanians, 1802' in Roy McLeod and Philip F. Rehbock, eds., *Nature in Its Greatest Extent: Western Science in the Pacific* (Honolulu: University of Hawaii Press, 1988), pp. 65–86.

Hunt, Susan, 'Southern Discomfort' in Susan Hunt, Martin Terry and Nicholas Thomas, *Lure of the Southern Seas: The Voyages of Dumont D'Urville 1826–1840* (Sydney: Historic Houses of New South Wales Trust, 2002), pp. 11–19.

Ingleton, Geoffrey C., *Charting a Continent: A Brief Memoir on the History of Marine Exploration and Hydrographical Surveying in Australian Waters, from the Discoveries of Captain James Cook to the War Activities of the Royal Australian Navy* (Sydney: Angus & Robertson, 1944).

Ingleton, Geoffrey C., '"The First Navigation of Torres Strait": Some Comments,' *Journal of Navigation*, 31/2 (1978), pp. 232–43.

Ingleton, Geoffrey C., 'Flinders as Cartographer' in R. W. Russell, ed., *Matthew Flinders – The Ifs of History* (Bedford Park, SA: University Relations Unit, Flinders University, 1979), pp. 63–80.

Ingleton, Geoffrey C., *Matthew Flinders: Navigator and Chartmaker* (Guildford: Genesis Publications in association with Hedley Australia, 1986).

Jack-Hinton, C., *The Search for the Islands of Solomon* (Oxford: The Clarendon Press, 1969).

Jangoux, Michel, 'Les Zoologistes et Botanistes qui Accompagnerent le Capitaine Baudin aux Terres Australes,' *Australian Journal of French Studies*, 41/2 (2004), pp. 55–78.

Jangoux, Michel, 'La Première relâche du *Naturaliste* au Port Jackson (26 April–18 May 1802): le témoignage du capitaine Hamelin,' *Australian Journal of French Studies*, 41/2 (2004), pp. 126–51.

Jangoux, Michel, 'Nicolas Baudin par son contemporain André-Pierre Ledru: une autre perception du capitaine naturaliste' in Sophie Linon-Chipon and Daniela Vaj, eds., *Relations savants, voyages et discours scientifiques* (Paris: Presses de l'Université de Paris-Sorbonne, 2006), pp. 107–20.

Jennings, William, 'Self and Other: Gonneville's Encounters in Terra Australis and Brazil,' *Viator: Medieval and Renaissance Studies*, 39/2 (2008), pp. 215–26.

Jennings, William, 'Gonneville's *Terra Australis*: Too Good to Be True?' *Australian Journal of French Studies*, 50/1 (2013), pp. 75–86.

Jack, Robert Logan, *Northmost Australia: Three Centuries of Exploration, Discovery, and Adventure in and around the Cape York Peninsula, Queensland*, 2 vols. (London: Simpkin, Marshall, Hamilton, Kent & Co., 1921).

Johnson, Clare, 'François Péron and the Passion for Objects' in Anne Chittleborough, Gillian Dooley, Brenda Glover and Rick Hosking, eds., *Alas, for the Pelicans! Flinders, Baudin & Beyond* (Kent Town, SA: Wakefield Press, 2003), pp. 31–44.

Johnson, Richard, *The Search for the Inland Sea: John Oxley, Explorer, 1783–1828* (Melbourne: Melbourne University Press, 2001).

Jones, Diana S., 'A Lasting Legacy: The Baudin Expedition in Australian Waters (1801–1803),' *The Great Circle*, 39/2 (2017), pp. 56–85.

Jones, Rhys, 'Images of Natural Man' in Jacqueline Bonnemains, Elliott Forsyth and Bernard Smith, eds., *Baudin in Australian Waters: The Artwork of the French Voyage of Discovery to the Southern Lands, 1801–1804* (Melbourne: Oxford University Press, 1988), pp. 35–64.

Joppien, Rüdiger and Chambers, Neil, 'The Scholarly Library and Collections of Knowledge of Sir Joseph Banks' in Giles Mandelbrote and Barry Taylor, eds., *Libraries within the Library: The Origins of the British Library's Printed Collections* (London: The British Library, 2009), pp. 222–43.

Jouanin, C., 'Les emeus de l'expédition Baudin,' *L'Oiseau et la Revue Française d'Ornithologie*, 29 (1959), pp. 168–201.

Jouanin, C., 'Nicolas Baudin chargé de réunir une collection pour la future impératrice Joséphine,' *Australian Journal of French Studies*, XLI/2 (2004), pp. 43–54.

Kantvilas, Gintaras, 'Labillardière and the Beginnings of Botanical Exploration in Tasmania' in John Mulvaney and Hugh Tyndale-Biscoe, eds., *Rediscovering Recherche Bay* (Canberra: National Academies Forum, 2007), pp. 35–44.

Kaye, Stuart B., *The Torres Strait* (The Hague: M. Nijhoff, 1997).

Keighery, Greg and Gibson, Neil, 'The Flinders Expedition in Western Australia: Robert Brown, the Plants and Their Influence on W.A. Botany' in Juliet Wege, Alex George, Jan Gathe, Kris Lemson and Kath Napier, eds., *Matthew Flinders and His Scientific Gentlemen: The Expedition of HMS Investigator to Australia, 1801–1805* (Welshpool, WA: Western Australian Museum, 2005), pp. 106–13.

Kemp, John, 'William Dampier: Navigator Extraordinary,' *Journal of Navigation*, 67/4 (2014), pp. 545–67.

Ketelaar, Eric, 'Exploration of the Archived World: From de Vlamingh's Plate to Digital Realities,' *Archives and Manuscripts*, 36/2 (2008), pp. 13–33.

King, Hilary, 'The Marine Chronometers of the Baudin Expedition to Australia, 1800–1804,' *Antiquarian Horology*, 23/6 (1997), pp. 508–21.

King, Robert J., 'Terra Australis, New Holland and New South Wales: The Treaty of Tordesillas and Australia,' *The Globe*, 47 (1998), pp. 35–55.

King, Robert J., 'What Brought Lapérouse to Botany Bay?' *Journal of the Royal Australian Historical Society*, 85/2 (1999), pp. 140–7.

King, Robert J., 'William Bolts and the Austrian Origins of the Lapérouse Expedition,' *Terrae Incognitae*, 40 (2008), pp. 1–28.

King, Robert J., 'The Jagiellonian Globe, a Key to the Puzzle of Jave la Grande,' *The Globe*, 62 (2009), pp. 1–50.

King, Robert J., 'Regio Patalis: Australia on the Map in 1531? (Early South Sea Voyages, or merely Cartographic Evolution?)' *The Portolan*, 82 (2011), pp. 8–17.

King, Robert J., 'Terra Australis Not Yet Known' and "The Mercator Projection"' in *Mapping Our World: Terra Incognita to Australia* (Canberra: National Library of Australia, 2013), pp. 83, 90.

King, Robert J., 'Havre de Sylla on Jave La Grande,' *Terrae Incognitae*, 45/1 (2013), pp. 30–61.

King, Robert J., 'Dirk Hartog Lands on Beach, the Gold-Bearing Province,' *The Globe*, 77 (2015), pp. 12–52.

King, Robert J., 'From Beach to Western Australia: Dirk Hartog and the Transition from Speculative to Actual Geography,' *The Great Circle*, 38/1 (2016), pp. 45–71.

King, Robert J., 'Marco Polo's Java and Locach on Mercator's World Maps of 1538 and 1569, and Globe of 1541,' *The Globe*, 81 (2017), pp. 41–61.

King, Robert J., 'Henri Peyroux de la Coudrenière and His Plan for a Colony in Van Diemen's Land,' *Map Matters*, 31 (2017), pp. 2–6.

King, Robert J., 'Finding Marco Polo's Locach,' *Terrae Incognitae*, 50/1 (2018), pp. 35–52.

King, Robert J., 'Cartographic Drift: Pulo Condor and the Ysles de Magna and Ye de Saill on the Dieppe Maps,' *The Globe*, 87 (2020), pp. 1–21.

Kingston, Ralph, 'A Not So Pacific Voyage: The "Floating Laboratory" of Nicolas Baudin,' *Endeavour*, 31/4 (2007), pp. 145–51.

Kinnear, N. B., 'Robert Brown's Zoological Collections Made during the Voyage of the "Investigator",' *Proceedings of the Linnean Society of London*, 144 (1931), pp. 36–8.

Knight, T. M., 'From Terra Incognita to New Holland,' *Cartography*, 6/2 (1967), pp. 82–9.

Kociumbas, Jan, *The Oxford History of Australia: Volume 2: Possessions, 1770–1860* (Oxford: Oxford University Press, 1992).

Konishi, Shino, 'Depicting Sexuality: A Case Study of the Baudin Expedition's Aboriginal Ethnography', *Australian Journal of French Studies*, 41/2 (2004), pp. 98–116.

Konishi, Shino, 'François Péron: An Unrequited Romance' in Ingereth Macfarlane and Mark Hannah, eds., *Transgressions: Critical Australian Indigenous Histories* (Canberra: ANU Press, 2007), pp. 1–18.

Konishi, Shino, 'Inhabited by a Race of Formidable Giants: French Explorers, Aborigines, and the Endurance of the Fantastic in the Great South Land, 1803', *Australian Humanities Review*, 44 (2008), pp. 7–22.

Konishi, Shino, *The Aboriginal Male in the Enlightenment World* (London: Pickering & Chatto, 2012).

Konishi, Shino, 'François Péron: Meditation on Death, Humanity and Savage Society' in Alexander Cook, Ned Curthoys and Shino Konishi, eds., *Representing Humanity in the Age of Enlightenment* (London: Pickering & Chatto, 2013), pp. 109–21, 209–11.

Konishi, Shino, 'Discovering the Savage Senses: French and British Explorers' Encounters with Aboriginal People' in John West-Sooby, ed., *Discovery and Empire: The French in the South Seas* (Adelaide: University of Adelaide Press, 2013), pp. 99–140.

Konishi, Shino, 'Early Encounters in Aboriginal Place: The Role of Emotions in French Readings of Indigenous Sites', *Australian Aboriginal Studies*, issue 2 (2015), pp. 12–23.

Lack, Clem, 'The Achievements of James Cook: Navigator, Humanist, and Anthropologist', *Journal of the Royal Historical Society of Queensland*, 9/1 (1970), pp. 7–77.

Lamb, Jonathan, 'Inchoate Possession: How Captain Kerguelen Claimed an Island', *Journal for Maritime Research*, 7/1 (2005), pp. 1–15.

Lee, Ida, 'Captain John Hayes – An Early Tasmanian Explorer', *The Tasmanian Mail* (11 December 1909), pp. 45–7.

Lee, Ida, *Captain Bligh's Second Voyage to the South Sea* (London: Longmans, Green, 1920).

Lee, Ida, *Early Explorers in Australia: From the Log-Books and Journals, Including the Diary of Allan Cunningham, Botanist, from March 1, 1817 to November 19, 1818* (London: Methuen & Co., 1925).

Lee, Ida, 'The First Sighting of Australia by the English', *Journal and Proceedings of the Royal Australian Historical Society*, 20/5 (1934), pp. 273–80.

Leupe, P. A., *De Reizen der Nederlanders naar het Zuidland of Nieuw-Holland in de 17e en 18e eeuw* (Amsterdam: G. Hulst van Keulen, 1868).

Lipscombe, Trevor, 'Lt. James Cook on the coast of Victoria 1770', *Victorian Historical Journal*, 89/1 (2018), pp. 137–51.

Lipscombe, Trevor, 'Cook Conspiracy at Point Hicks?' *The Globe*, 87 (2020), pp. 51–6.

Lipscombe, Trevor, 'Lt. James Cook's Misplaced Landmarks of the Coasts of Victoria and NSW', *The Globe*, 87 (2020), pp. 33–7.

Lipscombe, Trevor J., 'The Point Hicks Controversy – The Clouded Facts,' *Victorian Historical Journal*, 85 (2014), pp. 232–53.

Lipscombe, Trevor J., 'Cook's Cape Dromedary – Is It Montague Island?' and 'Is Cook's Cape Howe Really Telegraph Point?' *Map Matters*, 32 (2017), pp. 2–11.

Llewellyn, Patrick, 'Baudin's Chronometer' in Jean Fornasiero, Lindl Lawton and John West-Sooby, eds., *The Art of Science: Nicolas Baudin's Voyagers 1800–1804* (Adelaide: Wakefield Press, 2016), p. 115

Lodewyckx, 'The Name of Australia: Its Origin and Early Use,' *Victorian Historical Magazine*, XIII/3 (1929), pp. 99–115.

Lubbock, Adelaide, *Owen Stanley, R.N. 1811–1850, Captain of the 'Rattlesnake'* (Melbourne: William Heinemann, 1968).

Lysaght, A. M., 'Banks's Artists and His *Endeavour* Collections,' *The British Museum Yearbook*, 3 (London: British Museum Publications, 1979), pp. 9–80.

Mabberley, D. J., *Jupiter Botanicus: Robert Brown of the British Museum* (London: British Museum, Natural History, 1985).

Mabberley, D. J., 'The Legacy of Flinders' Naturalist [the Life and Work of Pioneering Botanist Robert Brown]' *Australian Geographic*, 60 (2000), pp. 48–63.

Mack, James D., *Matthew Flinders 1774–1814* (Melbourne: University of Melbourne Press, 1966).

Mackay, David, 'In the Shadow of Cook: The Ambition of Matthew Flinders' in John Hardy and Alan Frost, eds., *European Voyaging towards Australia* (Canberra: Australian Academy of the Humanities, 1990), pp. 99–111.

Mackay, David, 'The Burden of Terra Australis: Experiences of Real and Imagined Lands' in Robin Fisher and Hugh Johnston, eds., *From Maps to Metaphors: The Pacific World of George Vancouver* (Vancouver: University of British Columbia Press, 1993), pp. 263–89, 336–7.

Macknight, Campbell, 'A Useless Discovery: Australia and Its People in the Eyes of Others from Tasman to Cook,' *The Globe*, 61 (2008), pp. 1–10.

Macknight, C. C., *The Voyage to Marege': Macassan Trepangers in Northern Australia* (Melbourne: Melbourne University Press, 1976).

Macknight, C. C., 'On the Non-"discovery" of "Australia",' *Canberra Historical Journal*, 12 (1983), pp. 34–6.

Maps in Australia: Great Maps in Australia's History from the National Library's Collections (Canberra: National Library of Australia, 2008).

Marchant, Leslie R., 'Bruny D'Entrecasteaux, Joseph-Antoine Raymond (1739–1793)' in Douglas Pike, ed., *Australian Dictionary of Biography*, vol. 1 (Melbourne: Melbourne University Press, 1966), pp. 171–2.

Marchant, Leslie R., 'The Baudin Scientific Mission of Exploration and the French Contribution to the Maritime Discovery of Australia,' *The Globe*, 23 (1985), pp. 11–31.

Marchant, Leslie R., 'William Dampier's Significance in Australia's Maritime Discovery,' *Early Days: Journal and Proceedings of the Royal Western Australian Historical Society*, 9/4 (1986), pp. 54–9.

Marchant, Leslie R., *An Island unto Itself: The Life of William Dampier, Naturalist and Buccaneer* (Perth: Hesperian Press, 1988).

Marchant, Leslie R., 'The French Discovery and Survey of the Legendary North-west Cape and Willem River in Western New Holland,' *Imago Mundi*, 40 (1988), pp. 46–56.

Marchant, Leslie R., 'Hyperion and the Satyrs: French Monarchist and Revolutionary Scientists and Australian Discovery 1791–1795: The Accomplishments of the D'Entrecasteaux Expedition,' *Early Days: Journal of the Royal Western Australian Historical Society*, 11/1 (1995), pp. 11–32.

Marner, Serena K., 'William Dampier and His Botanical Collections' in Howard Morphy and Elizabeth Edwards, eds., *Australia in Oxford* (Oxford: Pitt Rivers Museum, 1988), pp. 1–2.

Marshall, P. J. and Williams, Glyndwr, *The Great Map of Mankind: British Perceptions of the World in the Age of Enlightenment* (London: J. M. Dent and Sons, 1982).

Maude, H. E., 'The Voyage of the Pandora's Tender,' *The Mariner's Mirror*, 50/3 (1964), pp. 217–35.

Mault, A., 'Notes on Charts of the Coast of Tasmania, Obtained from the Hydrographical Department, Paris, and Copied by Permission of the French Government,' *Papers and Proceedings of the Royal Society of Tasmania for 1889* (Hobart: Royal Society of Tasmania, 1890), pp. 107–15.

Mawer, G. A., 'Incognita: The Incredible Shrinking Continent,' *The Globe*, 69 (2011), pp. 41–50.

Mawer, G. A., *Incognita: The Invention and Discovery of Terra Australis* (Melbourne: Australian Scholarly, 2013).

Mawer, G. A., 'The Habitable World' *in Mapping Our World: Terra Incognita to Australia* (Canberra: National Library of Australia, 2013), p. 17.

Mawer, G. A., 'The Mysterious Absence of North West Cape,' *The Globe*, 81 (2016), pp. 105–8.

May, W. E., 'The "Reliance" Log Books of Matthew Flinders,' *Journal and Proceedings of the Royal Australian Historical Society*, 39/5 (1953), pp. 267–74.

Mayer, Wolf, 'The Geological Work of the Baudin Expedition in Australia (1801–1803): The Mineralogists, the Discoveries and the Legacy,' *Earth Sciences History*, 28/2 (2009), pp. 293–324.

McAleer, John and Rigby, Nigel, *Captain Cook and the Pacific: Art, Exploration & Empire* (New Haven: Yale University Press, 2017).

McCalman, Iain, *The Reef: A Passionate History: The Great Barrier Reef from Captain Cook to Climate Change* (New York: Scientific American / Farrar, Straus and Giroux, 2014).

McCarthy, F. D., 'The Cave Paintings of Groote Eylandt and Chasm Island' in C. P. Mountford, ed., *Records of the American-Australian Scientific Expedition to Arnhem Land* (Melbourne: Melbourne University Press, 1960), pp. 297–414.

McCarthy, James, *Monkey Puzzle Man: Archibald Menzies, Plant Hunter* (Dunbeath, Caithness: Whittles Publishing, 2008).

McCarthy, Michael, 'HM Ship *Roebuck* (1690–1701): Global Maritime Heritage?' *International Journal of Nautical Archaeology*, 33/2 (2004), pp. 330–7.

McCarthy, Michael, 'The Dutch on Australian Shores: The *Zuytdorp* Tragedy – An Unfinished Business' in Lindsey Shaw and Wendy Wilkins, eds., *Dutch Connections: 400 Years of Australian-Dutch Maritime Links, 1606–2006* (Sydney: Australian Maritime Museum, 2006), pp. 94–109.

McCarthy, Michael, 'Who Do You Trust? Discrepancies between the "Official and Unofficial" Sources Recording Explorers' Perceptions of Places and Their People' in Anne M. Scott, Alfred Hiatt, Claire McIlroy and Christopher Wortham, eds., *European Perceptions of Terra Australis* (Farnham: Ashgate, 2011), pp. 185–209.

McCarthy, Michael, '300 Years on: The Search for William Dampier and His Elusive Ship,' *The Great Circle*, 37/1 (2015), pp. 1–15.

McHugh, Evan, *1606: An Epic Adventure* (Sydney: University of New South Wales Press, 2006).

McIntyre, K. G., 'Portuguese Discoverers on the Australian Coast,' *Journal of the Royal Historical Society of Victoria*, 45/4 (1974), pp. 201–28.

McIntyre, K. G., *The Secret Discovery of Australia: Portuguese Ventures 250 Years before Captain Cook* (Sydney: Picador, 1982).

McKiggan, Ian, 'The Portuguese Expedition to Bass Strait in A.D. 1522,' *Journal of Australian Studies*, 1 (1977), pp. 2–32, and 'Jave-la-Grande: An Apologia,' ibid., 19 (1986), pp. 96–101.

McMinn, W. G., *Allan Cunningham: Botanist and Explorer* (Melbourne: Melbourne University Press, 1970).

Mellor, Doreen, 'Cook, His Mission and Indigenous Australia' in Michelle Hetherington and Howard Morphy, eds., *Discovering Cook's Collections* (Canberra: National Museum of Australia, 2009), pp. 112–26.

Menzies, Gavin, *1421: The Year China Discovered the World* (London: Bantam Press, 2002).

Mercer, F. R., *Amazing Career: The Story of Western Australia's First Surveyor-General* (Perth: Paterson Brokensha Pty. Ltd., n.d.).

Mitchell, Adrian, *Dampier's Monkey: The South Seas Voyages of William Dampier Including William Dampier's Unpublished Journal* (Kent Town, SA: Wakefield Press, 2010).

Moisés, Leyla Perrone, *Vinte Luas: Viagem de Paulmier Gonneville ao Brasil, 1503–1505* (São Paulo: Companhia das Letras, 1992).

Monteath, Peter, 'Contradictory Encounters: William Westall in Australia' in Anne Chittleborough, Gillian Dooley, Brenda Glover and Rick Hosking, eds., *Alas, for the Pelicans! Flinders, Baudin & Beyond* (Kent Town, SA: Wakefield Press, 2003), pp. 47–56.

Moon, Paul, 'From Tasman to Cook: The Proto-intelligence Phase of New Zealand's Colonisation,' *Journal of Intelligence History*, 18/2 (2019), pp. 253–68.

Moore, David T., 'Robert Brown on H.M.S. Investigator 1801–1805: An Overview of the Natural History Collecting Localities' in Juliet Wege, Alex George, Jan Gathe, Kris Lemson and Kath Napier, eds., *Matthew Flinders and His Scientific Gentlemen: The Expedition of H.M.S. Investigator to Australia 1801–5* (Welshpool, WA: Western Australian Museum, 2005), pp. 49–65.

Morgan, Kenneth, 'Sir Joseph Banks as Patron of the *Investigator* Expedition: Natural History, Geographical Knowledge and Australian Exploration,' *International Journal of Maritime History*, 26/2 (2014), pp. 235–64.

Morgan, Kenneth, 'From Cook to Flinders: The Navigation of Torres Strait,' *International Journal of Maritime History*, 27/1 (2015), pp. 41–60.

Morgan, Kenneth, *Matthew Flinders, Maritime Explorer of Australia* (London: Bloomsbury, 2016).

Morgan, Kenneth, 'A Historical Myth? Matthew Flinders and the Quest for a Strait,' *Australian Historical Studies*, 48/1 (2017), pp. 52–67.

Morgan, Kenneth, 'Finding Longitude: The Investigator expedition,' *International Journal of Maritime History*, 29/4 (2017), pp. 771–87.

Morgan, Kenneth, 'Matthew Flinders and the Charting of Australia's Coasts, 1798–1814,' *Terrae Incognitae*, 50/2 (2018), pp. 115–45.

Morrison-Scott, T. C. S. and Sawyer, F. C., 'The Identity of Captain Cook's Kangaroo,' *Bulletin of the British Museum (Natural History), Zoology*, 1/3 (1950), pp. 43–50.

Moyal, Ann, '*A Bright & Savage Land': Scientists in Colonial Australia* (Sydney: Collins, 1986).

Mulvaney, D. J., *The Prehistory of Australia* (London: Thames & Hudson, 1969).

Murray, Stuart, '"Notwithstanding Our Signs to the Contrary": Textuality and Authority at the Endeavour River, June to August 1771' in Glyndwr Williams, ed., *Captain Cook: Explorations and Reassessments* (Woodbridge: The Boydell Press, 2004), pp. 59–76.

Mutch, T. D., 'The First Discovery of Australia with Account of the Voyage of the Duyfken, and Career of Willem Jansz,' *Journal and Proceedings of the Royal Australian Historical Society*, XXVIII/V (1942), pp. 303–52.

Naish, John M., *The Interwoven Lives of George Vancouver, Archibald Menzies, Joseph Whidbey, and Peter Puget: Exploring the Pacific Northwest Coast* (Lewiston, NY: The Edwin Mellen Press, 1996).

Nicholson, Ian, *Via Torres Strait: A Maritime History of the Torres Strait Route and the Ships' Post Office at Booby Island, Roebuck Society Publications*, 48 (Nambour, QLD: Sunstrip Printers, 1996).

Norst, Marlene, *Ferdinand Bauer: The Australian Natural History Drawings* (London: British Museum [Natural History], 1989).

Norst, Marlene J., 'Recognition and Renaissance: Ferdinand Lucas Bauer 1760–1826,' *Australian Natural History*, 23/4 (1990), pp. 296–305.

Nugent, Maria, *Botany Bay: Where Histories Meet* (Crows Nest, NSW: Allen & Unwin, 2005).

Nugent, Maria, *Captain Cook Was Here* (Cambridge: Cambridge University Press, 2009).

O'Brien, Patty, 'Divine Browns and the Mighty Whiteman: Exotic Primitivism and the Baudin Voyage to Tasmania in 1802', *Journal of Australian Studies*, 23/63 (1999), pp. 13–21.

Orchard, A. E. and Orchard, T. A., *The Botanist and the Judge: Allan Cunningham in Tasmania 1818–1819* (Weston Creek, ACT: privately printed, 2014).

Osborn, T. G. B. and Gardner, C. A., 'Dampier's Australian Plants', *Proceedings of the Linnean Society of London*, 151/2 (1939), pp. 44–50.

Parry, J. H., *The Spanish Seaborne Empire* (London: Hutchinson, 1966).

Parthesius, Robert, 'Encounters of the Third Kind – Dutch Shipping in Asia and the Search for the South Land' in Lindsey Shaw and Wendy Wilkins, eds., *Dutch Connections: 400 Years of Australian-Dutch Maritime Links 1606–2006* (Sydney: Australian Maritime Museum, 2006), pp. 58–71.

Parthesius, Robert, *Dutch Ships in Tropical Waters: The Development of the Dutch East India Company (VOC) Network in Asia, 1595–1660* (Amsterdam: Amsterdam University Press, 2010).

Patton, Maggie, 'Tasman's Journal' in *Mapping Our World: Terra Incognita to Australia* (Canberra: National Library of Australia, 2013), p. 137.

Payne, Anthony, 'The Publication and Readership of Voyage Journals in the Age of Vancouver, 1730–1830' in Stephen Haycox, James Barnett and Caedman Liburd, eds., *Enlightenment and Exploration in the North Pacific 1741–1805* (Seattle: University of Washington Press, 1997), pp. 176–86.

Pearson, Michael, *Great Southern Land: The Maritime Exploration of Terra Australis* (Canberra: Department of the Environment and Heritage, 2005).

Pearson, Michael, '"Nothing Left Undone": The Hydrographic Surveys of Beautemps-Beaupré' in John Mulvaney and Hugh Tyndale-Biscoe, eds., *Rediscovering Recherche Bay* (Canberra: National Academies Forum, 2007), pp. 17–34.

Perera, Suvendrini, *Australia and the Insular Imagination: Beaches, Borders, Boats, and Bodies* (New York: Palgrave Macmillan, 2009).

Perry, T. M., *Australia's First Frontier: The Spread of Settlement in New South Wales, 1788–1829* (Melbourne: Melbourne University Press, 1963).

Perry, T. M., 'Seasons for Exploration. The Second Daniel Brock Memorial Lecture, 1975', *Proceedings of the Royal Geographical Society Australasia, South Australian Branch*, 76 (1975), pp. 51–8.

Perry, T. M., 'Matthew Flinders – The Man' in R. W. Russell, ed., *Matthew Flinders – The Ifs of History* (Bedford Park, SA: University Relations Unit, Flinders University, 1979), pp. 49–62.

Perry, T. M., *The Discovery of Australia: The Charts and Maps of the Navigators and Explorers* (Melbourne: Nelson, 1982).

Perry, T. M., 'Matthew Flinders and the Charting of the Australian Coast', *The Globe*, 23 (1985), pp. 1–10.

Perry, T. M., 'Charts and Views' in Bernard Smith and Alwyne Wheeler, eds., *The Art of the First Fleet and Other Early Australian Drawings* (New Haven: Yale University Press, 1988), pp. 70–108.

Perry, T. M., 'British Charting of Australian Waters' in Michael Richards and Maura O'Connor, eds., *Changing Coastlines: Putting Australia on the World Map 1493–1993* (Canberra: National Library of Australia, 1993), pp. 20–2.

Petrow, Stefan, 'Godfather of Tasmania: Commemorating Abel Tasman 1838 to 2012,' *Journal of Australian Studies*, 38/2 (2014), pp. 157–74.

Pfennigwerth, Stephanie, 'New Creatures Made Known: Some Animal Histories of the Baudin Expedition' in John West-Sooby, ed., *Discovery and Empire* (Adelaide: University of Adelaide Press, 2013), pp. 171–214.

Pinton, W. J., 'Some Mahogany Ship Relics Examined' in B. Potter, ed., *The Mahogany Ship: Relic or Legend? Proceedings of the Second Australian Symposium on the Mahogany Ship* (Warnambool, VIC: Warnambool Institute Press, 1987).

Playford, Phillip, 'The Wreck of the *Zuytdorp*,' *Journal and Proceedings of the Western Australian Historical Society*, 5/5 (1959), pp. 5–41.

Playford, Phillip, *Carpet of Silver: The Wreck of the Zuytdorp* (Crawley, WA: University of Western Australia Press, 1996).

Playford, Phillip, 'Aboriginal and European Discoveries of Australia,' *Early Days: Journal of the Royal Western Australian Historical Society*, 13/1 (2007), pp. 48–61.

Playford, Phillip E., *Voyage of Discovery to Terra Australis: By Willem De Vlamingh, 1696–1697* (Perth: Western Australian Museum, 1998).

Playford, Phillip E., 'Discoveries and Disasters – Early Dutch, French and British Exploration and Shipwrecks on the Coast of Western Australia' in Lindsey Shaw and Wendy Wilkins, eds., *Dutch Connections: 400 Years of Australian-Dutch Maritime Links 1606–2006* (Sydney: Australian Maritime Museum, 2006), pp. 26–39.

Plomley, N. J. B., *The Baudin Expedition and the Tasmanian Aborigines 1802* (Hobart: Blubber Head Press, 1983).

Plomley, N. J. B., 'The French and the Tasmanian Aborigines' in Maurice Blackman, ed., *Australian Aborigines and the French* (Kensington: University of New South Wales Press, 1990), pp. 25–36.

Powell, Alan, *John Stokes and the Men of the Beagle: Discoverers of Port Darwin* (Darwin: Library Services of the Northern Territory, 1986).

Powell, Alan, *Northern Voyagers: Australia's Monsoon Coast in Maritime History* (Melbourne: Australian Scholarly Publishing, 2010).

Preston, Diana and Michael Preston, *A Pirate of Exquisite Mind: The Life of William Dampier: Explorer, Naturalist and Buccaneer* (London: Corgi Books, 2005).

Protos, Alec, *The Road to Botany Bay: The Story of Frenchmans Road Randwick through the Journals of Lapérouse and the First Fleet Writers* (Randwick, NSW: Randwick & District Historical Society, 2000).

Rainaud, Armand, *Le Continent Austral: Hypothèses et Découvertes* (Paris: Armand Colin & Co., 1893).

Ralph, Robert, 'John MacGillivray – His Life and Work,' *Archives of Natural History*, 20/2 (1993), pp. 185–95.

Raven, H. C., 'The Identity of Captain Cook's Kangaroo,' *Journal of Mammalogy*, 20/1 (1939), pp. 50–7.

Reinhartz, Dennis, 'William Dampier and the Wreck of the *Roebuck* off Ascension Island in 1701,' *Terrae Incognitae*, 47/2 (2015), pp. 97–105.

Richard, Hélène, 'L'Expédition de D'Entrecasteaux (1791–1794) et les origins de L'Implantation Anglaise en Tasmanie,' *Revue française d'histoire d'outre-mer*, LXIX/257 (1982), pp. 289–306.

Richard, Hélène, *Le Voyage de Dentrecasteaux à la recherché de Lapérouse*, 2 vols. (Paris: Comité des travaux historiques et scientifiques, 1986).

Richards, Michael and O'Connor, Maura, eds., *Changing Coastlines: Putting Australia on the World Map 1493–1993* (Canberra: National Library of Australia, 1993).

Richards, Rhys, 'The Cruise of the *Kingston* and the *Elligood* in 1800 and the Wreck Found on King Island in 1802,' *The Great Circle*, 13/1 (1991), pp. 35–53.

Richardson, W. A. R., 'Is Java-la-Grande Australia? The Linguistic Evidence Concerning the West Coast,' *The Globe*, 19 (1983), pp. 9–46.

Richardson, W. A. R., 'Java-la-Grande: A Case Study of Place-Name Corruption,' *The Globe*, 22 (1984), pp. 9–32.

Richardson, W. A. R., 'Jave-la-Grande: A Place Name Chart of Its East Coast,' *The Great Circle*, 6/1 (1984), pp. 1–23.

Richardson, W. A. R., 'Mercator's Southern Continent: Its Origins, Influence and Gradual Demise,' *Terrae Incognitae*, 25/1 (1993), pp. 67–98.

Richardson, W. A. R. (Bill), 'Gavin Menzies' Cartographic Fiction: The Case of the Chinese "Discovery" of Australia,' *The Globe*, 56 (2004), pp. 1–11.

Richardson, W. A. R., *Was Australia Charted before 1606? The Jave la Grande Inscriptions* (Canberra: National Library of Australia, 2006).

Richardson, W.A.R. (Bill), 'Terra Australis, Jave la Grande and Australia: Identity Problems and Fiction' in Anne M. Scott, Alfred Hiatt, Claire McIlroy and Christopher Wortham, eds., *European Perceptions of Terra Australis* (Farnham: Ashgate, 2013), pp. 83–109.

Rigby, Nigel, '"The Whole of the Surveying Department Rested on Me": Matthew Flinders, Hydrography and the Navy' in Marc Serge Rivière and Kumari R. Issur, eds., *Baudin-Flinders dans L'Océan: Voyages, Découvertes, Rencontre: Voyages, Discoveries, Encounter* (Paris: L'Harmattan, 2006), pp. 259–70.

Ritchie, G. S., *The Admiralty Chart: British Naval Hydrography in the Nineteenth Century* (London: Hollis & Carter, 1967).

Robert, Willem C. H., *The Explorations, 1696–1697, of Australia by Willem de Vlamingh* (Amsterdam: Philo Press, 1972).

Robson, John, *Captain Cook's World: Maps of the Life and Voyages of James Cook R.N.* (London: Chatham Publishing, 2000).

Robson, Lloyd, *A History of Tasmania: Van Diemen's Land from the Earliest Times to 1855. Volume 1* (Melbourne: Oxford University Press, 1983).

Roe, Margriet, 'Hayes, Sir John (1768–1831)' in Douglas Pike, ed., *Australian Dictionary of Biography* (Melbourne: Melbourne University Press, 1966), I, p. 527.

Roe, Michael, 'New Light on George Bass, Entrepreneur and Intellectual,' *Journal of the Royal Australian Historical Society*, 72/4 (1987), pp. 251–72.

Rose, Deborah Bird, 'The Saga of Captain Cook: Morality in Aboriginal and European law,' *Aboriginal Studies*, 2 (1984), pp. 24–39.

Ross, Michael, 'The Mysterious Eastland Revealed,' *The Globe*, 53 (2002), pp. 1–22.

Roussier, Paul, 'Un projet de colonie française dans le Pacifique à la fin du XVIII siècle,' *Revue du Pacifique*, 6/1 (1927), pp. 726–33.

Ryan, Tom, 'Le Président des Terres Australes: Charles de Brosses and the French Enlightenment Beginnings of Oceanic Anthropology,' *Journal of Pacific History*, 37/2 (2002), pp. 157–86.

Salmond, Anne, *Aphrodite's Island: The European Discovery of Tahiti* (Berkeley and Los Angeles, CA: University of California Press, 2009).

Salmond, Anne, *Bligh: William Bligh in the South Seas* (Berkeley and Los Angeles, CA: University of California Press, 2011).

Sankey, Margaret, 'The Baudin Expedition in Port Jackson, 1802: Cultural Encounters and Enlightenment Politics,' *Explorations*, 31 (2001), pp. 5–36.

Sankey, Margaret, 'Est ou Ouest: le mythe des terres australes en France aux XVII et XVIII siècles' in Kumari R. Issur and Vinesh Y. Hookoomsing, eds., *L'Océan Indien dans les littératures francophones* (Paris: Editions Karthala, 2001), pp. 13–26.

Sankey, Margaret, 'The English Translation of the *Voyages de decouvertes aux Terres Australes* of François Péron: The Politics of Discovery in Early Nineteenth Century France and England' in Marc-Serge Rivière and Kumari R. Issur, eds., *Baudin-Flinders dans l'océan Indien: Voyages, Découvertes, Rencontre: Voyages, Discoveries, Encounter* (Paris: L'Harmattan, 2006), pp. 195–216.

Sankey, Margaret, 'Nationalism and Identity in Seventeenth-Century France: The Abbé Paulmier and the *Terres australes*,' *Australian Journal of French Studies*, 44/3 (2007), pp. 195–206.

Sankey, Margaret, 'Writing the Voyage of Scientific Exploration: The Logbooks, Journals and Notes of the Baudin Expedition (1800–1804),' *Intellectual History Review*, 20/3 (2010), pp. 401–13.

Sankey, Margaret, 'Mapping *Terra Australis* in the French Seventeenth Century: The Mémoires of the Abbé Jean Paulmier' in Anne M. Scott, Alfred Hiatt, Claire McIlroy and Christopher Wortham, eds., *European Perceptions of Terra Australis* (Farnham: Ashgate, 2011), pp. 111–34.

Sankey, Margaret, 'The Abbé Paulmier and the Rights of Man: The French Mission for the *Terres australes*,' *Australian Journal of French Studies*, 50/1 (2013), pp. 87–99.

Sankey, Margaret, 'The Abbé Jean Paulmier and the French Missions in the *Terres australes*: Myth and History,' *Australian Journal of French Studies*, 50/1 (2013), pp. 3–15.

Sankey, Margaret, 'The Abbé Paulmier's Mémoires and Early French Voyages in Search of Terra Australis,' in John West-Sooby, ed., *Discovery and Empire: The French in the South Seas* (Adelaide: University of Adelaide Press, 2013), pp. 42–66.

Schaffer, Simon, 'In Transit: European Cosmologies in the Pacific' in Kate Fullagar, ed., *The Atlantic World in the Antipodes: Effects and Transformations since the Eighteenth Century* (Newcastle upon Tyne: Cambridge Scholars Publishing, 2012), pp. 70–93.

Schilder, Günter, 'New Cartographical Contributions to the Coastal Exploration of Australia in the Course of the Seventeenth Century', *Imago Mundi*, 26/1 (1972), pp. 41–4.

Schilder, Günter, *Australia Unveiled: The Share of the Dutch Navigators in the Discovery of Australia* (Amsterdam: Theatris Orbis Terrarum, 1976).

Schilder, Günter, 'New Holland: The Dutch Discoveries' in Glyndwr Williams and Alan Frost, eds., *Terra Australis to Australia* (Melbourne: Oxford University Press, 1988), pp. 83–115.

Schilder, Günter, 'From Secret to Common Knowledge: The Dutch Discoveries' in John Hardy and Alan Frost, eds., *Studies from Terra Australis to Australia* (Canberra: Australian Academy of the Humanities, 1989), pp. 71–84, 250–3.

Schilder, Günter, 'A Continent Takes Shape: The Dutch Mapping of Australia' in Michael Richards and Maura O'Connor, eds., *Changing Coastlines: Putting Australia on the World Map 1493–1993* (Canberra: National Library of Australia, 1993), pp. 11–14.

Schilder, Günter, *Monumenta Cartographica Neerlandica, IX: Hessel Gerritsz (1580/81– 1632) Master Engraver and Map Maker, Who 'Ruled' the Seas* (Amsterdam: Hes & De Graaf, 2013).

Schilder, Günter and Kok, Hans, *Sailing for the East: History & Catalogue of Manuscript Charts on Vellum of the Dutch East India Company (VOC) 1602–1799* (Houten: Hes & De Graaf, 2010).

Schreiber, Roy E., *The Fortunate Adversities of William Bligh* (New York: Peter Lang, 1991).

Scott, Ernest, *Terre Napoléon: A History of French Explorations and Projects in Australia* (London: Methuen, 1910).

Scott, Ernest, 'English and French Navigators on the Victorian Coast', *Victorian Historical Magazine*, 2/4 (1912), pp. 145–76.

Scott, Ernest, *Lapérouse* (Sydney: Angus & Robertson, 1913).

Scott, Ernest, *The Life of Matthew Flinders* (Sydney: Angus & Robertson, 1914).

Scott, Ernest, 'The Maritime Exploration of Western Australia, with Especial Reference to the Voyages of Dampier and D'Entrecasteaux', *Report of the Eighteenth Meeting of the Australasian Association for the Advancement of Science* (Perth: Government Printer, 1928), pp. 402–16.

Seal, Graham, *The Savage Shore: Extraordinary Stories of Survival and Tragedy from the Early Voyages of Discovery* (New Haven, CT: Yale University Press, 2016).

Sexton, Robert, 'Dampier's *Roebuck*', *Bulletin of the Australasian Institute for Maritime Archaeology*, 35/1 (2011), pp. 28–38.

Sharp, Andrew, *The Discovery of Australia* (London: Oxford University Press, 1963).

Sharp, Andrew, *The Voyages of Abel Janszoon Tasman* (Oxford: Oxford University Press, 1968).

Shaw, Carlos Martinez, 'Terra Australis: The Spanish Quest' in John Hardy and Alan Frost, eds., *Studies from Terra Australis to Australia* (Canberra: Highland Press in association with the Australian Academy of the Humanities, 1989), pp. 57–69, 247–50.

Sheaffe, Stephen, 'Samuel Ashmore and Tracks through the Great Barrier Reef,' *Queensland History Journal*, 24/3 (2019), pp. 251–67.

Sheehan, Colin, 'Strangers and Servants of the Company: The United East India Company and Dutch Voyages to Australia' in Peter Veth, Peter Sutton and Margo Neale, eds., *Strangers on the Shore: Early Coastal Contacts in Australia* (Canberra: National Museum of Australia Press, 2008), pp. 6–34.

Shellam, Tiffany, *Shaking Hands on the Fringe: Negotiating the Aboriginal World at King George's Sound* (Crawley, WA: University of Western Australia Press, 2009).

Shellam, Tiffany, 'Mediating Encounters through Bodies and Talk' in Shino Konishi, Maria Nugent and Tiffany Shellam, eds., *Indigenous Intermediaries: New Perspectives on Exploration Archives* (Canberra: Australian National University Press, 2015), pp. 85–102.

Shellam, Tiffany, '"Thro' the Medium of Biscuits": Phillip Parker King and the Menang, 1821' in Gaye Sculthorpe, ed., *Yurlman: Mokare Mia Boodjar (Returning to Mokare's Home Country): Encounters and Collections in Menang Country* (Welshpool: Western Australian Museum, 2016), pp. 10–17.

Shellam, Tiffany, 'Ethnographic Inquiry on Phillip Parker King's Hydrographic Survey' in Martin Thomas and Amanda Harris, eds., *Expeditionary Anthropology: Teamwork, Travel and the 'Science of Man'* (New York: Berghahn, 2018), pp. 205–32.

Shipman, Joseph C., *William Dampier: Seaman-Scientist* (Lawrence, KS: University of Kansas Libraries, 1962).

Shirley, Rodney W., *The Mapping of the World: Early Printed World Maps 1472–1700* (London: The Holland Press, 1983).

Sigmond, J. P. and Zuiderbaan, L. H., *Dutch Discoveries of Australia: Shipwrecks, Treasures and Early Voyages Off the West Coast* (Adelaide: Rigby, 1978).

Sigmond, Peter, 'Two Pewter Plates' in Leo Akveld, Frank Broeze, Femme Gaastra, Gordon Jackson and Willem Mörzer Bruyns, eds., *In het kielzog: Maritiem-historisches studies aangeboden aan Jaap R. Bruijn bijzijn vertrek als hoogleraar zeegeschiedenis aande Universiteit Leiden* (Amsterdam: De Bataafsche Leeuw, 2003), pp. 245–56.

Skelton, R. A., *Explorers' Maps. Chapters in the Cartographic Record of Geographical Discovery* (London: Routledge and Kegan Paul, 1958).

Skelton, Raleigh A., 'Map Compilation, Production, and Research in Relation to Geographical Exploration' in Herman R. Friis, ed., *The Pacific Basin: A History of Its Geographical Exploration* (New York: American Geographical Society, 1967), pp. 40–56.

Slot, B. J., *Abel Tasman and the Discovery of New Zealand* (Amsterdam: Otto Cramwinckel, 1992).

Smith, Bernard, *European Vision and the South Pacific*, 2nd edn. (New Haven, CT: Yale University Press, 1985).

Smith, Bernard, 'The Intellectual and Artistic Framework of Pacific Exploration in the Eighteenth Century' in William Eisler and Bernard Smith, eds., *Terra Australis: The Furthest Shore* (Sydney: International Cultural Corporation of Australia, 1988), pp. 123–8.

Smith, Robert James, 'Matthew Flinders and the North Coast of New South Wales, 1799,' *Journal of the Royal Australian Historical Society*, 89/2 (1999), pp. 163–70.

Southwood, Jane, 'The Artwork of the Baudin Expedition to Australia (1800–1804): Nicolas-Martin Petit's 1802 Portrait of an Aboriginal Woman and Child from Van Diemen's Land' in Natalie Edwards, Ben McCann and Peter Poiana, eds., *Framing French Culture* (Adelaide: University of Adelaide Press, 2015), pp. 103–26.

Spate, O. H. K., 'Between Tasman and Cook: Bouvet's Place in the History of Exploration' in J. Andrews, ed., *Frontiers and Men: A Volume in Memory of Griffith Taylor (1880–1963)* (Melbourne: Cheshire, 1865), pp. 174–86.

Spate, O. H. K., 'De Lozier Bouvet and Mercantilist Expansion in the Pacific in 1740' in John Parker, ed., *Merchants and Scholars: Essays in the History of Exploration and Trade* (Minneapolis: University of Minnesota Press, 1965), pp. 221–37.

Spate, O. H. K., *Let Me Enjoy: Essays, Partly Geographical* (Canberra: Australian National University Press, 1965).

Spate, O. H. K., 'Amés Damnées,' *Overland*, 58 (1974), pp. 52–7.

Spate, O. H. K., 'Baudin and Flinders' in R. W. Russell, ed., *Matthew Flinders – The Ifs of History* (Bedford Park, SA: University Relations Unit, Flinders University, 1979), pp. 87–93.

Spate, O. H. K., *The Spanish Lake: The Pacific since Magellan*, vol. 1 (London: Croom Helm, 1979).

Sprod, Dan, 'Tobias Furneaux, RN, and His Pacific Voyaging,' *Tasmanian Historical Research Association, Papers and Proceedings*, 51/3 (2004), pp. 136–50.

Stallard, Avan Judd, 'Navigating Tasman's 1642 Voyage of Exploration: Cartographic Instruments and Navigational Decisions,' *The Portolan*, 69 (2007), pp. 24–43.

Stallard, Avan Judd, 'Better than *The Da Vinci Code*: The Theological Edifice That Is Gavin Menzies' 1421,' *History Australia*, 5/3 (2008), pp. 77.1–77.12.

Stallard, Avan Judd, 'Antipodes to Terra Australis' (University of Queensland PhD thesis, 2010).

Stallard, Avan Judd, *Antipodes: In Search of the Southern Continent* (Clayton, VIC: Monash University Publishing, 2016).

Stanbury, Myra, 'Louis Aleno de saint Alouarn (1738–1772): A Forgotten 18th-Century French Explorer,' *The Great Circle*, 39/2 (2017), pp. 25–55.

Starbuck, Nicole, 'Sir Joseph Banks and the Baudin Expedition: Exploring the Politics of the Republic of Letters,' *French History and Civilisation: Papers from the George Rudé Seminar*, 3 (2009), pp. 56–68.

Starbuck, Nicole, 'Nicolas Baudin: La relâche a Sydney et la deuxième campagne du *Géographe*' in Michel Jangoux, ed., *Portés par L'Air du Temps les Voyages du Capitaine Baudin* (Brussels: Editions de l'Université de Bruxelles, 2010), pp. 133–42.

Starbuck, Nicole, *Baudin, Napoléon and the Exploration of Australia* (London: Pickering & Chatto, 2013).

Starbuck, Nicole, 'Neither Civilised Nor Savage: The Aborigines of Colonial Port Jackson, through French Eyes, 1802' in Alexander Cook, Ned Curthoys and Shino Konishi, eds., *Representing Humanity in the Age of Enlightenment* (London: Pickering and Chatto, 2013), pp. 123–33, 212–15.

Starbuck, Nicole, 'Colonial Vision: French Voyager-Artists, Aboriginal Subjects and the British Colony at Port Jackson' in Natalie Edwards, Ben McCann and Peter Poiana, eds., *Framing French Culture* (Adelaide: University of Adelaide Press, 2015), pp. 29–52.

Starbuck, Nicole, 'Exploration, Observation and Regeneration: Voyagers' Perceptions of French and Tasmanian Families during the French Revolution,' *Annales Historiques de la Révolution Française*, no. 385 (2016), pp. 175–98.

Starbuck, Nicole, 'The Baudin Expedition and the Aborigines of "Botany Bay": Colonial Ethnography in the Era of Bonaparte,' *Zeitschrift für Australienstudien/Australian Studies Journal*, 32 (2018), pp. 29–43.

Stearn, William T., 'The Botanical Results of the *Endeavour* Voyage,' *Endeavour*, 27 (1968), 3–10.

Stearn, William T., 'The Botanical Explorations of Banks and Solander on Captain Cook's 1768–71 Voyage in the *Endeavour*' in *Captain Cook's Florilegium* (London: Lion and Unicorn Press, 1973), n.p.

Stearn, W. T., *The Australian Flower Paintings of Ferdinand Bauer* (London: Basilisk Press, 1976).

Stehn, Kay and George, Alex, 'Artist in a New Land: William Westall in New Holland' in Juliet Wege, Alex George, Jan Gathe, Kris Lemson and Kath Napier, eds., *Matthew Flinders and His Scientific Gentlemen: The Expedition of H.M.S. Investigator to Australia, 1801–5* (Welshpool, WA: Western Australian Museum, 2005), pp. 77–95.

Steven, Margaret, *First Impressions: The British Discovery of Australia* (London: British Museum [Natural History], 1988).

Stevenson, Edward Luther, *Terrestrial and Celestial Globes: Their History and Construction Including a Consideration of Their Value as Aids in the Study of Geography and Astronomy*, 2 vols. (New Haven, CT: Yale University Press, 1921).

Strong, Pauline Turner, 'Fathoming the Primitive: Australian Aborigines in Four Explorers' Journals, 1697–1845,' *Ethnohistory*, 33/2 (1986), pp. 175–94.

Sturma, Michael, 'Mutiny and Narrative: Francisco Pelsaert's Journals and the Wreck of the *Batavia*,' *The Great Circle*, 24/1 (2002), pp. 14–24.

Tardif, Philip John, *John Bowen's Hobart: The Beginning of European Settlement in Tasmania* (Hobart: Tasmanian Historical Research Association, 2003).

The Tasman Map of 1644: Historical Note and Description of the Manuscript Map in the Mitchell Library, Sydney (Sydney: The Trustees of the Public Library of New South Wales, 1948).

Taylor, Andrew, *The World of Gerald Mercator: The Mapmaker Who Revolutionised Geography* (London: Harper Collins, 2004).

Taylor, A. Carey, *Le President de Brosses et l'Australie* (Paris: Boivin, 1937).

Taylor, A. Carey, 'Charles de Brosses, the Man behind Cook' in Basil Greenhill, ed., *The Opening of the Pacific – Image and Reality, National Maritime Museum, Maritime Monographs and Reports*, no. 2 (Greenwich: National Maritime Museum, 1971), pp. 3–13.

Taylor, David, *The States of a Nation: The Politics and Surveys of the Australian State Borders* (Bathurst: NSW Department of Lands, 2006).

Taylor, James M. S., 'The Creation and Reception of William Westall's Admiralty Oil Paintings, Derived from His Voyage in H.M.S. Investigator, 1801–3' (University of Sussex D.Phil., 2015).

Taylor, James, *Picturing the Pacific; Joseph Banks and the Shipboard Artists of Cook and Flinders* (London: Adlard Coles, 2018).

Tent, Jan, 'Geographic and Linguistic Reflections on Moente and Dubbelde Ree: Two of Australia's First Recorded Placenames', *Geographical Research*, 44/4 (2006), pp. 372–85.

Tent, Jan and Helen Slatyer, 'Naming Places on the "Southland": European Place-Naming Practices from 1606 to 1803', *Australian Historical Studies*, 40/1 (2009), pp. 5–31.

Terry, Martin, 'The French and the Aborigines: A Decade of Depiction' in Maurice Blackman, ed., *Australian Aborigines and the French* (Kensington: University of New South Wales Press, 1990), pp. 111–33.

Terry, Martin, 'Early Mapping of the Pacific', *The Globe*, 37 (1992), pp. 22–4.

Terry, Martin, 'Encountering Dumont d'Urville' in Susan Hunt, Martin Terry and Nicholas Thomas, *Lure of the Southern Seas: The Voyages of Dumont D'Urville 1826–1840* (Sydney: Historic Houses of New South Wales Trust, 2002), pp. 23–34.

Thomas, Nicholas, *Discoveries: The Voyages of Captain Cook* (London: Allen Lane, 2003).

Tiley, Robert, *The Mermaid Tree: How a Tiny Unknown Ship Opened Australia's North and West to Development, Dreams and Disappointment* (Sydney: ABC Books, 2006).

Toft, Klaus, *The Navigators: Flinders vs. Baudin: The Race between Matthew Flinders and Nicolas Baudin to Discover the Fabled Passage through the Middle of Australia* (Potts Point, NSW: Duffy & Snellgrove, 2002).

Tooley, R. V., *The Printed Maps of New South Wales 1773–1873* (London: Map Collectors' Circle, 1968).

Tooley, R. V., *The Mapping of Australia* (London: Holland Press, 1979).

Toulouse, Sarah, 'Marine Cartography and Navigation in Renaissance France' in David Woodward, ed., *The History of Cartography. Volume Three. Cartography in the European Renaissance, Part 2* (Chicago: University of Chicago Press, 2007), pp. 1550–68.

Trickett, P., *Beyond Capricorn: How Portuguese Adventurers Discovered and Mapped Australia and New Zealand 250 Years before Captain Cook* (Adelaide: East Street Publications, 2007).

Tuckfield, Trevor, 'William Dampier – Where Did He Land?', *Journal and Proceedings of the Western Australian Historical Society*, V/I (1955), pp. 5–15.

Turnbull, Paul, *Science, Museums and Collecting the Indigenous Dead in Colonial Australia* (London: Palgrave Macmillan, 2017).

van den Boogaart, Ernst, 'The Mythical Symmetry in God's Creation: The Dutch and the Southern Continent, 1569–1756' in William Eisler and Bernard Smith, eds., *Terra Australis: The Furthest Shore* (Sydney: International Cultural Corporation of Australia, 1988), pp. 43–50.

van der Kraan, Alfons, 'Anthony Van Diemen: From Bankrupt to Governor-General, 1593–1636 (Part 1)', *The Great Circle*, 26/2 (2004), pp. 3–23.

van der Kraan, Alfons, 'Anthony Van Diemen: Patron of Discovery and Exploration, 1636–1645 (Part 2)', *The Great Circle*, 27/1 (2005), pp. 3–33.

van Duivenvoorde, Wendy, *Dutch East India Company Shipbuilding: The Archaeological Study of Batavia and Other Seventeenth-Century VOC Ships* (College Station: Texas A&M University Press, 2015).

van Duivenvoorde, Wendy, 'Dutch Seaman Dirk Hartog (1583–1621) and His Ship *Eendracht*,' *The Great Circle*, 38/1 (2016), pp. 1–31.

van Duivenvoorde, Wendy, 'Dirk Hartog Was Here! His 1616 Inscription Plate and Dutch Ship Communications' in Nonja Peters, ed., *A Touch of Dutch: Maritime, Military, Migration and Mercantile Connections on the Western Third 1616–2016* (Perth: Carina Hoang Communications, 2016), pp. 14–37.

Van Duzer, Chet, *The World for a King: Pierre Desceliers's World Map of 1550* (London: British Library, 2015).

van Huystee, Marit, *On the Yacht Duyfken (1601): The First European Ship to Explore the Australian Coast, Report*, Maritime Archaeology Department, Western Australian Maritime Museum No. 105 (1995), pp. 5–12.

Villiers, Alan, *Captain Cook, the Seamen's Seaman* (London: Hodder and Stoughton, 1967).

Walker, James Backhouse, *Abel Janszoon Tasman: His Life and Voyages* (Hobart: Government Printer, 1896).

Wallace, Colin, *The Lost Australia of François Péron* (London: Nottingham Court Press, 1984).

Wallis, Helen, 'The Exploration of the South Sea, 1519 to 1644. A Study of the Influence of Physical Factors, with a Reconstruction of the Routes of the Explorers' (University of Oxford D.Phil., 1954).

Wallis, Helen, 'The Dieppe Maps – The First Representation of Australia?' *The Globe*, 17 (1982), pp. 23–50.

Wallis, Helen, 'The Enigma of Java la Grande' in *Australia and the European Imagination: Papers from a Conference Held at the Humanities Research Centre, Australian National University*, May 1981 (Canberra: Australian National University, 1982), pp. 1–40.

Wallis, Helen, 'Did the Portuguese Discover Australia? The Map Evidence' in *Technical Papers of the 12th Conference of the International Cartographic Association, Perth, Western Australia*, 2 vols. (Perth, 1984), ii, pp. 203–20.

Wallis, Helen, 'Java la Grande: The Enigma of the Dieppe Maps' in Glyndwr Williams and Alan Frost, eds., *Terra Australis to Australia* (Melbourne: Australian Academy of the Humanities, 1988), pp. 39–81.

Wallis, Helen, 'Visions of Terra Australis in the Middle Ages and Renaissance' in William Eisler and Bernard Smith, eds., *Terra Australis: The Furthest Shore* (Sydney: International Cultural Corporation of Australia, 1988), pp. 35–42.

Wallis, Helen, 'The Challenge that Is an Australian Map,' *The Globe*, 37 (1992), pp. 4–5.

Ward, J. M., 'British Policy in the Exploration of the South Pacific, 1699–1793,' *Journal and Proceedings of the Royal Australian Historical Society*, XXXVII/1 (1947), pp. 25–49.

Waters, David W., 'Navigational Problems in Captain Cook's Day' in Antoinette Shalkop, ed., *Exploration in Alaska: Captain Cook Commemorative Lectures June–November 1978* (Anchorage, AK: Cook Inlet Historical Society, 1980), pp. 40–58.

Watts, Peter, Pomfrett, Jo Ann and Mabberley, David, *An Exquisite Eye: The Australian Flora & Fauna Drawings 1801–1820 of Ferdinand Bauer* (Glebe, NSW: Historic Houses Trust of New South Wales, 1997).

Webb, Joan, *George Caley, Nineteenth Century Naturalist* (Chipping Norton, NSW: Surrey Beatty, 1995).

Webb, Mark, 'Peter Good: Gardener on a Voyage of Discovery' in Juliet Wege, Alex George, Jan Gathe, Kris Lemson and Kath Napier, eds., *Matthew Flinders and His Scientific Gentlemen: The Expedition of H.M.S. Investigator to Australia 1801–1805* (Welshpool, WA: Western Australian Museum, 2005), pp. 97–103.

West-Sooby, John, 'Baudin, Flinders and the Scientific Voyage' in Marc-Serge Rivière and Kumari R. Issur, eds., *Baudin-Flinders dans L'Océan Indien: Voyages, Découvertes, Rencontre: Voyages, Discoveries, Encounter* (Paris: L'Harmattan, 2006), pp. 179–94.

West-Sooby, John, 'An Artist in the Making: The Early Drawings of Charles-Alexandre Lesueur during the Baudin Expedition to Australia' in Natalie Edwards, Ben McCann and Peter Poiana, eds., *Framing French Culture* (Adelaide: University of Adelaide Press, 2015), pp. 53–80.

West-Sooby, John and Fornasiero, Jean, 'Matthew Flinders through French Eyes: Nicolas Baudin's Lessons from Encounter Bay,' *Journal of Pacific History*, 52/1 (2017), pp. 1–14.

West-Sooby, John, Fornasiero, Jean and Sankey, Margaret, 'Nicolas Baudin (1754–1803), from Seafarer to Philosophical Voyager' in Eric Berti and Ivan Barko, eds., *French Lives in Australia* (Melbourne: Australian Scholarly Publishing, 2015), pp. 36–56.

Wheeler, Alwyne, 'Animals' in D. J. Carr, ed., *Sydney Parkinson: Artist of Cook's Endeavour Voyage* (London and Canberra: Croom Helm, 1983), pp. 195–249.

Wheeler, Alwyne, 'The Zoological Manuscripts of Robert Brown,' *Archives of Natural History*, 20/3 (1993), pp. 417–24.

White, Isobel, 'Birth and Death of a Ceremony', *Aboriginal History*, 4/1 (1980), pp. 33–42.

Whitehead, P. J. P., 'Zoological Specimens from Captain Cook's Voyages', *Journal of the Society for the Bibliography of Natural History*, 5/3 (1969), pp. 161–201.

Whittell, Hubert Massey, *The Literature of Australian Birds: A History and a Bibliography of Australian Ornithology* (Perth: Brokensha Pty. Ltd., 1954).

Wieder, Frederick Casper, ed., *Monumenta Cartographica: Reproductions of Unique and Rare Maps, Plans and Views in the Actual Size of the Originals: Accompanied by Cartographical Monographs* (The Hague: Martinus Nijhoff, 1925–33).

Williams, Gary C., 'William Dampier: Science, Exploration, and Literary Influence, Including His *Hydrographical Treatise* of 1699', *Proceedings of the California Academy of Sciences (Fourth Series)*, 59/14 (2008), pp. 592–602.

Williams, Gary C., 'The Historical Context and Influence of William Dampier's Hydrographic Science', *The Great Circle*, 37/1 (2016), pp. 53–81.

Williams, Glyn, *Voyages of Delusion: The Quest for the Northwest Passage* (New Haven, CT: Yale University Press, 2003).

Williams, Glyn, *Naturalists at Sea: From Dampier to Darwin* (New Haven, CT: Yale University Press, 2013).

Williams, Glyndwr, '"Far More Happier than We Europeans": Reactions to the Australian Aborigines on Cook's Voyage', *Historical Studies*, 19/77 (1981), pp. 499–512.

Williams, Glyndwr, 'New Holland – the English Approach' in John Hardy and Alan Frost, eds., *Studies from Terra Australis to Australia* (Canberra: Highland Press in association with the Australian Academy of the Humanities, 1988), pp. 85–92, 253–4.

Williams, Glyndwr, 'New Holland to New South Wales: The English Approaches' in Glyndwr Williams and Alan Frost, eds., *Terra Australis to Australia* (Melbourne: Oxford University Press in association with the Australian Academy of the Humanities, 1989), pp. 117–59.

Williams, Glyndwr, 'The Achievement of the English Voyages, 1650–1800' in Derek Howse, ed., *Background to Discovery: Pacific Exploration from Dampier to Cook* (Berkeley and Los Angeles: University of California Press, 1990), pp. 58–78.

Williams, Glyndwr, 'Buccaneers, Castaways, and Satirists: The South Seas in English Consciousness before 1750', *Eighteenth-Century Life*, 18/3 (1994), pp. 114–28.

Williams, Glyndwr, '"The Common Center of We Discoverers": Sir Joseph Banks, Exploration and Empire in the Late Eighteenth Century' in R. E. R. Banks, B. Elliott, J. G. Hawkes, D. King-Hele and G. L. Lucas, eds., *Sir Joseph Banks: A Global Perspective* (Kew: Royal Botanic Gardens, Kew, 1994), pp. 177–91.

Williams, Glyndwr, *The Great South Sea: English Voyages and Encounters 1570–1850* (New Haven, CT: Yale University Press, 1997).

Williams, Glyndwr, 'The Pacific: Exploration and Exploitation' in P. J. Marshall, ed., *The Oxford History of the British Empire. Volume 2. The Eighteenth Century* (Oxford: Oxford University Press, 1998), pp. 552–75.

Williams, Glyndwr, 'The *Endeavour* Voyage: A Coincidence of Motives' in Margarette Lincoln, ed., *Science and Exploration: European Voyages to the Southern Oceans in the Eighteenth Century* (Woodbridge: The Boydell Press, 1998), pp. 3–18.

Williams, Glyndwr and Frost, Alan, '*Terra Australis*: Theory and Speculation' in Glyndwr Williams and Alan Frost, eds., *Terra Australis to Australia* (Melbourne: Oxford University Press in association with the Australian Academy of the Humanities, 1988), pp. 1–38.

Williamson, A. R., *Eastern Traders: Some Men and Ships of Jardine, Matheson & Company and Their Contemporaries in the East India Company's Maritime Service* (Ipswich: Jardine Matheson & Co. Ltd., 1976).

Wintroub, Michael, 'The Translations of a Humanist Ship Captain: Jean Parmentier's 1529 Voyage to Sumatra,' *Renaissance Quarterly*, 68/1 (2015), pp. 98–132.

Withers, Charles W. J., *Placing the Enlightenment: Thinking Geographically about the Age of Reason* (Chicago: University of Chicago Press, 2007).

Withey, Lynne, *Voyages of Discovery: Captain Cook and the Exploration of the Pacific* (Berkeley and Los Angeles: University of California Press, 1987).

Wood, Frances, *Did Marco Polo Go to China?* (London: Secker and Warburg, 1995).

Wood, G. Arnold, rev. edn. J. C. Beaglehole, *The Discovery of Australia* (orig. pub. 1922; Melbourne: Macmillan, 1969).

Wood, Greg, 'Successive States: Aaron Arrowsmith's Chart of the Pacific Ocean, 1798–1832,' *The Globe*, 70 (2012), pp. 1–17.

Woods, Martin, 'The Southern Cross Revealed,' 'The First Modern Atlas,' 'New Holland's Birth Certificate,' 'The Last Great Dutch Voyage to Australia,' '"Terre Australe," East of New Holland' in *Mapping Our World: Terra Incognita to Australia* (Canberra: National Library of Australia, 2013), pp. 57, 96, 139, 143, 163.

Woodworth, Philip L. and Rowe, Glen H., 'The Tidal Measurements of James Cook during the Voyage of the Endeavour,' *History of Geo- and Space Sciences*, 9 (2018), pp. 85–103.

Worth, Howard, 'An Alternative View of Java la Grande: Approaches to Cartographic History and Their Impact on the Interpretation of the Dieppe Maps,' *The Great Circle*, 33/1 (2011), pp. 28–49.

Worth, Howard, 'The *Duyfken*: An Exploration of the Roles of a Replica Ship,' *The Great Circle*, 35/1 (2013), pp. 75–95.

Wroth, Lawrence C., *The Early Cartography of the Pacific* (New York: Bibliographical Society of America, 1944).

Yule, C. B., *The Australia Directory: Volume 2, East Coast, Torres Strait and Coral Sea ...* (London: Hydrographic Office, 1859).

Zandvliet, Kees, 'Golden Opportunities in Geopolitics: Cartography and the Dutch East India Company during the Lifetime of Abel Tasman' in William Eisler and Bernard Smith, eds., *Terra Australis: The Furthest Shore* (Sydney: Art Gallery of New South Wales, 1988), pp. 67–84.

Zandvliet, Kees, 'Mapping the Dutch World Overseas in the Seventeenth Century' in David Woodward, ed., *The History of Cartography. Volume Three. Cartography in the European Renaissance. Part 2* (Chicago: University of Chicago Press, 2007), pp. 1433–62.

Zuber, Mike A., 'The Armchair Discovery of the Unknown Southern Continent: Gerardus Mercator, Philosophical Pretensions and a Competitive Trade,' *Early Science and Medicine*, 16/6 (2011), pp. 505–41.

Index

Lightning Source UK Ltd.
Milton Keynes UK
UKHW020222220922
409222UK00003B/159